GUIDE TO ATLASES SUPPLEMENT:

World, Regional, National, Thematic

An International Listing of Atlases

Published 1971 through 1975

with Comprehensive Indexes

by

GERARD L. ALEXANDER

The Scarecrow Press, Inc.

Metuchen, N.J.   1977

Library of Congress Cataloging in Publication Data

Alexander, Gerard L
    Guide to atlases supplement, world, regional, national, the-
matic.

    Includes indexes.
    1. Atlases--Bibliography. I.   Title.
Z6021. A43   Suppl.   [GA300]   016. 912   70-157728
ISBN 0-8108-1011-5

CONTENTS

iii

v

vii

INTRODUCTION

Since the publication of the Guide to Atlases in 1971, some 2992 new entries have been added in this Supplement. Not only have I included atlases published during the years 1971 through 1975, but one will also find incorporated entries that were missed for the years 1950 through 1970. The entries are numbered consecutively throughout the work.

This Supplement continues the same general arrangement as the main volume (see below), numbering each entry beginning where the Guide to Atlases left off. Entries in the comprehensive indexes at the back of this volume refer to items in both the Guide and the Supplement (by entry number instead of page number).

This Supplement then, used together with the original Guide to Atlases, covers 25 years of atlas production, namely from 1950-1975.

In order to facilitate its use, perhaps a word is needed to explain the arrangement of the supplement volume. The entries have been divided as in the main volume into four distinct groups: (1) World Atlases, arranged chronologically by date and, within each year, alphabetically by publisher; (2) Regional Atlases, covering whole continents or major regions of same, listed within each continent alphabetically by publisher; (3) National Atlases, those of individual countries as a whole, located within each continent in alphabetic order by publisher; (4) Thematic Atlases, divided first alphabetically by subject, such as economy, geology, history, roads, and within each category alphabetically by publisher.

An atlas is listed more than once if it covers more than one area or subject. As an example, an historical atlas of Kenya, Tanzania and Uganda will have the following four entries: under "History" (a subdivision of Thematic Atlases) and also within "Africa" (a subdivision of National Atlases) under the name of each individual country. This facilitates the search for a certain type of atlas, as well as for the geographical area desired.

Each atlas entry lists the name of the publisher, title, edition, author, place of publication, date of publication, number of pages, colored maps and size of atlas.

In addition to a Publishers Index, arranged alphabetically and listing also the city and country of publication, there is a List of Publishers, divided first by continents, listing alphabetically by countries the various governmental agencies as well as private enterprises. Also provided is an alphabetic Authors, Cartographers, Editors Index. All of these are comprehensive indexes to both volumes, citing entry numbers, which run continuously from the Guide through the Supplement.

A great effort has been spent to date atlases accurately. The dates provided for undated atlases have been established from bibliographic sources, and when available, from internal evidence. Where a date is only deduced or conjectured it appeared in square brackets. The earliest and latest dates have been supplied for composite atlases. In many instances the actual number of pages in an atlas was doubtful; these have therefore been listed as "one volume." The dimensions of each atlas are given in centimeters, either height or width, whichever is greater.

Entries for atlases in Oriental and other languages in non-roman alphabets (Albanian, Arabic, Greek, Hebrew, Russian, Serbo-Croatian, etc.) have titles and names of publishers transliterated into roman characters. This was often problematic and made consistency difficult. The same applies to the use of accents and punctuations, some of which had to be omitted.

When I first undertook to compile the original volume of this international survey of atlases, irrespective of area and subject, published in every part of the world, in all languages, I knew only too well that I would be confronted with many problems. The vast number of atlases published over the years, and the unbelievable amount of research involved, made it imperative that I limit my work to the production of atlases since 1950. Another consideration was not to eliminate the possibility to purchase desired atlases. Many atlases published during the last 25 years may still be available, while others have long since gone out of print. Fortunately, however, the major library atlas collections throughout the world have preserved on their shelves a comprehensive selection for consultation.

As the work progressed, my task was made more difficult by the many conflicting data available to me. Invariably I found that different publishers in scattered corners of the world published the very same atlas as another with the identical title, but with their own imprint and date. Many atlases were translated from one language to another and reissued.

While I consulted literally thousands of possible sources, I was hard put to decide which seemed the most authoritative. Information varied frequently on titles, editions, names of publishers, number of pages, size of atlas, and dates; inconsistencies of spelling were the most confusing. I tried to make decisions based on the most authoritative source, but realize that occasional mistakes in judgment are unavoidable.

Additionally, a great handicap was the fact that I was unable personally to inspect physically each individual atlas listed.

The arduous nature of the task of bringing together titles of thousands of atlases, out of the enormous mass of literature from all over the world, in different languages, should be obvious. But the difficulties attending its performance by a single individual can only be estimated by those practically acquainted with the magnitude of this undertaking. Notwithstanding the time and care devoted, no one is more conscious than the compiler that the work cannot be free from errors and omissions. Suggestions for any factual corrections and additions, which may be appropriate for inclusion in a future edition, if and when one becomes a reality, would be much appreciated.

Gerard L. Alexander

Chief, Map Division
The Research Libraries
The New York Public Library

WORLD ATLASES

1950

5557 Hachette.
   Atlas mondial de poche. Paris, [1950].
   28p. col. maps. 18cm.

5558 IAC
   Le plus petit atlas du monde. By J. L. Sibert. Lyon,
   [1950].
   70p. col. maps. 11cm.

5559 Ksiaznica-Atlas.
   Maly atlas geograficzny. By Eugeniusz Romer. Wroclaw,
   1950.
   12p. col. maps. 30cm.

5560 Larousse.
   Le monde. [Atlas]. Paris, [1950].
   64p. col. maps. 38cm.

1951

5561 Mantnieks, P.
   Welt atlas. Bruxelles, 1951.
   32p. col. maps. 17cm.

1952

5562 Mantnieks, P.
   Welt atlas. Bruxelles, [1952].
   32p. col. maps. 17cm.

1953

5563 Perthes, Justus
   Taschenatlas der ganzen Welt. Gotha, 1953.
   148p. col. maps. 18cm.

1

1954

5564   Poland.   Centralny urząd geodezii i Kartografii
        Maly atlas geograficzny.   By Eugeniusz Romer.   Warszawa,
        1954.
        14p.   col.   maps.   30cm.

1955

5565   Rand McNally & Co.
        Rand McNally reader's world atlas.   Chicago, 1955.
        300p.   col.   maps.   25cm.

1956

5566   Rand McNally & Co.
        Standard world atlas.   Chicago, 1956.
        384p.   col.   maps.   28cm.

1957

5567   Maarif Basimevi.
        Orta atlas.   2ed.   Istanbul, 1957.
        52p.   col.   maps.   28cm.

5568   Učila.
        Politički atlas.   By Zvonimir Dugački.   Zagreb, 1957.
        128p.   col.   maps.   17cm.

1958

5569   Aguilar, S. A. de Ediciones.
        Atlas medio universal y de Colombia.   Madrid, 1958.
        140p.   col.   maps.   31cm.

5570   Denoyer-Geppert Co.
        The University atlas.   With Philip.   Chicago, 1958.
        200p.   col.   maps.   29cm.

5571   Kanaat Yayinlari.
        Yeni orta atlas.   Istanbul, [1958].
        40p.   col.   maps.   31cm.

1959

5572   Poland.   Państwowe przedsiębiorstwo wydawnictw Kartografi-
        cznych.
        Atlas geograficzny.   By Eugeniusz Romer.   Warszawa,

        1959.
        91p.   col. maps.   30cm.

5573   Poland.   Państwowe przedsiębiorstwo wydawnictw Kartografi-
       cznych.
       Maly atlas geograficzny.   By Eugeniusz Romer.   Warszawa,
       1959.
       14p.   col. maps.   30cm.

5574   Poland.   Państwowe przedsiębiorstwo wydawnictw Kartografi-
       cznych.
       Maly atlas swiata.   Warszawa, 1959.
       1 vol.   col. maps.   23cm.

                                 1960

5575   de Bussy, J. H.
       Politieke wereldatlas.   2ed.   By S. A. Leeflang.   Am-
       sterdam, 1960.
       65p.   21cm.

5576   Dell Pub. Co.
       The Hammond-Dell world atlas.   With Hammond.   New
       York, 1960.
       246p.   col. maps.   17cm.

5577   Dijkstra.
       Onze aarde; atlas van de werelddelen.   28ed.   By W. Bakker
       and H. Rusch.   Zeist, [1960].
       20p.   col. maps.   31cm.

5578   Golden Press.
       Golden book picture atlas of the world.   New York, 1960.
       6 vol.   col. maps.   25cm.

5579   Golden Press.
       The children's picture atlas of the world.   By Philip Ba-
       con.   New York, 1960.
       1 vol.   col. maps.   25cm.

5580   Hammond, C. S. & Co., Inc.
       Hammond comparative world atlas.   Maplewood, N. J.,
       1960.
       48p.   col. maps.   32cm.

5581   Oxford University Press.
       Oxford home atlas of the world.   London, 1960.
       124p.   col. maps.   27cm.

5582   Philip, George & Son, Ltd.
       Philips' practical atlas.   1 ed.   By Harold Fullard.   Lon-
       don, 1960.

1 vol.   col.   maps.   29cm.

5583   Poland.   Państwowe przedsiębiorstwo wydawnictw Kartografi-
       cznych.
       Maly atlas geograficzny.   By Eugeniusz Romer.   War-
       szawa, 1960.
       14p.   col.   maps.   30cm.

5584   Rand McNally & Co.
       Rand McNally classroom atlas.   Chicago, 1960.
       84p.   col.   maps.   25cm.

                                    1961

5585   Bartholomew, John & Son, Ltd.
       Meridian compact atlas of the world.   Edinburgh, 1961.
       144p.   col.   maps.   18cm.

5586   Edições Melhoramentos.
       Atlas geográfico Melhoramentos.   By Geraldo José
       Pauwels.   São Paulo, 1961.
       95p.   col.   maps.   35cm.

5587   Hammond, C. S. & Co., Inc.
       Modern world atlas.   Maplewood, N.J., 1961.
       48p.   col.   maps.   32cm.

5588   Milli Egitim Bakanligi.
       Yeni orta atlas.   Istanbul, [1961].
       40p.   col.   maps.   31cm.

5589   Poland.   Państwowe przedsiebiorstwo wydawnictw Kartografi-
       cznych.
       Atlas geograficzny.   By Eugeniusz Romer.   Warszawa,
       1961.
       91p.   col.   maps.   30cm.

5590   Poland.   Państwowe przedsiębiorstwo wydawnictw Kartografi-
       cznych.
       Maly atlas geograficzny.   By Eugeniusz Romer.   War-
       szawa, 1961.
       14p.   col.   maps.   30cm.

5591   Poland.   Państwowe przedsiębiorstwo wydawnictw Kartografi-
       cznych.
       Maly atlas swiata.   Warszawa, 1961.
       1 vol.   col.   maps.   23cm.

5592   Touring Club Italiano.
       Atlante internazionale.   Milano, 1961.
       2 vol.   col.   maps.   50cm.

1962

5593   Macmillan Co.
       Macmillan's world atlas for Liberian schools.   1 ed.
       London, 1962.
       32p.   col.   maps.   25cm.

5594   Poland.   Państwowe przedsiębiorstwo wydawnictw Kartografi-
       cznych.
       Atlas geograficzny dla Klasy IV.   Warszawa, 1962.
       35p.   col.   maps.   26cm.

5595   Poland.   Państwowe przedsiębiorstwo wydawnictw Kartografi-
       cznych.
       Maly atlas geograficzny.   By Eugeniusz Romer.   War-
       szawa, 1962.
       14p.   col.   maps.   30cm.

5596   Rand McNally & Co.
       Rand McNally reader's world atlas.   Chicago, 1962.
       300p.   col.   maps.   25cm.

1963

5597   Denóyer-Geppert Co.
       Visual relief atlas of world continents.   By Clarence B.
       Odell.   Chicago, 1963.
       32p.   col.   maps.   28cm.

5598   Editorial Vincens-Vives.
       Atlas de geografía general.   Barcelona, 1963.
       50p.   col.   maps.   32cm.

5599   Geographia Map Co.
       Geographia world atlas.   New York, 1963.
       40p.   col.   maps.   33cm.

5600   Gyldendal.
       Atlas uden navne.   By W. F. Hellner.   København, 1963.
       52p.   col.   maps.   24cm.

1964

5601   Istituto Geografico De Agostini.
       Atlash coğrafya ansiklopedisi.   By Besim Darkot.   Istan-
       bul, [1964].
       310p.   col.   maps.   34cm.

5602   Mexico.   Centro de Estudios y Documentación Sociales.
       Atlas del mundo actual.   2 ed.   Mexico, [1964].
       91p.   19cm.

5603   N. I. Sh.   Mjete Mesimore e Sportive "Hamid Shijaku."
       Atlas gjeografik.   Tiranë, 1964.
       56p.   col. maps.   30cm.

5604   Philip, George & Son, Ltd.
       Philip's first venture atlas.   British Isles edition.   By
       Harold Fullard.   London, [1964].
       30p.   col. maps.   23cm.

5605   Philip, George & Son, Ltd.
       Teach yourself atlas of the world.   By Harold Fullard.
       London, 1964.
       192p.   col. maps.   29cm.

5606   Poland.   Państwowe przedsiębiorstwo wydawnictw Kartografi-
       cznych.
       Maly atlas geograficzny.   By Eugeniusz Romer.   War-
       szawa, 1964.
       14p.   col. maps.   30cm.

5607   Reader's Digest Association, Ltd.
       The Reader's Digest great world atlas.   1 Canadian ed.
       Montreal, 1964.
       183p.   col. maps.   41cm.

                                1965

5608   Istituto Geografico De Agostini.
       La terra.   Grande atlante geografico economico storico.
       Novara, 1965.
       3 vol.   col. maps.   40cm.

5609   Oliver & Boyd.
       Intermediate school atlas.   With Bartholomew.   Edinburgh,
       1965.
       40p.   col. maps.   29cm.

5610   Philip, George & Son, Ltd.
       Philip's practical atlas.   2 ed.   By Harold Fullard.   Lon-
       don, 1965.
       1 vol.   col. maps.   29cm.

5611   Rand McNally & Co.
       Rand McNally continental world atlas.   Chicago, 1965.
       324p.   col. maps.   26cm.

1966

5612   Air Canada.
       Air Canada routes.   Ottawa, [1966].
       18p.   col. maps.   23cm.

5613   Bartholomew, John & Son, Ltd.
       The mini pocket atlas.   Edinburgh, 1966.
       164p.   col. maps.   15cm.

5614   Geokarta.
       Geografski atlas.   By Ratimir Kalmeta.   Beograd,
       1966.
       35p.   col. maps.   34cm.

5615   GEO Publishing Co.
       The Faber atlas.   By D. J. Sinclair.   With Hölzel.
       Oxford, 1966.
       201p.   col. maps.   31cm.

5616   Golden Press.
       Children's picture atlas of the world.   New York, 1966.
       544 p.   col. maps.   25cm.

5617   Oxford University Press.
       The shorter Oxford economic atlas of the world.   Lon-
       don, New York, 1966.
       128p.   col. maps.   26cm.

5618   Pergamon Press, Ltd.
       Wheaton-Pergamon secondary school atlas.   By Stanley
       Knight.   Oxford, 1966.
       110p.   col. maps.   26cm.

5619   Philip, George & Son, Ltd.
       Philips commercial course atlas.   By Harold Fullard.
       London, 1966.
       117p.   col. maps.   29cm.

5620   Poland.   Państwowe przedsiębiorstwo wydawnictw Kartografi-
       cznych.
       Atlas geograficzny dla Klasy IV.   Warszawa, 1966.
       1 vol.   col. maps.   26cm.

5621   Rand McNally & Co.
       Classroom atlas.   (World).   Philippine ed.   Chicago, 1966.
       1 vol.   col. maps.   25cm.

5622   Valistus.
       Valistuksen Koulukartasto.   Helsinki, 1966.
       36p.   col. maps.   26cm.

5623   Zanichelli, Nicola.

Atlante geografico.   By G. Nangeroni and L. Ricci.
Bologna, 1966.
244p.   col. maps.   34cm.

1967

5624   Aschehoug & Co.
       Skole-atlas.   Oslo, 1967.
       86p.   col. maps.   29cm.

5625   Bir Yayinevi.
       Modern orta atlasi.   With Istituto Geografico De Agostini.
       Istanbul, 1967.
       40p.   col. maps.   33cm.

5626   Bir Yayinevi.
       Resimli ilkokul atlasi.   With Istituto Geografico De
       Agostini.   Istanbul, 1967.
       28p.   col. maps.   27cm.

5627   Bir Yayinevi.
       Tarih atlasi.   With Istituto Geografico De Agostini.
       Istanbul, 1967.
       32p.   col. maps.   27cm.

5628   Collins, William, Sons & Co., Ltd.
       Collins children's atlas.   London, 1967.
       54p.   col. maps.   29cm.

5629   Czechoslovakia.   Kartografické nakladatelství.
       Školní zeměpisny atlas světa.   8ed.   By Vladimír Vokálek.
       Praha.   1967.
       27p.   col. maps.   29cm.

5630   Denoyer-Geppet Co.
       Our world, its geography in maps.   By Clarence B.
       Odell.   Chicago, 1967.
       97p.   col. maps.   28cm.

5631   Dent, J. M.
       Dent's Canadian school atlas.   Toronto, 1967.
       115p.   col. maps.   29cm.

5632   Editorial Codex.
       Geoatlas.   By José Aguilar.   Buenos Aires, 1967.
       3 vol.   col. maps.   32cm.

5633   Geokarta.
       Geografski atlas.   10ed.   By Ratimir Kalmeta.   Beograd,
       1967.
       35p.   col. maps.   34cm.

5634 Hammond, Inc.
      Hammond world atlas.   New perspective ed.   Maplewood,
      N. J., [1967].
      256p. col. maps. 29cm.

5635 Istituto Geografico De Agostini.
      Atlante della produzione e dei commerci.   By Umberto
      Bonapace and Giuseppe Motta.   Novara, [1967].
      120p. col. maps. 31cm.

5636 Kartografické nakladatelství.
      Atlas geográfico mundial de bolsillo.   With Centro Anglo-
      Mexicano del Libro and Bancroft & Co., Ltd.   Mexico,
      [1967].
      60p. col. maps. 17cm.

5637 Macmillan & Co., Ltd.
      Macmillan's world atlas for Liberian schools.   London,
      1967.
      32p. col. maps. 25cm.

5638 Meyer Kartographisches Institut.
      Rororo Weltatlas.   Taschenbuch ed.   Mannheim, 1967.
      152p. col. maps. 19cm.

5639 Oliver & Boyd.
      The advanced atlas of modern geography.   6ed.   With
      Bartholomew.   Edinburgh, [1967].
      1 vol. col. maps. 38cm.

5640 Oxford University Press.
      The Oxford junior atlas.   London, [1967].
      58p. col. maps. 26cm.

5641 Philip, George & Son, Ltd.
      Philip's elementary atlas.   104ed.   By Harold Fullard.
      London, 1967.
      64p. col. maps. 28cm.

5642 Philip, George & Son, Ltd.
      Philip's modern school atlas.   64ed.   By Harold Fullard.
      London, 1967.
      140p. col. maps. 29cm.

5643 Philip, George & Son, Ltd.
      Primary atlas.   London, 1967.
      1 vol. col. maps. 28cm.

5644 Philip, George & Son, Ltd.
      Visual atlas.   By Harold Fullard.   London, 1967.
      47p. col. maps. 23cm.

5645 Philip, George & Son, Ltd.

World wide atlas.   By Harold Fullard, London, [1967].
64p.   col.   maps.   29cm.

5646   Rand McNally & Co.
Rand McNally continental world atlas.   Chicago, 1967.
324p.   col.   maps.   26cm.

5647   U. S. S. R.   Nauchno-issledovatel'ski institut aeroklimatologii.
Atlas Kharakteristik vetra.   By I. G. Guterman and S. I.
Dunayeva.   Moskva, 1967-70.
2 vol.   35cm.

                                    1968

5648   Aldine Pub. Co.
Aldine University Atlas.   By Norton Ginsburg.   With
Philip.   Chicago, 1968.
310p.   col.   maps.   28cm.

5649   Aschehoug & Co.
Mitt første atlas.   4. skøear.   Oslo, 1968.
8p.   col.   maps.   24cm.

5650   Bancroft & Co.
The New Bancroft world atlas.   Rev. ed.   London,
[1968].
69p.   col.   maps.   17cm.

5651   Bir Yayinevi.
Ilkokul atlasi.   With Istituto Geografico De Agostini.
Istanbul, 1968.
28p.   col.   maps.   26cm.

5652   Bir Yayinevi.
Modern orta atlasi.   With Istituto Geografico De Agostini.
Istanbul, 1968.
40p.   col.   maps.   34cm.

5653   Bir Yayinevi.
Resimli ilkokul atlasi.   With Istituto Geografico De
Agostini.   Istanbul, 1968.
28p.   col.   maps.   27cm.

5654   Bir Yayinevi.
Tarih atlasi.   With Istituto Geografico De Agostini.
Istanbul, 1968.
32p.   col.   maps.   27cm.

5655   Cappelens, J. W. , Forlag, A. S.
Cappelens atlas for folkeskolen.   6ed.   Oslo, 1968.
55p.   col.   maps.   24cm.

5656 Cappelens, J. W., Forlag, A. S.
Mitt atlas for 4-6. skolear. Oslo, 1968.
24p. col. maps. 24cm.

5657 Dar al-Ma'Arif.
Al-Atlas, Al-Arabi. Cairo, 1968.
60p. col. maps. 30cm.

5658 De Sikkel.
Atlas. België en de wereld. By J. van den Branden
and M. Nouboers. With Hölzel. Antwerpen, [1968].
154p. col. maps. 33cm.

5659 Éditions du renouveau pédagogique.
Atlas du monde contemporain. By Pierre Gourou,
Fernand Grenier and Louis-Edmond Hamelin. Montréal,
1968.
88p. col. maps. 36cm.

5660 Ganaco, N. V.
Atlas nasional tentang, Indonesia. Djakarta, [1968].
72p. col. maps. 39cm.

5661 Generalstabens litografiska anstalt.
Stora internationella atlasen. Stockholm, 1968.
556p. col. maps. 38cm.

5662 GEO Publishing Co.
The Faber atlas. By D. J. Sinclair. With Hölzel.
Oxford, 1968.
201p. col. maps. 31cm.

5663 Gjellerups Forlag.
Mit første atlas. By Jørgen Clevin and Henry Holm.
København, 1968.
25p. col. maps. 25.5cm.

5664 Gyldendal.
Atlas 1 for folkeskolen. By W. F. Recato. København,
1968.
67p. col. maps. 27.5cm.

5665 Hachette.
Atlas contemporâneo. 1ed. By Nilo Bernardes and
Pierre Gourou. Paris, [1968].
56p. col. maps. 34cm.

5666 Hölzel, Ed. Verlag.
Österreichischer Atlas für höhere Schulen. 94ed. By
W. Strzygowski. Wien, 1968.
167p. col. maps. 32cm.

5667 Istituto Geografico De Agostini.

Atlante metodico.   By V. Bonapace and G. Motta.
Novara, 1968.
228p. col. maps. 33cm.

5668 Istituto Geografico De Agostini.
Atlante moderno.   By U. Bonapace and G. Motta.
Novara, 1968.
177p. col. maps. 33cm.

5669 Istituto Geografico De Agostini.
Geoatlante.   By Umberto Bonapace.   Novara, 1968.
106p. col. maps. 31cm.

5670 Istituto Geografico De Agostini.
Nuovo atlante.   By V. Bonapace.   Novara, 1968.
96p. col. maps. 30cm.

5671 Johnston, W. & A. K. and A. W. Bacon, Ltd.
World study atlas.   2ed.   Edinburgh, 1968.
64p. col. maps. 27cm.

5672 Kartográfiai Vállalat.
Földrajzi atlasz az általános iskolák számára.
By Sándor Radó.   Budapest, 1968.
32p. col. maps. 28cm.

5673 Kartográfiai Vállalat.
Földrajzi atlasz a középiskolak számára.   Budapest, 1968.
60p. col. maps. 29cm.

5674 Le livre de poche.
Atlas de poche.   With Kartografické nakladatelství.
Paris, 1968.
238p. col. maps. 17cm.

5675 Le livre de poche.
Atlas de poche.   With Kartografické nakladatelství.
Paris, 1968.
238p. col. maps. 17cm.

5676 Librairie Générale Française.
Atlas de poche.   Paris, 1968.
178p. col. maps. 16.5cm.

5677 Milli Eğitim Bakanliği.
Yeni orta atlas.   Istanbul, [1968].
40p. col. maps. 31cm.

5678 Nelson, Thomas & Sons, Ltd.
Nelson's Canadian school atlas.
By J. Wreford Watson.   Don Mills, Ont., 1968.
92p. col. maps. 29cm.

5679   Pergamon Press, Ltd.
       Wheaton atlas for the middle school.   By L. R. Hawkes.
       Oxford, 1968.
       54p.   col.   maps.   26cm.

5680   Philip, George & Son, Ltd.
       Modern commonwealth atlas.   3ed.   By Harold Fullard.
       London, [1968].
       72p.   col.   maps.   28cm.

5681   Poland.   Państwowe przedsiębiorstwo wydawnictw Kartografi-
       cznych.
       Atlas geograficzny dla Kl. IV.   Warszawa, 1968.
       36p.   col.   maps.   26cm.

5682   Poland.   Państwowe przedsiębiorstwo wydawnictw Kartografi-
       cznych.
       Atlas geograficzny V-VIII Klasy.   Warszawa, 1968.
       60p.   col.   maps.   26cm.

5683   Rand McNally & Co.
       Atlas advanced.   By J. Wreford Watson.   With Collins.
       London, 1968.
       227p.   col.   maps.   29cm.

5684   Rand McNally & Co.
       Students political atlas of the world.   Chicago, 1968.
       39p.   col.   maps.   28cm.

5685   Romania.   Editura di Stat Didactică şi Pedagogică.
       Atlas geografic scolar.   By N. Gheorghiu.   Bucuresti,
       1968.
       34p.   col.   maps.   33cm.

5686   Sélection du Reader's Digest, S. A. R. L.
       Atlas mondial de poche; mémento géographique.   With
       Kümmerly & Frey.   Paris, [1968].
       36p.   col.   maps.   18cm.

5687   Učila.
       Atlas za škole II stupnja.   3ed.   By Zvonimir Dugački.
       Zagreb, 1968.
       99p.   col.   maps.   34cm.

5688   U. S. S. R.   Glavnoe upravlenie geodezii i kartografii.
       Geograficheskii atlas.   3ed.   By N. I. Blinova.   Moskva,
       1968.
       198p.   col.   maps.   38cm.

5689   U. S. S. R.   Glavnoe upravlenie geodezii i kartografii.
       Malyi atlas mira.   Moskva, 1968.
       311p.   col.   maps.   19cm.

1969

5690   ADI Ltd.
       Atlas ha'olam vehe-halal.   (in Hebrew).   By Lurie.   Tel
       Aviv, 1969.
       350p.   col.   maps.   34cm.

5691   Aldine Pub. Co.
       Aldine university atlas.   By Norton Ginsburg.   Chicago,
       [1969].
       309p.   col.   maps.   29cm.

5692   Alves, Francisco.
       Nôvo atlas de geografia.   Rev. ed.   By J. Monteiro and
       F. d'Oliveira.   Rio de Janeiro, 1969.
       56p.   col.   maps.   31cm.

5693   Aschehoug & Co.
       Norge og rerden.   Oslo, 1969.
       71p.   col.   maps.   27cm.

5694   Bertelsmann, C.
       Neuer atlas der Welt.   Gütersloh, 1969.
       224p.   col.   maps.   32cm.

5695   Bulgaria.   Glavno upravlenie po geodeziâ kartografiâ.
       Geografski atlas za osmi Klas.   Sofia, 1969.
       66p.   col.   maps.   31cm.

5696   Cappelens, J. W. , Forlag, A. S.
       Cappelens atlas.   Større utgave for gymnaset.   Oslo, 1969.
       89p.   col.   maps.   32cm.

5697   Edições Melhoramentos.
       Atlas geográfico Melhoramentos.   28ed.   By Geraldo José
       Pauwels.   São Paulo, [1969].
       99p.   col.   maps.   35cm.

5698   Editorial Codex.
       Geoatlas.   By José Aguilar.   Buenos Aires, 1969.
       3 vol.   col.   maps.   42cm.

5699   Editorial F. T. D.
       Atlas universal y del Péru.   Lima, 1969.
       25p.   col.   maps.   28cm.

5700   Elsevier.
       Winkler Prins gezinsatlas.   By A. F. J. Wubbe.   Am-
       sterdam, Bruxelles, 1969.
       274p.   col.   maps.   33cm.

5701   Elsevier.

Winkler Prins wereldatlas.   Amsterdam, 1969.
293p. col. maps. 33cm.

5702   Encyclopaedia Britannica.
       Britannica atlas.   With Rand McNally.   Chicago, 1969.
       543p. col. maps. 39cm.

5703   Esselte Map Service.
       Stora internationella atlasen.   With Rand McNally.   Stock-
       holm, 1969.
       549p. col. maps. 38cm.

5704   Esselte Map Service.
       Verdens atlas.   Stockholm, 1969.
       160p. col. maps. 27.5cm.

5705   Freytag, Berndt & Artaria.
       Kleiner Weltatlas; die Staaten der Erde.   Wien, [1969].
       1 vol. col. maps. 15cm.

5706   Generalstabens litografiska anstalt.
       Stora internationella atlasen.   Stockholm, 1969.
       556p. col. maps. 38cm.

5707   Gyldendal.
       Gyldendals atlas for folkeskolen.   Oslo, 1969.
       26p. col. maps. 28cm.

5708   Gyldendal.
       Gyldendals reliefatlas.   2ed.   By Poul Holmelund and Ib
       Kejlbo.   København, 1969.
       126p. col. maps. 35cm.

5709   Haack, Hermann.
       Haack Kleiner Weltatlas.   By Rudolf Habel.   Gotha, 1969.
       408p. col. maps. 17cm.

5710   Haack, Hermann.
       Weltatlas.   Die Staaten der Erde und ihre Wirtschaft.   9ed.
       By Edgar Lehmann.   Gotha, Leipzig, 1969.
       176p. col. maps. 35cm.

5711   Hammond, Inc.
       Hammond discovery world atlas.   Maplewood, N.J.,
       [1969].
       64p. col. maps. 28cm.

5712   Hatier.
       Atlas mondial.   By André Journaux.   Paris, 1969.
       190p. col. maps. 35cm.

5713   Hölzel, Ed. Verlag.
       Österreichischer Atlas für höhere Schulen.   96ed.   By

W. Strzygowski.   Wien, 1969.
167p.   col. maps.   32cm.

5714   Jacaranda.
Jacaranda atlas.   By V. G. Honour.   Brisbane, 1969.
152p.   col. maps.   28cm.

5715   Johnston, W. & A. K. & G. W. Bacon, Ltd.
Dimension 3.   Political, physical and economic
world atlas.   Edinburgh, 1969.
64p.   col. maps.   28cm.

5716   Jugoslavenski leksikografski zavod.
Atlas svijeta.   4ed.   Zagreb, 1969.
501p.   col. maps.   30cm.

5717   Kümmerly & Frey.
Wirtschaftsgeographischer Weltatlas.   2ed.   By Hans
Boesch.   Bern, 1969.
89p.   col. maps.   34cm.

5718   List, P.
Harms atlas Deutschland und die Welt.   München, 1969.
125p.   col. maps.   32cm.

5719   Lloyd's Corp. of.
Lloyd's maritime atlas.   7ed.   London, 1969.
166p.   col. maps.   25cm.

5720   McGraw-Hill Book Co.
Man's domain, a thematic atlas of the world.   With General Drafting.   By Norman J. W. Thrower.   New York,
[1969].
76p.   col. maps.   34cm.

5721   Nelson, Thomas & Sons, Ltd.
World atlas of mountaineering.   By Wilfred Noyce and
Ian McMorrin.   London, 1969.
224p.   col. maps.   27cm.

5722   Nystrom.
Nystrom world atlas.   By Richard Edes Harrison.   Chicago, [1969].
62p.   col. maps.   26cm.

5723   Orell Füssli, A. G.
Atlante svizzero por le scuole medie.   By Edward Imhof.
Zürich, 1969.
152p.   col. maps.   33.5cm.

5724   Orell Füssli, A. G.
Schweizerischer Mittelschulatlas.   By Edward Imhof.
Zürich, 1969.
152p.   col. maps.   33.5cm.

5725 Otava.
Otavan maailmankartasto. 5ed. Helsinki, 1969.
172p. col. maps. 29cm.

5726 Otava.
Taskuatlas. Maailmankartasto ja tietohakemisto. Helsinki, 1969.
234p. col. maps. 18cm.

5727 Philip, George & Son, Ltd.
Philip's modern school atlas. 67ed. By Harold Fullard.
London, 1969.
132p. col. maps. 29cm.

5728 Poland. Państwowe przedsiębiorstwo wydawnictw Kartograficznych.
Atlas geograficzny. By H. Gorski. Warszawa, 1969.
159p. col. maps. 31cm.

5729 Poland. Państwowe przedsiębiorstwo wydawnictw Kartograficznych.
Atlas geograficzny dla Kl. IV. Warszawa, 1969.
36p. col. maps. 26cm.

5730 Poland. Państwowe przedsiębiorstwo wydawnictw Kartograficznych.
Atlas geograficzny dla Klas V-VIII. Warszawa, 1969.
1 vol. col. maps. 31cm.

5731 Poland. Państwowe przedsiębiorstwo wydawnictw Kartograficznych.
Kieszonkowy atlas świata. With Haack. Warszawa, 1969.
408p. col. maps. 16cm.

5732 Politikens forlag.
Politikens verdensatlas. København, 1969.
182p. col. maps. 28cm.

5733 Reader's Digest Association, Ltd.
The Readers Digest great world atlas. 2ed. London,
1969.
179p. col. maps. 41cm.

5734 Siemens, A. G.
Welt-Telex-Atlas. München, [1969].
373p. col. maps. 30cm.

5735 Söderström, Werner.
Kansakoulun Kartasto. Helsinki, 1969.
40p. col. maps. 27cm.

5736 U. S. S. R. Glavnoe upravlenie geodezii i kartografii.
Atlas mira. By L. N. Kolosova. Moskva, 1969.

65p.   col.   maps.   19cm.

5737   Vallardi, A.
       La terra i continenti extraeuropei.   By Cesare Saibene.
       Milano, [1969].
       39p.   col.   maps.   32cm.

5738   Wolters-Noordhoff.
       De Kleine Bosatlas.   53ed.   By F. J. Ormeling.
       Groningen, 1969.
       112p.   col.   maps.   31cm.

5739   W. S. O. J.
       Kansakoulon Kartasto.   Porvoo, Helsinki, 1969.
       38p.   col.   maps.   26cm.

1970

5740   Aguilar, S. A. de Ediciones.
       Atlas bachillerato, universal y de España.   24ed.   By
       Antonio López Gómez.   Madrid, 1970.
       117p.   col.   maps.   35cm.

5741   Aguilar, S. A. de Ediciones.
       Atlas bachillerato, universal y de España.   25ed.   By
       Antonio López Gómez.   Madrid, 1970.
       117p.   col.   maps.   35cm.

5742   Aguilar, S. A. de Ediciones.
       Atlas bachillerato, universal y de España.   26ed.   By
       Antonio López Gómez.   Madrid, 1970.
       117p.   col.   maps.   35cm.

5743   Aguilar, S. A. de Ediciones.
       Atlas bachillerato, universal y de España.   27ed.   By
       Antonio López Gómez.   Madrid, 1970.
       117p.   col.   maps.   35cm.

5744   Aguilar, S. A. de Ediciones.
       Atlas bachillerato, universal y de España.   28ed.   By
       Antonio López Gómez.   Madrid, 1970.
       117p.   col.   maps.   35cm.

5745   Aguilar, S. A. de Ediciones.
       Gran atlas Aguilar.   Madrid, 1970.
       3 vol.   col.   maps.   51cm.

5746   Bartholomew, John & Son, Ltd.
       Edinburgh world atlas.   7ed.   Edinburgh, 1970.
       160p.   col.   maps.   38cm.

5747   Bartholomew, John & Son, Ltd.
       Physical world atlas.   Edinburgh, [1970].
       168p.   col.   maps.   38cm.

5748   Beazley, Mitchell, Ltd.
       The atlas of the universe.   1ed.   By Patrick Moore.
       London, 1970.
       272p.   col.   maps.   36cm.

5749   Bertelsmann, C.
       Der grosse Bertelsmann Weltatlas.   Jubiläumsausgabe.
       By W. Bormann.   Gütersloh, 1970.
       440p.   col.   maps.   32cm.

5750   Bertelsmann, C.
       Neuer Atlas der Welt.   Gütersloh, [1970].
       224p.   col.   maps.   32cm.

5751   Blond Educational Ltd.
       The Blond world atlas.   By Jean de Varennes and Jean
       Lavallee.   With Holt, Rinehart and Winston.   London,
       1970.
       158p.   col.   maps.   34cm.

5752   Brazil.   Instituto Brasileiro de geografia et estatística.
       Atlas geográfico escolar.   6ed.   Rio de Janeiro, [1970].
       57p.   col.   maps.   31cm.

5753   Chambers, W. & R., Ltd.
       Historical atlas of the world.   By Oddvar Bjørklund.
       With Cappelen Forlag.   Edinburgh, 1970.
       134p.   col.   maps.   21cm.

5754   Clute, J. W.
       Atlas international.   Atlas mundial.   With Hammond.
       Mexico, D. F., [1970].
       224p.   col.   maps.   32cm.

5755   Collins, William, Sons & Co., Ltd.
       Collins-Longmans study atlas.   London, 1970.
       152p.   col.   maps.   28cm.

5756   Collins, William, Sons & Co., Ltd.
       Collins-Longmans visible regions atlas.   17ed.   By K. H.
       Huggins.   Glasgow, 1970.
       98p.   col.   maps.   29cm.

5757   Collins, William, Sons & Co., Ltd.
       Collins-Longmans atlas four.   By J. David Thompson.
       Glasgow, 1970.
       172p.   col.   maps.   27cm.

5758   Collins, William, Sons & Co., Ltd.

Collins graphic atlas.   London, 1970.
136p. col. maps.   28cm.

5759   Collins, William, Sons & Co. , Ltd.
Collins world atlas.   London, 1970.
160p. col. maps.   27cm.

5760   Companha Editofa Nacional.
Moderno atlas escolar; ensino médio.   By Henrique
Gamba.   São Paulo, [1970].
75p. col. maps.   31cm.

5761   Czechoslovakia.   Kartografické nakladelství.
Atlas svĕta.   Bratislava, 1970.
95p. col. maps.   32cm.

5762   Denoyer-Geppert Co.
Mapas historicos de Europa y del mundo.   By James H.
Breasted, Carl F. Huth and Samuel B. Harding.   Chicago,
1970.
55p. col. maps.   28cm.

5763   Doubleday.
Family reference world atlas.   With Hammond.   Garden
City, N.Y. , 1970.
256p. col. maps.   42cm.

5764   Edições Melhoramentos.
Atlas geográfico universal Melhoramentos.   29ed.   By
Geraldo José Pauwels.   São Paulo, 1970.
99p. col. maps.   35cm.

5765   Editions Bordas.
Atlas général Bordas.   By Pierre Serryn and René
Blaselle.   Paris, [1970].
168p. col. maps.   31cm.

5766   Editions Bordas.
Atlas illustré.   By Pierre Serryn and René Blasselle.
Paris, [1970].
272p. col. maps.   31cm.

5767   Editions Bordas.
Petit atlas Bordas.   La France, le monde.   By René
Cauët, Pierre Serryn and Marc Vincent.   Paris, 1970.
80p. col. maps.   32cm.

5768   Editions du renouveau pédagogique.
Atlas du monde contemporain.   2ed.   By Pierre Gourou,
Fernand Grenier and Louis-Edmond Hamelin.   Montreal,
[1970].
107p. col. maps.   36cm.

5769   Editions Stauffacher.
        Nouvel atlas mondial. By E. T. Rimli and R. Habel.
        Zürich, Lausanne, Paris, 1970.
        400p. col. maps. 28cm.

5770   Editorial Rivadeneyra.
        Atlas escolar Rivadeneyra. By Adolfo Maillo. Madrid,
        [1970].
        32p. col. maps. 32cm.

5771   Editorial Vincens-Vives.
        Atlas de geografía general. 10ed. By J. Vicens and S.
        Sobrequés. Barcelona, [1970].
        50p. col. maps. 32cm.

5772   Encyclopaedia Universalis.
        Atlas universalis. Paris, 1970.
        543p. col. maps. 38cm.

5773   Faber & Faber.
        The Faber atlas. 5ed. By D. J. Sinclair. London,
        [1970].
        154p. col. maps. 32cm.

5774   Generalstabens litografiska anstalt.
        Skolans världsatlas. Stockholm, 1970.
        98p. col. maps. 30cm.

5775   Generalstabens litografiska anstalt.
        Stora internationella atlasen. Stockholm, 1970.
        556p. col. maps. 38cm.

5776   Geokarta.
        Geografski atlas. By Mihailo Radovanović. Beograd,
        1970.
        35p. col. maps. 34cm.

5777   GEO Publishing Co.
        The Faber atlas. 5ed. By D. J. Sinclair. With Hölzel.
        Oxford, 1970.
        196p. col. maps. 31cm.

5778   Grolier International.
        Atlas mundial. With Rand McNally. Chicago, 1970.
        215p. col. maps. 37cm.

5779   Gyldendal.
        Atlas 2. København, 1970.
        65p. col. maps. 27.5cm.

5780   Gyldendal.
        Atlas for folkeskolen. Oslo, 1970.
        70p. col. maps. 28cm.

5781 Gyldendal.
      Gyldendals verdensatlas.   By G. Wicklund-Hansen.   With
      Philip.   Oslo, 1970.
      270p.   col. maps.   29cm.

5782 Haack, Hermann.
      Die Erde.   Haack Kleiner Atlas.   1ed.   By K. Breitfeld.
      Gotha, Leipzig, [1970].
      424p.   col. maps.   17cm.

5783 Hallwag, A. G.
      Der grosse Reader's Digest Weltraum-Atlas.   Bern,
      Stuttgart, 1970.
      272p.   col. maps.   37cm.

5784 Hammond, Inc.
      Atlas international.   Atlas mundial.   Maplewood, N.J.,
      1970.
      224p.   col. maps.   32cm.

5785 Hammond, Inc.
      Family reference world atlas.   Maplewood, N.J., 1970.
      256p.   col. maps.   32cm.

5786 Hammond, Inc.
      Hammond citation world atlas.   New perspective ed.
      Maplewood, N.J., [1970].
      352p.   col. maps.   32cm.

5787 Hammond, Inc.
      Hammond standard world atlas; latest and most authentic
      geographical and statistical information.   Maplewood,
      N.J., [1970].
      320p.   col. maps.   32cm.

5788 Hammond, Inc.
      World atlas.   Classics ed.   Maplewood, N.J., 1970.
      352p.   col. maps.   32cm.

5789 Hart-Davis.
      The atlas of world history.   By Colin and Sarah McEvedy.
      London, 1970-
      in parts.   col. maps.   29cm.

5790 Herder Verlag.
      Atlas universal Herder.   Barcelona, [1970].
      198p.   col. maps.   35cm.

5791 Herder Verlag.
      Herders grosser Weltatlas.   3ed.   Freiburg, [1970].
      250p.   col. maps.   40cm.

5792 Holt-Blond.

Atlas general Holt.   Toronto, 1970.
158p.   col. maps.   34cm.

5793   Holt-Blond.
The Holt world atlas.   Toronto, 1970.
158p.   col. maps.   34cm.

5794   Holt, Rinehart and Winston.
The Blond world atlas.   By Jean de Varennes and Jean
Lavallee.   With Blond Educational, Ltd.   Toronto, 1970.
158p.   col. maps.   34cm.

5795   Hölzel, Ed. Verlag.
Österreichischer Atlas für höhere Schulen.   97ed.   Wien,
1970.
165p.   col. maps.   32cm.

5796   International Bank for Reconstruction and Development.
World bank atlas; population, per capita product and
growth rate.   5ed.   Washington, D.C., 1970.
16p.   col. maps.   28cm.

5797   Istituto Geografico De Agostini.
Atlante della produzione e dei commerci.   By Umberto
Bonapace and Giuseppe Motta.   Novara, 1970.
120p.   col. maps.   31cm.

5798   Istituto Geografico De Agostini.
Atlante geografico metodico.   By Umberto Bonapace and
Giuseppe Motta.   Novara, 1970.
206p.   col. maps.   36cm.

5799   Istituto Geografico De Agostini.
Atlante geografico moderno.   By Umberto Bonapace.
Novara, 1970.
121p.   col. maps.   37cm.

5800   Istituto Geografico De Agostini.
Geoatlante.   By Umberto Bonapace.   Novara, [1970].
136p.   col. maps.   31cm.

5801   Istituto Geografico De Agostini.
Nuovo atlante mondiale.   By Umberto Bonapace.   Novara,
1970.
500p.   col. maps.   36cm.

5802   Johnston, W. & A. K. & G. W. Bacon, Ltd.
First school atlas.   London, 1970.
64p.   col. maps.   28cm.

5803   Journaux, A.
Atlas mondial.   Caen, 1970.
16p.   col. maps.   31cm.

5804 JRO Verlag.
      Der grosse JRO-Weltatlas. 26ed.   By Ernst Kremling and
      Helmut Kremling. München, 1970.
      246p. col. maps. 44cm.

5805 JRO Verlag.
      Grosser JRO-Weltatlas. Permanentausgabe. München,
      [1970].
      in parts. col. maps. 44cm.

5806 Jugoslavenski leksikografski zavod.
      Atlas svijeta. 4ed. By Petar Mardešić and Oto Oppitz.
      Zagreb, [1970].
      510p. col. maps. 30cm.

5807 Kartográfiai Vállalat.
      Földrajzi atlasz a középiskolák számára. Budapest, 1970.
      60p. col. maps. 29cm.

5808 Kartográfiai Vállalat.
      Kis világatlasz. 3ed. By Sándor Radó. Budapest, 1970.
      332p. col. maps. 19cm.

5809 Keysersche Verlagsbuchhandlung, GMBH.
      Lautensach Neuer Weltatlas, Schul-und Hausatlas.
      München, [1970].
      1 vol. col. maps. 31cm.

5810 Kümmerly & Frey.
      KF Atlas. Naturbild und Wirtschaft der Erde. By
      Georges Grosjean. Bern, 1970.
      206p. col. maps. 32cm.

5811 Laffont.
      L'Atlas de l'univers. By Patrick Moore. Paris, [1970].
      272p. col. maps. 37cm.

5812 Läromedelsförlagen.
      Nordisk skolatlas; läroverksupplagen. 12ed. By Hans
      W:son Ahlmann. With Generalstabens litografiska anstalt.
      Stockholm, [1970].
      85p. col. maps. 34cm.

5813 Lexicon Publications, Inc.
      Lexicon international atlas. With Hammond. Chicago,
      Ill., 1970.
      352p. col. maps. 32cm.

5814 Macmillan.
      Europe and the world: maps and mapwork. By John
      Moser. London, 1970.
      32p. col. maps. 28cm.

5815 McGraw-Hill Book Co.
Man's domain, a thematic atlas of the world. 2ed. By
Norman J. W. Thrower. With General Drafting Co.
New York, [1970].
80p. col. maps. 34cm.

5816 Meyer, Kartographisches Institut.
Das Grosse Duden-Lexikon, Band 10: Weltatlas. By
Adolf Hanle. Mannheim, Wien, Zürich, 1970.
627p. col. maps. 37cm.

5817 Meyer, Kartographisches Institut.
Meyers grosser Weltatlas. By Adolf Hanle. Mannheim,
Wien, Zürich, 1970.
422p. col. maps. 36cm.

5818 Meyer, Kartographisches Institut.
Meyers Universalatlas. Mannheim, 1970.
248p. col. maps. 37cm.

5819 National Geographic Society.
National Geographic atlas of the world. 3ed. Washington, D. C., 1970.
331p. col. maps. 49cm.

5820 N. I. Sh. Mjete Mësimore e Sportive "Hamid Shijaku."
Atlas për shkollat fillore. Tiranë, 1970.
19p. col. maps. 26cm.

5821 Oliver & Boyd.
Intermediate school atlas. 15ed. With Bartholomew.
Edinburgh, 1970.
40p. col. maps. 29cm.

5822 Oliver & Boyd.
The new comparative atlas. 49ed. With Bartholomew.
Edinburgh, [1970].
112p. col. maps. 29cm.

5823 Otava.
Taskuatlas. Maailmankartasto ja tietohakemisto. With
Kartografické nakladatelství. Helsinki, 1970.
234p. col. maps. 17cm.

5824 Oxford University Press.
Concise Oxford atlas. 2ed. By D. P. Bickmore. London, 1970.
288p. col. maps. 27cm.

5825 Oxford University Press.
Oxford home atlas of the world. 3ed. Oxford, 1970.
144p. col. maps. 27cm.

5826   Oxford University Press.
       The little Oxford atlas.   London, 1970.
       70p. col. maps. 26cm.

5827   Oxford University Press.
       The Oxford atlas.   By C. Lewis and J. D. Campbell.
       London, 1970.
       1 vol. col. maps. 27cm.

5828   Peuser, Ediciones Geográficas.
       Nuevo atlas geográfico metódico universal.   33ed.   By
       José Anesi.   Buenos Aires, 1970.
       96p. col. maps. 38cm.

5829   Philip, George & Son, Ltd.
       Glydendals verdensatlas.   By G. Wicklund-Hansen.   Lon-
       don, 1970.
       270p. col. maps. 32cm.

5830   Philip, George & Son, Ltd.
       Philips' commercial course atlas.   By Harold Fullard.
       London, [1970].
       30p. col. maps. 29cm.

5831   Philip, George & Son, Ltd.
       Philips' secondary school atlas.   London, 1970.
       1 vol. col. maps. 29cm.

5832   Philip, George & Son, Ltd.
       The atlas of the universe.   1ed.   By Patrick Moore.
       London, 1970.
       272p. col. maps. 36cm.

5833   Philip, George & Son, Ltd.
       The Library atlas.   By H. Fullard and H. C. Darby.
       London, 1970.
       320p. col. maps. 29cm.

5834   Poland.   Glowny urząd statystyczny.
       Atlas statystyczny.   1ed.   By Janusz Stępiński.   War-
       szawa, 1970.
       197p. col. maps. 28cm.

5835   Poland.   Państwowe przedsiębiorstwo wydawnictw Kartografi-
       cznych.
       Atlas geograficzny.   6ed.   By Henryk Górski and Wanda
       Jędrzejewska.   Warszawa, 1970.
       159p. col. maps. 32cm.

5836   Poland.   Państwowe przedsiębiorstwo wydawnictw Kartografi-
       cznych.
       Atlas geograficzny.   By Jan Rzędowski.   Warszawa, 1970.
       38p. col. maps. 32cm.

5837   Poland.   Państwowe przedsiębiorstwo wydawnictw Kartografi-
       cznych.
       Maly atlas swiata.   Warszawa, 1970.
       69p.   col.   maps.   23cm.

5838   Radio Amateur Callbook, Inc.
       Radio amateurs' world atlas.   Lake Bluff, Ill., 1970.
       16p.   col.   maps.   31cm.

5839   Rand McNally & Co.
       Atlas mundial.   With Grolier International.   Chicago,
       [1970].
       215p.   col.   maps.   37cm.

5840   Rand McNally & Co.
       Goode's world atlas.   13ed.   By Edward B. Espenshade,
       Jr.   Chicago, 1970.
       315p.   col.   maps.   29cm.

5841   Rand McNally & Co.
       Nuevo atlas del mundo.   Chicago, 1970.
       215p.   col.   maps.   36cm.

5842   Rand McNally & Co.
       Rand McNally classroom atlas.   6ed.   Chicago, 1970.
       84p.   col.   maps.   25cm.

5843   Rand McNally & Co.
       Rand McNally news atlas of the world.   Chicago, [1970].
       96p.   col.   maps.   36cm.

5844   Rand McNally & Co.
       Rand McNally pocket world atlas.   Chicago, 1970.
       316p.   col.   maps.   15cm.

5845   Rand McNally & Co.
       Standard world atlas.   Chicago, 1970.
       264p.   col.   maps.   31cm.

5846   Rand McNally & Co.
       The atlas of the universe.   By Patrick Moore.   Chicago,
       1970.
       272p.   col.   maps.   36cm.

5847   Rand McNally & Co.
       The International atlas.   Chicago, 1970.
       503p.   col.   maps.   38cm.

5848   Reader's Digest, AB.
       Det Bedstes store verdensatlas.   København, 1970.
       216p.   col.   maps.   40cm.

5849   Reader's Digest, N.V.

De Reader's Digest grote wereld atlas.   5ed.   By Frank
Debenham.   Amsterdam, [1970].
204p.   col.   maps.   40cm.

5850   Rikisútgáfa námsbóka.
       Landabréfabók.   By Helgi Elíasson, Einar Magnússon
       and Agúst Böovarsson.   Reykjavík, [1970].
       56p.   col.   maps.   25cm.

5851   Selection du Reader's Digest, S. A. R. L.
       Grand atlas mondial.   8ed.   By Frank Debenham and
       Henri Gossot.   Paris, 1970.
       272p.   col.   maps.   40cm.

5852   Slovenska Kartografia.
       Malý skolský atlas.   Bratislava, 1970.
       16p.   col.   maps.   17cm.

5853   Técnica Aérea e Fotogramétrica.
       Rotas/routes, TAP.   Lisboa, [1970].
       19p.   col.   maps.   26cm.

5854   U. S. S. R.   Glavnoe upravlenie geodezii i kartografii.
       Atlas mira.   Moskva, 1970.
       65p.   col.   maps.   19cm.

5855   U. S. S. R.   Glavnoe upravlenie geodezii i kartografii.
       Geograficheskii atlas materikov dlya 6-go klassa.
       Moskva, 1970.
       36p.   col.   maps.   28cm.

5856   U. S. S. R.   Glavnoe upravlenie geodezii i kartografii.
       Malyi atlas mira.   By V. N. Salmanova.   Moskva, 1970.
       311p.   col.   maps.   19cm.

5857   Velhagen & Klasing.
       Unsere Welt.   Atlas.   By Wilhelm Grotelüschen.   Berlin,
       1970.
       179p.   col.   maps.   33cm.

5858   Wesmael-Charlier.
       Atlas classique.   By Jean Tilmont and Marcel de Roeck.
       Namur, [1970].
       32p.   col.   maps.   36cm.

5859   Wesmael-Charlier.
       Cartographie des parties du monde.   By J. Tilmont.
       Namur, 1970.
       32p.   35cm.

5860   Westermann, Georg.
       Der Lebensraum des Menschen.   Ein Westermann Atlas
       für Schule und Haus.   3ed.   Braunschweig, 1970.

130p.   col.   maps.   30cm.

5861   Westermann, Georg.
       Westermann Schulatlas.   1ed.   Grosse Ausgabe.   By
       Ferdinand Mayer.   Braunschweig, [1970].
       192p.   col.   maps.   30cm.

5862   Westermann, Georg.
       Westermann Schulatlas.   2ed.   By Ferdinand Mayer.
       Braunschweig, 1970.
       196p.   col.   maps.   30cm.

5863   W. S. O. Y.
       Joka Kodin maailmankartasto.   Helsinki, [1970].
       180p.   col.   maps.   28cm.

5864   W. S. O. Y.
       Koulon omatoimikartat 1 & 2.   Helsinki, 1970.
       2 vol.   col.   maps.   26cm.

1971

5865   Aguilar, S. A. de Ediciones.
       Atlas bachillerato universal y de Colombia.   By Antonio
       López Gómez.   Madrid, 1971.
       120p.   col.   maps.   35cm.

5866   Aguilar, S. A. de Ediciones.
       Atlas bachillerato, universal y de España.   29ed.   By
       A. L. Gómez.   Madrid, 1971.
       117p.   col.   maps.   35cm.

5867   Aldine Pub. Co.
       World patterns: The Aldine College atlas.   By Norton
       Ginsburg.   With Philip.   Chicago, 1971.
       128p.   col.   maps.   28cm.

5868   Aldine Pub. Co.
       World patterns.   The Aldine college atlas.   By Harold
       Fullard.   With Philip.   Chicago, 1971.
       128p.   col.   maps.   28cm.

5869   Bartholomew, John & Son, Ltd.
       Mini atlas.   Edinburgh, 1971.
       128p.   col.   maps.   15cm.

5870   Bartholomew, John & Son, Ltd.
       New comparative atlas.   Edinburgh, 1971.
       1 vol.   col.   maps.   32cm.

5871   Beazley, Mitchell, Ltd.

The atlas of the universe.   By Patrick Moore.   London,
1971.
272p.   col. maps.   36cm.

5872   Beazley, Mitchell, Ltd.
       The world atlas of wine.   By Hugh Johnson.   London,
       1971.
       272p.   col. maps.   28cm.

5873   Bergvalls Förlag.
       Bergvalls atlas.   Stockholm, 1971.
       1 vol.   col. maps.   25cm.

5874   Bertelsmann, C.
       Bertelsmann Hausatlas.   Gütersloh, 1971.
       320p.   col. maps.   32cm.

5875   Bir Yayinevi.
       Büyük tarih atlasi.   With Istituto Geografico De Agostini.
       Istanbul, 1971.
       128p.   col. maps.   34cm.

5876   Bir Yayinevi.
       Ilkokul atlasi.   With Istituto Geografico De Agostini.
       Istanbul, 1971.
       20p.   col. maps.   26cm.

5877   Bir Yayinevi.
       Modern orta atlasi.   With Istituto Geografico De Agostini.
       Istanbul, 1971.
       32p.   col. maps.   34cm.

5878   Bir Yayinevi.
       Resimli ilkokul atlasi.   With Istituto Geografico De
       Agostini.   Istanbul, 1971.
       20p.   col. maps.   27cm.

5879   Bir Yayinevi.
       Tarih atlasi.   With Istituto Geografico De Agostini.
       Istanbul, 1971.
       32p.   col. maps.   27cm.

5880   British Sulphur Corp. Ltd.
       World sulphur and sulphuric acid atlas.   London, 1971.
       137p.   col. maps.   30cm.

5881   Cartographia.
       Illustrated political and economical world atlas.   3ed.
       Budapest, [1971].
       185p.   col. maps.   34cm.

5882   Cartographia.
       Pocket world atlas.   3ed.   Budapest, [1971].

     292p.   col.   maps.   18cm.

5883   Collins, William, Sons & Co., Ltd.
     Atlas two.   2ed.   London, 1971.
     76p.   col.   maps.   27cm.

5884   Collins, William, Sons & Co., Ltd.
     Collins clear school atlas.   London, 1971.
     64p.   col.   maps.   23cm.

5885   Collins, William, Sons & Co., Ltd.
     Collins-Longman study atlas.   17ed.   London, 1971.
     152p.   col.   maps.   28cm.

5886   Collins, William, Sons & Co., Ltd.
     Collins pocket atlas.   London, 1971.
     160p.   col.   maps.   17cm.

5887   Collins, William, Sons & Co., Ltd.
     The Collins world atlas.   Glasgow, [1971].
     334p.   col.   maps.   27cm.

5888   Cram, George F. Co.
     Cram modern world atlas.   With Hammond.   Indianapolis,
     Ind., [1971].
     358p.   col.   maps.   32cm.

5889   Cram, George F. Co.
     Student atlas: Earth science and outer space.   Indianapo-
     lis, Ind., [1971].
     34p.   col.   maps.   32cm.

5890   Curcio.
     Grande atlante internazionale.   Roma, 1971.
     99p.   col.   maps.   28cm.

5891   Czechoslovakia.   Kartografické nakladatelství.
     Kapesní atlas světa.   7ed.   By Dušan Trávníček and
     Jaroslav Vinař.   Praha, 1971.
     122p.   col.   maps.   17cm.

5892   Denoyer-Geppert Co.
     Denoyer's student atlas.   Chicago, 1971.
     88p.   col.   maps.   31cm.

5893   Dent, J. M.
     Dent's Canadian school atlas.   Rev. ed.   Toronto, [1971].
     115p.   col.   maps.   29cm.

5894   Djambatan.
     Atlas seluruh dunia.   Djakarta, [1971].
     67p.   col.   maps.   31cm.

5895 Doubleday.
      Family reference world atlas.   With Hammond.   Garden
      City, N. Y. , 1971.
      256p. col. maps. 29cm.

5896 Doubleday.
      Hammond contemporary world atlas.   New census ed.
      With Hammond.   Garden City, N. Y. , [1971].
      256p. col. maps. 29cm.

5897 Droemer.
      Knaurs grosser Weltatlas.   München, Zürich, [1971].
      536p. col. maps. 29cm.

5898 E. D. A. F.
      El universo en color.   Gran atlas y geografía Edaf físico-
      político-económico.   Madrid, [1971].
      395p. col. maps. 40cm.

5899 Edições Melhoramentos.
      Atlas geográfico Melhoramentos.   By Geraldo José
      Pauwels. São Paulo, 1971.
      100p. col. maps. 34cm.

5900 Editions Bordas.
      Grand atlas Bordas.   By Pierre Serryn.   Paris, Montreal,
      [1971].
      330p. col. maps. 40cm.

5901 Editions françaises.
      Atlas Larousse canadien.   By Benoit Brouillette and
      Maurice Saint-Yves.   Québec, [1971].
      161p. col. maps. 28cm.

5902 Fabbri.
      Atlante geografico scolastico.   Milano, 1971.
      64p. col. maps. 34cm.

5903 Fabbri.
      Atlante geografico universal.   By Piero Dagradi.   Milano,
      1971.
      110p. col. maps. 34cm.

5904 Fabbri.
      Nuovo atlante scolastico.   Milano, 1971.
      76p. col. maps. 30cm.

5905 Fabbri.
      Nuovo atlante universale.   Milano, 1971.
      149p. col. maps. 30cm.

5906 Faber & Faber.
      The Faber atlas.   By D. J. Sinclair.   London, 1971.

154p. col. maps. 32cm.

5907 Field Enterprises Educational Corp.
The world book atlas. With Rand McNally. Chicago,
1971.
392p. col. maps. 37cm.

5908 France. Centre de recherches historique.
Atlas des cultures vivrieres; atlas of food crops. By
Jacques Bertin. Paris, 1971.
41p. 61cm.

5909 Freytag, Berndt & Artaria.
Österreichischer Schulatlas. Wien, 1971.
90p. col. maps. 32cm.

5910 Generalstabens litografiska anstalt.
En delad varld. Stockholm, 1971.
1 vol. col. maps. 22cm.

5911 Geographical Pub. Co.
School and library atlas of the world. By Fred W.
Foster. Sycamore, Ill., [1971].
326p. col. maps. 57cm.

5912 Geokarta.
Geografski atlas. 13ed. By Ratimir Kalmeta. Beograd,
1971.
37p. col. maps. 34cm.

5913 GEO Publishing Co.
The Faber atlas. 5ed. By D. J. Sinclair. With
Hölzel. Oxford, 1971.
210p. col. maps. 31cm.

5914 Gyldendal.
Atlas I for folkeskolen. 2ed. København, 1971.
67p. col. maps. 27.5cm.

5915 Gyldendal.
Kulturgeografisk atlas. 7ed. By Johannes Humlum.
København, 1971.
2 vol. col. maps. 27cm.

5916 Haack, Hermann.
Atlas der Erdkunde fur die allgemeinbildenden poly-
technischen Oberschulen. Gotha, Leipzig, 1971.
128p. col. maps. 29cm.

5917 Haack, Hermann.
Atlas für die 4. und 5. Klasse. Gotha, 1971.
24p. col. maps. 29cm.

5918 Haase.
      Haases atlas. København, [1971].
      78p. col. maps. 26cm.

5919 Haase.
      Haases atlas for folkeskolen. 1ed. København, 1971.
      16p. col. maps. 26cm.

5920 Hachette.
      Atlas Hachette. By Pierre Gourou. Paris, [1971].
      223p. col. maps. 24cm.

5921 Hammond, Inc.
      Ambassador world atlas. Maplewood, N. J., 1971.
      496p. col. maps. 32cm.

5922 Hammond, Inc.
      Ambassador world atlas. New census ed. Maplewood,
      N. J., 1971.
      496p. col. maps. 32cm.

5923 Hammond, Inc.
      Atlas moderno universal con indice y nomenclador
      geografico. Maplewood, N. J., 1971.
      46p. col. maps. 32cm.

5924 Hammond, Inc.
      Family reference world atlas. Maplewood, N. J., 1971.
      256p. col. maps. 29cm.

5925 Hammond, Inc.
      Globemaster world atlas. Maplewood, N. J., 1971.
      112p. col. maps. 28cm.

5926 Hammond, Inc.
      Hammond citation world atlas. Maplewood, N. J., 1971.
      360p. col. maps. 32cm.

5927 Hammond, Inc.
      Hammond comparative world atlas. Maplewood, N. J.,
      1971.
      48p. col. maps. 32cm.

5928 Hammond, Inc.
      Hammond contemporary world atlas. New census ed.
      Maplewood, N. J. [1971].
      256p. col. maps. 29cm.

5929 Hammond, Inc.
      Hammond discovery world atlas. Maplewood, N. J.,
      [1971].
      48p. col. maps. 28cm.

5930 Hammond, Inc.
      Hammond headline world atlas. Maplewood, N. J. , 1971.
      48p. col. maps. 28cm.

5931 Hammond, Inc.
      Hammond standard world atlas; latest and most authentic
      geographical and statistical information. Maplewood,
      N. J. , 1971.
      320p. col. maps. 32cm.

5932 Hammond, Inc.
      Hammond world atlas. Maplewood, N. J. , [1971].
      208p. col. maps. 25cm.

5933 Hammond, Inc.
      Hammond world atlas. New census ed. Maplewood,
      N. J. , [1971].
      256p. col. maps. 29cm.

5934 Hammond, Inc.
      Intermediate world atlas. Maplewood, N. J. , [1971].
      63p. col. maps. 28cm.

5935 Hammond, Inc.
      International world atlas. Maplewood, N. J. , 1971.
      200p. col. maps. 32cm.

5936 Hammond, Inc.
      Man and history. [Atlas]. Maplewood, N. J. , [1971].
      192p. col. maps. 29cm.

5937 Hammond, Inc.
      Medallion world atlas. Maplewood, N. J. , 1971.
      672p. col. maps. 32cm.

5938 Hammond, Inc.
      Reference atlas for schools. Maplewood, N. J. , [1971].
      48p. col. maps. 28cm.

5939 Hammond, Inc.
      Standard world atlas. Maplewood, N. J. , 1971.
      192p. col. maps. 32cm.

5940 Hammond, Inc.
      World atlas. Classics ed. Maplewood, N. J. , 1971.
      352p. col. maps. 32cm.

5941 Hammond, Inc.
      World atlas. Hallmark ed. Maplewood, N. J. , 1971.
      2 vol. col. maps. 32cm.

5942 Hölzel, Ed. Verlag.
      Österreichischer Atlas für höhere Schulen. 98ed. By

H. Eckelt.   Wien, 1971.
165p. col. maps. 32cm.

5943 Houghton, Mifflin Co.
      The Times atlas of the world.   2ed.   With Bartholomew.
      Boston, 1971.
      394p. col. maps. 46cm.

5944 International Bank for Reconstruction and Development.
      World bank atlas: population, per capita product, and
      growth rate.   6ed.   Washington, D.C., 1971.
      13p. col. maps. 28cm.

5945 Istituto Geografico De Agostini.
      Atlante della produzione e dei commerci.   By Umberto
      Bonapace and Giuseppe Motta.   Novara, 1971.
      120p. col. maps. 31cm.

5946 Istituto Geografico De Agostini.
      Atlante geografico metodico.   By Umberto Bonapace and
      Giuseppe Motta.   Novara, 1971.
      206p. col. maps. 36cm.

5947 Istituto Geografico De Agostini.
      Atlante geografico moderno.   By Umberto Bonapace and
      Giuseppe Motta.   Novara, 1971.
      133p. col. maps. 37cm.

5948 Istituto Geografico De Agostini.
      Calendario atlante de Agostini.   Novara, 1971.
      827p. col. maps. 16cm.

5949 Istituto Geografico De Agostini.
      Nuovo atlante della scuola media unica.   By Umberto
      Bonapace and Giuseppe Motta.   Novara, 1971.
      64p. col. maps. 21.5cm.

5950 Istituto Geografico De Agostini.
      Nuovo atlante mondiale.   By Umberto Bonapace and
      Giuseppe Motta.   Novara, 1971.
      532p. col. maps. 36cm.

5951 Jacaranda.
      Jacaranda junior world atlas.   By V. G. Honour.   Milton,
      1971.
      91p. col. maps. 28cm.

5952 Jacaranda.
      The Jacaranda atlas.   2ed.   By V. G. Honour.   Milton,
      1971.
      144p. col. maps. 29cm.

5953 Jugoslavenski leksikografski zavod.

Naš svijet-zemljopisni atlas svijeta za VI i VII razved
osnovne skole. 4ed. Zagreb, 1971.
1 vol. col. maps. 32.5cm.

5954 Kantonaler Lehrmittel Verlag.
Schweizerischer Sekundarschulatlas. 11ed. By Eduard
Imhof. With Orell Füssli. Zürich, 1971.
88p. col. maps. 34cm.

5955 Kapelusz y Cía.
Coloratlas Kapelusz Mundi: físico, político, económico,
estadístico. Buenos Aires, 1971.
78p. col. maps. 32cm.

5956 Kaplán Cojano, Oscar.
Geografía atlas universal. Santiago de Chile, 1971.
347p. col. maps. 25cm.

5957 Kartográfiai Vállalat.
Földrajzi atlasz-az általános iskolák számára. Budapest,
1971.
32p. col. maps. 28cm.

5958 Kartográfiai Vállalat.
Földrajzi atlasz a középiskolák számára. Budapest, 1971.
60p. col. maps. 29cm.

5959 Kartográfiai Vállalat.
Képes politikai és gazdasági világatlasz. By Sándor Radó.
Budapest, 1971.
414p. col. maps. 34cm.

5960 Kartográfiai Vállalat.
Kis világatlasz. 3ed. By Sándor Radó. Budapest, 1971.
292p. col. maps. 19cm.

5961 Knaur, Th. Nachf.
Knaurs Grosser Weltatlas. München, 1971.
536p. col. maps. 46cm.

5962 Koninklijke Luchtvaart Maatschappij, N. V.
KLM flight companion. Amsterdam, [1971].
16p. col. maps. 26cm.

5963 Läromedelsförlagen.
Nordisk skolatlas; läroverksupplagen. By Hans W:son
Ahlmann. With Generalstabens litografiska anstalt.
Stockholm, 1971.
85p. col. maps. 34cm.

5964 Läromedelsförlagen.
Skolans världs atlas. Stockholm, 1971.
96p. col. maps. 32cm.

5965   Läromedelsförlagen.
       Skolatlas. By Magnus Lundqvist and Olof Hedbom.   Stock-
       holm, 1971.
       1 vol.   col.   maps.   34cm.

5966   Larousse.
       Atlas Larousse canadien.   By Benoît Brouillette and
       Maurice Saint-Ives.   Québec, [1971].
       168p.   col.   maps.   28cm.

5967   Livraria Sá da Costa.
       Novo atlas escolar português, histórico-geográfico.   11ed.
       By João Soares.   Lisboa, 1971.
       85p.   col.   maps.   34cm.

5968   Lloyd's Corp. of.
       Lloyd's maritime atlas.   8ed.   London, 1971.
       166p.   col.   maps.   25cm.

5969   Marketing International.
       International airline & road atlas.   1ed.   Frankfurt am
       Main, [1971].
       1 vol.   col.   maps.   30cm.

5970   Meyer, Kartographisches Institut.
       Meyers grosser physischer Weltatlas.   Band 4: Atlas zur
       physischen Geographie; Oreographie.   By Karlheinz Wagner.
       Mannheim, [1971].
       67p.   col.   maps.   30cm.

5971   Meyer, Kartographisches Institut.
       Weltatlas.   Mannheim, 1971.
       490p.   col.   maps.   30cm.

5972   Mondadori.
       Atlante internazionale.   Milano, 1971.
       126p.   col.   maps.   28cm.

5973   Mouton & Co.
       Atlas des cultures vivrières.   Atlas of food crops.   By
       Jacques Bertin.   Paris, [1971].
       59p.   col.   maps.   42cm.

5974   N. I. Sh. Mjete Mësimore e Sportive "Hamid Shijaku."
       Atlas gjeografik i shqipërisë.   By Ergjin Samimit.   Tiranë,
       1971.
       26p.   col.   maps.   32cm.

5975   Nystrom.
       Nystrom reference atlas for schools.   With Hammond.
       Chicago, 1971.
       48p.   col.   maps.   28cm.

5976 Nystrom.
Nystrom world atlas. By Richard Edes Harrison.
Chicago, [1971].
62p. col. maps. 26cm.

5977 Nystrom.
Reference atlas for schools. With Hammond. Chicago,
[1971].
48p. col. maps. 28cm.

5978 Oliver & Boyd.
The advanced atlas of modern geography. 9ed. With
Bartholomew. Edinburgh, 1971.
163p. col. maps. 38cm.

5979 Otava.
Kansakoulun Kartasto. Helsinki, 1971.
18p. col. maps. 27cm.

5980 Otava.
Otavan Koulukartasto. Helsinki, 1971.
44p. col. maps. 27cm.

5981 Oxford University Press.
Shorter Oxford economic atlas of the world. 4ed. London, 1971.
128p. col. maps. 26cm.

5982 Parey Verlag.
Weltforstatlas. By Claus Wiebecke. Hamburg, 1971.
in parts. col. maps. 42cm.

5983 Pembina.
Atlas Indonesia & dunia, untuk sekolah dasar di Djawa,
Bali, Nusatenggara Maluku. By Chalid Latif and M. J.
Ridwan. Djakarta, [1971].
28p. col. maps. 32cm.

5984 Pergamon Press, Ltd.
Wheaton primary atlas. By L. R. Hawkes. Oxford,
1971.
36p. col. maps. 26cm.

5985 Philip, George & Son, Ltd.
Around the world. A view from space [atlas].
London, [1971].
125p. col. maps. 29cm.

5986 Philip, George & Son, Ltd.
Modern commonwealth atlas. 6ed. By Harold Fullard.
London, 1971.
72p. col. maps. 28cm.

5987   Philip, George & Son, Ltd.
        Philips' elementary atlas.   107ed.   By Harold Fullard.
        London, 1971.
        52p.   col.   maps.   28cm.

5988   Philip, George & Son, Ltd.
        Philip's first venture atlas.   By Harold Fullard.   London,
        1971.
        24p.   col.   maps.   23cm.

5989   Philip, George & Son, Ltd.
        Philips' modern school atlas.   68ed.   By Harold Fullard.
        London, 1971.
        132p.   col.   maps.   29cm.

5990   Philip, George & Son, Ltd.
        Philips' new school atlas.   57ed.   By Harold Fullard.
        London, 1971.
        64p.   col.   maps.   29cm.

5991   Philip, George & Son, Ltd.
        Philips' practical atlas.   4ed.   By Harold Fullard.   Lon-
        don, 1971.
        177p.   col.   maps.   29cm.

5992   Philip, George & Son, Ltd.
        Philip's venture atlas.   By Harold Fullard.   London, 1971.
        50p.   col.   maps.   28cm.

5993   Philip, George & Son, Ltd.
        Pocket atlas of the world.   London, 1971.
        124p.   col.   maps.   17cm.

5994   Philip, George & Son, Ltd.
        Primary atlas.   London, 1971.
        16p.   col.   maps.   28cm.

5995   Philip, George & Son, Ltd.
        The atlas of the universe.   2ed.   By Patrick Moore.
        London, 1971.
        272p.   col.   maps.   36cm.

5996   Philip, George & Son, Ltd.
        The 'Observer' atlas of world affairs: a guide to major
        tensions and conflicts.   By Andrew Wilson.   London,
        1971.
        111p.   col.   maps.   28cm.

5997   Philip, George & Son, Ltd.
        Visual atlas.   By Harold Fullard.   London, [1971].
        47p.   col.   maps.   23cm.

5998   Philip, George & Son, Ltd.

World patterns; the Aldine college atlas. By Harold
Fullard. London, 1971.
128p. col. maps. 28cm.

5999 Poland. Państwowe przedsiębiorstwo wydawnictw Kartograficznych.
Atlas geograficzny. 7ed. By Jan Rzędowski. Warszawa,
1971.
151p. col. maps. 32cm.

6000 Poland. Państwowe przedsiębiorstwo wydawnictw Kartograficznych.
Atlas geograficzny licealny. 7ed. Warszawa, 1971.
151p. col. maps. 32cm.

6001 Poland. Państwowe przedsiębiorstwo wydawnictw Kartograficznych.
Atlas geograficzny, V-VIII Klasy. 8ed. Warszawa, 1971.
60p. col. maps. 31cm.

6002 Poland. Państwo przedsiębiorstwo wydawnictw Kartograficznych.
Kieszonkowy atlas świata. Warszawa, 1971.
402p. col. maps. 16cm.

6003 Rand McNally & Co.
Atlas of the universe. 1st Canadian ed. By Stuart Kaminsky and Charles Yoder. Chicago, 1971.
1 vol. col. maps. 36cm.

6004 Rand McNally & Co.
Cosmopolitan world atlas. Chicago, Ill., 1971.
428p. col. maps. 38cm.

6005 Rand McNally & Co.
Goode's world atlas. 13 rev. ed. By Edward B. Espenshade, Jr. Chicago, 1971.
315p. col. maps. 29cm.

6006 Rand McNally & Co.
Rand McNally premier world atlas. New census ed.
Chicago, 1971.
336p. col. maps. 37cm.

6007 Rand McNally & Co.
Rand McNally premier world atlas. New portrait ed.
Chicago, 1971.
350p. col. maps. 37cm.

6008 Rand McNally & Co.
Rand McNally regional atlas. 4ed. By Edward B.
Espenshade, Jr. Chicago, 1971.
64p. col. maps. 29cm.

6009   Rand McNally & Co.
       The atlas of the universe.   2ed.   By Patrick Moore.
       Chicago, 1971.
       272p.   col. maps.   36cm.

6010   Rand McNally & Co.
       The world book atlas.   With Field Enterprises Educational
       Corp.   Chicago, [1971].
       392p.   col. maps.   37cm.

6011   Rand McNally & Co.
       World atlas.   Family ed.   Chicago, Ill., 1971.
       328p.   col. maps.   32cm.

6012   Rand McNally & Co.
       World atlas.   Imperial ed.   Chicago, [1971].
       288p.   col. maps.   32cm.

6013   Rand McNally & Co.
       World atlas.   Reference ed.   Chicago, Ill., [1971].
       245p.   col. maps.   32cm.

6014   Rand McNally & Co.
       World master atlas.   Reference ed.   Chicago, Ill., 1971.
       248p.   col. maps.   32cm.

6015   Reader's Digest Association, Ltd.
       The Reader's Digest great world atlas.   3rd Canadian ed.
       Montreal, [1971].
       187p.   col. maps.   41cm.

6016   School and Library Publ. Co.
       School and Library atlas of the world.   By Fred W.
       Foster.   Sycamore, Ill., 1971.
       350p.   col. maps.   55cm.

6017   Scott, Foresman & Co.
       World patterns: The Aldine college atlas.   By Harold
       Fullard.   Chicago, 1971.
       128p.   col. maps.   28cm.

6018   Simon and Schuster.
       The world atlas of wine.   By Hugh Johnson and Mitchell
       Beazley.   London, New York, 1971.
       272p.   col. maps.   30cm.

6019   Školska Knjiga.
       Naš svijet.   Zemljopisni atlas svijeta za VI i VII razred
       osnovne škole.   Zagreb, [1971].
       52p.   col. maps.   33cm.

6020   Slovenska Kartografia.
       Školský zemepisný atlas.   8ed.   Bratislava, 1971.

51p.   col.   maps.   28cm.

6021   Teikoku-Shoin Co., Ltd.
       Social study atlas for middle-school pupils.   Tokyo, [1971].
       138p.   col.   maps.   31cm.

6022   Times of London.
       The Times atlas of the world.   2ed.   With Bartholomew.
       Edinburgh, 1971.
       394p.   col.   maps.   46cm.

6023   Učila.
       Atlas za škole II stupnja.   3ed.   By Zvonimir Dugački.
       Zagreb, 1971.
       107p.   col.   maps.   34cm.

6024   U. S. S. R.   Glavnoe upravlenie geodezii i kartografii.
       Atlas istorii dvernego mira dlya V klassa strednei shkoly.
       Moskva, 1971.
       12p.   col.   maps.   26cm.

6025   U. S. S. R.   Glavnoe upravlenie geodezii i kartografii.
       Atlas istorii strednich vekov dlya VI klassa stredneii shkoly.
       Moskva, 1971.
       16p.   col.   maps.   26cm.

6026   U. S. S. R.   Glavnoe upravlenie geodezii i kartografii.
       Atlas mira.   Moskva, 1971.
       184p.   col.   maps.   34cm.

6027   U. S. S. R.   Glavnoe upravlenie geodezii i kartografii.
       Atlas mira.   Pocket ed.   Moskva, 1971.
       64p.   col.   maps.   18cm.

6028   U. S. S. R.   Glavnoe upravlenie geodezii i kartografii.
       Atlas zaribechnich stran dlya srednei shkoly.   Moskva,
       1971.
       48p.   col.   maps.   28cm.

6029   U. S. S. R.   Glavnoe upravlenie geodezii i kartografii.
       Geograficheskii atlas dlya 5-go klassa.   Moskva, 1971.
       16p.   col.   maps.   28cm.

6030   U. S. S. R.   Glavnoe upravlenie geodezii i kartografii.
       Geograficheskii atlas materikov dlya 6-go klassa.
       Moskva, 1971.
       36p.   col.   maps.   28cm.

6031   U. S. S. R.   Glavnoe upravlenie geodezii i kartografii.
       Malyi atlas mira.   Moskva, 1971.
       159p.   col.   maps.   19cm.

6032   U. S. S. R.   Glavnoe upravlenie geodezii i kartografii.

Uchebnii atlas mira.   Moskva, 1971.
147p. col. maps. 34cm.

6033   U. S. S. R. Glavnoe upravlenie geodezii i kartografii.
       World Atlas. English ed. Moskva, 1971.
       184p. col. maps. 34cm.

6034   Velhagen & Klasing.
       Unsere Welt. Grundschulatlas. Berlin, [1971].
       39p. col. maps. 28cm.

6035   Vicens-Vives, Jaime.
       Atlas de geografía general. 11ed. By J. Vicens and S.
       Sobrequés. Barcelona, [1971].
       50p. col. maps. 24cm.

6036   Westermann, Georg.
       Diercke Weltatlas. 75ed. Braunschweig, 1971.
       228p. col. maps. 34cm.

6037   Westermann, Georg.
       Westermann Atlas für Dortmunder Schulen. 3ed. By
       Herbert Frommberger. Braunschweig, 1971.
       39p. col. maps. 34cm.

6038   Westermann, Georg.
       Westermann Atlas für Essener Schulen. Braunschweig,
       1971.
       28p. col. maps. 34cm.

6039   Westermann, Georg.
       Westermann-Grundschulatlas. Braunschweig, [1971].
       32p. col. maps. 30cm.

6040   Westermann, Georg.
       Westermann Schulatlas. Braunschweig, 1971.
       144p. col. maps. 30cm.

6041   Western Pub. Co.
       The golden book picture atlas of the world. Wayne, N. J.,
       1971.
       6 vol. col. maps. 32cm.

6042   Wolters-Noordhoff.
       De grote Bosatlas. 47ed. By F. J. Ormeling. Gronin-
       gen, 1971.
       202p. col. maps. 34cm.

6043   W. S. O. Y.
       Kansakoulun Kartasto. Porvoo, Helsinki, 1971.
       38p. col. maps. 26cm.

6044   Zanichelli, Nicola.

Atlante geografico generale Zanichelli.   Bologna, [1971].
227p.   col.   maps.   32cm.

6045   Zenkyozu.
New world atlas.   By Keiji Tanaka.   Tokyo, 1971.
186p.   col.   maps.   42cm.

1972

6046   Aguilar, S. A. de Ediciones.
Atlas general básico Aguilar.   32ed.   Madrid, 1972.
118p.   col.   maps.   35cm.

6047   Atlas and Maps Industries.
A world atlas for Ceylon students.   In Sinhala and Tamil.
Colombo, [1972].
1 vol.   28cm.

6048   Bartholomew, John & Son, Ltd.
Exploration universe; an atlas of our environment.   By
William Kinnear and James R. Carson.   Edinburgh, 1972.
47p.   col.   maps.   31cm.

6049   Bartholomew, John & Son, Ltd.
Mini atlas.   Edinburgh, 1972.
128p.   col.   maps.   15cm.

6050   Beazley, Mitchell, Ltd.
The atlas of the earth.   By Tony Loftas.   With Philip.
London, 1972.
447p.   col.   maps.   38cm.

6051   Bertelsmann, C.
Atlas international.   Gütersloh, [1972].
456p.   col.   maps.   39cm.

6052   Bertelsmann, C.
Der grosse Bertelsmann Weltatlas.   Jubiläumsausgabe.
By W. Bormann.   Gütersloh, 1972.
440p.   col.   maps.   32cm.

6053   Bir Yayinevi.
Modern orta atlasi.   With Istituto Geografico De Agostini.
Istanbul, [1972].
43p.   col.   maps.   34cm.

6054   Blondel La Rougery.
Atlas geographique la vie ouvriere.   Paris, 1972.
1 vol.   col.   maps.   28cm.

6055   Cappelens, J. W., Forlag, A. S.

Cappelens Norges atlas for skolen.   By K. B. Sollesnes.
Oslo, 1972.
37p.   col.   maps.   30cm.

6056   Cárdenas Associates.
       Atlas universal "Cosmos"; astronomía, geografía, geología,
       zoología, profusamente ilustrado.   By Eduardo Cárdenas.
       Fort Lauderdale, Fla., [1972].
       320p.   20cm.

6057   Collins, William, Sons & Co., Ltd.
       Collins-Longman study atlas.   18ed.   London, 1972.
       152p.   col.   maps.   28cm.

6058   Collins, William, Sons & Co., Ltd.
       Collins-Longman study atlas.   19ed.   London, 1972.
       152p.   col.   maps.   28cm.

6059   Collins, William, Sons & Co., Ltd.
       Collins graphic atlas.   London, 1972.
       136p.   col.   maps.   28cm.

6060   Collins, William, Sons & Co., Ltd.
       Collins pocket atlas.   London, 1972.
       96p.   col.   maps.   17cm.

6061   Cram, George F., Co.
       Cram's student quick reference atlas of the world.
       Indianapolis, Ind., 1972.
       27p.   col.   maps.   31cm.

6062   Czechoslovakia.   Kartografické nakladatelství.
       Atlas svéta.   Praha, 1972.
       94p.   col.   maps.   32cm.

6063   Czechoslovakia.   Kartografické nakladatelství.
       Školský atlas světových dějin.   6ed.   Praha, 1972.
       95p.   col.   maps.   31cm.

6064   Doubleday.
       Hammond contemporary world atlas.   New Census ed.
       With Hammond.   Garden City, N.Y., [1972].
       256p.   col.   maps.   29cm.

6065   Doubleday.
       Family reference world atlas.   With Hammond.   Garden
       City, N.Y., 1972.
       256p.   col.   maps.   29cm.

6066   Edições Melhoramentos.
       Atlas geográfico universal Melhoramentos.   By Geraldo
       José Pauwels.   São Paulo, 1972.
       100p.   col.   maps.   35cm.

6067   Editions Bordas.
       Atlas général Bordas, historique et géographique.   By
       Pierre Serryn and R. Blasselle.   With Hölzel.   Paris,
       Wien, 1972.
       215p.   col.   maps.   31cm.

6068   Editions Stauffacher.
       Neuer Weltatlas.   By E. T. Rimli.   With Haack.   Zürich,
       1972.
       444p.   col.   maps.   44cm.

6069   Editorial Teide.
       Atlas básico universal.   With Istituto Geografico De
       Agostini.   Barcelona, [1972].
       80p.   col.   maps.   31cm.

6070   Elsevier.
       Grote Winkler Prins atlas.   By A. F. J. Wubbe.   Amster-
       dam, Brussel, 1972.
       340p.   col.   maps.   38cm.

6071   Encyclopaedia Britannica.
       Britannica atlas.   With Rand McNally.   Chicago, [1972].
       541p.   col.   maps.   39cm.

6072   Fabritius.
       Fabritius verdensatlas.   By Fridtjov Isachsen and Hallstein
       Myklebost.   Oslo, 1972.
       72p.   col.   maps.   30cm.

6073   Field Enterprises Educational Corp.
       The world book atlas.   With Rand McNally.   Chicago,
       [1972].
       392p.   col.   maps.   37cm.

6074   Generalstabens litografiska anstalt.
       Oppikoulon kartasto.   Stockholm, 1972.
       63p.   col.   maps.   29cm.

6075   Geokarta.
       Geografski atlas.   15ed.   By Mihailo Radavanović.   Beo-
       grad, 1972.
       35p.   col.   maps.   34cm.

6076   Gyldendal.
       Lille erhvervsgeografisk atlas.   By Johannes Humlum.
       København, 1972.
       39p.   col.   maps.   31cm.

6077   Haack, Hermann.
       Die Erde.   Haack Kleiner Atlas.   2ed.   By K. Breitfeld.
       Gotha, Leipzig, 1972.
       440p.   col.   maps.   17cm.

6078   Haack, Hermann.
       <u>Haack Weltatlas.</u> 1ed. Gotha, Leipzig, 1972.
       412p. col. maps. 36cm.

6079   Hachette.
       <u>Atlas Hachette.</u> By Pierre Gourou. Paris, 1972.
       223p. col. maps. 24cm.

6080   Hachette.
       <u>Nouvel atlas illustré.</u> By C. Saibène. Paris, [1970].
       94p. col. maps. 32.5cm.

6081   Hammond, Inc.
       <u>Family reference world atlas.</u> Maplewood, N.J., 1972.
       256p. col. maps. 32cm.

6082   Hammond, Inc.
       <u>Hammond advanced reference atlas.</u> Maplewood, N.J.,
       <u>[1972].</u>
       172p. col. maps. 32cm.

6083   Hammond, Inc.
       <u>Hammond citation world atlas.</u> Maplewood, N.J., 1972.
       352p. col. maps. 32cm.

6084   Hammond, Inc.
       <u>Hammond comparative world atlas.</u> Maplewood, N.J.,
       <u>[1972].</u>
       48p. col. maps. 32cm.

6085   Hammond, Inc.
       <u>Hammond contemporary world atlas.</u> New census ed.
       <u>Maplewood, N.J., [1972].</u>
       256p. col. maps. 29cm.

6086   Hammond, Inc.
       <u>Hammond headline world atlas.</u> Maplewood, N.J., [1972].
       48p. col. maps. 28cm.

6087   Hammond, Inc.
       <u>Hammond standard world atlas; latest and most authentic</u>
       <u>geographical and statistical information.</u> Maplewood,
       N.J., 1972.
       320p. col. maps. 32cm.

6088   Hammond, Inc.
       <u>Hammond world atlas.</u> Collectors ed. Maplewood, N.J.,
       <u>[1972].</u>
       352p. col. maps. 32cm.

6089   Hammond, Inc.
       <u>Intermediate world atlas.</u> Maplewood, N.J., [1972].
       63p. col. maps. 28cm.

6090 Hammond, Inc.
Standard world atlas. Maplewood, N.J., 1972.
1 vol. col. maps. 32cm.

6091 Hammond, Inc.
Standard world atlas. Deluxe ed. Maplewood, N.J., 1972.
320p. col. maps. 32cm.

6092 Hammond, Inc.
World atlas. Collectors ed. Maplewood, N.J., 1972.
352p. col. maps. 32cm.

6093 Hammond, Inc.
World atlas. Classics ed. Maplewood, N.J., 1972.
1 vol. col. maps. 32cm.

6094 Hammond, Inc.
World atlas for students. Maplewood, N.J., 1972.
37p. col. maps. 32cm.

6095 Herder Verlag.
Herders grosser Weltatlas. 4ed. Freiburg, Basel, Wien,
1972.
250p. col. maps. 40cm.

6096 Heyden & Son, Ltd.
The Heyden new world atlas. New York, London, 1970.
270p. col. maps. 29cm.

6097 Hirt Verlag.
Hirts Taschenatlas. With Kartografie. Kiel, 1972.
178p. col. maps. 16cm.

6098 Hölzel, Ed. Verlag.
Atlas Belgie en de wereld. By J. van den Branden and
M. Nouboers. Wien, 1972.
141p. col. maps. 32cm.

6099 Hölzel, Ed. Verlag.
Österreichischer Atlas für höhere Schulen. 99ed. Wien,
1972.
165p. col. maps. 32cm.

6100 Hölzel, Ed. Verlag.
Österreichischer Hauptschulatlas. 10ed. Wien, 1972.
88p. col. maps. 33cm.

6101 Istituto Geografico De Agostini.
Atlante geografico metodico. By Umberto Bonapace and
Giuseppe Motta. Novara, [1972].
190p. col. maps. 37cm.

6102 Istituto Geografico De Agostini.

Atlante geografico moderno. By Umberto Bonapace and
Giuseppe Motta. Novara, [1972].
133p. col. maps. 37cm.

6103   Istituto Geografico De Agostini.
       Modern orta atlas. Istanbul, [1972].
       43p. col. maps. 34cm.

6104   Istituto Geografico De Agostini.
       Nuovo atlante mondiale. By Umberto Bonapace and
       Giuseppe Motta. Novara, 1972.
       532p. col. maps. 36cm.

6105   Jacaranda.
       Robinson's world atlas. Milton, Q. , 1972.
       130p. col. maps. 28cm.

6106   Jacaranda.
       The Jacaranda atlas. By V. G. Honour. Milton, 1972.
       145p. col. maps. 29cm.

6107   Johnston & Bacon.
       The traveller's world reference atlas. By Dan Hillman.
       Edinburgh, London, 1972.
       38p. col. maps. 27cm.

6108   JRO Verlag.
       JRO Taschen Weltatlas. München, [1972].
       196p. col. maps. 17cm.

6109   JRO Verlag.
       JRO Weltatlas. Handausgabe. München, 1972.
       232p. col. maps. 30cm.

6110   Kartográfiai Vállalat.
       Földrajzi atlasz a középiskolák számára. By Sándor
       Radó. Budapest, 1972.
       60p. col. maps. 29cm.

6111   Kartografie.
       Atlas svéta. 3ed. By Vladimir Vokálek. Praha, 1972.
       144p. col. maps. 29cm.

6112   Kartografie.
       Hirt's Taschenatlas. Praha, 1972.
       178p. col. maps. 16cm.

6113   Kartografie.
       Malý školní zemépisný atlas. 9ed. Praha, 1972.
       16p. col. maps. 17cm.

6114   Knaur, Th. Nachf.
       Knaurs Grosser Weltatlas. München, 1972.

        536p.   col. maps.   46cm.

6115   Kümmerly & Frey.
       KF Taschen-Weltatlas.   Bern, [1972].
       35p.   col. maps.   18cm.

6116   Meulenhoff, J. M.
       Atlas Belgie en den wereld.   By J. van den Branden and
       M. Nouboers.   Amsterdam, 1972.
       150p.   col. maps.   32cm.

6117   Mladinska Knjiga.
       Veliki atlas sveta.   By Jakob Medved.   Ljubljana, 1972.
       406p.   col. maps.   31cm.

6118   Nelson, Thomas & Sons, Ltd.
       My first picture atlas.   London, 1972.
       52p.   col. maps.   33cm.

6119   Nelson, Thomas & Sons, Ltd.
       World picture atlas.   London, 1972.
       112p.   col. maps.   32cm.

6120   Otava.
       Otavan peruskoulu-kartasto.   Helsinki, 1972.
       113p.   col. maps.   27cm.

6121   Oxford University Press.
       Oxford economic atlas of the world.   4ed.   By D. B.
       Jones.   London, 1972.
       415p.   col. maps.   38cm.

6122   Oxford University Press.
       The Canadian Oxford school atlas.   3ed.   By E. G. Pleva.
       Toronto, 1972.
       166p.   col. maps.   27cm.

6123   Oxford University Press.
       The Oxford school atlas.   London, 1972.
       202p.   col. maps.   25cm.

6124   Oxford University Press.
       The shorter Oxford school atlas.   3ed.   Oxford, 1972.
       64p.   col. maps.   25cm.

6125   Peuser, Ediciones Geográficas.
       Nuevo atlas universal.   Buenos Aires, [1972].
       80p.   col. maps.   37cm.

6126   Philip, George & Son, Ltd.
       Philips' concorde world atlas.   By Harold Fullard.   Lon-
       don, 1972.
       212p.   col. maps.   29cm.

6127   Philip, George & Son, Ltd.
        Philips' modern school atlas.   69ed.   By Harold Fullard.
        London, 1972.
        132p.   col.   maps.   29cm.

6128   Philip, George & Son, Ltd.
        Philips' modern school atlas.   70ed.   By Harold Fullard.
        London, 1972.
        132p.   col.   maps.   29cm.

6129   Philip, George & Son, Ltd.
        Philips' world horizons atlas.   By H. Fullard.   London,
        [1972].
        32p.   col.   maps.   28cm.

6130   Philip, George & Son, Ltd.
        Primary atlas.   London, 1972.
        18p.   col.   maps.   28cm.

6131   Philip, George & Son, Ltd.
        The atlas of the earth.   By Tony Loftas.   With Mitchell
        Beazley Ltd.   London, 1972.
        447p.   col.   maps.   38cm.

6132   Philip, George & Son, Ltd.
        The International atlas.   London, 1972.
        501p.   col.   maps.   39cm.

6133   Philip, George & Son, Ltd.
        The university atlas.   14ed.   By H. Fullard and H. C.
        Darby.   London, 1972.
        187p.   col.   maps.   29cm.

6134   Philip, George & Son, Ltd.
        World atlas of shipping.   By W. D. Ewart and H. Fullard.
        London, 1972.
        277p.   col.   maps.   29cm.

6135   Poland.   Państwowe przedsiębiorstwo wydawnictw Kartografi-
        cznych.
        Atlas geograficzny dla Kl. IV.   Warszawa, 1972.
        36p.   col.   maps.   26cm.

6136   Poland.   Pańtswowe przedsiębiorstwo wydawnictw Kartografi-
        cznych.
        Atlas geograficzny, V-VIII Klasy.   Warszawa, 1972.
        60p.   col.   maps.   31cm.

6137   Poland.   Państwowe przedsiębiorstwo wydawnictw Kartografi-
        cznych.
        Atlas geograficzny licealny.   9ed.   Warszawa, 1972.
        120p.   col.   maps.   32.5cm.

6138   Porto Editora.
         Atlas editora.   With Aguilar.   Porto, [1972].
         135p.   col.   maps.   32cm.

6139   Quadrangle Books.
         New York Times atlas of the world.   With Bartholomew.
         New York, 1972.
         268p.   col.   maps.   37cm.

6140   Radio Amateur Callbook, Inc.
         Radio amateurs world atlas.   6ed.   Lake Bluff, Ill.,
         [1972].
         19p.   col.   maps.   31cm.

6141   Rand McNally & Co.
         Cosmopolitan world atlas.   Chicago, 1972.
         428p.   col.   maps.   38cm.

6142   Rand McNally & Co.
         New cosmopolitan world atlas.   Chicago, 1972.
         420p.   col.   maps.   37cm.

6143   Rand McNally & Co.
         Rand McNally cosmopolitan world atlas.   Chicago, [1972].
         352p.   col.   maps.   27cm.

6144   Rand McNally & Co.
         Rand McNally one dollar fifty world atlas.   Chicago, 1972.
         28p.   col.   maps.   30cm.

6145   Rand McNally & Co.
         Rand McNally popular world atlas.   Chicago, 1972.
         201p.   col.   maps.   31cm.

6146   Rand McNally & Co.
         The earth and man: a Rand McNally world atlas.   Chi-
         cago, 1972.
         439p.   col.   maps.   38cm.

6147   Rand McNally & Co.
         The world book atlas.   With Field Enterprises Educational
         Corp.   Chicago, [1972].
         392p.   col.   maps.   37cm.

6148   Rand McNally & Co.
         World in Review.   [Atlas.]   By Lester Markel.   With The
         New York Times.   New York, 1972.
         156p.   col.   maps.   37cm.

6149   Reader's Digest Association, Ltd.
         The Reader's Digest great world atlas.   2ed.   3 rev.
         London, 1972.
         179p.   col.   maps.   40cm.

6150   Sahab.
       Atlas-i nuwīn-i gāhān dar asr-i fadā.   Teheran, [1972].
       130p.   col.   maps.   29cm.

6151   Slovenska Kartografia.
       Atlas sveta.   2ed.   By Vladimír Vokálek.   Bratislava,
       1972.
       151p.   col.   maps.   33cm.

6152   Slovenska Kartografia.
       Školský zemepisný atlas.   Bratislava, 1972.
       51p.   col.   maps.   32cm.

6153   Studi Geo-Cartografici.
       Atlante mondiale Grolier.   By Federico de Agostini.
       Milano, 1972.
       2 vol.   col.   maps.   33cm.

6154   Südwest Verlag.
       Neuer grosser Weltatlas für Heim, Unterricht und Reise.
       By Horst Mietzner.   München, [1972].
       168p.   col.   maps.   31cm.

6155   The New York Times.
       The New York Times atlas of the world.   With The Times
       of London and Bartholomew.   New York, 1972.
       268p.   col.   maps.   37cm.

6156   Times of London.
       The Times atlas of the world.   Comprehensive ed.   With
       Bartholomew.   London, 1972.
       123p.   col.   maps.   46cm.

6157   Times of London.
       The Times atlas of the world.   4ed.   With Bartholomew.
       London, 1972.
       400p.   col.   maps.   46cm.

6158   Times of London.
       The Times concise atlas of the world.   London, 1972.
       272p.   col.   maps.   38cm.

6159   Učila.
       Atlas za osnovnu školu.   4ed.   By Zvonimir Dugački.
       Zagreb, 1972.
       53p.   col.   maps.   33cm.

6160   Učila.
       Atlas za škole II stupnja.   4ed.   By Zvonimir Dugački.
       Zagreb, 1972.
       107p.   col.   maps.   34cm.

6161 Učila.
Atlas za škole II stupnja. 5ed. By Zvonimir Dugački.
Zagreb, 1972.
107p. col. maps. 34cm.

6162 U. S. S. R. Glavnoe upravlenie geodezii i kartografii.
Agroklimaticheskii atlas mira. Moskva, 1972.
115p. col. maps. 41cm.

6163 U. S. S. R. Glavnoe upravlenie geodezii i kartografii.
Atlas mira. Moskva, 1972.
64p. col. maps. 24cm.

6164 U. S. S. R. Glavnoe upravlenie geodezii i kartografii.
Atlas mira. Moskva, 1972.
66p. col. maps. 19cm.

6165 U. S. S. R. Glavnoe upravlenie geodezii i kartografii.
Malyi atlas mira. By V. N. Salmanova and L. N.
Kolosova. Moskva, 1972.
216p. col. maps. 20.5cm.

6166 Wesmael-Charlier.
Algemene atlas. Namur, 1972.
220p. col. maps. 26cm.

6167 Wesmael-Charlier.
Vereenvoudigde atlas. Namur, 1972.
100p. col. maps. 26cm.

6168 Westermann, Georg.
Westermann/Rand McNally International Atlas. Braunschweig, 1972.
526p. col. maps. 38cm.

6169 Westermann, Georg.
Westermann Schulatlas. Braunschweig, 1972.
183p. col. maps. 30cm.

6170 Wiley, John & Sons.
Atlas of world physical features. By Rodman Eldredge
Snead. New York, [1972].
176p. col. maps. 29cm.

6171 Wolters-Noordhoff.
De grote Bosatlas. 47ed. By F. J. Ormeling. Groningen, 1972.
400p. col. maps. 34cm.

6172 Zanichelli, Nicola.
Atlante geografico generale Zanichelli. Bologna, 1972.
232p. col. maps. 32cm.

1973

6173 Aguilar, S. A. de Ediciones.
      Atlas general básico Aguilar.   37ed. Madrid, 1973.
      117p. col. maps. 35cm.

6174 Aguilar, S. A. de Ediciones.
      85 atlas universal Aguilar. 1ed. Madrid, 1973.
      213p. col. maps. 21cm.

6175 Bartholomew, John & Son, Ltd.
      Mini atlas. Edinburgh, 1973.
      128p. col. maps. 15cm.

6176 Bartholomew, John & Son, Ltd.
      The Edinburgh world atlas. 8ed. Edinburgh, 1973.
      159p. col. maps. 38cm.

6177 Bartholomew, John & Son, Ltd.
      The world atlas. 9ed. Edinburgh, 1974.
      112p. col. maps. 38cm.

6178 Beazley, Mitchell, Ltd.
      Concise atlas of the earth. With Philip. London, 1973.
      258p. col. maps. 37cm.

6179 Beazley, Mitchell, Ltd.
      The Mitchell Beazley atlas of world wildlife. London,
      1973.
      208p. col. maps. 37cm.

6180 Berlitz.
      The Traveller's world reference atlas. By D. Hillman.
      London, 1973.
      28p. col. maps. 27cm.

6181 Bertelsmann, C.
      Bertelsmann Hausatlas. Gütersloh. 1973.
      320p. col. maps. 32cm.

6182 Bertelsmann, C.
      Länder Lexikon Weltatlas. Gütersloh, 1973.
      432p. col. maps. 18cm.

6183 Bertelsmann, C.
      Weltatlas. München, 1973.
      318p. col. maps. 33cm.

6184 British Sulphur Corp., Ltd.
      World fertilizer atlas. 4ed. London, 1973.
      103p. col. maps. 30cm.

6185   Collins, William, Sons & Co., Ltd.
       Atlas four.   Metric edition.   Glasgow, 1973.
       178p. col. maps. 27cm.

6186   Collins, William, Sons & Co., Ltd.
       Atlas three. 1ed. Glasgow, 1973.
       128p. col. maps. 26cm.

6187   Collins, William, Sons & Co., Ltd.
       Atlas two. New enlarged metric ed. Glasgow, 1973.
       86p. col. maps. 27cm.

6188   Collins, William, Sons & Co., Ltd.
       Daily Telegraph world atlas.   By D. L. Baker.   Glasgow,
       1973.
       115p. col. maps. 26cm.

6189   Collins, William, Sons & Co., Ltd.
       World atlas for Hong Kong.   Glasgow, [1973].
       1 vol. col. maps. 27cm.

6190   Dent, J. M.
       Dent's Canadian school atlas.   Toronto, [1973].
       115p. col. maps. 29cm.

6191   Deutscher Taschenbuch Verlag.
       DTV-Perthes-Weltatlas.   München, Darmstadt, 1973-
       in parts. col. maps. 20cm.

6192   Editorial Teide.
       Atlas universal geo-económico.   With Istituto Geografico
       De Agostini.   Barcelona, [1973].
       160p. col. maps. 31cm.

6193   Esselte Map Service.
       Bergvalls atlas. 5ed. By Olof Hedbom, Rune Hermansson
       and Anita Österberg. Stockholm, 1973.
       125p. col. maps. 26cm.

6194   Field Enterprises Educational Corp.
       The world book atlas.   With Rand McNally.   Chicago,
       1973.
       392p. col. maps. 37cm.

6195   Freytag, Berndt & Artaria.
       Neuer Schulatlas für Hauptschulen und Unterstufen der
       Höheren Schulen.   Wien, [1973].
       110p. col. maps. 32cm.

6196   Geographical Pub. Co.
       School and library atlas of the world.   By Fred W. Foster.
       Sycamore, Ill., [1973].
       326p. col. maps. 57cm.

6197 Goldmann Verlag.
      Goldmanns Handatlas. 12ed. With Visintin. München,
      1973.
      242p. col. maps. 41cm.

6198 Grange Batelière.
      Atlas geographique Alpha. Paris, 1973.
      80p. col. maps. 30cm.

6199 Haack, Hermann.
      Atlas der Erdkunde. 9ed. Gotha, Leipzig, 1973.
      128p. col. maps. 28cm.

6200 Haack, Hermann.
      Die Erde. Haack Kleiner Atlas. 2ed. By K. Breitfeld.
      Gotha, Leipzig, [1973].
      440p. col. maps. 17cm.

6201 Hammond, Inc.
      Hammond ambassador world atlas. Maplewood, N. J.,
      [1973].
      480p. col. maps. 33cm.

6202 Hammond, Inc.
      Hammond comparative world atlas. Maplewood, N. J.,
      [1973].
      48p. col. maps. 32cm.

6203 Hammond, Inc.
      Hammond headline world atlas. Maplewood, N. J., [1973].
      48p. col. maps. 28cm.

6204 Hammond, Inc.
      Hammond international world atlas. Maplewood, N. J.,
      [1973].
      192p. col. maps. 32cm.

6205 Hammond, Inc.
      Hammond standard world atlas; latest and most authentic
      geographical and statistical information. Maplewood,
      N. J., 1973.
      320p. col. maps. 32cm.

6206 Hammond, Inc.
      Hammond standard world atlas. Deluxe ed. Maplewood,
      N. J., 1973.
      320p. col. maps. 32cm.

6207 Hammond, Inc.
      Hammond world atlas. Superior ed. Maplewood, N. J.,
      [1973].
      184p. col. maps. 32cm.

6208 Hammond, Inc.
Medallion world atlas. Maplewood, N. J. , [1973].
1 vol. col. maps. 32cm.

6209 Hammond, Inc.
New world atlas: Hammond/Scholastic. Maplewood,
N. J. , [1973].
48p. col. maps. 28cm.

6210 Hammond, Inc.
The first book atlas. 2ed. Maplewood, N. J. , 1973.
96p. col. maps. 28cm.

6211 Herder Verlag.
Herders grosser Weltatlas. 5ed. Freiburg, Basel,
Wien, 1973.
250p. col. maps. 40cm.

6212 Hölzel, Ed. Verlag.
Österreichischer Atlas für höhere Schulen. 100ed. Wien,
1973.
167p. col. maps. 32cm.

6213 Hölzel, Ed. Verlag.
Österreichischer Hauptschulatlas. Wien, 1973.
107p. col. maps. 33cm.

6214 Istituto Geografico De Agostini.
Atlante della produzione e dei commerci. By Umberto
Bonapace and Giuseppe Motta. Novara, [1973].
120p. col. maps. 31cm.

6215 Istituto Geografico De Agostini.
Atlante mondiale. By U. Bonapace and G. Motta.
Novara, [1973].
530p. col. maps. 37cm.

6216 Istituto Geografico De Agostini.
Atlas universal geo-económico. Barcelona, [1973].
160p. col. maps. 31cm.

6217 Istituto Geografico De Agostini.
Calendario atlante de Agostini. Novara, 1973.
827p. col. maps. 16cm.

6218 Johnston & Bacon.
My second atlas. Edinburgh, London, 1973.
1 vol. col. maps. 27cm.

6219 Johnston & Bacon.
The travellers world reference atlas. 1ed. By Dan Hill-
man. London, 1973.
38p. col. maps. 27cm.

6220 JRO Verlag.
      Der grosse JRO-Weltatlas. 27ed. By Ernst Kremling
      and Helmut Kremling. München, 1973.
      221p. col. maps. 44cm.

6221 JRO Verlag.
      JRO Handatlas. 1ed. München, 1973.
      232p. col. maps. 30cm.

6222 JRO Verlag.
      JRO-Hausatlas. München, 1973.
      313p. col. maps. 31cm.

6223 Kartográfiai Vállalat.
      Földrajzi atlasz az általános iskolák számára. 17ed.
      Budapest, 1973.
      32p. col. maps. 28cm.

6224 Kartográfiai Vállalat.
      Földrajzi atlasz a középiskolák számára. 12ed. Buda-
      pest, 1973.
      60p. col. maps. 29cm.

6225 Kluwer.
      Oosthoek-Times wereldatlas. With Bartholomew. Wagen-
      ingen, [1973].
      275p. col. maps. 39cm.

6226 Larousse.
      Atlas général Larousse. By G. Reynaud-Dulaurier and
      H. Fullard. Paris, 1973.
      320p. col. maps. 29cm.

6227 Merriam, G. & C. Co.
      Webster's atlas and zipcode directory. With Hammond.
      Springfield, Mass., [1973].
      352p. col. maps. 32cm.

6228 Nathan, Fernand.
      Atlas du XXe siècle. By R. and M. Ozouf. Paris, 1973.
      1 vol. col. maps. 35cm.

6229 Oliver & Boyd.
      The advanced atlas of modern geography. 10 metric ed.
      With Bartholomew. Edinburgh, 1973.
      159p. col. maps. 38cm.

6230 Oosthoek.
      Oosthoek-Times Wereldatlas. With Bartholomew.
      Wageningen, 1973.
      283p. col. maps. 39cm.

6231 Oxford University Press.

Oxford home atlas of the world. 3ed. London, 1973.
124p. col. maps. 27cm.

6232 Oxford University Press.
Oxford world atlas. By Saul B. Cohen. London, 1973.
198p. col. maps. 38cm.

6233 Pan Books, Ltd.
World atlas. London, 1973.
85p. col. maps. 30cm.

6234 Philip, George & Son, Ltd.
Modern home atlas. London, 1973.
47p. col. maps. 28cm.

6235 Philip, George & Son, Ltd.
Philips' middle school atlas. By H. Fullard. London,
1973.
32p. col. maps. 28cm.

6236 Philip, George & Son, Ltd.
Philips' modern school atlas. 70ed. By Harold Fullard.
London, 1973.
132p. col. maps. 29cm.

6237 Philip, George & Son, Ltd.
Philips' modern school atlas. 71ed. By Harold Fullard.
London, 1973.
132p. col. maps. 29cm.

6238 Philip, George & Son, Ltd.
The Library atlas. 10ed. By H. Fullard and H. C.
Darby. London, 1973.
319p. col. maps. 29cm.

6239 Philip, George & Son, Ltd.
The university atlas. 15ed. By H. Fullard and H. C.
Darby. London, 1973.
187p. col. maps. 29cm.

6240 Philip, George & Son, Ltd.
Visual atlas. By Harold Fullard. London, 1973.
55p. col. maps. 23cm.

6241 Philip, George & Son, Ltd.
World atlas. By Harold Fullard. London, [1973].
127p. col. maps. 20cm.

6242 Philip, George & Son, Ltd.
World atlas of shipping. By W. D. Ewart and H. Fullard.
London, 1973.
277p. col. maps. 29cm.

6243   Poland. Państwowe predsiębiorstwo wydawnictw kartografi-
        cznych.
        Powszechny atlas świata.   1ed.   By Henryk Górski and
        Zofia Cukierska.   Warszawa, 1973.
        239p.   col. maps.   32cm.

6244   Rand McNally & Co.
        Rand McNally popular world atlas.   Chicago, [1973].
        201p.   col. maps.   31cm.

6245   Rand McNally & Co.
        The Rand McNally atlas of world wildlife.   Chicago,
        [1973].
        208p.   col. maps.   37cm.

6246   Rand McNally & Co.
        The world book atlas.   With Field Enterprises Educational
        Corp.   Chicago, 1973.
        392p.   col. maps.   37cm.

6247   Reise und Verkehrsverlag.
        RV-Weltatlas.   By K. Thieme.   With Bertelsmann.   Ber-
        lin, [1973].
        318p.   col. maps.   32cm.

6248   Školska Knjiga.
        Naš svijet.   Zemljopisni atlas svijeta za osnovu skolu.
        Zagreb, [1973].
        55p.   col. maps.   33cm.

6249   Slovenska Kartografia.
        Malý školský zemepisný atlas.   6ed.   Bratislava, 1973.
        16p.   col. maps.   17cm.

6250   Spectrum.
        Spectrum wereldatlas.   Informatie, cartografie, docu-
        mentatie.   Utrecht, [1973].
        394p.   col. maps.   32cm.

6251   Standaard Uitgeverij.
        Kleine Standaard schoolatlas.   By Michiel David.   Anvers,
        [1973].
        35p.   col. maps.   30cm.

6252   St. Martin's Press.
        World atlas of shipping; sea and shipping.   By W. D.
        Ewart and Harold Fullard.   With Philip.   New York,
        London, [1973].
        296p.   col. maps.   29cm.

6253   Teikoku-Shoin Co. , Ltd.
        New detailed atlas for high-school students.   Tokyo, [1973].
        136p.   col. maps.   31cm.

6254   U. S. S. R. Glavnoe upravlenie geodezii i kartografii.
       Atlas mira. Afrika. Moskva, 1973.
       21p. col. maps. 34cm.

6255   U. S. S. R. Glavnoe upravlenie geodezii i kartografii.
       Atlas mira. Zapadnaia Evropa. Moskva, 1973.
       40p. col. maps. 34cm.

6256   Velhagen & Klasing.
       Unsere Welt. Atlas für die Schule. Berlin, 1973.
       120p. col. maps. 33cm.

6257   Verbo.
       Atlas universal Verbo. 3ed. Lisboa, [1973].
       188p. col. maps. 33cm.

6258   Watts.
       The basic atlas. By Kenneth Ody. London, [1973].
       94p. col. maps. 28cm.

6259   Westermann, Georg.
       Westermann Schulatlas. Grosse Ausg. Braunschweig,
       1973.
       423p. col. maps. 30cm.

6260   Wheaton & Co., Ltd.
       Wheaton primary atlas. Exeter, 1973.
       1 vol. col. maps. 28cm.

6261   Wolters-Noordhoff.
       De grote Bosatlas. 47ed. By F. J. Ormeling. Gronin-
       gen, 1973.
       202p. col. maps. 34cm.

6262   Young Readers Press.
       World atlas. By Harold Fullard. With Philip. New
       York, [1973].
       127p. col. maps. 20cm.

                              1974

6263   Aguilar, S. A. de Ediciones.
       Atlas general básico Angiluar. 38ed. By A. L. Gómez.
       Madrid, 1974.
       117p. col. maps. 35cm.

6264   Aguilar, S. A. de Ediciones.
       Atlas general básico Aguilar. 39ed. By A. L. Gómez.
       Madrid, 1974.
       117p. col. maps. 35cm.

6265   Bartholomew, John & Son, Ltd.
       Mini atlas.   Edinburgh, 1974.
       128p. col. maps. 15cm.

6266   Bartholomew, John & Son, Ltd.
       Our world. A children's pictorial atlas.   By William
       Kinnear and James R. Carson.   With Holmes McDougall.
       Edinburgh, 1974.
       50p. col. maps. 30cm.

6267   Bertelsmann, C.
       Weltatlas.   München, 1974.
       191p. col. maps. 18cm.

6268   Cappelens, J. W. , Forlag, A. S.
       Verdensatlas for gymmaset.   Oslo, [1974].
       1 vol. col. maps. 30cm.

6269   Collins, William, Sons & Co. , Ltd.
       Daily Telegraph world atlas.   Glasgow, 1974.
       115p. col. maps. 26cm.

6270   Delagrave.
       Atlas Kienast et Bertrand.   2ed.   Paris, 1974.
       80p. col. maps. 31.5cm.

6271   Deutscher Bücherbund.
       Der neue Haus-Atlas.   Stuttgart, 1973.
       208p. col. maps. 35cm.

6272   Doubleday.
       Hammond contemporary world atlas.   New census ed.
       With Hammond.   Garden City, N. Y. , [1974].
       287p. col. maps. 29cm.

6273   Elsevier.
       Winkler Prins gezinsatlas.   Amsterdam, 1974.
       256p. col. maps. 33cm.

6274   Encyclopaedia Britannica.
       Britannica atlas.   With Rand McNally.   Chicago, 1974.
       534p. col. maps. 39cm.

6275   Grosset & Dunlap.
       The Grosset world atlas.   With Hammond.   New York,
       [1974].
       48p. col. maps. 28cm.

6276   Haack, Hermann.
       Die Erde.   4ed.   Gotha, Leipzig, 1974.
       429p. col. maps. 17cm.

6277   Haack, Hermann.

Haack Hausatlas.   Gotha, Leipzig, 1974.
296p.   col. maps.   35cm.

6278   Hamlyn.
The universal encyclopedic world atlas.   Sydney, [1974].
288p.   col. maps.   35cm.

6279   Hammond, Inc.
Hammond ambassador world atlas.   Maplewood, N.J.,
1974.
480p.   col. maps.   33cm.

6280   Hammond, Inc.
Hammond citation world atlas.   Maplewood, N.J., [1974].
352p.   col. maps.   32cm.

6281   Hammond, Inc.
Hammond global world atlas.   Maplewood, N.J., 1974.
31p.   col. maps.   24cm.

6282   Hammond, Inc.
Hammond standard world atlas.   Maplewood, N.J., [1974].
223p.   col. maps.   32cm.

6283   Hammond, Inc.
Hammond standard world atlas.   Deluxe ed.   Maplewood,
N.J., 1974.
320p.   col. maps.   32cm.

6284   Hammond, Inc.
The whole earth atlas.   Maplewood, N.J., 1974.
256p.   col. maps.   28cm.

6285   Herder Verlag.
Herders grosser Weltatlas.   6ed.   Freiburg, Basel, Wien,
[1974].
250p.   col. maps.   40cm.

6286   Istituto Geografico De Agostini.
Atlante geografico economico.   By Umberto Bonapace and
Giuseppe Motta.   Novara, 1974.
262p.   col. maps.   36cm.

6287   Istituto Geografico De Agostini.
Atlante geografico metodico.   By Umberto Bonapace and
Giuseppe Motta.   Novara, [1974].
190p.   col. maps.   37cm.

6288   Istituto Geografico De Agostini.
Atlante geografico moderno.   By Umberto Bonapace and
Giuseppe Motta.   Novara, [1974].
132p.   col. maps.   37cm.

6289 Istituto Geografico De Agostini.
Atlante mondiale. By U. Bonapace and G. Motta.
Novara, 1974.
532p. col. maps. 37cm.

6290 Istituto Geografico De Agostini.
Il nuovo atlante della scuola media. By Umberto Bonapace and Giuseppe Motta. Novara, [1974].
96p. col. maps. 31cm.

6291 Jacaranda.
Jacaranda junior world atlas. Sydney, 1974.
91p. col. maps. 28cm.

6292 Johnston & Bacon
World study atlas. Metric ed. Edinburgh, London, 1974.
64p. col. maps. 27cm.

6293 Jugoslavenski leksikografski zavod.
Atlas svijeta. 5ed. Zagreb, 1974.
604p. col. maps. 30cm.

6294 Lexicon Publications, Inc.
Lexicon international atlas. With Hammond. Chicago,
[1974].
352p. col. maps. 32cm.

6295 Lloyd's Corp. of.
Lloyd's maritime atlas. 9ed. London, 1974.
166p. col. maps. 25cm.

6296 Meyer. Kartographisches Institut.
Meyers grosser Weltatlas. 2ed. Mannheim, 1974.
621p. col. maps. 38cm.

6297 Meyer, Kartographisches Institut.
Meyers neuer Handatlas. By Adolf Hanle. Mannheim,
1974.
336p. col. maps. 38cm.

6298 Neguri Editorial.
Atlas geográfico. 1ed. Bilbao, 1974.
159p. col. maps. 26cm.

6299 Pembina.
Atlas Indonesia & Dunia. Djakarta, 1974.
28p. col. maps. 32cm.

6300 Penguin Books.
The Penguin world atlas. By Peter Hall. Harmondsworth,
Middlesex, 1974.
253p. col. maps. 21cm.

6301   Philip, George & Son, Ltd.
        The International atlas.   London, 1974.
        501p.   col.   maps.   39cm.

6302   Philip, George & Son, Ltd.
        The university atlas.   16ed.   By H. Fullard and H. C.
        Darby.   London, 1974.
        187p.   col.   maps.   29cm.

6303   Poland.   Państwowe przedsiębiorstwo wydawnictw Kartografi-
        cznych.
        Powszechny atlas świata.   2ed.   By Henryk Górski and
        Zofia Cukierska.   Warszawa, 1974.
        238p.   col.   maps.   32cm.

6304   Politikens forlag.
        Politikens verdensatlas.   København, 1974.
        184p.   col.   maps.   28cm.

6305   Rand McNally & Co.
        Giant world atlas.   Chicago, 1974.
        30p.   col.   maps.   33cm.

6306   Rand McNally & Co.
        Goode's world atlas.   14ed.   By Edward B. Espenshade,
        Jr. and Joel Morrison.   Chicago, 1974.
        372p.   col.   maps.   29cm.

6307   Rand McNally & Co.
        Rand McNally atlas del mundo de hoy.   Chicago, [1974].
        64p.   col.   maps.   28cm.

6308   Rand McNally & Co.
        Rand McNally cosmopolitan world atlas.   Chicago, [1974].
        352p.   col.   maps.   27cm.

6309   Rand McNally & Co.
        The international atlas.   Chicago, 1974.
        534p.   col.   maps.   38cm.

6310   Reader's Digest Association, Ltd.
        The Reader's Digest great world atlas.   4ed.   London,
        1974.
        179p.   col.   maps.   40cm.

6311   Reader's Digest Association Pty, Ltd.
        The great world atlas.   Sydney, 1974.
        192p.   col.   maps.   40cm.

6312   Reise und Verkehrsverlag.
        RV-Universal-Weltatlas.   By H. Albert.   Berlin, 1974.
        318p.   col.   maps.   32cm.

6313   Romania.   Editura di Stat Didactică și Pedagogică.
       Atlas geografic general.   Bucuresti, 1974.
       228p.   col. maps.   33cm.

6314   Scholastic Book Service.
       World atlas, Scholastic/Hammond.   New York, 1974.
       48p.   col. maps.   28cm.

6315   Standaard Uitgeverij.
       Standaard wereldatlas.   Anvers, 1974.
       164p.   col. maps.   31cm.

6316   U. S. S. R.   Glavnoe upravlenie geodezii i kartografii.
       Malyi atlas mira.   By L. N. Kolosova.   Moskva, 1974.
       181p.   col. maps.   20cm.

6317   U. S. S. R.   Glavnoe upravlenie geodezii i kartografii.
       Uchebnii atlas mira.   2ed.   Moskva, 1974.
       180p.   col. maps.   34cm.

6318   Velhagen & Klasing & Schroedel.
       Unsere Welt.   Berlin, [1974].
       180p.   col. maps.   33cm.

6319   Westermann, Georg.
       Diercke Weltatlas.   By Ferdinand Mayer.   Braunschweig,
       1974.
       232p.   col. maps.   30cm.

6320   Westermann, Georg.
       Internationaler Atlas.   Braunschweig, [1974].
       501p.   col. maps.   38cm.

6321   Westermann, Georg.
       Rororo Weltatlas.   Hamburg, [1974].
       224p.   col. maps.   32cm.

1975

6322   Bartholomew, John & Son, Ltd.
       Mini atlas.   Edinburgh, 1975.
       128p.   col. maps.   15cm.

6323   Bartholomew, John & Son, Ltd.
       Problems of our planet.   An atlas of earth and man.
       Edinburgh, 1975.
       1 vol.   col. maps.   38cm.

6324   Beazley, Mitchell, Ltd.
       The Mitchell Beazley world atlas of exploration.   London,
       1975.

1 vol. col. maps. 28cm.

6325 Bertelsmann, C.
Atlas international. Gütersloh, 1975.
580p. col. maps. 39cm.

6326 Bibliograf, S. A.
Atlas didactico universal SPES. Barcelona, [1975].
80p. col. maps. 28cm.

6327 BLV Verlagsgesellschaft.
Wirtschaftsgeographischer Weltatlas. 3ed. München,
Bern, Wien, 1975.
169p. col. maps. 33cm.

6328 Deutscher Taschenbuch Verlag.
Perthes Weltatlas. Darmstadt, 1975.
in parts. col. maps. 20cm.

6329 Esselte Map Service.
Bergvalls atlas. By Olof Hedbom, Rune Hermansson and
Anita Österberg. Stockholm, 1975.
125p. col. maps. 26cm.

6330 Gyldendal.
Atlas of economic geography. 7ed. By J. Humlum and
H. S. Thomsen. København, 1975.
139p. col. maps. 27cm.

6331 Gyldendal.
Kulturgeografisk atlas. By Johannes Humlum. København,
1975.
2 vol. col. maps. 27cm.

6332 Hamlyn.
Hamlyn Boy's and Girl's atlas. London, 1975.
1 vol. col. maps. 28cm.

6333 Hammond, Inc.
Hammond ambassador world atlas. Maplewood, N.J.,
1975.
480p. col. maps. 33cm.

6334 Hammond, Inc.
Hammond international world atlas. Maplewood, N.J.,
1975.
192p. col. maps. 32cm.

6335 Hammond, Inc.
Medallian world atlas. Maplewood, N.J., [1975].
655p. col. maps. 32cm.

6336 Hammond, Inc.

The whole earth atlas.   Maplewood, N.J. , 1975.
256p.   col. maps.   28cm.

6337   Lingen.
       Grosser atlas der Erde.   Köln, 1975.
       340p.   col. maps.   38cm.

6338   List, P.
       List grosser Weltatlas.   Mensch und Erde.   München,
       1975.
       295p.   col. maps.   32cm.

6339   McGraw-Hill Book Co.
       Man's domain, a thematic atlas of the world.   3ed.   By
       Norman J. W. Thrower.   With General Drafting Co.   New
       York, 1975.
       80p.   col. maps.   34cm.

6340   National Geographic Society.
       National Geographic atlas of the world.   4ed.   Washington,
       D.C. , 1975.
       331p.   col. maps.   49cm.

6341   Oxford University Press.
       The new Oxford atlas.   London, [1975].
       208p.   col. maps.   38cm.

6342   Pergamon Press, Ltd.
       The world ocean atlas.   By Sergei G. Gorshkov.   Oxford,
       New York, 1975.
       in parts.   col. maps.   46cm.

6343   Philip, George &, Son, Ltd.
       Modern school economic atlas.   By Harold Fullard.   Lon-
       don, 1975.
       176p.   col. maps.   23cm.

6344   Philip, George & Son, Ltd.
       Philips' concorde world atlas.   By Harold Fullard.   Lon-
       don, 1975.
       211p.   col. maps.   29cm.

6345   Philip, George & Son, Ltd.
       Philips' modern school atlas.   72ed.   By Harold Fullard.
       London, 1975.
       132p.   col. maps.   29cm.

6346   Philip, George & Son, Ltd.
       The university atlas.   17ed.   By H. Fullard and H. C.
       Darby.   London, 1975.
       187p.   col. maps.   29cm.

6347   Rand McNally & Co.

Cosmopolitan world atlas.   Chicago, 1975.
396p.   col.   maps.   38cm.

6348   Rand McNally & Co.
Family world atlas.   Chicago, 1975.
304p.   col.   maps.   32cm.

6349   Rand McNally & Co.
Goode's world atlas.   14ed.   By Edward B. Espenshade,
Jr. and Joel Morrison.   Chicago, 1975.
372p.   col.   maps.   29cm.

6350   Rand McNally & Co.
Illustrated world atlas.   Chicago, 1975.
224p.   col.   maps.   19cm.

6351   Rand McNally & Co.
Premier world atlas.   Chicago, 1975.
340p.   col.   maps.   38cm.

6352   Rand McNally & Co.
Rand McNally imperial world atlas.   Chicago, 1975.
324p.   col.   maps.   32cm.

6353   Rand McNally & Co.
Rand McNally popular world atlas.   Chicago, 1975.
204p.   col.   maps.   31cm.

6354   Rand McNally & Co.
Rand McNally world atlas of exploration.   By Eric Newby.
Chicago, 1975.
288p.   col.   maps.   28cm.

6355   Rand McNally & Co.
The international atlas.   Chicago, 1975.
557p.   col.   maps.   38cm.

6356   Spectrum.
Spectrum gezinsatlas.   By J. Buisman.   Utrecht, [1975].
259p.   col.   maps.   39cm.

6357   Springer Verlag.
Climate-diagram maps of the individual continents and the
ecological climate regions of the earth.   Berlin, Heidelberg, New York, 1975.
36p.   40cm.

6358   Thames and Hudson, Ltd.
Archaeological atlas of the world.   By David Whitehouse.
London, 1975.
272p.   25cm.

6359   Westermann, Georg.

Die Welt in Karten. Braunschweig, [1975].
44p. col. maps. 30cm.

6360 Westermann, Georg.
Diercke Weltatlas. 3ed. Braunschweig, 1975.
234p. col. maps. 30cm.

AFRICA

6361 African Magazine.
    The atlas of Africa. London, 1973.
    350p. col. maps. 40cm.

6362 Arnold, E.
    An atlas of African history. By J. D. Fage. London,
    [1970].
    64p. 29cm.

6363 Arnold, E.
    An atlas of African history. By J. D. Fage. London,
    1973.
    64p. 29cm.

6364 Automobile Association of South Africa.
    Road atlas and touring guide of southern Africa. 3ed.
    Johannesburg, [1968].
    200p. col. maps. 25cm.

6365 BP Southern Africa Pty., Ltd.
    BP padkaarte. Road maps. Cape Town, [195-].
    14p. col. maps. 29cm.

6366 BP Southern Africa Pty., Ltd.
    BP road maps. Padkaarte. Cape Town, [1970].
    22p. col. maps. 29cm.

6367 B. P. Southern Africa Pty., Ltd.
    Road maps-Padkaarte. Cape Town, [1967].
    22p. col. maps. 29cm.

6368 Denoyer-Geppert Co.
    The history of Africa in maps. By Harry A. Gailey.
    Chicago, [1971].
    96p. 28cm.

6369 Editions Jeune Afrique.
    Grand atlas du continent africain. 1ed. By Régine Van
    Chi-Bonnardel. Paris, [1973].
    335p. col. maps. 41cm.

6370 Free Press.

The atlas of Africa.   By Régine Van Chi-Bonnardel.   1ed.
New York, 1973.
335p. col. maps. 41cm.

6371 Free Press.
      The atlas of the African continent.   By Régine Van Chi-
      Bonnardel.   New York, 1974.
      336p. col. maps. 41cm.

6372 Macmillan.
      A map book of Africa.   2ed.   By A. Ferriday.   London,
      1971.
      80p. 25cm.

6373 Macmillan.
      A map book of Eastern Africa, Zambia, and Malawi.
      Nairobi, 1974.
      1 vol. col. maps. 25cm.

6374 Macmillan.
      My second book of maps.   An atlas of Ghana and the rest
      of Africa.   London, 1974.
      33p. col. maps. 28cm.

6375 Map Studio Productions, pty. , Ltd.
      Road atlas of Southern Africa.   With Shell South Africa.
      Johannesburg, 1970.
      64p. col. maps. 27.5cm.

6376 McGraw-Hill Book Co.
      Africa on maps dating from the twelfth to the eighteenth
      century.   New York, 1970.
      77p. col. maps. 53cm.

6377 Nelson, Thomas & Sons, Ltd.
      West African secondary school atlas.   3ed.   By J.
      Wreford Watson, A. K. Wareham, and E. A. Boateng.
      London, [1968].
      84p. col. maps. 29cm.

6378 Organisation of African Unity.
      International Atlas of West Africa.   Dakar, 1968.
      in parts. col. maps. 54cm.

6379 Oxford University Press.
      Oxford atlas for East Africa.   By F. C. A. McBain.
      London, 1971.
      65p. col. maps. 26cm.

6380 Oxford University Press.
      Oxford regional economic atlas.   Africa.   Paperback ed.
      London, 1970.
      1 vol. col. maps. 25cm.

6381 Oxford University Press.
Oxford regional economic atlas of the Middle East and
North Africa. London, 1960.
135p. col. maps. 27cm.

6382 Oxford University Press.
Oxford regional economic atlas. The Middle East and
North Africa. London, 1970.
135p. col. maps. 27cm.

6383 Oxford University Press.
Oxford regional economic atlas. The Middle East and
North Africa. Paperback ed. London, 1970.
1 vol. col. maps. 25cm.

6384 Philip, George & Son, Ltd.
Philip se kollege atlas vir Suidelike Afrika. 6ed. By
Harold Fullard. London, 1971.
168p. col. maps. 29cm.

6385 Philip, George & Son, Ltd.
Philips' college atlas for southern Africa. London, 1971.
168p. col. maps. 29cm.

6386 Philip, George & Son, Ltd.
Philips' modern college atlas for Africa. 9ed. By
Harold Fullard. London, 1968.
167p. col. maps. 29cm.

6387 Philip, George & Son, Ltd.
Philips' modern college atlas for Africa. 10ed. By
Harold Fullard. London, 1971.
167p. col. maps. 29cm.

6388 Philip, George & Son, Ltd.
Philips' modern college atlas for Africa. 11ed. By
Harold Fullard. London, [1972].
167p. col. maps. 29cm.

6389 Philip, George & Son, Ltd.
Philips' modern college atlas for Africa. 12ed. By
Harold Fullard. London, 1974.
168p. col. maps. 29cm.

6390 Rand McNally & Co.
Africa: Africa mini-atlas. Chicago, [1973].
8p. col. maps. 36cm.

6391 University of London Press.
A student's atlas of African history. By Derek A. Wilson.
London, 1971.
64p. 28cm.

6392   University of Wales Press.
       Tropical Africa. An atlas for rural development.   By
       H. R. J. Davies.   Cardiff, 1973.
       81p. col. maps. 42cm.

6393   University Tutorial Press.
       A student's atlas of African history.   By Derek A. Wilson.
       London, 1971.
       1 vol. 28cm.

6394   U. S. S. R. Akademia nauk.
       Klimaticheskii atlas Afriki.   Moskva, 1972.
       137p. col. maps. 35cm.

6395   U. S. S. R. Glavnoe upravlenie geodezii i kartografii.
       Atlas mira. Afrika. Moskva, 1973.
       21p. col. maps. 34cm.

6396   Varia Books.
       Varia atlas for Southern Africa.   Alberton, 1972.
       1 vol. col. maps. 28cm.

6397   Vilo.
       Le grand atlas du continent Africain.   Pans, 1973.
       340p. col. maps. 41cm.

ANTARCTICA

6398   American Geographical Society.
       Antarctic map folio series.   New York, 1969-
       in portf. col. maps. 44cm.

6399   U. S. Naval Oceanographic Office.
       Oceanographic atlas of the polar seas.   Part I: Antarctic.
       Washington, D. C. , 1970.
       69p. col. maps. 40cm.

ASIA

6400   Denoyer-Geppert Co.
       South Asia in maps.   By Robert C. Kingsbury.   Chicago,
       1969.
       96p. 28cm.

6401   Denoyer-Geppert Co.
       South Asia in maps.   2ed.   By Robert C. Kingsbury.
       Chicago, 1974.
       96p. 28cm.

6402   Denoyer-Geppert Co.
       Southeast Asia in maps.   By Thomas Frank Barton.
       Chicago, [1973].
       96p. 28cm.

6403   Generalstrabens litografiska anstalt.
       Var värld sydasien; politisk-ekonomisk atlas.   By Eivor
       Samuelsson.   Stockholm, [1973].
       72p.   col. maps.   22cm.

6404   Macmillan.
       A map book of Asia.   6ed.   By Alan Ferriday.   London,
       1971.
       64p.   25cm.

6405   Macmillan Education, Ltd.
       A map book of Australasia.   By A. Ferriday.   London,
       1974.
       52p.   col. maps.   25cm.

6406   Oxford University Press.
       Australasian school atlas.   By John Bartholomew and K.
       R. Cramp.   Oxford, 1966.
       64p.   col. maps.   28cm.

6407   United Nations.
       Energy atlas of Asia and the Far East.   New York, 1970.
       28p.   col. maps.   38cm.

6408   U. S. Army Natick Laboratories.
       Mainland Southeast Asia.   A folio of thematic maps for
       military users.   Natick, Mass., 1969.
       78p.   col. maps.   46cm.

6409   U. S. Geological Survey.
       Atlas of Asia and Eastern Europe to support detection of
       underground nuclear testing.   Washington, D. C., 1966-69.
       5 vol.   col. maps.   62cm.

AUSTRALASIA

6410   Macmillan Education, Ltd.
       A map book of Australasia.   By A. Ferriday.   London,
       1974.
       52p.   col. maps.   25cm.

6411   Reed, A. H. & A. W.
       A descriptive atlas of the Pacific Islands.   New Zealand,
       Australia, Polynesia, Melanesia, Micronesia, Philippines.
       By T. F. Kennedy.   Wellington, [1968].
       64p.   24cm.

6412   University Press.
       Australasian school atlas.   By John Bartholomew and K.
       R. Cramp.   Oxford, 1966.
       64p.   col. maps.   28cm.

EUROPE

6413   Bartholomew, John & Son, Ltd.
       Atlas of Europe.   With Scribner's.   New York, 1974.
       128p.   col.   maps.   30cm.

6414   Bartholomew, John & Son, Ltd.
       Road atlas Europe.   Edinburgh, [1970].
       136p.   col.   maps.   30cm.

6415   Bartholomew, John & Son, Ltd.
       Road atlas Europe.   Edinburgh, 1971.
       136p.   col.   maps.   30cm.

6416   Bartholomew, John & Son, Ltd.
       Road atlas Europe.   Edinburgh, 1972.
       136p.   col.   maps.   30cm.

6417   Bartholomew, John & Son, Ltd.
       Road atlas Europe.   Edinburgh, 1973.
       136p.   col.   maps.   30cm.

6418   Bartholomew, John & Son, Ltd.
       Road atlas Europe.   Edinburgh, 1974.
       136p.   col.   maps.   30cm.

6419   Bartholomew, John & Son, Ltd.
       Road atlas Europe.   Edinburgh, 1975.
       136p.   col.   maps.   30cm.

6420   Bartholomew, John & Son, Ltd.
       The Bartholomew/Warne atlas of Europe.   By Geoffrey
       S. Browne and Robert M. Croucher.   Edinburgh, [1974].
       118p.   col.   maps.   31cm.

6421   Bernces Förlag.
       Bernces reseatlas.   Malmö, [1972].
       190p.   col.   maps.   31cm.

6422   Bertelsmann, C.
       Autoatlas Bertelsmann.   Deutschland-Europa.   Gütersloh,
       1970.
       386p.   col.   maps.   27cm.

6423   Bertelsmann, C.
       Autoatlas Bertelsmann.   Deutschland-Europa.   Gütersloh,
       1971.
       386p.   col.   maps.   27cm.

6424   Bertelsmann, C.
       Autoatlas Bertelsmann.   Deutschland-Europa.   Gütersloh,
       [1973].
       380p.   col.   maps.   27cm.

6425 Blackie & Son, Ltd.
Atlas of European political history. 1ed. By P. G.
Dickson Jones. Glasgow, 1973.
30p. col. maps. 25cm.

6426 Cartographia.
Climatic atlas of Europe. With Unesco. Budapest, 1970-
in parts. col. maps. 60cm.

6427 Continental Gummiwerke Kartographischer Verlag.
Continental Atlas. Deutschland, Europa. 36ed. Hannover,
1969.
555p. col. maps. 26cm.

6428 Continental Gummiwerke Kartofraphischer Verlag.
Continental Atlas. Deutschland, Europa. 37ed. Hannover, 1970.
611p. col. maps. 26cm.

6429 Continental Gummiwerke Kartographischer Verlag.
Der grosse Continental-Atlas. Hannover, Stuttgart, 1971.
639p. col. maps. 26cm.

6430 Continental Gummiwerke Kartographischer Verlag.
Der grosse Continental-Atlas. 39ed. Hannover, Stuttgart,
1972.
601p. col. maps. 26cm.

6431 Das Beste, G. M. B. H.
Reader's Digest ADAC Autoreisebuch. Atlas von den
Alpen bis zur Nordsee. Stuttgart, Zürich, Wien, 1968.
440p. col. maps. 31cm.

6432 Das Beste, G. M. B. H.
Reader's Digest ADAC Autoreisebuch. Atlas von den
Alpen bis zur Nordsee. 4ed. Stuttgart, Zürich, Wien,
1970.
440p. col. maps. 31cm.

6433 Denoyer-Geppert Co.
Mapas historicos de Europa y del Mundo. By James H.
Breasted, Carl F. Huth and Samuel B. Harding. Chicago,
1970.
55p. col. maps. 28cm.

6434 Det Bedste fra Reader's Digest AS.
Det Bedste fra Reader's Digest. København, 1969.
516p. col. maps. 29cm.

6435 Dutton, E. P. & Co.
EURoad; the complete guide to motoring in Europe. By
Bert W. Lief. New York, 1971.
72p. col. maps. 28cm.

6436   Editions Bordas.
       Atlas routier et touristique.   Paris, 1970.
       1 vol.   col. maps.   28cm.

6437   Esso, A. G.
       Europe Atlas.   Hamburg, 1968.
       96p.   col. maps.   30cm.

6438   Esso, A. G.
       Europa-Atlas.   Hamburg, [1969].
       96p.   col. maps.   30cm.

6439   Esso, A. G.
       Europa-Atlas.   Ausgabe 1970/71.   Hamburg, [1970].
       96p.   col. maps.   30cm.

6440   Esso, A. G.
       Europa-Atlas.   Hamburg, [1971].
       96p.   col. maps.   30cm.

6441   European Road Guide, Inc.
       1971-1972 Motoring atlas, Europe and Israel.   Larchmont,
       N.Y., 1971.
       78p.   28cm.

6442   Falk Verlag.
       Europa.   Auto-Atlas.   Hamburg, 1975.
       41p.   col. maps.   25cm.

6443   Fietz, W. G.
       Strassenatlas: Deutschland und Europa.   Frankfurt, [1972].
       71p.   col. maps.   27cm.

6444   France.   Direction des ports maritimes et des voies
       navigables.
       Liaisons fluviales Mer-du-Nord--Mediterranée.   Paris,
       [1969].
       1 vol.   col. maps.   42cm.

6445   Freytag, Berndt & Artaria.
       Europa Auto Atlas: Europe et Méditerranée.   Road atlas.
       Wien, [1972].
       216p.   col. maps.   26cm.

6446   Generalstabens litografiska anstalt.
       Europa camping and caravaning.   Stockholm, 1966/67.
       1 vol.   col. maps.   30cm.

6447   Geographia, Ltd.
       European motoring atlas and guide.   London, [1970].
       89p.   col. maps.   29cm.

6448   Geokarta.

Evropa, shkolni atlas. By Dragomir Božić. Beograd,
[1957].
12p. col. maps. 30cm.

6449 Geokarta.
Van evropski kontinenti, shkolni atlas. By Ilija Melentijević. Beograd, [1957].
12p. col. maps. 32cm.

6450 Germany. Militärgeographisches Amt.
BW-Kraftfahrer Atlas. Bonn, 1969.
2 vol. col. maps. 30cm.

6451 Gower Economic Publications.
Business atlas of Western Europe. Epping, 1974.
144p. col. maps. 29cm.

6452 Hallwag, A. G.
Autropa atlas. Bern, 1970.
89p. col. maps. 25cm.

6453 Hallwag, A. G.
Autropa atlas. Bern, [1971].
89p. col. maps. 25cm.

6454 Hallwag, A. G.
Autropa atlas. Bern, 1972.
84p. col. maps. 25cm.

6455 Hallwag, A. G.
Europa-Auto-Atlas. Bern, [1970].
210p. col. maps. 26cm.

6456 Hallwag, A. G.
Europa-Auto-Atlas. Bern, Stuttgart, [1971].
210p. col. maps. 26cm.

6457 Hallwag, A. G.
Europa-Auto-Atlas. Bern, [1972].
216p. col. maps. 26cm.

6458 Hallway, A. G.
Europa-Auto-Atlas. Bern, [1973].
224p. col. maps. 26cm.

6459 Hallwag, A. G.
Europa-Auto-Atlas. Bern, 1974.
220p. col. maps. 26cm.

6460 Hallwag, A. G.
Europa-Auto-Atlas. Bern, 1975.
220p. col. maps. 26cm.

6461   Hallwag, A. G.
       Europa Touring.   Automobilführer von Europa.   Bern,
       Stuttgart, [1970].
       822p. col. maps.   26cm.

6462   Hallwag, A. G.
       Europa Touring.   Automobilführer von Europa.   Bern,
       Stuttgart, [1971].
       822p. col. maps.   26cm.

6463   Hallwag, A. G.
       Europa Touring.   Automobilführer von Europa.   Bern,
       Stuttgart, 1972.
       822p. col. maps.   26cm.

6464   Hallwag, A. G.
       Europa Touring.   Automobilführer von Europa.   Bern,
       Stuttgart, [1973].
       822p. col. maps.   26cm.

6465   Hallwag, A. G.
       Europa Touring.   Automobilführer von Europa.   Bern,
       Stuttgart, 1974.
       822p. col. maps.   26cm.

6466   Hallwag, A. G.
       Europa Touring.   Automobilführer von Europa.   Bern,
       Stuttgart, 1975.
       865p. col. maps.   26cm.

6467   Harrap.
       A sketch map geography of North-West Europe.   By
       Dorothy E. Cocks.   London, 1971.
       48p.   25cm.

6468   International Road Federation.
       Main European arteries (E roads): traffic census maps,
       1965.   Grands itinéraires européens; Europäische Haupt-
       verkehrsadern.   Geneva, 1968.
       19p. col. maps.   29cm.

6469   JRO Verlag.
       Grosser JRO Strassenatlas.   Deutschland, Alpenländer,
       Europa.   Munchen, 1973.
       120p. col. maps.   30cm.

6470   JRO Verlag.
       JRO Autoatlas.   Deutschland, Europäische Reiseländer.
       München, [1971].
       1 vol. col. maps.   25cm.

6471   König, Hans, Verlag.
       Fina Europa Atlas.   Bergen-Enkheim, 1969.

          114p.   col.   maps.   25cm.

6472   König, Hans, Verlag.
       Strassenatlas Deutschland-Europa.   Frankfurt am Main,
       1971.
       1 vol.   col.   maps.   29cm.

6473   Kümmerly & Frey.
       Auto Europa, road atlas.   Bern, [1971].
       241p.   col.   maps.   25cm.

6474   Kümmerly & Frey.
       Auto-Europa.   Strassenatlas.   Bern, 1969.
       218p.   col.   maps.   25cm.

6475   Kümmerly & Frey.
       Europa.   Europe.   Strassenatlas.   Bern, 1969.
       84p.   col.   maps.   23cm.

6476   Kümmerly & Frey.
       Europa.   Europe.   Strassenatlas.   Bern, 1970.
       260p.   col.   maps.   26cm.

6477   Kümmerly & Frey.
       Europa, Europe.   Strassenatlas.   Bern, 1971.
       260p.   col.   maps.   26cm.

6478   Kümmerly & Frey.
       Europa, Europe.   Strassenatlas.   Bern, [1972].
       260p.   col.   maps.   26cm.

6479   Kümmerly & Frey.
       Europa.   Europe.   Strassenatlas.   Bern, [1973].
       266p.   col.   maps.   26cm.

6480   Kümmerly & Frey.
       Europa.   Grosser Strassen- und Reiseatlas.   Bern, 1973.
       165p.   col.   maps.   30cm.

6481   Kümmerly & Frey.
       Europe, atlas routier.   Bern, [1968].
       140p.   col.   maps.   23cm.

6482   Kümmerly & Frey.
       Europe road atlas.   Bern, [1971].
       140p.   col.   maps.   23cm.

6483   Lademann forlagsaktieselskab.
       Lademanns rejseatlas.   By Svend-Aage Hansen.   With
       Kümmerly & Frey.   København, 1972.
       192p.   col.   maps.   31cm.

6484   Lief, B. W.

EURoad: the complete guide to motoring in Europe.
New York, [1971].
72p. col. maps. 28cm.

6485   Lief, B. W.
       Volvo road atlas; the complete guide to motoring in
       Europe. New York, [1971].
       72p. col. maps. 28cm.

6486   Longmans.
       Europe in maps. By R. Knowles and P. W. E. Stowe.
       London, 1969.
       96p. col. maps. 28cm.

6487   Longmans.
       Europe in maps. 2ed. By R. Knowles and P. W. E.
       Stowe. London, 1970.
       96p. col. maps. 28cm.

6488   Longmans.
       Europe in maps. 3ed. By R. Knowles and P. W. E.
       Stowe. London, 1971.
       96p. col. maps. 28cm.

6489   Macdonald & Evans.
       Western Europe in maps and diagrams. By J. E. Heath
       and I. K. James. London, 1973.
       47p. 28cm.

6490   Macdonald Education.
       Macdonald atlas library. Europe. London, 1970.
       44p. col. maps. 27cm.

6491   Macmillan.
       Europe and the world: maps and mapwork. By John
       Moser. London, 1970.
       32p. col. maps. 28cm.

6492   Macmillan Education, Ltd.
       A picture map book of Europe. Basingstoke, 1971.
       1 vol. col. maps. 28cm.

6493   Mairs Geographischer Verlag.
       Der grosse Continental-Atlas. Deutschland, Europa.
       Stuttgart, 1971.
       576p. col. maps. 26cm.

6494   Mairs Geographischer Verlag.
       Der grosse Continental-Atlas Deutschland, Europa.
       Stuttgart, 1972.
       576p. col. maps. 26cm.

6495   Mairs Geographischer Verlag.

Der grosse Continental-Atlas.   Deutschland, Europa.
Stuttgart, 1973.
576p.   col. maps.   26cm.

6496   Mairs Geographischer Verlag.
Der grosse Continental-Atlas.   Deutschland, Europa.
Stuttgart, 1974.
576p.   col. maps.   26cm.

6497   Mairs Geographischer Verlag.
Der grosse Continental-Atlas.   Deutschland, Europa.
Stuttgart, 1975.
576p.   col. maps.   26cm.

6498   Mairs Geographischer Verlag.
Der grosse Shell Atlas.   Deutschland, Europa.   1970/71.
Stuttgart, 1970.
317p.   col. maps.   27cm.

6499   Mairs Geographischer Verlag.
Der grosse Shell-Atlas.   Deutschland, Europa.   1971/72.
Stuttgart, 1971.
317p.   col. maps.   27cm.

6500   Mairs Geographischer Verlag.
Der grosse Shell Atlas.   Deutschland und Europa.   Stuttgart, 1972.
526p.   col. maps.   27cm.

6501   Mairs Geographischer Verlag.
Der grosse Shell Atlas.   Deutschland und Europa.   Stuttgart, 1973.
513p.   col. maps.   27cm.

6502   Mairs Geographischer Verlag.
Der grosse Shell Atlas.   Deutschland und Europa.   Stuttgart, 1974.
513p.   col. maps.   27cm.

6503   Mairs Geographischer Verlag.
Der grosse Shell Atlas.   Deutschland und Europa.   Stuttgart, 1975.
513p.   col. maps.   27cm.

6504   Mairs Geographischer Verlag.
Shell atlas of Europe.   Stuttgart, [1971].
229p.   col. maps.   27cm.

6505   Mairs Geographischer Verlag.
VARTA Atlas Deutschland/Europa.   Stuttgart, [1974].
1 vol.   col. maps.   30cm.

6506   Miller Freeman.

Atlas of Western European pulp and paper industry.
Brussels, 1974.
9p.   29cm.

6507 Mondadori.
      Rand McNally road atlas of Europe.   Chicago, 1973.
      104p.   col. maps.   28cm.

6508 Nathan, Fernand.
      Europe atlas.   Paris, 1973.
      1 vol.   col. maps.   37.5cm.

6509 N. I. Sh. Mjete Mësimore e Sportive "Hamid Shijaku."
      Historia e mejestes per klasen e vi te shkolles tetevjecare
      harta.   Tiranë, 1970.
      16p.   col. maps.   29cm.

6510 Oxford University Press.
      Atlas of European history.   By Edward Whiting Fox.
      London, 1956.
      64p.   col. maps.   26cm.

6511 Oxford University Press.
      Oxford regional economic atlas of Western Europe.   By
      K. M. Clayton and I. B. F. Kormoss.   London, 1971.
      160p.   col. maps.   26cm.

6512 Oxford University Press.
      Oxford regional economic atlas of Western Europe.   By
      K. M. Clayton and I. B. F. Kormoss.   London, 1972.
      160p.   col. maps.   26cm.

6513 Philip, George & Son, Ltd.
      Philips' road atlas Europe.   1ed.   London, 1972.
      239p.   col. maps.   29cm.

6514 Rad.
      Evropa.   Atlas nemih karata za nastavu geografije.   By
      Radovin Nedeljković.   Beograd, 1970.
      60p.   34cm.

6515 Rand McNally & Co.
      Europe; a Rand McNally atlas.   Chicago, 1974.
      69p.   col. maps.   28cm.

6516 Rand McNally & Co.
      Rand McNally road atlas of Europe.   Chicago, 1971.
      96p.   col. maps.   28cm.

6517 Rand McNally & Co.
      Rand McNally road atlas of Europe.   Chicago, 1972.
      104p.   col. maps.   28cm.

6518   Rand McNally & Co.
       Rand McNally road atlas of Europe.   Chicago, 1973.
       104p. col. maps. 28cm.

6519   Rand McNally & Co.
       Rand McNally road atlas of Europe.   Chicago, 1974.
       104p. col. maps. 28cm.

6520   Rand McNally, GMBH.
       Rand McNally road atlas of Europe.   Chicago, 1971.
       96p. col. maps. 28cm.

6521   Rand McNally, GMBH.
       Rand McNally road atlas of Europe.   Chicago, 1972.
       104p. col. maps. 28cm.

6522   Ravenstein Geographische Verlagsanstalt.
       Reiseatlas Deutschland und Europa.   Frankfurt, 1971.
       67p. col. maps. 29cm.

6523   Ravenstein Geographische Verlagsanstalt.
       Reiseatlas Deutschland und Europa.   Frankfurt, 1975.
       66p. col. maps. 29cm.

6524   Ravenstein Geographische Verlagsanstalt.
       Strassen; der aktuelle Auto-Atlas Deutschland und Europa.
       Frankfurt am Main, [1968].
       66p. col. maps. 29cm.

6525   Ravenstein Geographische Verlagsanstalt.
       Strassen; der aktuelle Auto-Atlas Deutschland und Europa.
       Frankfurt am Main, 1969.
       66p. col. maps. 29cm.

6526   Ravenstein Geographische Verlagsanstalt.
       Strassen; der aktuelle Auto-Atlas. Deutschland und Europa.
       Frankfurt, 1970.
       66p. col. maps. 29cm.

6527   Ravenstein Geographische Verlagsanstalt.
       Strassen; der aktuelle Auto-Atlas Deutschland und Europa.
       Frankfurt, 1971.
       66p. col. maps. 29cm.

6528   Ravenstein Geographische Verlagsanstalt.
       Strassen; der aktuelle Auto-Atlas Deutschland und Europa.
       Frankfurt, 1972.
       66p. col. maps. 29cm.

6529   Ravenstein Geographische Verlagsanstalt.
       Strassen; der aktuelle Auto-Atlas Deutschland und Europa.
       Frankfurt, 1973.
       68p. col. maps. 29cm.

6530   Ravenstein Geographische Verlagsanstalt.
       Strassen; der aktuelle Auto-Atlas Deutschland und Europa.
       Frankfurt, 1974.
       66p.   col.   maps.   29cm.

6531   Ravenstein Geographische Verlagsanstalt.
       Strassen; der aktuelle Auto-Atlas Deutschland und Europa.
       Frankfurt, 1975.
       66p.   col.   maps.   29cm.

6532   Reader's Digest, N. V.
       Het Beste boek voor de weg.   Amsterdam, [1969].
       1 vol.   col.   maps.   29cm.

6533   Reader's Digest, N. V.
       Het Beste boek voor de weg.   2ed.   Amsterdam, [1970].
       1 vol.   col.   maps.   29cm.

6534   Reise und Verkehrsverlag.
       Grosser Auto-Atlas: international.   Stuttgart, 1975.
       503p.   col.   maps.   27cm.

6535   Reise und Verkehrsverlag.
       Strassenatlas: Deutschland, Europa.   Berlin, [1973].
       169p.   col.   maps.   26cm.

6536   Reise und Verkehrsverlag.
       Strassenatlas: Deutschland, Europa.   Berlin, 1974.
       208p.   col.   maps.   26cm.

6537   Royal Automobile Club.
       Road atlas of Europe.   London, 1972.
       124p.   col.   maps.   28cm.

6538   Scribner.
       The Bartholomew/Scribner atlas of Europe: A profile of
       Western Europe.   By Geoffrey S. Browne and Robert M.
       Croucher.   New York, 1974.
       128p.   col.   maps.   30cm.

6539   Sélection du Reader's digest, S. A. R. L.
       Guide de la route Europe.   Paris, [1969].
       1 vol.   col.   maps.   29cm.

6540   Spectrum.
       Spectrum wegenatlas.   Utrecht, 1974.
       104p.   col.   maps.   39cm.

6541   Tammi.
       Euroopan autoilukartasto.   Helsinki, 1969.
       225p.   col.   maps.   31cm.

6542   Unesco.

Climatic atlas of Europe. Atlas climatique de l'Europe.
By F. Steinhauser. Geneva, Paris, 1970-
in parts. col. maps. 60cm.

6543 United Nations. Economic Commission for Europe.
Census of motor traffic on main international traffic
arteries, 1965. [Atlas.] Geneva, [1967].
10p. col. maps. 28cm.

6544 U. S. S. R. Glavnoe upravlenie geodezii i kartografii.
Atlas mira. Zapadnaia Evropa. Moskva, 1973.
40p. col. maps. 34cm.

6545 U. S. S. R. Glavnoe upravlenie geodezii i kartografii.
Automobilinie marshrute europeiskaya chaste. Moskva,
1973.
39p. col. maps. 27cm.

6546 Warne, F.
Atlas of Europe. With Bartholomew. London, 1974.
128p. col. maps. 30cm.

6547 World Meteorological Organization.
Climatic atlas of Europe. By F. Steinhauser. With
Cartographia. Budapest, 1970-
in parts. col. maps. 60cm.

NORTH AMERICA

6548 American Oil Co.
American road atlas. With Diversified Map Corp.
Racine, Wisc., [1971].
114p. col. maps. 28cm.

6549 American Youth Hostels.
North American bicycle atlas. By Virginia Ward and
Mary Williams. With Hammond. Maplewood, N.J., [1969].
127p. 24cm.

6550 American Youth Hostels.
North American bicycle atlas. 2ed. By Virginia Ward
and Mary Williams. New York, [1971].
191p. 24cm.

6551 American Youth Hostels.
North American bicycle atlas. 3ed. By Virginia Ward
and Mary Williams. New York, [1973].
191p. 24cm.

6552 Artists & Writers Press.
Holiday Inn travel guide and road atlas. With General
Drafting. New York, [1961].
80p. col. maps. 28cm.

6553 Donnelley, R. R. & Sons Co.
Best Western 1969 travel guide and atlas. Chicago, 1969.
48p. col. maps. 31cm.

6554 Donnelley, R. R. & Sons Co.
Best Western 1970 travel guide and atlas. Chicago, 1970.
48p. col. maps. 31cm.

6555 Donnelley, R. R. & Sons Co.
Best Western 1971 travel guide and atlas. Chicago, [1971].
48p. col. maps. 31cm.

6556 Donnelley, R. R. & Sons Co.
Best Western motels, 1972 travel guide and atlas. [North America]. Chicago, 1972.
48p. col. maps. 31cm.

6557 General Drafting Co.
Travel atlas. With Exxon Travel Club. Houston, Tex., [1973].
84p. col. maps. 29cm.

6558 General Drafting Co.
Travel atlas [North America]. With Humble Travel Club. New York, [1970].
84p. col. maps. 29cm.

6559 General Drafting Co.
Travel atlas [North America]. With Humble Travel Club. New York, [1971].
84p. col. maps. 29cm.

6560 Generalstabens litografiska anstalt.
Vär värld Nordamerika. Politsk-ekonomisk atlas. By Leif Söderström and Gunnar Schalin. Stockholm, 1971.
70p. col. maps. 22cm.

6561 Goushá, H. M. Co.
American highway atlas. Chicago, [1955].
98p. col. maps. 46cm.

6562 Goushá, H. M. Co.
American highway atlas. Chicago, [1956].
98p. col. maps. 46cm.

6563 Goushá, H. M. Co.
American highway atlas. 3ed. New York, [1957].
102p. col. maps. 46cm.

6564 Goushá, H. M. Co.
American highway atlas. 4ed. New York, [1959].
103p. col. maps. 46cm.

6565 Goushá, H. M. Co.
      American highway atlas. 5ed. New York, [1960].
      103p. col. maps. 46cm.

6566 Goushá, H. M. Co.
      American highway atlas. Chicago, [1961].
      103p. col. maps. 46cm.

6567 Hammond, Inc.
      American Youth Hostels' North American bicycle atlas.
      Maplewood, N. J., [1969].
      127p. 24cm.

6568 Hammond, Inc.
      Nature atlas of America. By Roland C. Clement.
      Maplewood, N. J., 1973.
      255p. col. maps. 32cm.

6569 Hammond, Inc.
      Pictorial travel atlas of scenic America. By E. L.
      Jordan. Maplewood, N. J., 1973.
      288p. col. maps. 28cm.

6570 Kapelusz y Cía.
      Atlas Humboldt: Américan del Norte, del Sur, Central y
      Antillana, físico, político, económico. 10ed. Buenos
      Aires, [1959].
      66p. col. maps. 26cm.

6571 Kapelusz y Cía.
      Atlas Humboldt: América del Norte, del Sur, central y
      Antillana, físico, político, económico. 10ed. Buenos
      Aires, [1964].
      66p. col. maps. 26cm.

6572 Kapelusz y Cía.
      Coloratlas Kapelusz, América central y Antillas: físico,
      político, económico, estadístico. Buenos Aires, [1970].
      28p. col. maps. 32cm.

6573 Macmillan.
      A map book of North America. By A. Ferriday. Basing-
      stoke, 1975.
      1 vol. col. maps. 25cm.

6574 Methuen.
      An atlas of North American affairs. By D. K. Adams
      and H. B. Rodgers. Toronto, 1970.
      136p. 22cm.

6575 Rand McNally & Co.
      Texaco international road atlas. New York, 1959.
      48p. col. maps. 25cm.

6576 Rand McNally & Co.
      Texaco international road atlas.   New York, 1961.
      48p. col. maps. 25cm.

6577 Skelly Oil Co.
      Skelly highway atlas.   With H. M. Goushá.   Tulsa,
      Okla., [1959].
      56p. col. maps. 26cm.

6578 Wiley, John & Sons.
      Atlas of paleogeographic maps of North America.   By
      Charles Schuchert.   New York, [1955].
      177p. 30cm.

SOUTH AMERICA

6579 Generalstabens litografiska anstalt.
      Vär värld Latinamerika.   Politisk-ekonomisk atlas.   By
      Leif Söderström and Gunnar Schalin.   Stockholm, 1968.
      1 vol. col. maps. 22cm.

6580 Kapelusz y Cía.
      Atlas Humboldt: América del Norte, del Sur, Central y
      Antillana, físico, político, económico.   10ed.   Buenos
      Aires, [1959].
      66p. col. maps. 26cm.

6581 Kapelusz y Cía.
      Atlas Humboldt: América del Norte, del Sur, central y
      Antillana, físico, político, económico.   10ed.   Buenos
      Aires, [1964].
      66p. col. maps. 26cm.

6582 Pan American Institute of Geography & History.
      Atlas de América.   Buenos Aires, 1955.
      66p. col. maps. 36cm.

6583 Praeger, Frederick A.
      An atlas of Latin American affairs.   By Ronald M.
      Schneider.   New York, 1966.
      136p. 22cm.

6584 Praeger, Frederick A.
      An atlas of Latin American affairs.   By Ronald M.
      Schneider.   New York, 1970.
      136p. 22cm.

6585 Uruguay. Comisión de Integración Eléctrica Regional.
      Atlas del desarrollo energético de América de Sur.   3ed.
      Montevideo, 1971.
      43p. col. maps. 76cm.

NATIONAL ATLASES

AFRICA

Botswana

6586 Botswana. Govt. Printer.
Botswana: an atlas for secondary schools. By R.
Gardner. Gaborone, 1972.
15p. col. maps. 31cm.

6587 Collins, William, Sons & Co., Ltd.
Atlas for Botswana. Johannesburg, [1973].
67p. col. maps. 27cm.

Chad

6588 Chad. Institut National Tchadien pour les Sciences Humaines.
Atlas pratique du Tchad. 1ed. Paris, 1972.
77p. col. maps. 39cm.

Congo see Zaire

Egypt see U.A.R.

Ethiopia

6589 Mariam, Mesfin Wolde.
An atlas of Ethiopia. Addis Ababa, [1970].
84p. col. maps. 28cm.

6590 Mariam, Mesfin Wolde.
An atlas of Ethiopia. Rev. ed. Addis Ababa, 1970.
84p. col. maps. 28cm.

6591 Mariam, Mesfin Wolde.
Ethiopia: maps and figures. Addis Ababa, [1961].
14p. 28cm.

Ghana

6592 Collins, William, Sons & Co., Ltd.
Collins-Longmans Ghana atlas. 1ed. Glasgow, 1963.
65p. col. maps. 22.5cm.

6593   Ghana.   Meteorological Services.
       Climatic maps of Ghana for agriculture.   By Anthony
       K. L. Usscher.   Legon, [1969].
       36p.   32cm.

6594   Ghana.   Survey Dept.
       National atlas of Ghana.   By E. A. Boateng.   Accra,
       1960-1970.
       15p.   col.   maps.   64cm.

6595   Ghana.   Survey Dept.
       Portfolio of Ghana maps.   Accra, [1969].
       13p.   col.   maps.   44cm.

6596   Macmillan.
       My second book of maps.   An atlas of Ghana and the rest
       of Africa.   London, 1974.
       33p.   col.   maps.   28cm.

6597   Nelson, Thomas & Sons, Ltd.
       Ghana junior atlas.   By E. A. Boateng.   London, 1968.
       33p.   col.   maps.   29cm.

Ivory Coast

6598   Ivory Coast.   Ministère du plan de Côte D'Ivoire.
       Atlas de Côte D'Ivoire.   Abidjan, 1971-
       1 vol.   col.   maps.   57cm.

Kenya

6599   Carleton University.
       A Computer atlas of Kenya.   By D. R. F. Taylor.   Ot-
       tawa, 1971.
       121p.   28cm.

6600   Collins, William, Sons & Co., Ltd.
       The new Kenya atlas.   By R. B. Ogendo.   Nairobi,
       [1971].
       48p.   col.   maps.   27cm.

6601   Philip, George & Son, Ltd.
       The first Kenya atlas.   By H. J. Nyamn and Harold
       Fullard.   London, 1973.
       36p.   col.   maps.   28cm.

6602   Survey of Kenya.
       National atlas of Kenya.   3ed.   Nairobi, 1970.
       103p.   col.   maps.   41cm.

6603   Survey of Kenya.
       National atlas of Kenya.   Nairobi, 1971.
       103p.   col.   maps.   41cm.

Liberia

6604 Africana Pub. Corp.
Liberia in maps: graphic perspectives of a developing country. By Stefan von Gnielinski. New York, [1972]. 111p. 29cm.

6605 Macmillan & Co., Ltd.
Macmillan's world atlas for Liberian schools. 1ed. London, 1962. 32p. col. maps. 25cm.

6606 Macmillan & Co., Ltd.
Macmillan's world atlas for Liberian schools. London, 1967. 32p. col. maps. 25cm.

6607 University of London Press.
Liberia in maps. By Stefan von Gnielinski. London, 1972. 111p. 29cm.

Lybia

6608 Collins, William, Sons & Co., Ltd.
Arabic atlas for Libya. Glasgow, [1970]. 1 vol. col. maps. 27cm.

Malagasy Republic

6609 Malagasy. L'Association des Géographes de Madagascar.
Atlas de Madagascar. Tananarive, [1969-]. in parts. col. maps. 40cm.

6610 Malagasy. L'Association des Géographes de Madagascar.
Atlas de Madagascar. Tananarive, [1971]. 70p. col. maps. 40cm.

Malawi

6611 Collins, William, Sons & Co., Ltd.
Atlas for Malawi. Rev. ed. By A. MacGregor Hutcheson. Limbe, 1969. 36p. col. maps. 27cm.

6612 Collins, William, Sons & Co., Ltd.
Atlas for Malawi. Blantyre, [1971]. 41p. col. maps. 27cm.

6613 Macmillan.
A map book of Eastern Africa, Zambia, and Malawi. Nairobi, 1974. 1 vol. col. maps. 25cm.

6614 Malawi. Dept. of Surveys.

Maps illustrating development projects, 1970-1973.
Blantyre, [1970].
17p. col. maps. 49cm.

6615   Malawi. Dept. of Surveys.
Maps illustrating development projects, 1972-1973/4.
Blantyre, [1972].
25p. col. maps. 49cm.

6616   Malawi. Geological Survey.
Geological atlas of Malawi. By R. T. Cannon. Zomba,
1970-
in parts. col. maps. 64cm.

6617   University of London Press.
Malawi in maps. By Swanzie Agnew and Michael Stubbs.
London, 1972.
143p. 35cm.

Mali

6618   Nathan, Fernand.
République du Mali, mon livret de cartographie. Paris,
1970.
16p. col. maps. 32cm.

Mauritius

6619   Macmillan Education, Ltd.
Atlas for Mauritius. London, 1971.
33p. col. maps. 29cm.

6620   Macmillan Education, Ltd.
Atlas for Mauritius. London, 1973.
33p. col. maps. 29cm.

Morocco

6621   France. Centre national de la recherche scientifique.
Atlas préhistorique du Maroc. Paris, 1973-
in parts. col. maps. 46cm.

Mozambique

6622   Shell Moçambique, Ltd.
Estradas de Moçambique. Lourenço Marques, [1969].
12p. col. maps. 23cm.

Nigeria

6623   Macmillan Education, Ltd.
Macmillan junior atlas for Nigeria. Lagos, 1975.
1 vol. col. maps. 29cm.

6624   Macmillan Education, Ltd.
          The Nigeria school atlas.   London, Basingstoke, 1972.
          32p.   col. maps.   29cm.

6625   Macmillan Education, Ltd.
          The Nigeria school atlas.   London, Basingstoke, 1973.
          32p.   col. maps.   29cm.

6626   Macmillan Education, Ltd.
          The Nigeria school atlas.   London, Basingstoke, 1974.
          32p.   col. maps.   29cm.

6627   Nigeria.   Federal Surveys.
          Nigeria.   Lagos, [1961].
          13p.   col. maps.   54cm.

6628   Nigeria.   Federal Surveys.
          Nigeria.   Lagos, 1970-
          1 vol.   col. maps.   56cm.

6629   Oxford University Press.
          Oxford atlas for Nigeria.   London, 1968.
          98p.   col. maps.   26cm.

6630   Oxford University Press.
          Oxford atlas for Nigeria.   London, 1971.
          77p.   col. maps.   26cm.

Sierra Leone

6631   Africana Pub. Corp.
          Sierra Leone in maps: graphic perspectives of a develop-
          ing country.   2ed.   By John Innes Clarke.   New York,
          1972.
          120p.   29cm.

6632   Collins, William, Sons & Co., Ltd.
          School atlas for Sierra Leone.   By Milton Harvey.   Glas-
          gow, [1973].
          30p.   col. maps.   27cm.

Somalia

6633   Collins, William, Sons & Co., Ltd.
          Atlas for Somalia.   Glasgow, London, [1970].
          1 vol.   col. maps.   27cm.

South Africa

6634   Automobile Association of South Africa.
          Road atlas and touring guide of Southern Africa.   3ed.
          Johannesburg, [1968].
          200p.   col. maps.   25cm.

6635   BP Southern Africa Pty., Ltd.
       BP padkaarte. Road maps.   Cape Town, [195-].
       14p. col. maps. 29cm.

6636   BP Southern Africa Pty., Ltd.
       BP road maps. Padkaarte. Cape Town, [1970].
       22p. col. maps. 29cm.

6637   B.P. Southern Africa Pty., Ltd.
       Road maps. Padkaarte. Cape Town, [1967].
       22p. col. maps. 29cm.

6638   Macmillan South Africa, Ltd.
       Junior secondary atlas for South African schools.
       Basingstoke, 1972.
       1 vol. col. maps. 28cm.

6639   Map Studio Productions, pty., Ltd.
       Road atlas of Southern Africa. With Shell South Africa.
       Johannesburg, 1970.
       64p. col. maps. 27.5cm.

6640   Philip, Georg & Son, Ltd.
       Philip se kollege atlas vir Snidelike Afrika.   6ed.   By
       Harold Fullard. London, 1971.
       168p. col. maps. 29cm.

6641   Philip, George & Son, Ltd.
       Philips' college atlas for southern Africa.   London, 1971.
       168p. col. maps. 29cm.

Swaziland

6642   Military Vehicles & Engineering Establishment.
       A land system atlas of Swaziland.   By G. Murdoch.
       Christchurch, 1971.
       49p. col. maps. 47.5cm.

Tanzania

6643   Africana Pub. Corp.
       Tanzania in maps: graphic perspectives of a developing
       country. By L. Berry. New York, 1972.
       172p. 29cm.

6644   Tanzania. Bureau of Resource Assessment and Land--Use
       Planning.
       Regional economic atlas, mainland Tanzania.   Dar Es
       Salaam, 1968.
       70p. 25cm.

6645   Tanzania Publishing House, Ltd.
       Atlasi yenye picha kwa shule za msingi za Tanzania.

Dar Es Salaam, 1969.
32p. col. maps. 29cm.

6646 University of London Press.
Tanzania in Maps. By L. Berry. London, 1971.
172p. 29cm.

Uganda

6647 Collins, William, Sons & Co., Ltd.
Atlas for Uganda. London, [1971].
1 vol. col. maps. 27cm.

U. A. R. -Egypt

6648 U. A. R. -Egypt. al-Jihaz al-Markazi lil-Ta'bi'ah al'Ammah
wa-al-Ihsa.
United Arab Republic statistical atlas, 1952-1966. Cairo,
1968.
123p. col. maps. 35cm.

6649 U. A. R. -Egypt. Survey of Egypt.
U. A. R. tourist atlas. Cairo, [1971].
69p. col. maps. 30cm.

Upper Volta

6650 Editions Jeune Afrique.
Atlas de la Haute-Volta. Paris, 1975.
48p. col. maps. 29cm.

Zaire

6651 Congo. Commissariat Général au Plan.
Atlas du Congo. Brazzaville, 1969.
15p. col. maps. 62cm.

6652 Congo. Institut national pour l'étude agronomique.
Atlas climatique du bassin Congolais. By Franz Bultot.
Bruxelles, 1971-
4 vol. col. maps. 33cm.

Zambia

6653 Africana Pub. Corp.
Zambia in maps: graphic perspectives of a developing
country. By D. Hywel Davies. New York, 1971.
128p. 29cm.

6654 Africana Pub. Corp.
Zambia in maps: graphic perspectives of a developing
country. By D. Hywel Davies. New York, 1972.
128p. 29cm.

6655   Collins, William, Sons & Co., Ltd.
       Atlas for Zambia. Glasgow, 1973.
       49p. col. maps. 27cm.

6656   Collins, William, Sons & Co., Ltd.
       Primary atlas for Zambia. Glasgow, [1973].
       1 vol. col. maps. 27cm.

6657   Macmillan.
       A map book of Eastern Africa, Zambia, and Malawi.
       Nairobi, 1974.
       1 vol. col. maps. 25cm.

6658   University of London Press.
       Zambia in Maps. By D. Hywel Davies. London, 1971.
       128p. 29cm.

6659   Zambia. National Council for Scientific Research.
       Atlas of the population of Zambia. By Mary E. Jackman
       and D. Hywel Davies. Lusaka, 1971.
       10p. col. maps. 54cm.

Afghanistan

6660   Afghanistan.   Cartographic Inst.
       Preliminary atlas of the provinces of Afghanistan.   Kabul,
       1970.
       55p.   27.5cm.

6661   Geographic & Drafting Institute.
       General atlas of Afghanistan.   Teheran, 1975.
       1 vol.   col.   maps.   32cm.

6662   Sahab.
       General atlas of Afghanistan.   By Abbas Sahab.   Teheran,
       1974.
       201p.   col.   maps.   32cm.

Bangla Desh

6663   Oxford University Press.
       Oxford school atlas for Pakistan.   London, Oxford, 1966.
       60p.   col.   maps.   26cm.

6664   Oxford University Press.
       Oxford school atlas for Pakistan.   Lahore, London, [1973].
       57p.   col.   maps.   26cm.

6665   Ramnarain Sons Limited.
       Cotton map of India & Pakistan; silver jubilee publication.
       Bombay, [1953].
       27p.   31cm.

6666   State University of New York.
       Computer atlas of Bangla Desh.   By Paul R. Baumann and
       Charles W. Woolever.   Oneonta, N.Y., 1972.
       84p.   29cm.

Cambodia

6667   U.S. Central Intelligence Agency.
       Cambodia: provincial maps.   Washington, D.C., 1971.
       22p.   col.   maps.   26cm.

6668   U.S. Central Intelligence Agency.
       Indochina atlas.   Washington, D.C., 1970.

14p.   col.   maps.   46cm.

6669   Vietnam.   National Geographic Center.
       Geological atlas of Vietnam, Cambodia and Laos.   Saigon,
       1962-63.
       in parts.   col.   maps.   33cm.

Ceylon   see   Sri Lanka

China

6670   McGraw-Hill Book Co.
       Atlas of China.   By Chiao-min Hsieh and Christopher L.
       Salter.   New York, [1973].
       282p.   31cm.

6671   Rand McNally & Co.
       Rand McNally illustrated atlas of China.   Chicago, 1972.
       80p.   col.   maps.   39cm.

6672   The New York Times.
       The Times atlas of China.   By P. J. M. Geelan and D.
       C. Twitchett.   New York, [1974].
       232p.   col.   maps.   37cm.

6673   U. S. Central Intelligence Agency.
       People's Republic of China atlas.   Washington, D. C.,
       1971.
       82p.   col.   maps.   43cm.

6674   U. S. Central Intelligence Agency.
       People's Republic of China.   Administrative atlas.
       Washington, D. C., 1975.
       68p.   col.   maps.   38cm.

Hong Kong

6675   Collins, William, Sons & Co., Ltd.
       World atlas for Hong Kong.   Glasgow, [1973].
       1 vol.   col.   maps.   27cm.

6676   Macmillan Publishers, (H. K.), Ltd.
       Hong Kong Certificate Atlas.   Hong Kong, 1970.
       1 vol.   28cm.

India

6677   India Book House.
       School atlas for India.   Bombay, 1974.
       64p.   col.   maps.   29cm.

6678   India.   Census Commission.
       Census of India 1961.   Census Atlas.   By A. Mitra.

New Delhi, 1970.
423p. col. maps. 52cm.

6679 India. Census Commission.
      Census of India 1960. Census Atlas. By Sen Gupta.
      Delhi, 1971.
      423p. col. maps. 52cm.

6680 India. Meteorological Dept.
      Climatological atlas of India, abridged. New Delhi, 1971.
      40p. col. maps. 38cm.

6681 India. Ministry of Agriculture.
      An agricultural atlas of India. By J. Singh. Delhi,
      1974.
      356p. col. maps. 25cm.

6682 India. Ministry of Irrigation and Power.
      Irrigation atlas of India. Delhi, 1969.
      1 vol. 30cm.

6683 India. Ministry of Irrigation and Power.
      Irrigation atlas of India. Calcutta, 1972.
      1 vol. 30cm.

6684 India. National Atlas Organisation.
      Tourist atlas of India. By S. P. Dasgupta. Delhi, 1974.
      25p. col. maps. 56cm.

6685 Indian Central Jute Committee.
      The Indian jute atlas. Calcutta, 1959.
      89p. 31cm.

6686 Ramnarain Sons Limited.
      Cotton map of India & Pakistan; Silver jubilee publication.
      Bombay, [1953].
      27p. 31cm.

Indonesia

6687 Anikasari.
      Atlas Indonesia. [In Indonesian.] Djakarta, [1971-].
      in parts. 35cm.

6688 Collins, William, Sons & Co., Ltd.
      Atlas dunja sekolah menegah. Glasgow, [1973].
      1 vol. col. maps. 27cm.

6689 Djambatan.
      Atlas seluruh dunia. Djakarta, [1971].
      67p. col. maps. 31cm.

6690 Djambatan.

Alas untuk sekolah landjutan.   Djakarta, 1970.
56p.   col.   maps.   32cm.

6691   Ganaco, N. V.
       Atlas nasional tentang, Indonesia.   Djakarta, [1968].
       72p.   col.   maps.   39cm.

6692   Indonesia.   Badan Atlas Nasional.
       Badan atlas nasional.   Djakarta, [1968].
       in parts.   30cm.

6693   Indonesia.   Direktorat Land Use.
       Atlas Indonesia, buku kedua ekonomi.   [Indonesian
       economic atlas.]   (In Indonesian).   By I. Made Sandy.
       Djakarta, 1971.
       26p.   col.   maps.   35cm.

6694   Madju, Firma.
       Atlas Indonesia dan dunia untuk sekolah dasar.   Medan,
       [1972].
       32p.   col.   maps.   28cm.

6695   Pembina.
       Atlas Indonesia & Dunia.   Djakarta, 1974.
       28p.   col.   maps.   32cm.

6696   Pembina.
       Atlas Indonesia & dunia, untuk sekolah dasar di Djawa,
       Bali, Nusatenggara, Maluku.   By Chalid Latif and M. J.
       Ridwan.   Djakarta, [1971].
       28p.   col.   maps.   32cm.

Iran

6697   Geographic and Drafting Institute.
       Atlas of Iran.   White Revolution Proceeds and Progresses.
       Teheran, 1971.
       190p.   col.   maps.   35cm.

6698   Iran.   Danishgah.
       Atlas-i-tarikhi Iran.   Historical atlas of Iran.   Teheran,
       1971.
       76p.   col.   maps.   28cm.

6699   Iran.   Ministry of Interior.
       Atlas of Iran.   White Revolution.   2ed.   Teheran, 1973.
       197p.   col.   maps.   35cm.

6700   Sahab.
       Atlas of ancient and historical maps of Iran.   Teheran,
       [1973].
       200p.   col.   maps.   35cm.

6701   Sahab.
       Atlas of Iran.   White Revolution Proceeds and Progresses.
       Teheran, 1971.
       191p.   col. maps.   35cm.

6702   Sahab.
       Atlas of Iran.   White Revolution Proceeds and Progresses.
       2ed.   Teheran, 1974.
       197p.   col. maps.   35cm.

6703   Sahab.
       Climatic atlas of Iran.   With Univ. of Teheran.   By M. H.
       Ganji.   Teheran, [1972].
       117p.   col. maps.   42cm.

6704   Sahab.
       Travel atlas of Iran.   Teheran, 1970.
       99p.   col. maps.   24cm.

6705   University of Teheran.
       Climatic atlas of Iran.   By Ahmad Mostofi.   In English
       and Persian.   Teheran, 1965.
       117p.   col. maps.   44cm.

6706   University of Teheran.
       Climatic atlas of Iran.   By M. H. Ganji.   Teheran,
       [1972].
       117p.   col. maps.   42cm.

6707   University of Teheran.
       Historical atlas of Iran.   Teheran, 1971.
       1 vol.   col. maps.   28cm.

Israel

6708   ADI Ltd.
       Atlas ha'olam vehe-halal (in Hebrew).   By B. Lurie.
       Tel Aviv, 1969.
       350p.   col. maps.   34cm.

6709   Carta.
       Carta's Israel motor atlas.   Jerusalem, [1970].
       57p.   col. maps.   21cm.

6710   Carta.
       Carta's Israel road guide.   2ed.   Jerusalem, 1965.
       68p.   col. maps.   24cm.

6711   Carta.
       Carta's Israel road guide.   Jerusalem, [1972].
       75p.   col. maps.   28cm.

6712   Elsevier.

        Atlas of Israel. [English ed.] With Survey of Israel.
        Amsterdam, 1971.
        140p. col. maps. 50cm.

6713   European Road Guide, Inc.
        1971-1972 Motoring atlas, Europe and Israel.   Larchmont,
        N. Y. , 1971.
        78p. 28cm.

6714   Israel. Central Bureau of Statistics.
        Israel. Atlas of industry and crafts. Jerusalem, 1965.
        1 vol. col. maps. 29cm.

6715   Israel. Mahleket ha-medidot.
        Israel in 14 pictorial maps. Jerusalem, [1953].
        23p. col. maps. 32cm.

6716   Yavneh.
        Atlas fisi, medini vekalkali. By Moshe Brawer. Tel
        Aviv, 1969.
        128p. col. maps. 35cm.

Japan

6717   Buyōdō Co. , Ltd.
        Road atlas. Japan. (in Japanese). Tokyo, 1970.
        4 vol. col. maps. 26cm.

6718   Heibonsha.
        Heibonsha Japan atlas. 2ed. Tokyo, 1972.
        327p. col. maps. 32cm.

6719   Heibonsha.
        Japan: the pocket atlas. Tokyo, 1970.
        275p. col. maps. 20cm.

6720   International Society for Educational Information.
        Atlas of Japan. Physical, economic and social.   1ed.
        (in English). By R. Isida. Tokyo, 1970.
        128p. col. maps. 37cm.

6721   International Society for Educational Information.
        Atlas of Japan. Physical, economic and social.   2ed.
        (in English). By R. Isida. Tokyo, 1974.
        128p. col. maps. 37cm.

6722   International Society for Educational Information.
        Simple atlas of Japan. Tokyo, [1969].
        12p. col. maps. 30cm.

6723   Japan. Geographical Survey Institute.
        National atlas of Japan. Tokyo, 1972.
        1 vol. col. maps. 80cm.

6724   Japan.   Meteorological Agency.
       Climatic atlas of Japan.   Tokyo 1971-72.
       2 vol.   col.   maps.   54cm.

6725   Kokusai Kyōiku Jōhō Sentā.
       Atlas of Japan: physical, economic, and social.   By R.
       Isida.   Tokyo, 1970.
       128p.   col.   maps.   37cm.

6726   Teikoku-Shoin Co., Ltd.
       Teikoku's complete atlas of Japan.   3ed.   (in English).
       By Yoshio Moriya.   Tokyo, 1969.
       55p.   col.   maps.   31cm.

6727   Warajiya Kabushiki Kaisha.
       Zenkoku Doro Chizucho.   (Japan road atlas).   Osaka,
       1970.
       250p.   col.   maps.   26cm.

Jordan

6728   Jordan.   Meteorological Dept.
       Climatic atlas of Jordan.   Amman, 1971.
       127p.   30cm.

Laos

6729   Laos.   National Geographic Center.
       Complete atlas of Laos.   With U.S. Army Map Service.
       Vientiane, [1955].
       28p.   col.   maps.   73cm.

6730   U.S. Central Intelligence Agency.
       Indochina atlas.   Washington, D.C., 1970.
       14p.   col.   maps.   46cm.

6731   Vietnam.   National Geographic Center.
       Geological atlas of Vietnam, Cambodia and Laos.   Saigon,
       1962-63.
       in parts.   col.   maps.   33cm.

Lebanon

6732   Lebanon.   Wizārat al-Taşmin al-'Āmm.
       Atlas du Liban.   Beyrouth, 1969.
       20p.   col.   maps.   49cm.

Malaysia

6733   Automobile Association of Malaya.
       Malaysia road atlas; road atlas showing all motor roads
       in Malaysia.   3ed.   Penang, 1971.
       28p.   col.   maps.   25cm.

6734   Borneo Literature Bureau.
        Buka peta negeri Malaysia.   By P. Collenette.   Kuching
        [1970].
        26p.   31cm.

6735   Collins, William, Sons & Co., Ltd.
        Collins-Longmans new secondary atlas for Malaysia and
        Singapore.   1ed.   By R. B. Bunnett.   Glasgow, 1966.
        88p.   col. maps.   29cm.

6736   Collins, William, Sons & Co., Ltd.
        Collins-Longmans new secondary atlas for Malaysia and
        Singapore.   3ed.   By R. B. Bunnett.   Glasgow, London,
        1969.
        88p.   col. maps.   29cm.

6737   Collins, William, Sons & Co., Ltd.
        Primary atlas for Malaysia.   Chinese ed.   Glasgow,
        [1970].
        1 vol.   col. maps.   29cm.

6738   Jacaranda.
        Atlas sekolah menengah Malaysia.   Atlas for secondary
        schools.   Milton, 1971.
        106p.   col. maps.   28cm.

6739   Jacaranda.
        Secondary atlas for Malaysia and Singapore.   By J. A.
        Johnson.   Brisbane, 1971.
        106p.   col. maps.   28cm.

6740   Murray, J.
        Secondary atlas for Malaysia and Singapore.   London, 1971.
        1 vol.   col. maps.   28cm.

Pakistan   see   Bangla Desh

Philippines

6741   Rand McNally & Co.
        Classroom atlas.   (World).   Philippine ed.   Chicago, 1966.
        1 vol.   col. maps.   25cm.

6742   Reed, A. H. & A. W.
        A descriptive atlas of the Pacific Islands, New Zealand,
        Australia, Polynesia, Melanesia, Micronesia, Philippines.
        By T. F. Kennedy.   Wellington, [1968].
        64p.   24cm.

Singapore

6743   Collins, William, Sons & Co., Ltd.
        Collins-Longmans new secondary atlas for Malaysia and

Singapore. 1ed. By R. B. Bunnett. Glasgow, 1966.
88p. col. maps. 29cm.

6744   Collins, William, Sons & Co., Ltd.
Collins-Longmans new secondary atlas for Malaysia and
Singapore. 3ed. By R. B. Bunnett. Glasgow, London,
1969.
88p. col. maps. 29cm.

6745   Jacaranda.
Secondary atlas for Malaysia and Singapore. By J. A.
Johnson. Brisbane, 1971.
106p. col. maps. 28cm.

6746   Macmillan & Co., Ltd.
New pictorial atlas for Singapore. Singapore, 1972.
1 vol. col. maps. 28cm.

6747   Murray, J.
Secondary atlas for Malaysia and Singapore. London, 1971.
1 vol. col. maps. 28cm.

Sri Lanka

6748   Atlas and Maps Industries.
A concise atlas geography of Ceylon. Colombo, [1971].
35p. 29cm.

6749   Atlas and Maps Industries.
A concise atlas geography of Ceylon. Sinhala and Tamil
ed. Colombo, [1972].
35p. 29cm.

6750   Atlas and Maps Industries.
A world atlas for Ceylon students. In Sinhala and Tamil.
Colombo, [1972].
1 vol. 28cm.

Thailand

6751   Thailand. Royal Thai Survey Department.
Topical maps of Thailand. Bangkok, 1964.
16p. 30cm.

6752   U. S. Engineer Resources Inventory Center.
Resource atlas project--Thailand. Washington, D. C.,
1969-71.
2 vol. col. maps. 34cm.

Vietnam

6753   U. S. Central Intelligence Agency.

Indochina atlas. Washington, D. C. , 1970.
14p. col. maps. 46cm.

6754 U. S. Engineer Agency of Resources Inventories.
Vietnam subject index maps. Washington, D. C. , 1970.
182p. 32cm.

6755 Vietnam, Information Section.
An annotated atlas of the Republic of Vietnam. Washington, D. C. , 1972.
62p. col. maps. 28cm.

6756 Vietnam. National Geographic Center.
Complete administrative atlas of South Vietnam. Dalat,
1971.
44p. col. maps. 43cm.

6757 Vietnam. National Geographic Center.
Complete physical atlas of Vietnam (North and South).
Dalat, 1965-1966.
12p. col. maps. 43cm.

6758 Vietnam. National Geographic Center.
Geological atlas of Vietnam, Cambodia and Laos. Saigon,
1962-63.
in parts. col. maps. 33cm.

6759 Vietnam. National Geographic Center.
Maps of the provinces of the Republic of Vietnam. Dalat,
1971-72.
46p. 43cm.

Australia

6760 Gregory's Guides & Maps Pty. Ltd.
      The Ampol touring atlas of Australia. Sydney, 1969.
      122p. col. maps. 32cm.

6761 Gregory's Guides & Maps Pty. Ltd.
      The Ampol touring atlas of Australia. 2ed. Sydney,
      [1970].
      122p. col. maps. 32cm.

6762 Gregory's Guides & Maps Pty. Ltd.
      The Ampol touring atlas of Australia. 3ed. Sydney,
      1971.
      122p. col. maps. 32cm.

6763 Gregory's Guides & Maps Pty. Ltd.
      Touring atlas of Australia. By Charles Sriber. Sydney,
      [1970].
      122p. col. maps. 32cm.

6764 Hamlyn.
      Gemhunting atlas of Australia. Sydney, New York, 1973.
      260p. col. maps. 27cm.

6765 Hamlyn.
      Road atlas of Australia. Sydney, 1972.
      128p. col. maps. 26cm.

6766 Hammond, Inc.
      Illustrated atlas of Australia. Maplewood, N.J., [1972].
      16p. col. maps. 31cm.

6767 Heinemann.
      Australia. A map geography. London, 1972.
      1 vol. 21cm.

6768 Jacaranda.
      Jacaranda atlas. By V. G. Honour. Brisbane, 1969.
      152p. col. maps. 28cm.

6769 Jacaranda.
      Jacaranda junior world atlas. By V. G. Honour. Milton,
      1971.

111

91p. col. maps. 28cm.

6770 Jacaranda.
      The Jacaranda atlas. 2ed. By V. G. Honour. Milton,
      1971.
      144p. col. maps. 29cm.

6771 Jacaranda.
      The Jacaranda atlas. By V. G. Honour. Milton, 1972.
      145p. col. maps. 29cm.

6772 Oxford University Press.
      A map history of Australia. 2ed. By Ian Wynd and Joyce
      Wood. Melbourne, London, [1967].
      60p. col. maps. 25cm.

6773 Reed, A. H. & A. W.
      A descriptive atlas of the Pacific Islands. New Zealand,
      Australia, Polynesia, Melanesia, Micronesia, Philippines.
      By T. F. Kennedy. Wellington, [1968].
      64p. 24cm.

New Zealand

6774 Hamlyn.
      AA road atlas of New Zealand. Auckland, 1974.
      124p. col. maps. 29cm.

6775 Jacaranda.
      The Jacaranda atlas for New Zealand prepared for
      secondary schools. By T. T. Ryder. Auckland, 1971.
      144p. col. maps. 29cm.

6776 Jacaranda.
      The Jacaranda social studies resources atlas for New
      Zealand. 1ed. By E. R. Bloomfield and C. A. Watson.
      Milton, 1972.
      92p. col. maps. 28cm.

6777 New Zealand. Government Printing Office.
      New Zealand atlas. By I. McL. Wards. Auckland,
      [1975].
      176p. col. maps. 32cm.

6778 New Zealand. Local Government Commission.
      Regions and districts of New Zealand. Wellington, 1973.
      86p. 30cm.

6779 Reed, A. H. & A. W.
      A descriptive atlas of the Pacific Islands. New Zealand,
      Australia, Polynesia, Melanesia, Micronesia, Philippines.
      By T. F. Kennedy. Wellington, [1968].
      64p. 24cm.

6780   Shell Co. of New Zealand.
       Shell road maps of New Zealand.   Wellington, 1972.
       44p.   col. maps.   28cm.

Papua and New Guinea

6781   Collins, William, Sons & Co., Ltd.
       An atlas of Papua and New Guinea.   By R. G. Ward and
       D. A. M. Lea.   Glasgow, 1970.
       101p.   26cm.

6782   Jacaranda.
       Papua New Guinea resource atlas.   By Edgard Ford.
       Milton, Q., 1974.
       56p.   col. maps.   60cm.

6783   University of Papua and New Guinea.
       An atlas of Papua and New Guinea.   By R. Gerard Ward
       and David A. M. Lea.   With Collins.   Port Moresby,
       [1970].
       101p.   26cm.

6784   University of Papua and New Guinea.
       Atlas of Papua and New Guinea.   Port Moresby, 1970-
       in parts.   32cm.

EUROPE

Albania

6785 N. I. Sh. Mjete Mësimore e Sportive "Hamid Shijaku."
Atlas gjeografik. Tiranë, 1964.
56p. col. maps. 30cm.

6786 N. I. Sh. Mjete Mësimore e Sportive "Hamid Shijaku."
Atlas gjeografik i shqipërisë. By Ergjin Samimit.
Tiranë, 1971.
26p. col. maps. 32cm.

6787 N. I. Sh. Mjete Mësimore e Sportive "Hamid Shijaku."
Atlas për shkollat fillore. Tiranë, 1970.
19p. col. maps. 26cm.

6788 N. I. Sh. Mjete Mësimore e Sportive "Hamid Shijaku."
Historia e mejestes per Klasen e vi te shkolles
tetevjecare harta. Tiranë, 1970.
16p. col. maps. 29cm.

Austria

6789 Austria. Bundesdenkmalamt.
Atlas der historischen Schutzzonen in Österreich. Graz,
1970.
1 vol. 35cm.

6790 Freytag, Berndt & Artaria.
Auto-Atlas. Österreich 1:200,000. Wien, [1970].
111p. col. maps. 26cm.

6791 Freytag, Berndt & Artaria.
Auto-Atlas Österreich 1:200,000. Wien, [1972].
111p. col. maps. 26cm.

6792 Freytag, Berndt & Artaria.
Auto-Atlas Österreich 1:200,000. Wien, 1975.
103p. col. maps. 26cm.

6793 Freytag, Berndt & Artaria.
Neuer Schulatlas für Hauptschulen und Unterstufen der
Höheren Schulen. Wien, [1973].
110p. col. maps. 32cm.

6794   Freytag, Berndt & Artaria.
       Österreichischer Schulatlas.   Wien, 1971.
       90p.   col.   maps.   32cm.

6795   Hölder, Pichler, Tempsky.
       Historischer Weltatlas zur allgemeinen und Österreichischen
       Geschichte.   46ed.   By Egon Lendl, Wilhelm Wagner,
       Rudolf Klein.   Wien, 1969.
       146p.   col.   maps.   27cm.

6796   Hölzel, Ed. Verlag.
       Österreichischer Atlas für höhere Schulen.   94ed.   By W.
       Strzygowski.   Wien, 1968.
       167p.   col.   maps.   32cm.

6797   Hölzel, Ed. Verlag.
       Österreichischer Atlas für höhere Schulen.   96ed.   By W.
       Strzygowski.   Wien, 1969.
       167p.   col.   maps.   32cm.

6798   Hölzel, Ed. Verlag.
       Österreichischer Atlas für höhere Schulen.   97ed.   Wien,
       1970.
       165p.   col.   maps.   32cm.

6799   Hölzel, Ed. Verlag.
       Österreichischer Atlas für höhere Schulen.   98ed.   By
       H. Eckelt.   Wien, 1971.
       165p.   col.   maps.   32cm.

6800   Hölzel, Ed. Verlag.
       Österreichischer Atlas für höhere Schulen.   99ed.   Wien,
       1972.
       165p.   col.   maps.   32cm.

6801   Hölzel, Ed. Verlag.
       Österreichischer Atlas für höhere Schulen.   100ed.   Wien,
       1973.
       167p.   col.   maps.   32cm.

6802   Hölzel, Ed. Verlag.
       Österrcichischer Hauptschulatlas.   10ed.   Wien, 1972.
       88p.   col.   maps.   33cm.

6803   Hölzel, Ed. Verlag.
       Österreichischer Hauptschulatlas.   Wien, 1973.
       107p.   col.   maps.   33cm.

Belgium

6804   De Sikkel.
       Atlas België en de wereld.   By J. van den Branden and
       M. Nouboers.   With Hölzel.   Antwerpen, [1968].

154p.   col.   maps.   33cm.

6805   Hachette.
       Atlas routier et touristique: France, Belgique, Luxem-
       bourg, Suisse.   With Bordas.   Paris, [1970].
       76p.   col.   maps.   30cm.

6806   Hölzel, Ed. Verlag.
       Atlas Belgie en de wereld.   By J. van den Branden and
       M. Nouboers.   Wien, 1972.
       141p.   col.   maps.   32cm.

6807   Institut cartographique européan.
       Carte politique de la Belgique.   Atlas des élections
       législatives du 31 mars 1968.   By Wilfried Dewachter.
       Bruxelles, 1970.
       79p.   col.   maps.   30cm.

6808   Macmillan & Co., Ltd.
       A map book of the Benelux countries.   By A. J. B.
       Tussler and A. J. L. Alden.   London, 1970.
       64p.   28cm.

6809   Meulenhoff, J. M.
       Atlas Belgie en den wereld.   By J. van den Branden and
       M. Nouboers.   Amsterdam, 1972.
       150p.   col.   maps.   32cm.

6810   Scriptoria.
       Politieke kaart van Belgie.   By Wilfried Dewachter.
       Antwerpen, 1969.
       79p.   col.   maps.   29cm.

6811   Sélection du Reader's digest, S. A. R. L.
       Guide de la route: France, Belgique, Suisse.   Paris,
       [1969].
       455p.   col.   maps.   29cm.

6812   Standaard Uitgeverij.
       Kleine Standaard schoolatlas.   By Michiel David.
       Anvers, [1973].
       35p.   col.   maps.   30cm.

6813   Standaard Uitgeverij.
       Standaard wereldatlas.   Anvers, 1974.
       164p.   col.   maps.   31cm.

6814   Wesmael-Charlier.
       Atlas der algemene geschiedenis.   By Franz Hayt.
       Namur, [1971].
       152p.   col.   maps.   26cm.

6815   Wesmael-Charlier.

Atlas der algemene geschiedenis. By Franz Hayt. Namur, 1974.
151p. col. maps. 26cm.

6816 Wesmael-Charlier.
Atlas d'histoire universelle (et d'histoire de Belgique).
By Franz Hayt. Namur, [1969].
152p. col. maps. 26cm.

6817 Wesmael-Charlier.
Atlas d'histoire universelle et d'histoire de Belgique. By
Franz Hayt. Namur, 1970.
144p. col. maps. 26cm.

Bulgaria

6818 Balkanturist.
Automobile map of Bulgaria. Sofia, 1958.
32p. col. maps. 17cm.

6819 Bulgaria. Akademiya na naukite.
Atlas narodna republika Bulgariya. Sofia, 1973.
168p. col. maps. 50cm.

6820 Bulgaria. Akademiya na naukite.
Bulgarski dialekten atlas. (In Bulgarian). Sofia, 1964-
in parts. col. maps. 50cm.

6821 Bulgaria. Glavno upravlenie po geodeziâ i kartografiâ.
Avtomobilei atlas Bulgaria. Sofia, 1970.
51p. col. maps. 21cm.

6822 Bulgaria. Glavno upravlenie po geodeziâ i kartografiâ.
Avtomobilei atlas Bulgaria. 2ed. Sofia, 1971.
52p. col. maps. 21cm.

6823 Bulgaria. Glavno upravlenie po geodeziâ i kartografiâ.
Geografski atlas na Bulgarija za 10. Klas. Sofia, 1970.
48p. col. maps. 29cm.

Czechoslovakia

6824 Czechoslovakia. Akademia věd.
Atlas chekhoslovatskoy istorii. (in Russian). Praha, 1972.
40p. col. maps. 32cm.

6825 Czechoslovakia. Kartografické nakladatelství.
Autoatlas ČSSR. Praha, 1971.
171p. col. maps. 31cm.

6826 Czechoslovakia. Ústřední správa geodézie a kartografie.
Školní atlas Československých dějin. 5ed. Praha, 1969.

75p.   col.   maps.   31cm.

6827   Czechoslovakia.   Ústřední správa geodézie a kartografie.
       Školní atlas Československých dějin.   Praha, 1971.
       75p.   col.   maps.   31cm.

6828   Delta éditions.
       Tchécoslovaquie.   Cartes et plans.   By Philippe Froment.
       Paris, 1968.
       144p.   col.   maps.   18cm.

6829   Kartografie.
       Atlas CSSR.   1ed.   Praha, 1972.
       58p.   col.   maps.   32cm.

6830   Kartografie.
       Atlas CSSR.   2ed.   Praha, 1973.
       58p.   col.   maps.   32cm.

6831   Kartografie.
       Autoatlas ČSSR.   7ed.   Praha, 1973.
       183p.   col.   maps.   25cm.

6832   Kartografie.
       Školský atlas Československých dějin.   9ed.   Praha, 1973.
       44p.   col.   maps.   30cm.

6833   Kartografie.
       Školský zemepisný atlas Československskej Socialistickej
       republicky.   8ed.   Bratislava, 1972.
       55p.   col.   maps.   30cm.

6834   Slovenska Kartografia.
       Atlas Československskej Socialistickej republicky.
       Bratislava, 1971.
       35p.   col.   maps.   30cm.

6835   Slovenska Kartografia.
       Autoatlas CSSR.   1ed.   Bratislava, 1971.
       18p.   col.   maps.   25cm.

6836   Slovenska Kartografia.
       Autoatlas ČSSR.   2ed.   Bratislava, 1972.
       18p.   col.   maps.   25cm.

6837   Slovenska Kartografia.
       Autoatlas CSSR.   3ed.   Bratislava, 1973.
       169p.   col.   maps.   25cm.

6838   Slovenska Kartografia.
       Skolský atlas Československých dejin.   9ed.   Bratislava,
       1973.
       75p.   col.   maps.   33cm.

Denmark

6839   Denmark.   Geodaetisk Institut.
       Denmark.   24ed.   København, 1970.
       1 vol.   col.   maps.   27.5cm.

6840   Denmark.   Geodaetisk Institut.
       Geodaetisk Instituts Kort, Denmark.   København, 1968.
       32p.   col.   maps.   27.5cm.

6841   Denmark.   Geodaetisk Institut.
       Geodaetisk Instituts Kort, Denmark.   København, 1969.
       32p.   col.   maps.   27.5cm.

6842   Det Beste A. S.
       Det Bestes bilbok.   Oslo, 1969.
       392p.   col.   maps.   29cm.

6843   Gjellerups Forlag.
       Mit første atlas.   By Jørgen Clevin and Henry Holm.
       København, 1968.
       25p.   col.   maps.   25.5cm.

6844   Gyldendal.
       Atlas 1 for folkeskolen.   By W. F. Recato.   København,
       1968.
       67p.   col.   maps.   27.5cm.

6845   Reader's Digest A. B.
       Det Bästas bilbok.   Stockholm, [1969].
       392p.   col.   maps.   29cm.

Finland

6846   Generalstabens litografiska anstalt.
       Oppikoulon Kartasto.   Stockholm, 1972.
       63p.   col.   maps.   29cm.

6847   Maanmittaushallitus.
       Suomi.   Finland.   Yleiskartta 1:400,000.   Helsinki, 1966-
       72.
       31p.   col.   maps.   35cm.

6848   Maanmittaushallitus.
       Suomi.   Finland.   Yleiskartta 1:400,000 general karta.
       6ed.   Helsinki, 1968.
       121p.   col.   maps.   25cm.

6849   Maanmittaushallitus.
       Suomi.   Finland.   Yleiskarttalehtio 1:400,000 general-
       kartblocket.   Helsinki, [1968-72].
       31p.   col.   maps.   35cm.

6850 Maanmittaushallitus.
      Suomi. Finland. Yleiskarttalehtiö 1:400,000. Finland;
      generalkartblocket. Helsinki, [1969].
      34p. col. maps. 35cm.

6851 Maanmittaushallitus.
      Yleiskarttalehtiö-Generalkartblocket. Helsinki, 1968.
      31p. col. maps. 35cm.

6852 Otava.
      Kansakoulun Kartasto. Helsinki, 1971.
      18p. col. maps. 27cm.

6853 Otava.
      Otavan maailmankartasto. 5ed. Helsinki, 1969.
      172p. col. maps. 29cm.

6854 Otava.
      Otavan peruskoulu-kartasto. Helsinki, 1972.
      113p. col. maps. 27cm.

6855 Otava.
      Taskuatlas. Maailmankartasto ja tietohakemisto. Helsinki,
      [1969].
      234p. col. maps. 18cm.

6856 Otava.
      Taskuatlas. Maailmankartasto ja tietohakemisto. With
      Kartograficke nakladatelství. Helsinki, 1970.
      234p. col. maps. 17cm.

6857 Söderström, Werner.
      Kansakoulun Kartasto. Helsinki, 1969.
      40p. col. maps. 27cm.

6858 Valistus.
      Valistuksen Koulukartasto. Helsinki, 1966.
      36p. col. maps. 26cm.

6859 W. S. O. Y.
      Joka kodin maailmankartasto. Helsinki, [1970].
      180p. col. maps. 28cm.

6860 W. S. O. Y.
      Historisk atlas. By Jarl Gustafson. Porvoo, Helsinki,
      1971.
      38p. col. maps. 26cm.

6861 W. S. O. Y.
      Kansakoulon Kartasto. Porvoo, Helsinki, 1969.
      38p. col. maps. 26cm.

6862 W. S. O. Y.

Kansakoulun Kartasto.   Porvoo, Helsinki, 1971.
38p. col. maps. 26cm.

6863   W. S. O. Y.
Koulon omatoimikartat 1 & 2.   Helsinki, 1970.
2 vol. col. maps. 26cm.

France

6864   Automobile Association.
Road book of France.   1ed.   London, 1969.
535p. col. maps. 25cm.

6865   Automobile Association.
Road book of France.   2ed.   London, 1970.
535p. col. maps. 25cm.

6866   Blondel La Rougery.
Atlas des routes de France.   Paris, 1968.
32p. col. maps. 24cm.

6867   Blondel La Rougery.
Atlas des routes de France.   Paris, 1969.
32p. col. maps. 24cm.

6868   Colin.
Atlas des circonscriptions électorales en France depuis
1875.   By Marie-Thérèse Lancelot and Alain Lancelot.
Paris, 1970.
95p. 35cm.

6869   Editions André Lesot.
Atlas départemental de la France à lusage des statisticiens;
commerçants, industriels, agents de publicité, administra-
tions publiques ou privées, etc.   Paris, [1970].
1 vol. 23cm.

6870   Editions Bordas.
Petit atlas Bordas.   La France, le monde.   By René
Cauët, Pierre Serryn and Marc Vincent.   Paris, 1970.
80p. col. maps. 32cm.

6871   France.   Centre national de la recherche scientifique.
Atlas de la population rurale.   France.   Paris, 1968.
176p. col. maps. 34cm.

6872   France.   Centre national de la recherche scientifique.
Atlas linguistique de la France par régions.   Vol. 1:
de l'ouest.   Paris, 1971-
in parts. col. maps. 45.5cm.

6873   France.   Centre national de la recherche scientifique.
Atlas linguistique et ethnographique.   Paris, 1972-

in parts.   col. maps.   50cm.

6874   France.   Direction de la météorologie nationale.
       Atlas climatique de la France.   By Jean Bessemoulin.
       Paris, 1969.
       45p.   col. maps.   53cm.

6875   France.   Direction de la météorologie nationale.
       Atlas climatique de la France.   By Jean Bessemoulin.
       Paris, 1974.
       29p.   col. maps.   30cm.

6876   France.   Electricité de France.
       Atlas: réseau général d'énergie électrique de France.
       Paris, 1969.
       1 vol.   col. maps.   34cm.

6877   France.   Electricité de France.
       Atlas, réseau géneral d'énergie électrique de France.
       Paris, 1971.
       116p.   col. maps.   34cm.

6878   France.   La Documentation Française.
       Atlas de la formation professionelle.   France.   Paris,
       [1969].
       2 vol.   col. maps.   65cm.

6879   France.   La Documentation Française.
       Atlas économique et social pour l'aménagement du terri-
       toire.   By T. Hautreux.   Paris, 1966-69.
       3 vol.   col. maps.   56cm.

6880   France.   Ministère de l'Éducation nationale.
       Atlas de l'Éducation nationale.   La Celle-Saint Cloud,
       1970.
       3 vol.   col. maps.   72cm.

6881   France.   Ministère des postes et télécommunications.
       Mémento de nomenclature géographique.   Paris, 1967.
       87p.   31cm.

6882   France.   Service de l'économie forestière.
       Atlas forestier.   Paris, 1968.
       79p.   col. maps.   32cm.

6883   Hachette.
       Atlas routier et touristique: France, Belgique, Luxem-
       bourg, Suisse.   With Bordas.   Paris, [1970].
       76p.   col. maps.   30cm.

6884   Imprimeries Oberthur.
       Atlas des départements français.   Rennes, 1969.
       138p.   col. maps.   27cm.

6885 Imprimeries Oberthur.
      Atlas des départements français.   Rennes, 1971.
      396p. col. maps. 27cm.

6886 Imprimeries Oberthur.
      Index-atlas des départments français.   Rennes, 1969.
      227p. col. maps. 26cm.

6887 Imprimeries Oberthur.
      Index atlas des départments français.   Rennes, 1971.
      227p. col. maps. 26cm.

6888 Map Productions, Ltd.
      Pocket Atlas. Vols 1: France, 2: Germany, 3: Spain,
      4: Italy. London, [1970].
      4 vol. col. maps. 19cm.

6889 Michelin et Cie.
      Atlas des routes de France.   Paris, [1971].
      1 vol. col. maps. 26cm.

6890 Michelin et Cie.
      Michelin atlas des autoroutes de France.   Paris, 1970.
      46p. col. maps. 26cm.

6891 Michelin et Cie.
      Michelin atlas des autoroutes de France.   Paris, [1971].
      54p. col. maps. 26cm.

6892 Michelin et Cie.
      Michelin atlas des autoroutes de France.   Paris, [1973].
      66p. col. maps. 26cm.

6893 Oxford Polytechnic.
      France. A socio-economic atlas.   Oxford, 1972.
      48p. col. maps. 28cm.

6894 Sélection du Reader's Digest, S. A. R. L.
      Grand atlas de la France. 2ed. Paris, 1970.
      244p. col. maps. 41cm.

6895 Sélection du Reader's Digest, S. A. R. L.
      Guide de la route: France, Belgique, Suisse. Paris,
      [1969].
      455p. col. maps. 29cm.

Germany

6896 Bertelsmann, C.
      Autoatlas Bertelsmann. Deutschland-Europa. Gütersloh,
      1970.
      386p. col. maps. 27cm.

6897 Bertelsmann, C.
      Autoatlas Bertelsmann: Deutschland-Europa. Gütersloh,
      1971.
      386p. col. maps. 27cm.

6898 Bertelsmann, C.
      Autoatlas Bertelsmann: Deutschland-Europa. Gütersloh,
      [1973].
      380p. col. maps. 27cm.

6899 Continental Gummiwerke Kartographischer Verlag.
      Continental Atlas. Deutschland, Europa. 36ed. Han-
      nover, 1969.
      555p. col. maps. 26cm.

6900 Continental Gummiwerke Kartographischer Verlag.
      Continental Atlas. Deutschland, Europa. 37ed. Han-
      nover, 1970.
      611p. col. maps. 26cm.

6901 Continental Gummiwerke Kartographischer Verlag.
      Conti-Strassenatlas Deutschland. Hannover, 1973.
      239p. col. maps. 26cm.

6902 Continental Gummiwerke Kartographischer Verlag.
      Der grosse Continental-Atlas. Hannover, Stuttgart, 1971.
      639p. col. maps. 26cm.

6903 Continental Gummiwerke Kartographischer Verlag.
      Der grosse Continental-Atlas. 39ed. Hannover, Stutt-
      gart, 1972.
      601p. col. maps. 26cm.

6904 Esso, A. G.
      Taschen-Atlas Deutschland. Hamburg, [1972].
      64p. col. maps. 25cm.

6905 Falk Verlag.
      Autostrassen Atlas der Bundesrepublik Deutschland. Ham-
      burg, [1968].
      68p. col. maps. 25cm.

6906 Falk Verlag.
      Autostrassen Atlas der Bundesrepublik Deutschland. Ham-
      burg, 1969.
      68p. col. maps. 25cm.

6907 Falk Verlag.
      Autostrassen Atlas der Bundesrepublik Deutschland.
      72p. col. maps. 25cm.

6908 Falk Verlag.
      Phoenix Autoatlas Bundesrepublik Deutschland. Hamburg,

        1973.
        72p. col. maps. 25cm.

6909 Falk Verlag.
        Phoenix Autoatlas Bundesrepublik Deutschland.   Hamburg,
        1974.
        72p. col. maps. 25cm.

6910 Falk Verlag.
        Phoenix Autoatlas Bundesrepublik Deutschland.   Hamburg,
        1975.
        72p. col. maps. 25cm.

6911 Fietz, W. G.
        Strassenatlas 1972: Deutschland und Europa.   Frankfurt,
        [1972].
        71p. col. maps. 27cm.

6912 Germany. Deutsche Reichsbahn.
        Deutsche Reichsbahn. Wegkarten.   Berlin, [1968].
        42p. col. maps. 32cm.

6913 Germany. Militärgeographisches Amt.
        BW-Kraftfahrer Atlas. Bonn, 1969.
        2 vol. col. maps. 30cm.

6914 Germany: Statistisches Bundesamt.
        Die Bundesrepublik Deutschland in Karten.   Mainz, 1965-
        69.
        102p. col. maps. 63cm.

6915 Haack, Hermann.
        Deutsche Demokratische Republik: Kartenband.   By Hel-
        mut Busch. Gotha, Leipzig, [1967].
        57p. col. maps. 23cm.

6916 Haack, Hermann.
        Haack Kleiner Atlas; Deutsche Demokratische Republik.
        1ed. Gotha, Leipzig, 1971.
        230p. col. maps. 18cm.

6917 Haack, Hermann.
        Verkehrsatlas. Deutsche Demokratische Republik.   1ed.
        By H. Langer. Gotha, 1971.
        216p. col. maps. 18cm.

6918 Haack, Hermann.
        Verkehrsatlas. Deutsche Demokratische Republik.   By
        H. Langer. Gotha, 1972.
        220p. col. maps. 18cm.

6919 Institut für Thematische Kartographie der Deutschen Kreis-
        kartenverlagsanstalt.

Atlas zur Kleinen Deutschlandkunde.   By Rudolf Ernst.
München, 1968.
144p. col. maps. 21cm.

6920 JRO Verlag.
      Der Grosse JRO Auto Atlas.   JRO Autofuhrer der
      Bundesrepublik Deutschland.   24ed. München, 1964.
      658p. col. maps. 24. 5cm.

6921 JRO Verlag.
      Grosser JRO Strassenatlas.   Deutschland, Alpenländer,
      Europa. München, 1973.
      120p. col. maps. 30cm.

6922 JRO Verlag.
      JRO Autoatlas.   Deutschland, Europäische Reiseländer.
      München, [1971].
      1 vol. col. maps. 25cm.

6923 König, Hans, Verlag.
      Deutscher Ferien Atlas.   Frankfurt am Main, 1969.
      105p. col. maps. 24cm.

6924 König, Hans, Verlag.
      Strassenatlas Deutschland-Europa.   Frankfurt am Main,
      1971.
      1 vol. col. maps. 29cm.

6925 Landkartenverlag, VEB.
      Atlas für Motortouristik der Deutschen Demokratischen
      Republik. Berlin, [1973].
      224p. col. maps. 26cm.

6926 Landkartenverlag, VEB.
      Reiseatlas der Deutschen Demokratischen Republik.   4ed.
      Berlin, 1970.
      176p. col. maps. 26cm.

6927 Landkartenverlag, VEB.
      Reiseatlas der Deutschen Demokratischen Republik.   4ed.
      Berlin, [1971].
      176p. col. maps. 26cm.

6928 Landkartenverlag, VEB.
      Reiseatlas der Deutschen Demokratischen Republik.   4ed.
      Berlin, 1972.
      176p. col. maps. 26cm.

6929 Landkartenverlag, VEB.
      Reiseatlas der Deutschen Demokratischen Republik.   5ed.
      Berlin, 1973.
      176p. col. maps. 26cm.

6930   Landkartenverlag, VEB.
       Reiseatlas der Deutschen Demokratischen Republik.   6ed.
       Berlin, 1973.
       176p. col. maps. 26cm.

6931   List, P.
       Harms atlas Deutschland und die Welt.   München, 1969.
       125p. col. maps. 32cm.

6932   Mairs Geographischer Verlag.
       Der grosse Continental-Atlas.   Deutschland, Europa.
       Stuttgart, 1971.
       576p. col. maps. 26cm.

6933   Mairs Geographischer Verlag.
       Der grosse Continental-Atlas.   Deutschland, Europa.
       Stuttgart, 1972.
       576p. col. maps. 26cm.

6934   Mairs Geographischer Verlag.
       Der grosse Continental-Atlas.   Deutschland, Europa.
       Stuttgart, 1973.
       576p. col. maps. 26cm.

6935   Mairs Geographischer Verlag.
       Der grosse Continental-Atlas.   Deutschland, Europa.
       Stuttgart, 1974.
       576p. col. maps. 26cm.

6936   Mairs Geographischer Verlag.
       Der grosse Continental-Atlas.   Deutschland, Europa.
       Stuttgart, 1975.
       576p. col. maps. 26cm.

6937   Mairs Geographischer Verlag.
       Der Grosse Shell Atlas.   Deutschland, Europa.   1970/71.
       Stuttgart, 1970.
       317p. col. maps. 27cm.

6938   Mairs Geographischer Verlag.
       Der Grosse Shell-Atlas.   Deutschland, Europa.   1971/72.
       Stuttgart, 1971.
       317p. col. maps. 27cm.

6939   Mairs Geographischer Verlag.
       Der Grosse Shell Atlas.   Deutschland und Europa.   Stutt-
       gart, 1972.
       526p. col. maps. 27cm.

6940   Mairs Geographischer Verlag.
       Der Grosse Shell Atlas.   Deutschland und Europa.   Stutt-
       gart, 1973.
       513p. col. maps. 27cm.

6941   Mairs Geographischer Verlag.
       Der Grosse Shell Atlas. Deutschland und Europa.   Stutt-
       gart, 1974.
       513p. col. maps. 27cm.

6942   Mairs Geographischer Verlag.
       Der Grosse Shell Atlas. Deutschland und Europa.   Stutt-
       gart, 1975.
       513p. col. maps. 27cm.

6943   Mairs Geographischer Verlag.
       Deutscher Generalatlas. Stuttgart, [1974].
       302p. col. maps. 27cm.

6944   Mairs Geographischer Verlag.
       Shell Reiseatlas Deutschland.   Stuttgart, 1975.
       206p. col. maps. 30cm.

6945   Mairs Geographischer Verlag.
       VARTA Atlas Deutschland/Europa.   Stuttgart, [1974].
       1 vol. col. maps. 30cm.

6946   Map Productions, Ltd.
       Pocket Atlas.   Vols 1: France, 2: Germany, 3: Spain,
       4: Italy.   London, [1970].
       4 vol. col. maps. 19cm.

6947   Ravenstein Geographische Verlagsanstalt.
       Reiseatlas Deutschland und Europa.   Frankfurt, 1971.
       67p. col. maps. 29cm.

6948   Ravenstein Geographische Verlagsanstalt.
       Reiseatlas Deutschland und Europa.   Frankfurt, 1975.
       66p. col. maps. 29cm.

6949   Ravenstein Geographische Verlagsanstalt.
       Strassen; der aktuelle Auto-Atlas Deutschland und Europa.
       Frankfurt am Main, [1968].
       66p. col. maps. 29cm.

6950   Ravenstein Geographische Verlagsanstalt.
       Strassen; der aktuelle Auto-Atlas Deutschland und Europa.
       Frankfurt am Main, 1969.
       66p. col. maps. 29cm.

6951   Ravenstein Geographische Verlagsanstalt.
       Strassen; der aktuelle Auto-Atlas.   Deutschland und
       Europa.   Frankfurt, 1970.
       66p. col. maps. 29cm.

6952   Ravenstein Geographische Verlagsanstalt.
       Strassen; der aktuelle Auto-Atlas Deutschland und Europa.
       Frankfurt, 1971.
       66p. col. maps. 29cm.

6953 Ravenstein Geographische Verlagsanstalt.
      Strassen; der aktuelle Auto-Atlas Deutschland und Europa.
      Frankfurt, 1972.
      66p. col. maps. 29cm.

6954 Ravenstein Geographische Verlagsanstalt.
      Strassen; der aktuelle Auto-Atlas Deutschland und Europa.
      Frankfurt, 1973.
      68p. col. maps. 29cm.

6955 Ravenstein Geographische Verlagsanstalt.
      Strassen; der aktuelle Auto-Atlas Deutschland und Europa.
      Frankfurt, 1974.
      66p. col. maps. 29cm.

6956 Ravenstein Geographische Verlagsanstalt.
      Strassen; der aktuelle Auto-Atlas Deutschland und Europa.
      Frankfurt, 1975.
      66p. col. maps. 29cm.

6957 Reise und Verkehrsverlag.
      Strassenatlas: Deutschland, Europa. Berlin, [1973].
      169p. col. maps. 26cm.

6958 Reise und Verkehrsverlag.
      Strassenatlas: Deutschland, Europa. Berlin, 1974.
      208p. col. maps. 26cm.

6959 Verlag Zeit im Bild.
      Deutsche Demokratische Republik: Kartenband. By Hel-
      mut Busch. With Haack. Dresden, [1967].
      57p. col. maps. 23cm.

Greece

6960 Al-Ma-Prisma, Ltd.
      Mobil road maps of Greece: Hellas. Athens, [1971].
      16p. col. maps. 24cm.

6961 Mobil Oil Hellas.
      Mobil road maps of Greece. Athens, 1971.
      20p. col. maps. 24cm.

Great Britain

6962 Allan.
      British rail atlas. London, 1965.
      83p. col. maps. 24cm.

6963 Allan.
      British railways pre-grouping atlas and gazetteer.
      Shepperton, 1972.
      84p. col. maps. 24cm.

6964   Allan.
       British railways pre-grouping atlas and gazetteer.   5ed.
       London, [1973].
       84p.   col.   maps.   24cm.

6965   Bartholomew, John & Son, Ltd.
       Bartholomew road atlas Britain.   Edinburgh, 1971-72.
       112p.   col.   maps.   30cm.

6966   Bartholomew, John & Son, Ltd.
       Bartholomew road atlas Britain.   Edinburgh, 1973.
       112p.   col.   maps.   30cm.

6967   Bartholomew, John & Son, Ltd.
       Companion road atlas of British Isles.   Edinburgh, [1971].
       112p.   col.   maps.   30cm.

6968   Bartholomew, John & Son, Ltd.
       Motorway atlas of Great Britain.   Edinburgh, 1972.
       48p.   col.   maps.   31cm.

6969   Bartholomew, John & Son, Ltd.
       Motorways atlas of Great Britain.   Edinburgh, 1973.
       48p.   col.   maps.   31cm.

6970   Bartholomew, John & Son, Ltd.
       Road atlas Britain.   Edinburgh, [1971].
       112p.   col.   maps.   28cm.

6971   Bartholomew, John & Son, Ltd.
       Road atlas Britain.   Edinburgh, 1974.
       112p.   col.   maps.   28cm.

6972   Bartholomew, John & Son, Ltd.
       Road atlas Britain.   Edinburgh, 1975.
       112p.   col.   maps.   28cm.

6973   Bartholomew, John & Son, Ltd.
       Road atlas of Great Britain.   Edinburgh, 1969.
       112p.   col.   maps.   25cm.

6974   Bartholomew, John & Son, Ltd.
       Roadmaster travel maps of Britain.   Edinburgh, 1970.
       1 vol.   col.   maps.   25cm.

6975   Bee Research Organisation.
       Preliminary bumble bee atlas.   London, 1973.
       31p.   20.5cm.

6976   British Bureau of Television Advertising, Ltd.
       The BBTA Marketing Manual of the United Kingdom 1970.
       1ed.   London, 1970.
       1 vol.   col.   maps.   49cm.

6977   British Bureau of Television Advertising, Ltd.
       The BBTA Marketing Manual of the United Kingdom.   2ed.
       London, 1971.
       1 vol. col. maps. 49cm.

6978   British Bureau of Television Advertising, Ltd.
       The BBTA Marketing Manual of the United Kingdom.   3ed.
       London, [1973].
       1 vol. col. maps. 49cm.

6979   Collins, William, Sons & Co., Ltd.
       Collins road atlas, Britain & Ireland.   Glasgow, 1974.
       97p. col. maps. 28cm.

6980   Collins, William, Sons & Co., Ltd.
       Collins road atlas, Britain & Ireland.   Glasgow, 1975.
       97p. col. maps. 28cm.

6981   Cranfield & Bonfiel Books.
       Waterways atlas of the British Isles.   2ed.   London, 1968.
       53p. col. maps. 24cm.

6982   David & Charles.
       A literary atlas and gazetteer of the British Isles.   By
       Michael Hardwick.   Newton Abbot, 1973.
       216p. col. maps. 24cm.

6983   Esso Petroleum Co., Ltd.
       Esso road atlas of Great Britain and Ireland.   1972/73 ed.
       With Edward Stanford, Ltd.   London, 1971.
       254p. col. maps. 28cm.

6984   Faber & Faber.
       An agricultural atlas of England and Wales.   2ed.   By
       J. T. Coppock.   London, 1974.
       255p. 25cm.

6985   Gale Research Co.
       A literary atlas and gazetteer of the British Isles.   By
       Michael Hardwick and Alan G. Hodgkiss.   Detroit, [1973].
       215p. col. maps. 25cm.

6986   Geographia, Ltd.
       AA Great Britain road atlas.   London, [1973].
       247p. col. maps. 30cm.

6987   Geographia, Ltd.
       Geographia commercial gazetteer and atlas of Great
       Britain.   London, 1970.
       2 vol. col. maps. 25cm.

6988   Geographia, Ltd.
       Geographia commercial gazetteer and atlas of Great

Britain.   London, [1972].
2 vol.   col. maps.   25cm.

6989 Geographia, Ltd.
      Geographia road atlas of Great Britain.   Commercial
      atlas of Great Britain.   London, [1969].
      94p.   col. maps.   28cm.

6990 Geographia, Ltd.
      Geographia road atlas of Great Britain.   GB motoring
      atlas.   London, [1969].
      94p.   col. maps.   28cm.

6991 Geographia, Ltd.
      Geographia road atlas of Great Britain.   London, [1972].
      94p.   col. maps.   28cm.

6992 Geographia, Ltd.
      Great Britain touring atlas and guide.   8ed.   London,
      [1972].
      68p.   col. maps.   28cm.

6993 Gt. Britain.   Ministry of Housing and Local Government.
      Atlas of planning maps of England and Wales.   London,
      1965-70.
      in parts.   col. maps.   44cm.

6994 Gower Economic Publications.
      Business atlas of Great Britain.   Epping, Essex, [1974].
      186p.   28cm.

6995 Hamlyn.
      The motorists touring maps and gazetteer.   London, 1972.
      163p.   col. maps.   28cm.

6996 Heinemann.
      A map history of the British people, 1700 to 1970.   By
      Brian Catchpole.   London, 1971.
      170p.   26cm.

6997 Johnston, W. & A. K. & G. W. Bacon, Ltd.
      Autoway atlas.   Great Britain and Ireland.   London, 1969.
      1 vol.   col. maps.   26cm.

6998 Johnston & Bacon.
      A & B roads and motorways atlas of Great Britain.
      4ed.   Edinburgh, 1973.
      48p.   col. maps.   33cm.

6999 Johnston & Bacon.
      3 miles to 1 inch road atlas of Great Britain.   Edinburgh,
      London, [1971].
      112p.   col. maps.   30cm.

7000   Johnston & Bacon.
        3 miles to 1 inch road atlas of Great Britain.   7ed.
        Edinburgh, London, 1973.
        373p.   col.   maps.   30cm.

7001   Macdonald Education.
        British Isles [atlas].   London, 1971.
        44p.   col.   maps.   27cm.

7002   Macmillan & Co., Ltd.
        A map book of the British Isles.   2ed.   By A. Ferriday.
        London, 1952.
        69p.   25cm.

7003   Macmillan & Co., Ltd.
        A map book of the British Isles.   3ed.   By A. Ferriday.
        London, 1955.
        69p.   25cm.

7004   Macmillan & Co., Ltd.
        A map book of the British Isles.   4ed.   By A. Ferriday.
        London, 1957.
        69p.   25cm.

7005   Macmillan & Co., Ltd.
        A map book of the British Isles.   4ed.   By A. Ferriday.
        London, 1959.
        69p.   25cm.

7006   Macmillan & Co., Ltd.
        A map book of the British Isles.   5ed.   By A. Ferriday.
        London, 1962.
        69p.   25cm.

7007   Macmillan.
        A map book of the British Isles.   6ed.   By A. Ferriday.
        London, 1971.
        69p.   25cm.

7008   Macmillan.
        A picture map book of the British Isles.   By Alan Fer-
        riday.   London, 1971.
        48p.   col.   maps.   25cm.

7009   Macmillan.
        British history atlas.   By Martin Gilbert.   New York,
        1968.
        118p.   24cm.

7010   Macmillan.
        British history atlas.   By Martin Gilbert.   New York,
        [1971].
        118p.   24cm.

7011   Macmillan.
       British weather in maps.   2ed.   By James A. Taylor and
       R. A. Yates.   London, 1967.
       304p.   col. maps.   23cm.

7012   Map Productions, Ltd.
       BMC Route Planner.   London, [1970].
       64p.   col. maps.   28cm.

7013   Map Productions, Ltd.
       Fina route planning atlas.   Great Britain.   London, 1969.
       64p.   col. maps.   28cm.

7014   Map Productions, Ltd.
       Fina route planning atlas.   Great Britain, London, [1970].
       64p.   col. maps.   28cm.

7015   Map Productions, Ltd.
       Great Britain.   Motorways.   London, [1972].
       1 vol.   col. maps.   27cm.

7016   Map Productions, Ltd.
       Great Britain.   Route Planning [atlas].   London, [1971].
       64p.   col. maps.   28cm.

7017   Map Productions, Ltd.
       Great Britain.   Route planning maps.   London, [1972].
       139p.   col. maps.   28cm.

7018   Map Productions, Ltd.
       Motorways: A new atlas to illustrate the motorway system
       of Great Britain.   London, [1970].
       1 vol.   col. maps.   27cm.

7019   National Trust.
       The what to see atlas, showing places of historic, archi-
       tectural & scenic interest in England, Wales, and Northern
       Ireland.   5ed.   With Bartholomew.   London, [1970].
       60p.   col. maps.   25cm.

7020   National Trust.
       The what to see atlas, showing places of historic, archi-
       tectural and scenic interest in England, Wales and Northern
       Ireland.   With Bartholomew.   London, 1971.
       60p.   col. maps.   25cm.

7021   National Trust.
       The what to see atlas, showing places of historic, archi-
       tectural and scenic interest in England, Wales and Northern
       Ireland.   5ed.   With Bartholomew.   London, [1974].
       60p.   col. maps.   25cm.

7022   Nelson, Thomas & Sons, Ltd.

Critical supplement to the Atlas of British flora.   By
F. H. Perring and P. D. Sell.   London, [1970].
168p.   38cm.

7023   Philip, George & Son, Ltd.
       BP road atlas of Great Britain.   London, 1971.
       160p.   col. maps.   28cm.

7024   Philip, George & Son, Ltd.
       BP road atlas of Great Britain.   London, 1972.
       160p.   col. maps.   28cm.

7025   Philip, George & Son, Ltd.
       Esso road atlas of Great Britain and Ireland.   London,
       1972.
       253p.   col. maps.   29cm.

7026   Philip, George & Son, Ltd.
       Esso road atlas of Great Britain and Ireland.   London,
       1974.
       260p.   col. maps.   29cm.

7027   Philip, George & Son, Ltd.
       Motorist's touring maps and gazetteer.   London, [1971].
       146p.   col. maps.   29cm.

7028   Philip, George & Son, Ltd.
       National atlas.   Road maps and town plans--Great Britain.
       London, 1971.
       192p.   col. maps.   29cm.

7029   Philip, George & Son, Ltd.
       National road atlas of Great Britain.   London, [1971].
       103p.   col. maps.   28cm.

7030   Philip, George & Son, Ltd.
       Philip's first venture atlas.   British Isles edition.   By
       Harold Fullard.   London, [1964].
       30p.   col. maps.   23cm.

7031   Philip, George & Son, Ltd.
       Shell road atlas, Great Britain: with special London sec-
       tion.   London, 1971.
       160p.   col. maps.   29cm.

7032   Philip, George & Son, Ltd.
       Shell road atlas, Great-Britain: with special London sec-
       tion.   London, 1972.
       160p.   col. maps.   29cm.

7033   Philip, George & Son, Ltd.
       Shell road atlas of Great Britain.   London, [1971].
       144p.   col. maps.   28cm.

7034   Reader's Digest Association, Ltd.
        The Reader's Digest A. A. book of the road.   3ed.   Lon-
        don, [1972].
        412p.   col.   maps.   28cm.

7035   Shell-Mex & BP Ltd.
        Shell golfer's atlas of England, Scotland and Wales.   Lon-
        don, 1968.
        1 vol.   col.   maps.   28cm.

7036   Stanford, Edward.
        Esso road atlas of Great Britain and Ireland.   1970-71 ed.
        London, 1970.
        253p.   col.   maps.   28cm.

7037   Stanford, Edward.
        Esso road atlas of Great Britain and Ireland.   1972-73 ed.
        London, 1971.
        254p.   col.   maps.   28cm.

7038   Stanford, Edward.
        Esso road atlas of Great Britain and Ireland.   London,
        1973.
        254p.   col.   maps.   28cm.

7039   Stanford, Edward.
        Stanford's geological atlas of Great Britain.   By T.
        Eastwood.   London, 1966.
        296p.   25cm.

7040   Stanford, Edward.
        The 'What to See' Atlas.   London, [1972].
        79p.   col.   maps.   25cm.

7041   Warne, F.
        Warne's natural history atlas of Great Britain.   By
        Charles King.   London, 1970.
        50p.   col.   maps.   25cm.

7042   Wheaton & Co., Ltd.
        Wheaton's atlas of British and world history.   2ed.
        Exeter, 1972.
        52p.   col.   maps.   25cm.

Hungary

7043   Cartographia.
        Autoatlas von Ungarn.   Road atlas of Hungary.   Budapest,
        1973.
        118p.   col.   maps.   26cm.

7044   Cartographia.
        Road atlas of Hungary.   Budapest, 1972.

118p.   col.   maps.   26.5cm.

7045   Cartographia.
       Road atlas of Hungary.   By Hegyi Gyula.   Budapest,
       1973.
       118p.   col.   maps.   26.5cm.

7046   Kartográfiai Vállalat.
       Földrajzi atlasz a középiskolák Számára.   Budapest, 1970.
       60p.   col.   maps.   29cm.

7047   Kartográfiai Vállalat.
       Földrajzi atlasz a középiskolák Számára.   Budapest, 1971.
       60p.   col.   maps.   29cm.

7048   Kartográfiai Vállalat.
       Földrajzi atlasz a középiskolák Számára.   By Sándor Radó.
       Budapest, 1972.
       60p.   col.   maps.   29cm.

7049   Kartográfiai Vállalat.
       Földrajzi atlasz a középiskolák Számára.   12ed.   Buda-
       pest, 1973.
       60p.   col.   maps.   29cm.

7050   Kartográfiai Vállalat.
       Hungary.   [Pocket Atlas].   (in English).   Budapest, [1970].
       17p.   col.   maps.   20cm.

7051   Kartográfiai Vállalat.
       Magyarország autóatlasza.   1ed.   Budapest, 1972.
       220p.   col.   maps.   21cm.

7052   Kartográfiai Vállalat.
       Magyarország autóatlasza.   Budapest, 1973.
       220p.   col.   maps.   21cm.

7053   Kartográfiai Vállalat.
       Magyarország: Földrajzi atlasz az általános iskolák
       számára.   Budapest, 1972.
       32p.   col.   maps.   28cm.

7054   Kartográfiai Vállalat.
       Magyarország regionális atlaszai.   Budapest, 1968.
       1 vol.   col.   maps.   40cm.

Iceland

7055   Rikisútgáfa námsbóka.
       Landabréfabók.   By Helgi Elíasson, Einar Magnússon and
       Agúst Böovarsson.   Reykjavik, [1970].
       56p.   col.   maps.   25cm.

Ireland

7056   Collins, William, Sons & Co., Ltd.
        Collins road atlas, Britain & Ireland.   Glasgow, 1974.
        97p.   col.   maps.   28cm.

7057   Collins, William, Sons & Co., Ltd.
        Collins road atlas, Britain & Ireland.   Glasgow, 1975.
        97p.   col.   maps.   28cm.

7058   David & Charles.
        A railway atlas of Ireland.   1ed.   Newton Abbot, 1972.
        40p.   25cm.

7059   David & Charles.
        A railway atlas of Ireland.   Newton Abbot, 1974.
        40p.   25cm.

7060   Educational Company of Ireland, Ltd.
        Certificate atlas for Irish schools.   Dublin, [1970].
        110p.   col.   maps.   28cm.

7061   Educational Company of Ireland, Ltd.
        Irish primary school atlas.   Dublin, [1973].
        20p.   col.   maps.   28cm.

7062   Educational Company of Ireland, Ltd.
        Irish school and college atlas.   Dublin, [1971].
        32p.   col.   maps.   28cm.

7063   Educational Company of Ireland, Ltd.
        Irish student atlas.   By E. Butler.   Dublin, [1972].
        66p.   col.   maps.   28cm.

7064   Esso Petroleum Co., Ltd.
        Esso road atlas of Great Britain and Ireland.   1972/73 ed.
        With Stanford.   London, 1971.
        254p.   col.   maps.   28cm.

7065   Johnston, W. & A. K. & G. W. Bacon, Ltd.
        Autoway atlas.   Great Britain and Ireland.   London, 1969.
        1 vol.   col.   maps.   26cm.

7066   Johnston, W. & A. K. & G. W. Bacon, Ltd.
        Pocket road atlas of Ireland.   London, 1968.
        1 vol.   col.   maps.   18cm.

7067   Methuen.
        An atlas of Irish history.   By Ruth Dudley Edwards.
        London, 1973.
        261p.   25cm.

7068   Philip, George & Son, Ltd.
        Esso road atlas of Great Britain and Ireland.   London, 1972.

253p. col. maps. 29cm.

7069 Philip, George & Son, Ltd.
        Esso road atlas of Great Britain and Ireland. London,
        1974.
        260p. col. maps. 29cm.

7070 Royal Automobile Club.
        Road map of Ireland. With Bartholomew, London, [1969].
        16p. col. maps. 22cm.

7071 Stanford, Edward.
        Esso road atlas of Great Britain and Ireland. 1970-71 ed.
        London, 1970.
        253p. col. maps. 28cm.

7072 Stanford, Edward.
        Esso road atlas of Great Britain and Ireland. 1972-73 ed.
        London, 1971.
        254p. col. maps. 28cm.

7073 Stanford, Edward.
        Esso road atlas of Great Britain and Ireland. London,
        1973.
        254p. col. maps. 28cm.

Italy

7074 Automobile club d'Italia.
        Autostrade italiane. Roma, [1973].
        44p. col. maps. 26cm.

7075 Innocenti.
        Carta automobilistica d'Italia. With De Agostini. Milano,
        [1972].
        28p. col. maps. 22cm.

7076 Istituto Geografico De Agostini.
        Atlante stradale d'Italia. Novara, 1969.
        182p. col. maps. 27cm.

7077 Istituto Geografico De Agostini.
        Atlante stradale d'Italia. Novara, 1971.
        1 vol. col. maps. 27cm.

7078 Istituto Geografico De Agostini.
        Atlante stradale d'Italia. Novara, [1972].
        188p. col. maps. 27cm.

7079 Istituto Geografico De Agostini.
        Atlantino di rotta. Alitalia. Roma, Novara, 1968.
        16p. col. maps. 22.5cm.

7080   Istituto Geografico De Agostini.
       Atlantino di rotta. Alitalia. Roma, Novara, 1971.
       16p. col. maps. 22.5cm.

7081   Istituto Geografico De Agostini.
       Carta automobilistica d'Italia. Novara, [1971].
       20p. col. maps. 29cm.

7082   Istituto Geografico De Agostini.
       Guida del servizio Fiat Italia. Novara, [1970].
       114p. col. maps. 25cm.

7083   Istituto Geografico De Agostini.
       Guida del servizio Fiat Italia. Novara, [1971].
       86p. col. maps. 25cm.

7084   Istituto Geografica De Agostini.
       Route maps, Alitalia. Novara, [1971].
       16p. col. maps. 22cm.

7085   Istituto Geografico De Agostini.
       Route maps, Alitalia. Novara, [1973].
       16p. col. maps. 22cm.

7086   Map Productions, Ltd.
       Pocket Atlas. Vols. 1: France, 2: Germany, 3: Spain,
       4: Italy. London, [1970].
       4 vol. col. maps. 19cm.

7087   Touring Club Italiano.
       Atlante automobilistico. Milano, 1971.
       in parts. col. maps. 32cm.

7088   Touring Club Italiano.
       Atlante automobilistico. Milano, 1974.
       3 vol. col. maps. 32cm.

Luxembourg

7089   Hachette.
       Atlas routier et touristique: France, Belgique, Luxem-
       bourg, Suisse. With Bordas. Paris, [1970].
       76p. col. maps. 30cm.

7090   Luxembourg. Ministère de l'Education Nationale.
       Atlas du Luxembourg. Luxembourg, 1971-
       1 vol. col. maps. 50cm.

7091   Macmillan & Co., Ltd.
       A map book of the Benelux countries. By A. J. B.
       Tussler and A. J. L. Alden. London, 1970.
       64p. 28cm.

Netherlands

7092   Macmillan & Co., Ltd.
       A map book of the Benelux countries.   By A. J. B. Tus-
       sler and A. J. L. Alden.   London, 1970.
       64p.   28cm.

7093   Netherlands.   Meteorologisch Institut.
       Klimaatlas van Nederland.   de Bilt, 1972.
       77p.   col. maps.   40cm.

7094   Nijgh & van Ditmar.
       Atlas van de Nederlandse democratie.   By T. Faber de
       Heer.   Amsterdam, 1973.
       64p.   29cm.

7095   Omnium.
       Nederland en overzeese rijksdelen.   Waalwijk, [1973].
       29p.   col. maps.   33cm.

7096   Oxford Polytechnic.
       The Netherlands.   A reference atlas.   Oxford, 1971.
       1 vol.   col. maps.   28cm.

7097   Wyt.
       Atlas van de tramwegen in Nederland.   Rotterdam, 1973.
       32p.   28cm.

Norway

7098   Aschehoug & Co.
       Mitt første atlas.   4. skøer.   Oslo, 1968.
       8p.   col. maps.   24cm.

7099   Aschehoug & Co.
       Norge og verden.   Oslo, 1969.
       71p.   col. maps.   27cm.

7100   Cappelens, J. W., Forlag, A. S.
       Cappelens atlas for folkeskolen.   6ed.   Oslo, 1968.
       55p.   col. maps.   24cm.

7101   Cappelens, J. W., Forlag, A. S.
       Cappelens Norges atlas for skolen.   By K. B. Sollesnes.
       Oslo, 1972.
       37p.   col. maps.   30cm.

7102   Cappelens, J. W., Forlag, A. S.
       Mittatlas for 4.-6. skolear.   Oslo, 1968.
       24p.   col. maps.   24cm.

7103   Det Beste A. S.
       Det Bestes bilbok.   Oslo, 1969.

392p.   col. maps.   29cm.

7104   Dreyers forlag.
        Økonomisk atlas.   By Tor Wisting.   Oslo, [1969].
        79p.   col. maps.   29cm.

7105   Kongelik Norsk automobilklub.
        KNA Kart-og reisehändbok.   Oslo, 1971.
        327p.   col. maps.   26cm.

7106   Läromedelsförlagen.
        Nordisk skolatlas; läroverksupplagen.   12ed.   By Hans
        W:son Ahlmann.   With Generalstabens litografiska anstalt.
        Stockholm, [1970].
        85p.   col. maps.   34cm.

7107   Läromedelsförlagen.
        Nordisk stolatlas; läroverksupplagen.   By Hans W:son
        Ahlmann.   With Generalstabens litografiska anstalt.
        Stockholm, 1971.
        85p.   col. maps.   34cm.

7108   Norway.   Postdirektoratet.
        Pensumoversikt i utenriks postgeografi for kontoraspiranter;
        postassistenkursene.   Oslo, [1970].
        16p.   32cm.

7109   Norway.   Vassdrags-og Elektrisitetsvesen.
        Glacier atlas of Southern and Northern Norway.   Oslo,
        1968-73.
        2 vol.   col. maps.   42cm.

7110   Poståpnernes Landsforbund.
        Post-, rej-og fylkeskarte.   Oslo, [1960].
        44p.   col. maps.   23cm.

7111   Reader's Digest AB.
        Det Bästas bilbok.   Stockholm, [1969].
        392p.   col. maps.   29cm.

Poland

7112   Poland.   Akademia nauk.
        Atlas historyczny Polski.   1ed.   Warszawa, [1961].
        2 vol.   col. maps.   31cm.

7113   Poland.   Akademia nauk.
        Polski atlas etnograficzny.   Zeszyt próbny.   Wroclaw,
        1958.
        in parts.   col. maps.   49cm.

7114   Poland.   Glowny urząd statystyczny.
        Atlas statystyczny.   1ed.   By Janusz Stepiński.   War-

szawa, 1970.
197p. col. maps. 28cm.

7115 Poland. Instytut geologiczny.
Atlas mineralogiczny Polski. Warszawa, 1971.
1 portf. col. maps. 30cm.

7116 Poland. Państwowe przedsiębiorstwo wydawnictw kartograficznych.
Atlas do historii Polski. Warszawa, 1966-
in parts. col. maps. 30cm.

7117 Poland. Państwowe przedsiębiorstwo wydawnictw kartograficznych.
Atlas geograficzny. By Henryk Górski. Warszawa, 1972.
37p. col. maps. 32cm.

7118 Poland. Państwowe przedsiębiorstwo wydawnictw kartograficznych.
Atlas historyczny Polski. 2ed. By Wladyslaw Czaplinski
and Tadeusz Ladogroski. Warszawa, [1970].
54p. col. maps. 32cm.

7119 Poland. Państwowe przedsiębiorstwo wydawnictw kartograficznych.
Atlas historyczny Polski. 3ed. Warszawa, 1973.
55p. col. maps. 32cm.

7120 Poland. Państwowe przedsiębiorstwo wydawnictw kartograficznych.
Atlas klimatyczny Polski. Warszawa, 1973.
141p. col. maps. 47cm.

7121 Poland. Państwowe przedsiębiorstwo wydawnictw kartograficznych.
Atlas samochodowy Polski. 2ed. Warszawa, 1959.
155p. col. maps. 23cm.

7122 Poland. Państwowe przedsiębiorstwo wydawnictw kartograficznych.
Atlas samochodowy Polski. Warszawa, 1970.
156p. col. maps. 23cm.

7123 Poland. Państwowe przedsiębiorstwo wydawnictw kartograficznych.
Atlas samochodowny Polski. Warszawa, 1971.
156p. col. maps. 23cm.

7124 Poland. Pánstwowe przedsiębiorstwo wydawnictw kartograficznych.
Atlas samochodowny Polski. Warszawa, 1972.
201p. col. maps. 23cm.

7125 Poland. Państwowe przedsiębiorstwo wydawnictw kartograficznych.
      Geograficzny atlas Polski, Warszawa, 1960.
      28p. col. maps. 34cm.

7126 Poland. Państwowe przedsiębiorstwo wydawnictw kartograficznych.
      Geograficzny atlas Polski. Warszawa, 1962.
      28p. col. maps. 34cm.

7127 Poland. Państwowe przedsiębiorstwo wydawnictw kartograficznych.
      Geograficzny atlas Polski. Warszawa, 1965.
      28p. col. maps. 34cm.

7128 Poland. Państwowe przedsiębiorstwo wydawnictw kartograficznych.
      Geograficzny atlas Polski. Warszawa, 1974.
      37p. col. maps. 34cm.

7129 Poland. Państwowe przedsiębiorstwo wydawnictw kartograficznych.
      Narodowy atlas Polski. Warszawa, 1973-75.
      in parts. col. maps. 40cm.

7130 Poland. Państwowe zakłady wydawnicta szkolnych.
      Polska XXV; ludność, przemyśl, rolnictwo, transport,
      kultura, oświata, zdrowie, na mapach. 1ed. By J.
      Ostrowski. Warszawa, [1969].
      16p. col. maps. 29cm.

7131 Poland. Wydawn. Geologiczne.
      Atlas litologiczno-paleogeograficzny obszarów platformowych
      Polski. Warszawa, 1974-
      in parts. 31cm.

7132 Poland. Wydawn. Geologiczne.
      Atlas litologiczno-surowcowy Polski. Warszawa, 1973-
      in parts. 31cm.

7133 Poland. Wydawn. Geologiczne.
      Atlas map górniczych. Katowice, 1971.
      17p. col. maps. 31cm.

7134 Poland. Wydawn. Geologiczne.
      Atlas mineralogeniczny Polski. By Roman Osika.
      Warszawa, 1970.
      16p. col. maps. 30cm.

7135 Poland. Wydawn. Geologiczne.
      Mineralogenic atlas of Poland. By Roman Osika. Warszawa, 1970.
      20p. col. maps. 30cm.

Portugal

7136   Editorial Everest.
       Mapa Everest de carreteras España y Portugal.   Leon,
       [1971].
       86p.   col. maps.   25cm.

7137   Firestone-Hispania, S. A.
       Firestone-Hispania atlas de España y Portugal.   San
       Sebastián, [1971].
       80p.   col. maps.   27cm.

7138   Firestone-Hispania, S. A.
       Firestone-Hispania atlas de España y Portugal.   San
       Sebastián, [1972].
       79p.   col. maps.   27cm.

7139   Firestone-Hispania, S. A.
       Firestone-Hispania atlas de España y Portugal.   San
       Sebastián, 1974.
       79p.   col. maps.   27cm.

7140   Livraria Sá da Costa.
       Novo atlas escolar português, histórico-geográfico.   11ed.
       By João Soares.   Lisboa, 1971.
       85p.   col. maps.   34cm.

7141   Portugal.   Ministerio do trabalho.
       Atlas sócio-económico.   Lisboa, 1974-
       in parts.   44cm.

7142   Selecções do Reader's Digest.
       O livro da estrada; selecções do Reader's Digest.   Lisboa,
       [1969].
       338p.   col. maps.   29cm.

7143   Spain.   Ministerio de Obras Públicas.
       España: Mapa oficial de carreteras.   8ed.   Madrid,
       [1969].
       114p.   col. maps.   32cm.

7144   Spain.   Ministerio de Obras Públicas.
       España: Mapa oficial de carreteras.   9ed.   Madrid,
       [1971].
       90p.   col. maps.   32cm.

7145   Spain.   Ministerio de Obras Públicas.
       España: Mapa oficial de carreteras.   9ed.   Madrid,
       1972.
       90p.   col. maps.   32cm.

7146   Spain.   Ministerio de Obras Públicas.
       España: Mapa oficial de carreteras.   10ed.   Madrid,
       1973.

86p.   col.   maps.   32cm.

7147   Spain.   Ministerio de Obras Públicas.
       España: Mapa oficial de carreteras.   11ed.   Madrid,
       1974.
       86p.   col.   maps.   32cm.

Romania

7148   Editura Stadion.
       România.   Ghid-atlas turistic.   By Mihai Iancu and D.
       Popescu.   Bucureşti, 1971.
       160p.   col.   maps.   24cm.

7149   Editura Stadion.
       România.   Tourist guide and atlas.   Bucureşti, 1971.
       80p.   col.   maps.   32cm.

7150   Romania.   Academia Republicii Socialiste.
       Atlasul lingvistic român.   Serie nova.   Vol. VII.
       Bucureşti, 1972.
       398p.   col.   maps.   37cm.

7151   Romania.   Editura Academiei Republicii Populare Romîne.
       Atlasul republicii socialiste România.   Bucureşti, 1973-78.
       in parts.   col.   maps.   63cm.

7152   Romania.   Editura di Stat Didactică şi Pedagogică.
       Atlas geografic scolar.   By N. Gheorghiu.   Bucureşti,
       1968.
       34p.   col.   maps.   33cm.

7153   Romania.   Editura di Stat Didactică şi Pedagogică.
       Atlas istoric.   Bucureşti, 1971.
       200p.   col.   maps.   34cm.

Scotland

7154   American Heritage.
       AA Illustrated road book of Scotland; with gazetteer,
       itineraries, maps and town plans.   New York, 1971.
       288p.   col.   maps.   25cm.

7155   Automobile Association.
       AA Illustrated road book of Scotland; with gazetteer,
       itineraries, maps and town plans.   London, 1971.
       288p.   col.   maps.   25cm.

7156   Scotland.   Scottish Development Dept.
       Planning maps series: Scotland.   Edinburgh, 1970-
       1 vol.   col.   maps.   43cm.

7157   Shell-Mex & BP Ltd.

Shell golfer's atlas of England, Scotland and Wales.
London, 1968.
1 vol. col. maps. 28cm.

Spain

7158 Aguilar, S. A. de Ediciones.
Atlas bachillerato, universal y de España. 24ed. By
Antonio López Gómez. Madrid, 1970.
117p. col. maps. 35cm.

7159 Aguilar, S. A. de Ediciones.
Atlas bachillerato, universal y de España. 25ed. By
Antonio López Gómez. Madrid, 1970.
117p. col. maps. 35cm.

7160 Aguilar, S. A. de Ediciones.
Atlas bachillerato, universal y de España. 26ed. By
Antonio López Gómez. Madrid, 1970.
117p. col. maps. 35cm.

7161 Aguilar, S. A. de Ediciones.
Atlas bachillerato, universal y de España. 27ed. By
Antonio López Gómez. Madrid, 1970.
117p. col. maps. 35cm.

7162 Aguilar, S. A. de Ediciones.
Atlas bachillerato, universal y de España. 28ed. By
Antonio López Gómez. Madrid, 1970.
117p. col. maps. 35cm.

7163 Aguilar, S. A. de Ediciones.
Atlas bachillerato, universal y de España. 29ed. By
A. L. Gómez. Madrid, 1971.
117p. col. maps. 35cm.

7164 Aguilar, S. A. de Ediciones.
Ciento veintiún atlas de España. 1ed. Madrid, [1973].
235p. col. maps. 21cm.

7165 Anubar.
Atlas historico; cómo se formó España. 2ed. By Antonio
Ubieto Arteta. Valencia, 1970.
148p. col. maps. 31cm.

7166 Cartografía Pirelli.
Guía Pirelli de carreteras: España. Barcelona, [1971].
40p. col. maps. 31cm.

7167 Editorial Everest.
Mapa Everest de carreteras España y Portugal. Leon,
[1971].
86p. col. maps. 25cm.

7168   Editorial Luis Vives, S. A.
        Atlas universal y de España.   Zaragoza, [1959].
        1 vol. col. maps. 32cm.

7169   Editorial Teide.
        Atlas de historia de España.   Barcelona, 1973.
        102p. col. maps. 28cm.

7170   Firestone-Hispania, S. A.
        Firestone-Hispania atlas de España y Portugal.   San
        Sebastián, [1971].
        80p. col. maps. 27cm.

7171   Firestone-Hispania, S. A.
        Firestone-Hispania atlas de España y Portugal.   San
        Sebastián, [1972].
        79p. col. maps. 27cm.

7172   Firestone-Hispania, S. A.
        Firestone-Hispania atlas de España y Portugal.   San
        Sebastián, 1974.
        79p. col. maps. 27cm.

7173   Jover.
        Atlas de geografía de España.   By R. M. Bofill Fransí.
        Barcelona, [1972].
        1 vol. col. maps. 20cm.

7174   Map Productions, Ltd.
        Pocket Atlas. Vols 1: France, 2: Germany, 3: Spain,
        4: Italy. London, [1970].
        4 vol. col. maps. 19cm.

7175   Selecções do Reader's Digest.
        O livro da estrada; selecções do Reader's Digest.   Lisboa,
        [1969].
        338p. col. maps. 29cm.

7176   Spain. Ministerio de Obras Públicas.
        España: Mapa oficial de carreteras.   8ed. Madrid,
        [1969].
        114p. col. maps. 32cm.

7177   Spain. Ministerio de Obras Públicas.
        España: Mapa oficial de carreteras.   9ed. Madrid,
        [1971].
        90p. col. maps. 32cm.

7178   Spain. Ministerio de Obras Públicas.
        España: Mapa oficial de carreteras.   9ed. Madrid,
        1972.
        90p. col. maps. 32cm.

7179   Spain.   Ministerio de Obras Públicas.
       España: Mapa oficial de carreteras.   10ed.   Madrid,
       1973.
       86p.   col. maps.   32cm.

7180   Spain.   Ministerio de Obras Públicas.
       España: Mapa oficial de carreteras.   11ed.   Madrid,
       1974.
       86p.   col. maps.   32cm.

Sweden

7181   Det Beste A. S.
       Det Bestes bilbok.   Oslo, 1969.
       392p.   col. maps.   29cm.

7182   Generalstabens litografiska anstalt.
       KAK Bilatlas.   Stockholm, 1969.
       296p.   col. maps.   31cm.

7183   Generalstabens litografiska anstalt.
       KAK Bilatlas.   Stockholm, [1972].
       1 vol.   col. maps.   31cm.

7184   Generalstabens litografiska anstalt.
       KAK Bilatlas.   Stockholm, 1973.
       1 vol.   col. maps.   31cm.

7185   Generalstabens litografiska anstalt.
       KAK bilkartor.   Road atlas of Sweden.   Autoatlas von
       Schweden.   Atlas routier de Suède.   Stockholm, [1969].
       1 vol.   col. maps.   31cm.

7186   Generalstabens litografiska anstalt.
       Post-och järnvägs karta över Sverige.   Stockholm, 1973.
       10p.   col. maps.   23cm.

7187   Kartlitografen, AB.
       Mobil bilkarta.   Danderyd, [1970].
       29p.   col. maps.   33cm.

7188   Kartlitografen, AB.
       Mobil bilkarta.   Danderyd, [1971].
       29p.   col. maps.   33cm.

7189   Läromedelsförlagen.
       Skolatlas.   By Magnus Lundqvist and Olof Hedbom.
       Stockholm, 1971.
       1 vol.   col. maps.   34cm.

7190   Mobil Oil, AB.
       Mobil bilkarta.   Danderyd, [1971].
       29p.   col. maps.   33cm.

7191   Motormännens riksförbund.
       M:s vagvisare:Sverige.   9ed.   By Harry Ljunberg.   Stock-
       holm, 1971.
       304p.   col. maps.   25cm.

7192   Reader's Digest A. B.
       Det Bästas bilbok.   Stockholm, [1969].
       392p.   col. maps.   29cm.

7193   Svenska bokförlaget.
       Atlas till historien.   3ed.   By Bengt Y. Gustafson.
       Stockholm, [1970].
       60p.   col. maps.   30cm.

Switzerland

7194   Hachette.
       Atlas routier et touristique: France, Belgique, Luxem-
       bourg, Suisse.   With Bordas.   Paris, [1970].
       76p.   col. maps.   30cm.

7195   Kümmerly & Frey.
       Computer atlas der Schweiz.   By A. Kilchenmann, D.
       Steiner, O. Matt and E. Gächter.   Bern, 1972.
       72p.   30cm.

7196   Kümmerly & Frey.
       Computer atlas of Switzerland.   Population; Housing; Oc-
       cupation; Agriculture.   Bern, 1972.
       72p.   30cm.

7197   Kümmerly & Frey.
       Schweiz und angrenzende Länder; Strassenatlas.   Bern,
       [1963].
       60p.   col. maps.   23cm.

7198   Sauerländer, H. R.
       Historischer atlas zur Welt- und Schweizer Geschichte.
       7ed.   By F. W. Putzger.   Aarau, 1969.
       146p.   col. maps.   27cm.

7199   Sélection du Reader's digest, S. A. R. L.
       Guide de la route: France, Belgique, Suisse.   Paris,
       [1969].
       455p.   col. maps.   29cm.

Turkey

7200   Bir Yayinevi.
       Ilkokul atlasi.   With Istituto Geografico De Agostini.
       Istanbul, 1968.
       28p.   col. maps.   26cm.

7201 Bir Yayinevi.
      Modern orta atlasi.   With Istituto Geografico De Agostini.
      Istanbul, 1967.
      40p. col. maps. 33cm.

7202 Bir Yayinevi.
      Modern orta atlasi.   With Istituto Geografico De Agostini.
      Istanbul, 1968.
      40p. col. maps. 34cm.

7203 Bir Yayinevi.
      Resimli ilkokul atlasi.   With Istituto Geografico De
      Agostini. Istanbul, 1967.
      28p. col. maps. 27cm.

7204 Bir Yayinevi.
      Resimli ilkokul atlasi.   With Istituto Geografico De
      Agostini. Istanbul, 1968.
      28p. col. maps. 27cm.

7205 Bir Yayinevi.
      Tarih atlasi.   With Istituto Geografico De Agostini.   Istan-
      bul, 1967.
      32p. col. maps. 27cm.

7206 Bir Yayinevi.
      Tarih atlasi.   With Istituto Geografico De Agostini.   Istan-
      bul, 1968.
      32p. col. maps. 27cm.

7207 Istituto Geografico De Agostini.
      Atlash coğrafya ansiklopedisi.   By Besim Darkot. Istanbul,
      [1964].
      310p. col. maps. 34cm.

7208 Istituto Geografico De Agostini.
      Modern orta atlas. Istanbul, [1972].
      43p. col. maps. 34cm.

7209 Kanaat Yayinlari.
      Yeni orta atlas. Istanbul, [1958].
      40p. col. maps. 31cm.

7210 Maarif Basimevi.
      Orta atlas. 2ed. Istanbul, 1957.
      52p. col. maps. 28cm.

7211 Milli Eğitim Bakanliği.
      Yeni orta atlas. Istanbul, [1961].
      40p. col. maps. 31cm.

7212 Milli Eğitim Bakanliği.
      Yeni orta atlas. Istanbul, [1968].

40p. col. maps. 31cm.

7213 Shell Co. of Turkey Ltd.
      Motorist guide to Turkey. Istanbul, [1971].
      228p. col. maps. 21cm.

U. S. S. R.

7214 Denoyer-Geppert Co.
      Soviet Union in maps. By Harold Fullard. With Philip.
      Chicago, 1972.
      33p. col. maps. 26cm.

7215 Macmillan Co.
      Russian history atlas. 1ed. By Martin Gilbert. New
      York, [1972].
      188p. 25cm.

7216 Oxford University Press.
      Oxford regional economic atlas of the U. S. S. R. and East-
      ern Europe. London, [1960].
      134p. col. maps. 26cm.

7217 Oxford University Press.
      Oxford regional economic atlas. The U. S. S. R. and
      Eastern Europe. London, [1969].
      134p. col. maps. 26cm.

7218 Oxford University Press.
      Oxford regional economic atlas. The U. S. S. R. and East-
      ern Europe. Paperback ed. London, 1969.
      134p. col. maps. 20cm.

7219 Oxford University Press.
      The U. S. S. R. and Eastern Europe. [Atlas.] With
      Economist Intelligence Unit, Ltd. London, [1969].
      134p. col. maps. 27cm.

7220 Philip, George & Son, Ltd.
      Soviet Union in maps. By Harold Fullard. London,
      1972.
      33p. col. maps. 25cm.

7221 University of Michigan Press.
      Economic atlas of the Soviet Union. 2ed. By George
      Kish. Ann Arbor, Mich., [1971].
      90p. col. maps. 27cm.

7222 U. S. Central Intelligence Agency.
      U. S. S. R. agricultural atlas. Washington, D. C., 1974.
      59p. col. maps. 57cm.

7223 U. S. Central Intelligence Agency.

U. S. S. R. atlas of transmission pipelines for natural gas.
Washington, D. C. , 1963.
66p. col. maps. 57cm.

7224 U. S. Military Academy.
Landscape atlas of the U. S. S. R. (in English). By Thomas
F. Plummer, Jr. , William G. Hanne, Edward F. Bruner,
and Christian C. Thudium, Jr. West Point, N. Y. , 1971.
197p. 45cm.

7225 U. S. S. R. Akademia nauk.
Klimaticheskii atlas S. S. S. R. Moskva, 1960-62.
2 vol. col. maps. 34cm.

7226 U. S. S. R. Glavnoe upravlenie geodezii i kartografii.
Atlas avtomobilnykh dorog S. S. S. R. 1ed. Moskva, 1959.
165p. col. maps. 27cm.

7227 U. S. S. R. Glavnoe upravlenie geodezii i kartografii.
Atlas avtomobilnykh dorog S. S. S. R. 2ed. Moskva, 1960.
165p. col. maps. 27cm.

7228 U. S. S. R. Glavnoe upravlenie geodezii i kartografii.
Atlas avtomobilnykh dorog S. S. S. R. 3ed. Moskva, 1960.
165p. col. maps. 27cm.

7229 U. S. S. R. Glavnoe upravlenie geodezii i kartografii.
Atlas avtomobilnykh dorog S. S. S. R. 2ed. Moskva, 1969.
167p. col. maps. 27cm.

7230 U. S. S. R. Glavnoe upravlenie geodezii i kartografii.
Atlas avtomobilnykh dorog S. S. S. R. 2ed. By N. T.
Markova. Moskva, 1970.
171p. col. maps. 27cm.

7231 U. S. S. R. Glavnoe upravlenie geodezii i kartografii.
Atlas avtomobilnykh dorog S. S. S. R. 3ed. By N. T.
Markova. Moskva, 1971.
167p. col. maps. 27cm.

7232 U. S. S. R. Glavnoe upravlenie geodezii i kartografii.
Atlas avtomobilnykh dorog S. S. S. R. 4ed. By N. T.
Markova. Moskva, 1972.
171p. col. maps. 27cm.

7233 U. S. S. R. Glavnoe upravlenie geodezii i kartografii.
Atlas avtomobilnykh dorog S. S. S. R. 4ed. Moskva, 1973.
167p. col. maps. 27cm.

7234 U. S. S. R. Glavnoe upravlenie geodezii i kartografii.
Atlas istorii S. S. S. R. dlya IV klassa. Moskva, 1971.
12p. col. maps. 26cm.

7235 U. S. S. R. Glavnoe upravlenie geodezii i kartografii.
Atlas istorii S. S. S. R. Part I. dlya VII klassa. Moskva,
1971.
16p. col. maps. 25cm.

7236 U. S. S. R. Glavnoe upravlenie geodezii i kartografii.
Atlas istorii S. S. S. R. Part II. dlya VIII klassa.
Moskva, 1971.
11p. col. maps. 26cm.

7237 U. S. S. R. Glavnoe upravlenie geodezii i kartografii.
Atlas istorii S. S. S. R. Part III, dlya IX-X klassov.
Moskva, 1971.
20p. col. maps. 26cm.

7238 U. S. S. R. Glavnoe upravlenie geodezii i kartografii.
Atlas obrazovania i razvitiya S. S. S. R. Moskva, 1972.
112p. col. maps. 34cm.

7239 U. S. S. R. Glavnoe upravlenie geodezii i kartografii.
Atlas skhem zheleznykh dorog S. S. S. R. Moskva, 1972.
101p. col. maps. 16cm.

7240 U. S. S. R. Glavnoe upravlenie geodezii i kartografii.
Atlas S. S. S. R. Moskva, 1971.
148p. col. maps. 38cm.

7241 U. S. S. R. Glavnoe upravlenie geodezii i kartografii.
Atlas S. S. S. R. dlya 8-go klassa. Moskva, 1971.
48p. col. maps. 28cm.

7242 U. S. S. R. Glavnoe upravlenie geodezii i kartografii.
Atlas S. S. S. R.-v deviatoi piatiletke. Moskva, 1972.
40p. col. maps. 29cm.

7243 U. S. S. R. Glavnoe upravlenie geodezii i kartografii.
Geograficheskii atlas S. S. S. R. dlya 7-go klassa. Moskva,
1971.
32p. col. maps. 28cm.

7244 U. S. S. R. Glavnoe upravlenie geodezii i kartografii.
Malyi atlas S. S. S. R. 1ed. Moskva, 1973.
197p. col. maps. 20cm.

7245 U. S. S. R. Glavnoe upravlenie geodezii i kartografii.
Nasha rodina: Geograficheskii atlas dlya 4-go klassa.
Moskva, 1971.
16p. col. maps. 28cm.

7246 U. S. S. R. Glavnoe upravlenie geodezii i kartografii.
Zheleznye dorogi S. S. S. R. 4ed. Moskva, 1969.
148p. col. maps. 16cm.

7247 U.S.S.R. Glavnoe upravlenie geodezii i kartografii.
      Zheleznye dorogi S.S.S.R. 5ed. Moskva, 1970.
      148p. col. maps. 16cm.

7248 U.S.S.R. Glavnoe upravlenie geodezii i kartografii.
      Zheleznye dorogi S.S.S.R. 6ed. Moskva, 1971.
      150p. col. maps. 16cm.

7249 Yale University Press.
      Atlas of Russian history: eleven centuries of changing
      borders. Rev. ed. By Allen F. Chew. New Haven,
      1970.
      127p. 28cm.

Wales

7250 Faber & Faber.
      An agricultural atlas of England and Wales. 2ed. By J.
      T. Coppock. London, 1974.
      255p. 25cm.

7251 Faber & Faber.
      An historical atlas of Wales. By William Rees. London,
      1972.
      71p. 26cm.

7252 Faber & Faber.
      An historical atlas of Wales from early to modern times.
      By William Rees. London, 1972.
      141p. 25cm.

7253 Gt. Britain. Ministry of Housing and Local Government.
      Atlas of planning maps of England and Wales. London,
      1965-70.
      in parts. col. maps. 44cm.

7254 National Trust.
      The what to see atlas, showing places of historical,
      architectural & scenic interest in England, Wales, and
      Northern Ireland. 5ed. With Bartholomew. London,
      [1970].
      60p. col. maps. 25cm.

7255 National Trust.
      The what to see atlas, showing places of historic,
      architectural and scenic interest in England, Wales and
      Northern Ireland. With Bartholomew. London, 1971.
      60p. col. maps. 25cm.

7256 National Trust.
      The what to see atlas, showing places of historic,
      architectural and scenic interest in England, Wales and
      Northern Ireland. 5ed. With Bartholomew. London,

[1974].
60p.   col. maps.   25cm.

7257   Shell-Mex & BP Ltd.
       Shell golfer's atlas of England, Scotland and Wales.   Lon-
       don, 1968.
       1 vol.   col. maps.   28cm.

7258   University of Wales Press.
       Historical atlas of Wales.   2ed.   By J. Idwal Jones (in
       Welsh).   Cardiff, 1972.
       137p.   25cm.

Yugoslavia

7259   Jugoslavenski leksikografski zavod.
       Jugoslavija; auto atlas.   By Petar Mardešić.   Zagreb,
       [1969].
       1 vol.   col. maps.   24cm.

7260   Jugoslavenski leksikografski zavod.
       Jugoslavija; auto atlas.   5ed.   Zagreb, 1970.
       56p.   col. maps.   24cm.

7261   Jugoslavenski leksikografski zavod.
       Jugoslavija; auto atlas.   7ed.   Zagreb, [1971].
       56p.   col. maps.   24cm.

7262   Jugoslavenski leksikografski zavod.
       Jugoslavija; auto atlas.   8ed.   Zagreb, [1971].
       52p.   col. maps.   24cm.

7263   Jugoslavenski leksikografski zavod.
       Jugoslavija; auto atlas.   10ed.   Zagreb, [1971].
       56p.   col. maps.   24cm.

7264   Jugoslavenski leksikografski zavod.
       Jugoslavija; auto atlas.   1ed.   Zagreb, 1973.
       110p.   col. maps.   24cm.

7265   Rad.
       Jugoslavija.   Atlas nemih karata za nastavu geografije.
       By Radovin Nedeljković.   Beograd, 1970.
       64p.   34cm.

7266   Turistička štampa.
       Road map, Yugoslavia.   2ed.   Beograd, 1958.
       132p.   col. maps.   29cm.

7267   Učila.
       Autoatlas Jugoslavijc.   Zagreb, 1965.
       27p.   col. maps.   23cm.

7268   Učila.
     Politički atlas.   By Zvonimir Dugački.   Zagreb, 1957.
     128p.   col. maps.   17cm.

7269   Učila.
     Povijesni atlas.   By Zvonimir Dugački.   Zagreb, 1969.
     66p.   col. maps.   30cm.

Bahama

7270 Collins, William Sons & Co., Ltd.
Atlas for Bahamas. London, 1971.
1 vol. col. maps. 28cm.

Barbados

7271 Macmillan Education, Ltd.
Atlas for Barbados, Windwards and Leewards. London,
1974.
55p. col. maps. 29cm.

Bermuda

7272 Collins, William, Sons & Co., Ltd.
Atlas for Bermuda. London, 1972.
1 vol. col. maps. 28cm.

Canada

7273 Air Canada.
Air Canada routes. Ottawa, [1966].
18p. col. maps. 23cm.

7274 Alpine Geographical Press.
Campground atlas of the United States and Canada. By
James A. Bier and Henry A. Raup. Champaign, Ill.,
1971.
320p. col. maps. 28cm.

7275 American Hotel Register Co.
Leahy's hotel-motel guide and travel atlas of the United
States, Canada and Mexico. 96ed. Chicago, 1971.
278p. col. maps. 38cm.

7276 American Hotel Register Co.
Leahy's hotel-motel guide and travel atlas of the United
States, Canada and Mexico. 97ed. Chicago, 1972.
278p. col. maps. 38cm.

7277 American Hotel Register Co.
Leahy's hotel-motel guide and travel atlas of the United
States, Canada and Mexico. 98ed. Chicago, 1973.
278p. col. maps. 38cm.

7278   American Hotel Register Co.
       Leahy's hotel-motel guide and travel atlas of the United
       States, Canada and Mexico.   99ed.   Chicago, 1974.
       296p.   col. maps.   38cm.

7279   American Hotel Register Co.
       Leahy's hotel-motel guide and travel atlas of the United
       States, Canada and Mexico.   100ed.   Chicago, 1975.
       296p.   col. maps.   38cm.

7280   American Map Co., Inc.
       Cleartype business control atlas of the United States and
       Canada.   New York, [1962].
       120p.   28cm.

7281   American Map Co., Inc.
       Cleartype business control atlas of the United States and
       Canada.   New York, 1970.
       120p.   29cm.

7282   American Map Co., Inc.
       Cleartype business control atlas of the United States and
       Canada.   New York, 1971.
       120p.   28cm.

7283   American Map Co., Inc.
       Cleartype business control atlas of the United States and
       Canada.   New York, 1972.
       128p.   28cm.

7284   American Map Co., Inc.
       Cleartype business control atlas of the United States and
       Canada.   New York, 1973.
       128p.   28cm.

7285   American Map Co., Inc.
       Cleartype business control atlas of the United States and
       Canada.   New York, 1974.
       128p.   28cm.

7286   American Map Co., Inc.
       Cleartype transcontinental highway atlas; United States,
       Canada, Mexico.   New York, [1950].
       16p.   col. maps.   40cm.

7287   Camping Maps, U.S.A.
       Camping maps, Canada.   By Glenn and Dale Rhodes.
       Upper Montclair, N.J., 1961.
       58p.   22cm.

7288   Canada.   Dept. of Citizenship and Immigration.
       Canada: Descriptive atlas.   Ottawa, 1951.
       102p.   col. maps.   28cm.

7289   Canada.   Department of Energy, Mines & Resources.
       Atlas et toponymie du Canada.   Ottawa, 1969.
       104p.   col.   maps.   38cm.

7290   Canada.   Dept. of Indian Affairs and Northern Development.
       Atlas of Indian reserves & settlements of Canada.   Ottawa,
       1971.
       1 vol.   col.   maps.   39cm.

7291   Canada.   Department of Mines and Technical Surveys.
       Atlas du Canada.   3ed.   Ottawa, 1957.
       110p.   col.   maps.   54cm.

7292   Canada.   Dept. of Transport.
       Atlas of climatic maps.   Ottawa, 1970.
       1 vol.   col.   maps.   39cm.

7293   Canada.   Inland Waters Branch.
       Hydrological atlas of Canada; preliminary maps.   Ottawa,
       1969.
       1 portf.   31cm.

7294   Canada.   Surveys and Mapping Branch.
       L'atlas national du Canada.   4ed.   Ottawa, 1974.
       284p.   col.   maps.   38cm.

7295   Canada.   Surveys and Mapping Branch.
       National atlas of Canada.   4ed.   Ottawa, 1970-
       in parts.   col.   maps.   38cm.

7296   Canada.   Surveys and Mapping Branch.
       The National atlas of Canada.   4ed.   Ottawa, 1974.
       284p.   col.   maps.   38cm.

7297   Centre de Psychologie et de Pédagogie.
       Atlas historique du Canada.   By D. G. G. Kerr.   Transl.
       by Pierre Tousignant.   Montreal, 1967.
       120p.   col.   maps.   31cm.

7298   Cram, George F., Co.
       Cram's road atlas of the United States, Canada, Mexico.
       Indianapolis, Ind., 1958.
       64p.   col.   maps.   31cm.

7299   Cram, George F., Co.
       Cram's road atlas of the United States, Canada, Mexico.
       Indianapolis, Ind., [1960].
       64p.   col.   maps.   31cm.

7300   Dent, J. M.
       Dent's Canadian school atlas.   Toronto, 1967.
       115p.   col.   maps.   29cm.

7301   Dent, J. M.
          Dent's Canadian school atlas.   Rev. ed.   Toronto, [1971].
          115p.   col.   maps.   29cm.

7302   Dent, J. M.
          Dent's Canadian school atlas.   Toronto, [1973].
          115p.   col.   maps.   29cm.

7303   Diversified Map Corporation.
          Interstate atlas.   United States, Canada, Mexico.   St.
          Louis, Mo., 1969.
          64p.   col.   maps.   23cm.

7304   Diversified Map Corporation.
          Pocket road atlas of the United States, Canada and Mexico.
          St. Louis, Mo., 1969.
          64p.   col.   maps.   21.5cm.

7305   Diversified Map Corporation.
          Road atlas of the United States, Canada, and Mexico.   St.
          Louis, Mo., 1968.
          144p.   col.   maps.   34cm.

7306   Diversified Map Corporation.
          The new Grosset road atlas of the United States, Canada
          and Mexico.   St. Louis, [1973].
          128p.   col.   maps.   34cm.

7307   Editions françaises.
          Atlas Larousse canadien.   By Benoît Brouillette and
          Maurice Saint-Yves.   Québec, [1971].
          161p.   col.   maps.   28cm.

7308   Elving, Bruce F.
          FM atlas and station directory, U.S., Canada.   Duluth,
          Minn., 1971.
          48p.   28cm.

7309   Gousha, H. M., Co.
          National road atlas, United States, Canada, Mexico.
          Chicago, San Jose, Calif., [1957].
          48p.   col.   maps.   26cm.

7310   Gousha, H. M., Co.
          Vacation guide and road atlas.   United States, Canada,
          Mexico.   With Brown & Bigelow.   Chicago, San Jose,
          Calif., [1957].
          48p.   col.   maps.   26cm.

7311   Gousha, H. M., Co.
          Vacation guide and road atlas.   United States, Canada and
          Mexico.   With Brown & Bigelow.   Chicago, San Jose,
          Calif., [1958].

           48p.   col. maps.   26cm.

7312   Hammond, C. S. & Co., Inc.
           Hammond's road atlas and city street guide of the United
           States, Canada, Mexico.   Maplewood, N. J., 1962.
           96p.   col. maps.   31cm.

7313   Hammond, C. S. & Co., Inc.
           Hammond road atlas of the United States, Canada, Mexico.
           Maplewood, N. J., 1966.
           48p.   col. maps.   32cm.

7314   Hartford Fire Insurance Co.
           United States road atlas, including Canada and Mexico.
           With H. M. Gousha.   Hartford, Conn., [1959].
           56p.   col. maps.   26cm.

7315   Hartford Fire Insurance Co.
           United States road atlas including Canada and Mexico.
           With H. M. Gousha.   Hartford, Conn., [1960].
           56p.   col. maps.   26cm.

7316   Larousse.
           Atlas Larousse canadien.   By Benoît Brouillette and
           Maurice Saint-Yves.   Québec, [1971].
           168p.   col. maps.   28cm.

7317   National Bus Traffic Association.
           Atlas of motor bus routes; showing operations of intercity
           bus carriers in the United States, Canada, Mexico.   Chi-
           cago, [1953].
           81p.   46cm.

7318   Nelson, Thomas & Sons, Ltd.
           Nelson's Canadian school atlas.   By J. Wreford Watson.
           Don Mills, Ont., 1968.
           92p.   col. maps.   29cm.

7319   Oxford University Press.
           Oxford regional economic atlas of the U. S. and Canada.
           2ed.   London, 1975.
           180p.   col. maps.   27cm.

7320   Oxford University Press.
           The Canadian Oxford school atlas.   3ed.   By E. G. Pleva.
           Toronto, 1972.
           166p.   col. maps.   27cm.

7321   Rand McNally & Co.
           Atlas Canada.   Chicago, 1962.
           15p.   col. maps.   31cm.

7322   Rand McNally & Co.

Canada road atlas. By Paul Tiddens. Chicago, 1974.
64p. col. maps. 38cm.

7323 Rand McNally & Co.
Rand McNally road atlas, United States, Canada, Mexico.
Chicago, 1971.
118p. col. maps. 40cm.

7324 Rand McNally & Co.
Rand McNally road atlas, United States, Canada, Mexico.
Chicago, 1972.
128p. col. maps. 40cm.

7325 Rand McNally & Co.
Rand McNally road atlas, United States, Canada, Mexico.
Chicago, 1973.
128p. col. maps. 40cm.

7326 Rand McNally & Co.
Rand McNally road atlas, United States, Canada, Mexico.
Chicago, 1974.
160p. col. maps. 40cm.

7327 Rand McNally & Co.
Rand McNally road atlas, United States, Canada, Mexico.
Chicago, 1975.
160p. col. maps. 40cm.

7328 Rand McNally & Co.
Rand McNally road atlas, U.S., Canada, Mexico.   50
anniversary ed. Chicago, 1974.
136p. col. maps. 40cm.

7329 Rand McNally & Co.
Road atlas & travel guide, United States, Canada, Mexico.
Chicago, 1971.
96p. col. maps. 27cm.

7330 Rand McNally & Co.
Road atlas & travel guide, United States, Canada, Mexico.
Chicago, 1972.
96p. col. maps. 27cm.

7331 Rand McNally & Co.
Texaco travel atlas: United States, Canada, Mexico.
Chicago, [1971].
224p. col. maps. 38cm.

7332 Rand McNally & Co.
Texaco travel atlas: United States, Canada, Mexico.
Chicago, 1972.
224p. col. maps. 38cm.

7333   Rand McNally & Co.
       Texaco travel atlas: United States, Canada, Mexico.
       Chicago, [1973].
       224p. col. maps. 38cm.

7334   Reader's Digest Association, Ltd.
       The Reader's Digest great world atlas.   1 Canadian ed.
       Montreal, 1964.
       183p. col. maps. 41cm.

7335   Reader's Digest Association, Ltd.
       The Reader's Digest great world atlas.   3 Canadian ed.
       Montreal, [1971].
       187p. col. maps. 41cm.

7336   Rolph-McNally, Ltd.
       Canadian road atlas.   Bramalea, Ont., 1972.
       48p. col. maps. 37cm.

Costa Rica

7337   U.S. Engineer Resources Inventory Center.
       Costa Rica: análisis regional de recursos físicos,
       Centroamérica y Panamá. 1ed. Washington, D.C., 1965.
       1 vol. col. maps. 34cm.

Cuba

7338   Cuba. Academia de Ciencias.
       Atlas nacional de Cuba, en el décimo aniversario de la
       Revolución. La Habana, 1970.
       132p. col. maps. 49cm.

7339   Cuba. Academia de Ciencias.
       Natsionalnyi atlas Kuby. Havana, 1970.
       143p. col. maps. 48cm.

7340   Cuba. Instituto Cubano de Cartografía y Catastro.
       Red de carreteras de la República de Cuba en planos
       provinciales y accesos de la ciudad de la Habana. Havana,
       1957.
       8p. 35cm.

7341   Cuba. Oficina Nacional de los Censos Demográfico y Electoral.
       Atlas censo 1953. La Habana, [1958].
       160p. 49cm.

7342   Instituto Cubano del Libro.
       Atlas de Cuba. Havana, 1972.
       144p. col. maps. 48cm.

7343   U.S. Department of Commerce.
       National atlas of Cuba. Springfield, Va., 1971.

309p.   27cm.

7344   U. S. S. R.   Glavnoe upravlenie geodezii i kartografii.
       Natsionalnyi atlas Kuby.   Moskva, 1972.
       154p.   col.   maps.   48cm.

Dominican Republic

7345   Editorial Seix Barral, S. A.
       Atlas escolar de la República Dominicana.   Barcelona,
       [1956].
       24p.   col.   maps.   29cm.

El Salvador

7346   Salvador.   Estadistica y cencos.
       El Salvador-atlas de resursos fisicos.   San Salvador,
       1969.
       1 vol.   col.   maps.   72cm.

Guatemala

7347   Guatemala.   Instituto Geográfico Nacional.
       Atlas nacional de Guatemala.   1ed.   Guatemala, [1972].
       1 vol.   col.   maps.   56cm.

Guyana

7348   Macmillan Education, Ltd.
       Atlas for Guyana and Trinidad and Tobago.   Basingstoke,
       1975.
       1 vol.   col.   maps.   28cm.

Jamaica

7349   Collins, William, Sons & Co., Ltd.
       Atlas for Jamaica and the western Caribbean.   London,
       1971.
       57p.   col.   maps.   26cm.

7350   Jamaica Pub. House.
       School atlas for Jamaica.   By Enid B. Johnston.   With
       Macmillan Education, Ltd.   Kingston, [1971].
       33p.   col.   maps.   29cm.

7351   Jamaica.   Scientific Research Council.
       The Rainfall of Jamaica.   [Atlas.]   Kingston, 1963.
       19p.   col.   maps.   43cm.

7352   Jamaica.   Town Planning Dept.
       National atlas of Jamaica.   Kingston, 1971.
       79p.   col.   maps.   46cm.

7353   Macmillan Education, Ltd.
       School atlas for Jamaica.   By Enid B. Johnston.   King-
       ston, [1971].
       33p. col. maps. 29cm.

7354   University of London Press.
       Jamaica in maps. By Colin G. Clarke.   London, 1974.
       104p. 23cm.

Mexico

7355   American Hotel Register Co.
       Leahy's hotel-motel guide and travel atlas of the United
       States, Canada and Mexico. 96ed. Chicago, 1971.
       278p. col. maps. 38cm.

7356   American Hotel Register Co.
       Leahy's hotel-motel guide and travel atlas of the United
       States, Canada and Mexico. 97ed. Chicago, 1972.
       278p. col. maps. 38cm.

7357   American Hotel Register Co.
       Leahy's hotel-motel guide and travel atlas of the United
       States, Canada and Mexico. 98ed. Chicago, 1973.
       278p. col. maps. 38cm.

7358   American Hotel Register Co.
       Leahy's hotel-motel guide and travel atlas of the United
       States, Canada and Mexico. 99ed. Chicago, 1974.
       296p. col. maps. 38cm.

7359   American Hotel Register Co.
       Leahy's hotel-motel guide and travel atlas of the United
       States, Canada and Mexico. 100ed. Chicago, 1975.
       296p. col. maps. 38cm.

7360   American Map Co., Inc.
       Cleartype transcontinental highway atlas; United States,
       Canada, Mexico. New York, [1950].
       16p. col. maps. 40cm.

7361   Asociación Nacional Automovilística.
       Atlas: rutas de México; routes of Mexico. 5ed. México,
       1971.
       2 vol. col. maps. 24cm.

7362   Asociación Nacional Automovilística.
       Atlas: rutas de Mexico; routes of Mexico. 6ed. México,
       [1973].
       2 vol. col. maps. 24cm.

7363   Climatic Data Press.
       Mexico campground guide and trailer atlas. By Frederick

L. Wernstedt. Lemont, Pa. , [1974].
54p. col. maps. 31cm.

7364 Cram, George F. , Co.
Cram's road atlas of the United States, Canada, Mexico.
Indianapolis, Ind. , 1958.
64p. col. maps. 31cm.

7365 Cram, George F. , Co.
Cram's road atlas of the United States, Canada, Mexico.
Indianapolis, Ind. , [1960].
64p. col. maps. 31cm.

7366 Diversified Map Corporation.
Interstate atlas. United States, Canada, Mexico.   St.
Louis, Mo. , 1969.
64p. col. maps. 23cm.

7367 Diversified Map Corporation.
Pocket road atlas of the United States, Canada and Mexico.
St. Louis, Mo. , 1969.
64p. col. maps. 21.5cm.

7368 Diversified Map Corporation.
Road atlas of the United States, Canada, and Mexico.
St. Louis, Mo. , 1968.
144p. col. maps. 34cm.

7369 Diversified Map Corporation.
The new Grosset road atlas of the United States, Canada
and Mexico. St. Louis, Mo. , [1973].
128p. col. maps. 34cm.

7370 Editorial Porrúa, S. A.
Nuevo atlas Porrúa de la República Mexicana. México,
1972.
197p. col. maps. 34cm.

7371 Editorial Porrúa, S. A.
Nuevo atlas Porrúa de la República Mexicana. 2ed.
México, 1974.
197p. col. maps. 34cm.

7372 Editorial Progreso.
La República Mexicana; geografía y atlas. 8ed. By
Thomás Zepeda. México, 1966.
159p. col. maps. 30cm.

7373 Goushá, H. M. , Co.
National road atlas, United States, Canada, Mexico.
Chicago, San Jose, Calif. , [1957].
48p. col. maps. 26cm.

7374   Goushá, H. M., Co.
       Vacation guide and road atlas. United States, Canada,
       Mexico. With Brown & Bigelow. Chicago, San Jose,
       Calif., [1957].
       48p. col. maps. 26cm.

7375   Goushá, H. M., Co.
       Vacation guide and road atlas. United States, Canada
       and Mexico. With Brown & Bigelow. Chicago, San Jose,
       Calif., [1958].
       48p. col. maps. 26cm.

7376   Hammond, C. S. & Co., Inc.
       Hammond's road atlas and city street guide of the United
       States, Canada, Mexico. Maplewood, N.J., 1962.
       96p. col. maps. 31cm.

7377   Hammond, C. S. & Co., Inc.
       Hammond road atlas of the United States, Canada, Mexico.
       Maplewood, N.J., 1966.
       48p. col. maps. 32cm.

7378   Hartford Fire Insurance Co.
       United States road atlas, including Canada and Mexico.
       With H. M. Goushá. Hartford, Conn., [1959].
       56p. col. maps. 26cm.

7379   Hartford Fire Insurance Co.
       United States road atlas, including Canada and Mexico.
       With H. M. Goushá. Hartford, Conn., [1960].
       56p. col. maps. 26cm.

7380   Kartografické nakladatelství.
       Atlas geográfico mundial de bolsillo. With Centro Anglo-
       Mexicano del Libro and Bancroft & Co., Ltd. México,
       [1967].
       60p. col. maps. 17cm.

7381   México. Comisión Federal de Electricidad.
       Red nacional eléctrica y centrales generadoras en la
       República Mexicana. México, 1971.
       10p. 39cm.

7382   Mexico. Ministerio de Comunicaciones y Obras Públicas.
       Atlas de la república Mexicana con los caminos a cargo
       de la dirección nacional de caminos. México, 1952.
       31p. 42cm.

7383   Mexico. Secretaría de Comunicaciones y Transportes.
       Cartas e información sobre vías generales de comunica-
       ción de las entidades federativas. México, 1964.
       2 vol. 44cm.

7384   National Bus Traffic Association.
        Atlas of motor bus routes; showing operations of intercity
        bus carriers in the United States, Canada, Mexico.   Chi-
        cago, [1953].
        81p.   46cm.

7385   Rand McNally & Co.
        Rand McNally road atlas, United States, Canada, Mexico.
        Chicago, 1971.
        118p.   col. maps.   40cm.

7386   Rand McNally & Co.
        Rand McNally road atlas, United States, Canada, Mexico.
        Chicago, 1972.
        128p.   col. maps.   40cm.

7387   Rand McNally & Co.
        Rand McNally road atlas, United States, Canada, Mexico.
        Chicago, 1973.
        128p.   col. maps.   40cm.

7388   Rand McNally & Co.
        Rand McNally road atlas, United States, Canada, Mexico.
        Chicago, 1974.
        160p.   col. maps.   40cm.

7389   Rand McNally & Co.
        Rand McNally road atlas, United States, Canada, Mexico.
        Chicago, 1975.
        160p.   col. maps.   40cm.

7390   Rand McNally & Co.
        Rand McNally road atlas, U.S., Canada, Mexico.   50
        anniversary ed.   Chicago, 1974.
        136p.   col. maps.   40cm.

7391   Rand McNally & Co.
        Road atlas & travel guide, United States, Canada, Mexico.
        Chicago, 1971.
        96p.   col. maps.   27cm.

7392   Rand McNally & Co.
        Road atlas & travel guide, United States, Canada, Mexico.
        Chicago, 1972.
        96p.   col. maps.   27cm.

7393   Rand McNally & Co.
        Texaco travel atlas: United States, Canada, Mexico.
        Chicago, [1971].
        224p.   col. maps.   38cm.

7394   Rand McNally & Co.
        Texaco travel atlas: United States, Canada, Mexico.

Chicago, 1972.
224p.   col. maps.   38cm.

7395   Rand McNally & Co.
       Texaco travel atlas: United States, Canada, Mexico.
       Chicago, [1973].
       224p.   col. maps.   38cm.

7396   University of Texas.
       Atlas of Mexico.   2ed.   Austin, Texas, 1975.
       165p.   col. maps.   36cm.

Nicaragua

7397   U. S. Engineer Resources Inventory Center.
       Nicaragua; análisis regional de recursos físicos,
       Centroamérica y Panamá.   1ed.   Washington, D. C. , 1966.
       1 vol.   col. maps.   34cm.

Panama

7398   Ediciones Oasis.
       Pequeño atlas geográfico de Panamá.   4ed.   [Panamá],
       1955.
       63p.   col. maps.   23cm.

7399   Editora Istmeña.
       Pequeño atlas geográfco de Panamá.   4ed.   Panamá, 1955.
       70p.   col. maps.   23cm.

7400   Panama.   Asesoría en geografía y ecología.
       Atlas de geografía médica.   Salud, 1970.
       60p.   col. maps.   74cm.

7401   Sanchez y Herrera.
       Pequeño atlas geográfico de Panamá.   Panamá, 1950.
       27p.   col. maps.   28cm.

U. S. A.

7402   Alpine Geographical Press.
       Campground atlas of the United States and Canada.   By
       James A. Bier and Henry A. Raup.   Champaign, Ill. ,
       1971.
       320p.   col. maps.   1971.

7403   American Hotel Register Co.
       Leahy's hotel-motel guide and travel atlas of the United
       States, Canada and Mexico.   96ed.   Chicago, 1971.
       278p.   col. maps.   38cm.

7404   American Hotel Register Co.
       Leahy's hotel-motel guide and travel atlas of the United

States, Canada and Mexico.   97ed.   Chicago, 1972.
278p.   col. maps.   38cm.

7405   American Hotel Register Co.
Leahy's hotel-motel guide and travel atlas of the United
States, Canada and Mexico.   98ed.   Chicago, 1973.
278p.   col. maps.   38cm.

7406   American Hotel Register Co.
Leahy's hotel-motel guide and travel atlas of the United
States, Canada and Mexico.   99ed.   Chicago, 1974.
296p.   col. maps.   38cm.

7407   American Hotel Register Co.
Leahy's hotel-motel guide and travel atlas of the United
States, Canada and Mexico.   100ed.   Chicago, 1975.
296p.   col. maps.   38cm.

7408   American Map Co., Inc.
Cleartype business control atlas of the United States and
Canada.   New York, [1962].
120p.   28cm.

7409   American Map Co., Inc.
Cleartype business control atlas of the United States and
Canada.   New York, 1970.
120p.   29cm.

7410   American Map Co., Inc.
Cleartype business control atlas of the United States and
Canada.   New York, 1971.
120p.   28cm.

7411   American Map Co., Inc.
Cleartype business control atlas of the United States and
Canada.   New York, 1972.
128p.   28cm.

7412   American Map Co., Inc.
Cleartype business control atlas of the United States and
Canada.   New York, 1973.
128p.   28cm.

7413   American Map Co., Inc.
Cleartype business control atlas of the United States and
Canada.   New York, 1974.
128p.   28cm.

7414   American Map Co., Inc.
Cleartype transcontinental highway atlas; United States,
Canada, Mexico.   New York, [1950].
16p.   col. maps.   40cm.

7415   American Oil Co.
       American road atlas.   With Diversified Map Corp.   Ra-
       cine, Wisc., [1971].
       114p.   col.   maps.   28cm.

7416   Artists & Writers Press.
       Holiday Inn travel guide and road atlas.   With General
       Drafting.   New York, [1961].
       80p.   col.   maps.   28cm.

7417   Brown & Bigelow.
       Automobile Travl-map road atlas for easier traveling.
       St. Paul, Minn., [1950].
       48p.   col.   maps.   26cm.

7418   Brown & Bigelow.
       Travl-map road atlas.   St. Paul, Minn., [1951].
       48p.   col.   maps.   26cm.

7419   Camping Maps, U.S.A.
       Camping maps, U.S.A.   By Glenn and Dale Rhodes.
       Upper Montclair, N.J., [1957].
       70p.   22cm.

7420   Camping Maps, U.S.A.
       Camping maps, U.S.A.   By Glenn and Dale Rhodes.
       Upper Montclair, N.J., [1961].
       206p.   22cm.

7421   Camping Maps, U.S.A.
       Private campgrounds and overnight trailer parks.   Palos
       Verdes Peninsula, Calif., 1968.
       256p.   22cm.

7422   Cram, George F., Co.
       Cram's easy reference business-man's atlas of the United
       States.   4ed.   Indianapolis, Ind., [1952].
       264p.   col.   maps.   38cm.

7423   Cram, George F., Co.
       Cram's easy reference business-man's atlas of the United
       States.   5ed.   Indianapolis, Ind., [1962].
       248p.   col.   maps.   38cm.

7424   Cram, George F., Co.
       Cram's road atlas of the United States, Canada, Mexico.
       Indianapolis, Ind., 1958.
       64p.   col.   maps.   31cm.

7425   Cram, George F., Co.
       Cram's road atlas of the United States, Canada, Mexico.
       Indianapolis, Ind., [1960].
       64p.   col.   maps.   31cm.

7426   Czechoslovakia. Ústřední správa geodézie a kartografie.
        Spojené státy americké. 1ed.   By Jiří Novotný.   Praha,
        1962.
        68p.   col.   maps.   27cm.

7427   Czechoslovakia. Ústřední správa geodézie a kartografie.
        Spojené státy americké. 2ed.   By Jiří Novotný.   Praha,
        1965.
        75p.   col.   maps.   27cm.

7428   Denoyer-Geppert Co.
        American history atlas.   9ed.   Chicago, [1953].
        48p.   col.   maps.   28cm.

7429   Denoyer-Geppert Co.
        Denoyer-Geppert atlas of American history.   1ed.   By
        Edgar B. Wesley.   Chicago, [1957].
        32p.   col.   maps.   28cm.

7430   Denoyer-Geppert Co.
        Our United States; its history in maps.   By Edgar B.
        Wesley.   Chicago, [1957].
        96p.   col.   maps.   28cm.

7431   Denoyer-Geppert Co.
        Our United States; its history in maps.   2ed.   By Edgar
        B. Wesley.   Chicago, [1961].
        96p.   col.   maps.   28cm.

7432   Denoyer-Geppert Co.
        Our United States; its history in maps.   3ed.   By Edgar
        B. Wesley.   Chicago, [1965].
        96p.   col.   maps.   28cm.

7433   Denoyer-Geppert Co.
        Our United States; its history in maps.   By Edgar Bruce
        Wesley.   Chicago, 1968.
        96p.   col.   maps.   28cm.

7434   Denoyer-Geppert Co.
        Our United States; its history in maps.   4ed.   By Edgar
        Bruce Wesley.   Chicago, 1971.
        96p.   col.   maps.   28cm.

7435   Diversified Map Corporation.
        American road atlas.   [U.S.]   With American Oil Co.
        St. Louis, Mo., 1971.
        114p.   col.   maps.   28cm.

7436   Diversified Map Corporation.
        American road atlas.   With Western Pub. Co., St. Louis,
        Mo., [1971].
        114p.   col.   maps.   28cm.

7437   Diversified Map Corporation.
       Diversified Map Corporation road atlas.   St. Louis, Mo.,
       1968.
       84p.   col. maps.   23cm.

7438   Diversified Map Corporation.
       Interstate atlas.   United States, Canada, Mexico.   St.
       Louis, Mo., 1969.
       64p.   col. maps.   23cm.

7439   Diversified Map Corporation.
       Pocket road atlas of the United States, Canada and Mexico.
       St. Louis, Mo., 1969.
       64p.   col. maps.   21.5cm.

7440   Diversified Map Corporation.
       Road atlas of the United States, Canada, and Mexico.
       St. Louis, Mo., 1968.
       144p.   col. maps.   34cm.

7441   Diversified Map Corporation.
       The new Grosset road atlas of the United States, Canada
       and Mexico.   St. Louis, [1973].
       128p.   col. maps.   34cm.

7442   Donnelley, R. R. & Sons, Co.
       1973 travel guide and atlas.   Chicago, [1973].
       48p.   col. maps.   31cm.

7443   Donnelley, R. R. & Sons, Co.
       Shell USA travel guide.   Chicago, [1970].
       31p.   col. maps.   26cm.

7444   Donnelley, R. R. & Sons, Co.
       Shell USA travel guide.   Chicago, 1971.
       31p.   col. maps.   26cm.

7445   Elving, Bruce F.
       FM atlas and station directory, U.S., Canada.   Duluth,
       Minn., 1971.
       48p.   28cm.

7446   Farmers Insurance Group.
       National road atlas.   With H. M. Gousha.   Los Angeles,
       Calif., 1961.
       64p.   col. maps.   26cm.

7447   General Drafting Co.
       HTC travel atlas.   With Humble Travel Club.   Houston,
       Texas, 1970.
       96p.   col. maps.   29cm.

7448   General Drafting Co.

HTC travel atlas. With Humble Travel Club. Houston, Texas, [1971].
84p. col. maps. 29cm.

7449 General Drafting Co.
Travel atlas. With Exxon Travel Club. Houston, Tex., [1973].
84p. col. maps. 29cm.

7450 Goushá, H. M., Co.
American highway atlas. Chicago, [1955].
98p. col. maps. 46cm.

7451 Goushá, H. M., Co.
American highway atlas. Chicago, [1956].
98p. col. maps. 46cm.

7452 Goushá, H. M., Co.
American highway atlas. 3ed. New York, [1957].
102p. col. maps. 46cm.

7453 Goushá, H. M., Co.
American highway atlas. 4ed. New York, [1959].
103p. col. maps. 46cm.

7454 Goushá, H. M., Co.
American highway atlas. 5ed. New York, [1960].
103p. col. maps. 46cm.

7455 Goushá, H. M., Co.
American highway atlas. Chicago, [1961].
103p. col. maps. 46cm.

7456 Goushá, H. M., Co.
National road atlas, United States, Canada, Mexico.
Chicago, San Jose, Calif., [1957].
48p. col. maps. 26cm.

7457 Goushá, H. M., Co.
New redi-map road atlas. With Brown & Bigelow.
Chicago, San Jose, Calif., [1951].
32p. col. maps. 26cm.

7458 Goushá, H. M., Co.
New redi-map; maps of the 48 states. With Brown & Bigelow. Chicago, [1952].
32p. col. maps. 26cm.

7459 Goushá, H. M., Co.
New redi-map road atlas with maps of 48 states. With Brown & Bigelow. Chicago, San Jose, Calif., [1954].
48p. col. maps. 26cm.

7460   Goushá, H. M., Co.
       Redi-map road atlas with maps of 48 states.   With Brown
       & Bigelow.   Chicago, San Jose, Calif., [1955].
       48p.   col. maps.   26cm.

7461   Goushá, H. M., Co.
       Redi-map road atlas with maps of 48 states.   With Brown
       & Bigelow.   Chicago, San Jose, Calif., [1956].
       48p.   col. maps.   26cm.

7462   Goushá, H. M., Co.
       United States road atlas.   San Jose, Calif., [1962].
       64p.   col. maps.   26cm.

7463   Goushá, H. M., Co.
       Vacation guide and road atlas.   United States, Canada,
       Mexico.   With Brown & Bigelow.   Chicago, San Jose,
       Calif., [1957].
       48p.   col. maps.   26cm.

7464   Goushá, H. M., Co.
       Vacation guide and road atlas.   United States, Canada and
       Mexico.   With Brown & Bigelow.   Chicago, San Jose,
       Calif., [1958].
       48p.   col. maps.   26cm.

7465   Hammond, C. S. & Co., Inc.
       Hammond's indexed atlas of the United States.   New York,
       1952.
       160p.   col. maps.   32cm.

7466   Hammond, C. S. & Co., Inc.
       Hammond's popular atlas of the United States.   Maplewood,
       N.J., [1958].
       112p.   col. maps.   32cm.

7467   Hammond, C. S. & Co., Inc.
       Hammond's popular atlas of the United States.   Maplewood,
       N.J., [1960].
       112p.   col. maps.   32cm.

7468   Hammond, C. S. & Co., Inc.
       Hammond's road atlas and city street guide of the United
       States, Canada, Mexico.   Maplewood, N.J., 1962.
       96p.   col. maps.   31cm.

7469   Hammond, C. S. & Co., Inc.
       Hammond road atlas of the United States, Canada, Mexico.
       Maplewood, N.J., 1966.
       48p.   col. maps.   32cm.

7470   Hammond, Inc.
       American history atlas.   Maplewood, N.J., 1969.

40p.   col.   maps.   31cm.

7471   Hammond, Inc.
       Hammond compact road atlas and vacation guide.   Maple-
       wood, N. J., [1973].
       48p.   col.   maps.   22cm.

7472   Hammond, Inc.
       History atlas of America.   Maplewood, N. J., [1971].
       31p.   col.   maps.   26cm.

7473   Hammond, Inc.
       Road atlas and travel guide, U. S.   Maplewood, N. J., 1971.
       48p.   col.   maps.   28cm.

7474   Hammond, Inc.
       United States history atlas.   Maplewood, N. J., [1971].
       64p.   col.   maps.   31cm.

7475   Hammond, Inc.
       United States history atlas.   Maplewood, N. J., 1973.
       64p.   col.   maps.   31cm.

7476   Hartford Fire Insurance Co.
       United States road atlas, including Canada and Mexico.
       With H. M. Gousha.   Hartford, Conn., [1959].
       56p.   col.   maps.   26cm.

7477   Hartford Fire Insurance Co.
       United States road atlas, including Canada and Mexico.
       With H. M. Gousha.   Hartford, Conn., [1960].
       56p.   col.   maps.   26cm.

7478   Humble Travel Club.
       HTC travel atlas.   With General Drafting Co.   Houston,
       Texas, [1971].
       84p.   col.   maps.   29cm.

7479   Macmillan & Co., Ltd.
       Camping maps U. S. A.   By Glenn and Dale Rhodes.   New
       York, 1968.
       436p.   26cm.

7480   Merriam, G. & C., Co.
       Webster's atlas and zipcode directory.   With Hammond.
       Springfield, Mass., [1973].
       352p.   col.   maps.   32cm.

7481   National Bus Traffic Association.
       Atlas of motor bus routes and express blocks no. A-602.
       Chicago, 1956.
       72p.   40cm.

7482   National Bus Traffic Association.
       Atlas of motor bus routes; showing operations of intercity
       bus carriers in the United States, Canada, Mexico.   Chi-
       cago, [1953].
       81p.   46cm.

7483   National Safety Council.
       National Safety Council road atlas, travel safety guide.
       With H. M. Gousha.   Chicago, [1964].
       64p.   col. maps.   28cm.

7484   National Safety Council.
       Travel safety guide and road atlas.   With Gousha.   Chi-
       cago, [1967].
       64p.   col. maps.   28cm.

7485   Oxford University Press.
       Oxford regional economic atlas of the U. S. and Canada.
       2ed.   London, 1975.
       180p.   col. maps.   27cm.

7486   Rand McNally & Co.
       Chevrolet's family travel guide.   Chicago, 1968.
       128p.   col. maps.   28cm.

7487   Rand McNally & Co.
       Rand McNally book of the United States; an illustrated
       atlas of today's world.   Chicago, [1963].
       176p.   col. maps.   29cm.

7488   Rand McNally & Co.
       Rand McNally commercial atlas and marketing guide.
       102ed.   Chicago, 1971.
       657p.   col. maps.   53cm.

7489   Rand McNally & Co.
       Rand McNally commercial atlas and marketing guide.
       103ed.   Chicago, 1972.
       667p.   col. maps.   53cm.

7490   Rand McNally & Co.
       Rand McNally commercial atlas and marketing guide.
       104ed.   Chicago, 1973.
       667p.   col. maps.   53cm.

7491   Rand McNally & Co.
       Rand McNally commercial atlas and marketing guide.
       105ed.   Chicago, 1974.
       669p.   col. maps.   53cm.

7492   Rand McNally & Co.
       Rand McNally commercial atlas and marketing guide.
       106ed.   Chicago, 1975.

669p.   col. maps.   53cm.

7493 Rand McNally & Co.
      Rand McNally handy railroad atlas of the United States.
      Chicago, 1971.
      64p.   31cm.

7494 Rand McNally & Co.
      Rand McNally handy railroad atlas of the United States.
      Chicago, 1973.
      64p.   31cm.

7495 Rand McNally & Co.
      Rand McNally illustrated road guide.   Chicago, 1956.
      48p.   col. maps.   23cm.

7496 Rand McNally & Co.
      Rand McNally interstate highway atlas.   Pocket ed.   Chi-
      cago, 1971.
      32p.   col. maps.   20cm.

7497 Rand McNally & Co.
      Rand McNally interstate highway atlas.   Pocket ed.   Chi-
      cago, 1972.
      32p.   col. maps.   20cm.

7498 Rand McNally & Co.
      Rand McNally interstate road atlas.   Chicago, 1974.
      96p.   col. maps.   28cm.

7499 Rand McNally & Co.
      Rand McNally road atlas and radio guide of the United
      States.   Chicago, 1950.
      88p.   col. maps.   27cm.

7500 Rand McNally & Co.
      Rand McNally road atlas and radio guide of the United
      States.   Chicago, 1951.
      88p.   col. maps.   27cm.

7501 Rand McNally & Co.
      Rand McNally road atlas and radio guide of the United
      States.   Chicago, 1952.
      96p.   col. maps.   27cm.

7502 Rand McNally & Co.
      Rand McNally road atlas and radio guide of the United
      States.   Chicago, 1957.
      96p.   col. maps.   27cm.

7503 Rand McNally & Co.
      Rand McNally road atlas and radio guide of the United
      States.   Chicago, 1958.

96p. col. maps. 27cm.

7504 Rand McNally & Co.
      Rand McNally road atlas. Golden anniversary ed. Chi-
      cago, 1974.
      160p. col. maps. 40cm.

7505 Rand McNally & Co.
      Rand McNally road atlas, United States, Canada, Mexico.
      Chicago, 1971.
      118p. col. maps. 40cm.

7506 Rand McNally & Co.
      Rand McNally road atlas, United States, Canada, Mexico.
      Chicago, 1972.
      128p. col. maps. 40cm.

7507 Rand McNally & Co.
      Rand McNally road atlas, United States, Canada, Mexico.
      Chicago, 1973.
      128p. col. maps. 40cm.

7508 Rand McNally & Co.
      Rand McNally road atlas, United States, Canada, Mexico.
      Chicago, 1974.
      160p. col. maps. 40cm.

7509 Rand McNally & Co.
      Rand McNally road atlas, United States, Canada, Mexico.
      Chicago, 1975.
      160p. col. maps. 40cm.

7510 Rand McNally & Co.
      Rand McNally road atlas, U.S., Canada, Mexico. 50 an-
      niversary ed. Chicago, 1974.
      136p. col. maps. 40cm.

7511 Rand McNally & Co.
      Rand McNally sales control atlas of the United States.
      New York, Chicago, 1959.
      96p. col. maps. 31cm.

7512 Rand McNally & Co.
      Rand McNally travel atlas. Chicago, 1974.
      224p. col. maps. 27cm.

7513 Rand McNally & Co.
      Rand McNally zip code atlas; state maps and marketing
      data for the newest system of marketing units--the 561
      zip code sectional areas. By Richard L. Forstall. Chi-
      cago, [1970].
      136p. col. maps. 28cm.

7514   Rand McNally & Co.
       Road atlas & travel guide, United States, Canada, Mexico.
       Chicago, 1971.
       96p.   col. maps.   27cm.

7515   Rand McNally & Co.
       Road atlas & travel guide, United States, Canada, Mexico.
       Chicago, 1972.
       96p.   col. maps.   27cm.

7516   Rand McNally & Co.
       Texaco international road atlas.   New York, 1959.
       48p.   col. maps.   25cm.

7517   Rand McNally & Co.
       Texaco international road atlas.   New York, 1961.
       48p.   col. maps.   25cm.

7518   Rand McNally & Co.
       Texaco touring maps.   New York, [1952].
       72p.   col. maps.   82cm.

7519   Rand McNally & Co.
       Texaco travel atlas: United States, Canada, Mexico.
       Chicago, [1971].
       224p.   col. maps.   38cm.

7520   Rand McNally & Co.
       Texaco travel atlas: United States, Canada, Mexico.
       Chicago, 1972.
       224p.   col. maps.   38cm.

7521   Rand McNally & Co.
       Texaco travel atlas: United States, Canada, Mexico.
       Chicago, [1973].
       224p.   col. maps.   38cm.

7522   Rand McNally & Co.
       These states united: atlas of American history.   Chicago,
       [1974].
       64p.   col. maps.   29cm.

7523   Rand McNally & Co.
       Zip code atlas.   Chicago, 1970.
       130p.   col. maps.   27cm.

7524   Skelly Oil Co.
       Skelly highway atlas.   With H. M. Gousha.   Tulsa, Okla.,
       [1959].
       56p.   col. maps.   26cm.

7525   U.S. Department of Agriculture.
       Atlas of the river basins of the United States.   2ed.

Washington, D.C., 1970.
82p. col. maps. 56cm.

7526 U.S. Department of Agriculture.
      Atlas of United States trees. By Elbert L. Little, Jr.
      Washington, D.C., 1971.
      in parts. 36cm.

7527 U.S. Department of Commerce.
      Congressional district atlas. Washington, D.C., [1960].
      99p. 29cm.

7528 U.S. Department of Commerce.
      Congressional district atlas. Washington, D.C., 1970.
      218p. 29cm.

7529 U.S. Department of Commerce.
      Congressional district atlas. Washington, D.C., 1973.
      1 vol. 29cm.

7530 U.S. Forest Service.
      Atlas of United States trees. By Elbert L. Little, Jr.
      Washington, D.C., 1971-
      in parts. 36cm.

7531 Water Information Center, Inc.
      Water atlas of the United States. 3ed. Port Washington,
      N.Y., 1973.
      200p. col. maps. 34cm.

7532 Western Pub. Co.
      American road atlas. With Diversified Map Corp. Wayne,
      N.J., [1971].
      114p. col. maps. 28cm.

SOUTH AMERICA

Argentina

7533 Argentina. Departmento de Agrometeorología.
Atlas agroclimático argentino. Buenos Aires, 1953.
15p. col. maps. 32cm.

7534 Argentina. Instituto Geográfico Militar.
Atlas de la República Argentina, físico, político y
estadístico. 1ed. Buenos Aires, 1953.
90p. col. maps. 49cm.

7535 Argentina. Instituto Geográfico Militar.
Atlas de la República Argentina. 2ed. Buenos Aires,
1959.
20p. col. maps. 40cm.

7536 Argentina. Instituto Geográfico Militar.
Atlas de la República Argentina. 4ed. Buenos Aires,
[1970].
28p. col. maps. 40cm.

7537 Argentina. Instituto Geográfico Militar.
Atlas de la República Argentina. Buenos Aires, 1972.
122p. col. maps. 31cm.

7538 Argentina. Instituto Geográfico Militar.
Atlas del potencial Argentino. 1ed. By J. Quargnolo.
Buenos Aires, 1972.
159p. col. maps. 33cm.

7539 Argentina. Ministerio de Agricultura y Gandaría.
Mapa ecológico de la República Argentina. [Atlas.]
By Juan Papadakis. Buenos Aires, 1951.
2 vol. col. maps. 33cm.

7540 Argentina. Servicio Meteorológico Nacional.
Atlas climático de la República Argentina. Buenos Aires,
1960.
85p. col. maps. 48cm.

7541 Ediciones G. L. G.
Compendio geográfico y atlas Argentina. By Roberto
Manuel Cayo. Buenos Aires, 1965.
70p. col. maps. 26cm.

7542   Editorial Estrada.
       Atlas del potencial Argentino.   1ed.   By J. Quargnolo.
       Buenos Aires, 1972.
       159p. col. maps. 33cm.

7543   Firestone de la Argentina, S. A.
       Mapa Firestone; red caminera de la República Argentina.
       Buenos Aires, [1950].
       15p. col. maps. 28cm.

7544   Industrias Kaiser Argentina, S. A.
       Atlas vial IKA. Buenos Aires, 1960.
       111p. col. maps. 23cm.

7545   Kapelusz y Cía.
       Coloratlas Kapelusz Mundi: físico, político, económico,
       estadístico. Buenos Aires, 1971.
       78p. col. maps. 32cm.

7546   Kapelusz y Cía.
       Coloratlas Kapelusz: República Argentina.   Buenos Aires,
       [1971].
       1 vol. col. maps. 32cm.

7547   Kapelusz y Cía.
       Coloratlas regional Argentina: físico, político, económico.
       1ed. Buenos Aires, [1973].
       68p. col. maps. 32cm.

7548   Peuser, Ediciones Geográficas.
       Nuevo atlas geográfico de la Argentina.   5ed.   By José
       Anesi. Buenos Aires, 1958.
       27p. col. maps. 37cm.

7549   Peuser, Ediciones Geográficas.
       Nuevo atlas geográfico de la Argentina.   8ed.   By José
       Anesi. Buenos Aires, 1969.
       24p. col. maps. 37cm.

7550   Peuser, Ediciones Geográficas.
       Nuevo atlas universal. Buenos Aires, [1972].
       80p. col. maps. 37cm.

Bolivia

7551   Gisbert y Cía, S. A.
       Atlas económico de Bolivia.   By Alfredo Ayala Z.   La
       Paz, 1954.
       10p. col. maps. 30cm.

7552   Gisbert y Cía, S. A.
       Atlas escolar de Bolívia.   By Alfredo Ayala Z.   La
       Paz, 1953.

       25p. col. maps. 29cm.

7553 Gisbert y Cía, S. A.
     Atlas escolar de Bolívia. By Alfredo Ayala Z. La Paz,
     [1960].
     25p. col. maps. 29cm.

Brazil

7554 Alves, Francisco.
     Nôvo atlas de geografia. Rev. ed. By J. Monteiro and
     F. d'Oliveira. Rio de Janeiro, 1969.
     56p. col. maps. 31cm.

7555 Brazil. Departamento nacional de estradas de rodagem.
     Atlas rodoviário provisório. Rio de Janeiro, [1970].
     2 vol. 49cm.

7556 Brazil. Instituto brasileiro de geografia et estatística.
     Atlas geográfico escolar. 6ed. Rio de Janeiro, [1970].
     57p. col. maps. 31cm.

7557 Brazil. Instituto brasileiro de geografia e estatística.
     Carta do Brasil ao milionésimo. Rio de Janeiro, 1960.
     190p. col. maps. 55cm.

7558 Brazil. Ministério da educação e cultura.
     Atlas histórico e geográfico brasileiro. 2ed. Rio de
     Janeiro, 1970.
     66p. col. maps. 32cm.

7559 Edições Melhoramentos.
     Atlas das potencialidades brasileiras. 1ed. Rio de
     Janeiro, [1974].
     158p. 38cm.

7560 Edições Melhoramentos.
     Atlas geográfico Melhoramentos. By Geraldo José Pau-
     wels. São Paulo, 1961.
     95p. col. maps. 35cm.

7561 Edições Melhoramentos.
     Atlas geográfico Melhoramentos. 28ed. By Geraldo José
     Pauwels. São Paulo, [1969].
     99p. col. maps. 35cm.

7562 Edições Melhoramentos.
     Atlas geográfico universal Melhoramentos. 29ed. By
     Geraldo José Pauwels. São Paulo, 1970.
     99p. col. maps. 35cm.

7563 Edições Melhoramentos.
     Atlas geográfico Melhoramentos. By Geraldo José Pau-

wels.   São Paulo, 1971.
100p.   col. maps.   34cm.

7564   Edições Melhoramentos.
       Atlas geográfico universal Melhoramentos.   By Geraldo
       José Pauwels.   São Paulo, 1972.
       100p.   col. maps.   35cm.

7565   Editôra Globo.
       Atlas do Brasil, Globo.   By Rudolf Ira and Edgar Klettner.
       Rio de Janiero, [1953].
       67p.   col. maps.   45cm.

7566   Livros Cadernos.
       Brasil, geografia regional; caderno de mapas.   By Levino
       de Moura and Heloisa Fortes de Oliveira.   Rio de Janeiro,
       [1970].
       42p.   col. maps.   33cm.

Chile

7567   Automóvil Club de Chile.
       Atlas caminero de Chile.   1ed.   By José Francisco Silva
       C.   Santiago, 1971.
       1 vol.   col. maps.   33cm.

7568   Chile.   Departamento de Caminos.
       Cartas camineras provinciales.   Santiago de Chile, 1951.
       1 vol.   col. maps.   33cm.

7569   Chile.   Instituto geográfico militar.
       Album con cartas preliminares.   Santiago de Chile, 1954-
       1970.
       102p.   col. maps.   56cm.

7570   Chile.   Instituto geográfico militar.
       Atlas de la República de Chile.   2ed.   Santiago de Chile,
       [1970].
       249p.   col. maps.   41cm.

7571   Chile.   Instituto hydrografico de la armada.
       Atlas oceanografico de Chile.   Valparaiso, 1972.
       21p.   col. maps.   45cm.

Colombia

7572   Aguilar, S. A. de Ediciones.
       Atlas bachillerato universal y de Colombia.   By Antonio
       López Gómez.   Madrid, 1971.
       120p.   col. maps.   35cm.

7573   Aguilar, S. A. de Ediciones.
       Atlas medio universal y de Colombia.   Madrid, 1958.

140p.   col.   maps.   31cm.

7574   Codazzi, Instituto Geográfico.
       Atlas básico de Colombia.   Bogotá, 1970.
       106p.   col.   maps.   32cm.

7575   Codazzi, Instituto Geográfico.
       Atlas de Colombia.   2ed.   Bogotá, 1969.
       216p.   col.   maps.   45cm.

7576   Colombia.   Departmento Administrativo Nacional de Estadistica.
       División político-administrativa de Colombia.   By Ernesto
       Rojas Morales.   Bogotá, [1970].
       180p.   col.   maps.   27cm.

7577   Editorial Colina.
       Atlas de Colombia.   Medellín, [1963].
       1 vol.   col.   maps.   15cm.

7578   Litografía Arco.
       Atlas de mapas antiguos de Colombia.   By Eduardo
       Acevedo Latorre.   Bogotá, 1971.
       169p.   col.   maps.   46cm.

Ecuador

7579   Ecuador.   Junta Nacional de Plantificación y Coordinación
       Económica.
       Principales aspectos socio económicos del país; informa-
       ción gráfica.   Quito, 1967.
       27p.   col.   maps.   58cm.

7580   Publicaciones Educativas Ariel.
       Atlas del Ecuador.   Guayaquil, [1970].
       16p.   col.   maps.   22cm.

Paraguay

7581   Ferreira Gubetich, Hugo.
       Paraguay.   [Atlas.]   Asunción, [1960].
       12p.   col.   maps.   26cm.

7582   Ponte, Alberto da.
       Atlas de la República de Paraguay por departmentos.
       Asunción, [1950].
       16p.   col.   maps.   28cm.

Peru

7583   Compañia de Seguros "Atlas."
       Atlas geográfico de Perú.   Lima, [1955].
       19p.   50cm.

7584   Editorial F. T. D.
       Atlas universal y del Peru.   Lima, 1969.
       25p.   col. maps.   28cm.

7585   Peru.   Instituto Nacional de Planificación.
       Atlas histórico geográfico y de paisajes peruanos.   By
       Carlos Peñaherrera del Aguila.   Lima, [1970].
       737p.   col. maps.   58cm.

7586   Peru.   Ministerio de Trabajo y Asuntos Indigenas.
       Atlas comunal.   Republica del Peru.   Lima, 1964.
       2 vol.   col. maps.   29cm.

Surinam

7587   Kessel, M. S. van.
       Atlas van Suriname.   7ed.   Paramaribo, [1960].
       24p.   32cm.

Uruguay

7588   Barreiro & Ramos.
       Atlas del Uruguay.   By Pedro Martín.   Montevideo, [1971].
       23p.   col. maps.   22cm.

7589   Martín, Pedro.
       Atlas del Uruguay.   Montevideo, [1957].
       23p.   col. maps.   22cm.

7590   Uruguay.   Dirección General de Estadística y Censos.   De-
       partmento de Cartografía.
       Mapas departmentales.   Montevideo, [1969].
       22p.   29cm.

Venezuela

7591   Compañia Shell de Venezuela.
       Carreteras de Venezuela.   3ed.   Caracas, [1960].
       23p.   19cm.

7592   Ediciones Nueva Cádiz.
       Atlas de bolsillo de Venezuela; datos geográficos, división
       política, vías de comunicatión.   6ed.   Caracas, 1952.
       73p.   col. maps.   14cm.

7593   Ediciones Nueva Cádiz.
       Atlas de bolsillo de Venezuela; datos geográficos, división
       política, vías de comunicatión.   7ed.   Caracas, 1953.
       73p.   col. maps.   14cm.

7594   Ediciones Nueva Cádiz.
       Atlas de bolsillo de Venezuela; datos geográficos, división
       política, vías de comunicacion.   8ed.   Caracas, 1954.

        145p.   col. maps.   14cm.

7595   Litografía Miangolarra Hnos.
        Atlas de bolsillo de Venezuela.   8ed.   By Juan Jones
        Parra.   Caracas, 1954.
        157p.   col. maps.   15cm.

7596   Litografía Miangolarra Hnos.
        Atlas de bolsillo de Venezuela.   9ed.   By Juan Jones
        Parra.   Caracas, 1957.
        157p.   col. maps.   15cm.

7597   Litografía Miangolarra Hnos.
        Pocket atlas of Venezuela.   (English ed.)   Caracas, 1957.
        160p.   col. maps.   15cm.

7598   Shell Caribbean Petroleum Company.
        Carreteras de Venezuela.   Caracas, [1951].
        19p.   18cm.

7599   Società Cartografica G. De Agostini.
        Atlas escolar de Venezuela.   Milano, 1950.
        94p.   col. maps.   24cm.

7600   Venezuela.   Dirección de cartografía nacional.
        Atlas de Venezuela.   Caracas, [1972].
        210p.   col. maps.   45cm.

AGRICULTURE

7601 Beazley, Mitchell, Ltd.
      The world atlas of wine. By Hugh Johnson. London,
      1971.
      272p. col. maps. 28cm.

7602 British Sulphur Corp. , Ltd.
      World fertilizer atlas. 4ed. London, 1973.
      103p. col. maps. 30cm.

7603 British Sulphur Corp, Ltd.
      World sulphur and sulphuric acid atlas. London, 1971.
      137p. col. maps. 30cm.

7604 Congo. Commissarial Général au Plan.
      Atlas du Congo. Brazzaville, 1969.
      15p. col. maps. 62cm.

7605 Faber & Faber.
      An agricultural atlas of England and Wales. 2ed. By
      J. T. Coppock. London, 1974.
      255p. 25cm.

7606 France. Centre de recherches historique.
      Atlas des cultures vivrières; atlas of food crops. By
      Jacques Bertin. Paris, 1971.
      41p. 61cm.

7607 Ghana. Meteorological Services.
      Climatic maps of Ghana for agriculture. By Anthony
      K. L. Usscher. Legon, [1969].
      36p. 32cm.

7608 India. Ministry of Agriculture.
      An agricultural atlas of India. By J. Singh. Delhi, 1974.
      356p. col. maps. 25cm.

7609 Indian Central Jute Committee.
      The Indian jute atlas. Calcutta, 1959.
      89p. 31cm.

7610 Mouton & Co.
      Atlas des cultures vivrières. Atlas of food crops. By

Jacques Bertin.   Paris, [1971].
59p. col. maps. 42cm.

7611   Ramnarain Sons Limited.
Cotton map of India & Pakistan; silver jubilee publication.
Bombay, [1953].
27p. 31cm.

7612   Simon and Schuster.
The world atlas of wine.   By Hugh Johnson and Mitchell
Beazley.   London, New York, 1971.
272p. col. maps. 30cm.

7613   U. S. Central Intelligence Agency.
U. S. S. R. agricultural atlas.   Washington, D. C., 1974.
59p. col. maps. 57cm.

7614   U. S. Department of Agriculture.
Agricultural conservation program maps, 1955.   Washington, D. C., 1957.
49p. 28cm.

7615   U. S. S. R. Glavnoe upravlenie geodezii i kartografii.
Agroklimaticheskii atlas mira.   Moskva, 1972.
115p. col. maps. 41cm.

AIRWAYS see TRANSPORTATION

ARCHAEOLOGY

7616   McGraw Hill Book Co.
Atlas of ancient archaeology.   By J. Hawkes.   New York,
[1974].
272p. col. maps. 28cm.

7617   Thames and Hudson, Ltd.
Archaeological atlas of the world.   By David Whitehouse.
London, 1975.
272p. 25cm.

ASTRONOMY

7618   Beazley, Mitchell, Ltd.
The atlas of the universe.   1ed.   By Patrick Moore.
London, 1970.
272p. col. maps. 36cm.

7619   Beazley, Mitchell, Ltd.
The atlas of the universe.   By Patrick Moore.   London,
1971.
272p. col. maps. 36cm.

7620   Philip, George & Son, Ltd.

The atlas of the universe. 1ed. By Patrick Moore.
London, 1970.
272p. col. maps. 36cm.

7621 Philip, George & Son, Ltd.
      The atlas of the universe. 2ed. By Patrick Moore.
      London, 1971.
      272p. col. maps. 36cm.

7622 Rand McNally & Co.
      Atlas of the universe. 1st Canadian ed. By Stuart Kamin-
      sky and Charles Yoder. Chicago, 1971.
      1 vol. col. maps. 36cm.

7623 Rand McNally & Co.
      The atlas of the universe. By Patrick Moore. Chicago,
      1970.
      272p. col. maps. 36cm.

7624 Rand McNally & Co.
      The atlas of the universe. 2ed. By Patrick Moore.
      Chicago, 1971.
      272p. col. maps. 36cm.

BIBLE

7625 Baker.
      Pocket atlas of the bible. By Charles F. Pfeiffer. Grand
      Rapids, Mich., 1973.
      1 vol. col. maps. 29cm.

7626 Cappelens, J. W., Forlag, A. S.
      Cappelens atlas til kristendomsundervisning. By Kare
      Valle. Oslo, 1971.
      23p. col. maps. 28cm.

7627 Gyldendal.
      Gyldendals bibel-atlas. With Philip. København, 1968.
      1 vol. col. maps. 29cm.

7628 Herder Verlag.
      Atlas zur Kirchengeschichte; die christlichen Kirchen in
      Geschichte und Gegenwart. By Hubert Jedin. Freiburg,
      [1970].
      272p. col. maps. 34cm.

7629 Macmillan.
      Jewish history atlas. By Martin Gilbert. New York,
      1973.
      126p. 24cm.

7630 Macmillan.
      Historical atlas of the religions of the world. By Ismail

Ragi al Faruqi. New York, 1974.
346p. col. maps. 29cm.

7631 Nomi Forlag. ~
Bibelatlas; en oversikt over kirkens historie og utvikling.
By H. H. Rowley. Oslo, Stavanger, [1970].
49p. col. maps. 26cm.

7632 Office Général du Livre.
Atlas biblique. By G. Pesce. Paris, 1972.
252p. col. maps. 31cm.

7633 Oxford University Press.
Oxford bible atlas. 2ed. By Herbert G. May. New
York, 1974.
144p. col. maps. 26cm.

7634 Pont. institutum orientalium studi orum.
Atlas hierarchicus ecclesiarum catholicarum orientalium.
3ed. By Michael Lacko. Rome, 1972.
24p. 25cm.

7635 Religious Education Press.
Atlas of man and religion. By Gordon K. Hawes. Oxford, New York, 1970.
127p. col. maps. 28cm.

7636 World Pub. Co.
Atlas of the Biblical world. By Denis Baly and A. D.
Tushingham. New York, 1971.
209p. col. maps. 29cm.

BOTANY

7637 Nelson, Thomas & Sons, Ltd.
Critical supplement to the Atlas of British flora. By
F. H. Perring and P. D. Sell. London, [1970].
168p. 38cm.

7638 U. S. Department of Agriculture.
Atlas of United States trees. By Elbert L. Little, Jr.
Washington, D. C., 1971.
in parts. 36cm.

7639 U. S. Forest Service.
Atlas of United States trees. By Elbert L. Little, Jr.
Washington, D. C., 1971-
in parts. 36cm.

CAMPING

7640 Alpine Geographical Press.
Campground atlas of the United States and Canada. By

James A. Bier and Henry A. Raup. Champaign, Ill.,
1971.
320p. col. maps. 28cm.

7641   Camping Maps, U.S.A.
       Camping maps, Canada. By Glenn and Dale Rhodes.
       Upper Montclair, N.J., 1961.
       58p. 22cm.

7642   Camping Maps, U.S.A.
       Camping maps, U.S.A. By Glenn and Dale Rhodes.
       Upper Montclair, N.J., [1957].
       70p. 22cm.

7643   Camping Maps, U.S.A.
       Camping maps, U.S.A. By Glenn and Dale Rhodes.
       Upper Montclair, N.J., [1961].
       206p. 22cm.

7644   Camping Maps, U.S.A.
       Private campgrounds and overnight trailer parks. Palos
       Verdes Peninsula, Calif., 1968.
       256p. 22cm.

7645   Climatic Data Press.
       Mexico campground guide and trailer atlas. By Frederick
       L. Wernstedt. Lemont, Pa., [1974].
       54p. col. maps. 31cm.

7646   Generalstabens litografiska anstalt.
       Europa camping and caravaning. Stockholm, 1966/67.
       1 vol. col. maps. 30cm.

7647   Macmillan & Co., Ltd.
       Camping maps U.S.A. By Glenn and Dale Rhodes. New
       York, 1968.
       436p. 26cm.

CLIMATE

7648   Argentina. Departamento de Agrometeorología.
       Atlas agroclimático argentino. Buenos Aires, 1953.
       15p. col. maps. 32cm.

7649   Argentina. Servicio Meteorológico Nacional.
       Atlas climático de la República Argentina. Buenos Aires,
       1960.
       85p. col. maps. 48cm.

7650   Brown, W. C., Co.
       Workbook of weather maps. 2ed. By John T. Hidore.
       Dubuque, Iowa, [1971].
       71p. 28cm.

7651   Canada.   Dept. of Transport.
       Atlas of climatic maps.   Ottawa, 1970.
       1 vol.   col.   maps.   39cm.

7652   Cartographia.
       Climatic atlas of Europe.   With Unesco.   Budapest, 1970-
       in parts.   col.   maps.   60cm.

7653   Congo.   Commissariat Général au Plan.
       Atlas du Congo.   Brazzaville, 1969.
       15p.   col.   maps.   62cm.

7654   Congo.   Institut national pour l'étude agronomoque.
       Atlas climatique du bassin congolais.   By Franz Bultot.
       Bruxelles, 1971-
       4 vol.   col.   maps.   33cm.

7655   France.   Direction de la météorologie nationale.
       Atlas climatique de la France.   By Jean Bessemoulin.
       Paris, 1969.
       45p.   col.   maps.   53cm.

7656   France.   Direction de la météorologie nationale.
       Atlas climatique de la France.   By Jean Bessemoulin.
       Paris, 1974.
       29p.   col.   maps.   30cm.

7657   Ghana.   Meteorological Services.
       Climatic maps of Ghana for agriculture.   By Anthony K.
       L. Usscher.   Legon, [1969].
       36p.   32cm.

7658   India.   Meteorological Dept.
       Climatological atlas of India, abridged.   New Delhi, 1971.
       40p.   col.   maps.   38cm.

7659   Jamaica.   Scientific Research Council.
       The Rainfall of Jamaica.   [Atlas.]   Kingston, 1963.
       19p.   col.   maps.   43cm.

7660   Japan.   Meteorological Agency.
       Climatic atlas of Japan.   Tokyo, 1971-72.
       2 vol.   col.   maps.   54cm.

7661   Jordan.   Meteorological Dept.
       Climatic atlas of Jordan.   Amman, 1971.
       127p.   30cm.

7662   Macmillan.
       British weather in maps.   2ed.   By James A. Taylor
       and R. A. Yates.   London, 1967.
       304p.   col.   maps.   23cm.

7663   Netherlands.   Meteorologisch Institut.
       Klimaatlas van Nederland.   de Bilt, 1972.
       77p.   col.   maps.   40cm.

7664   Poland.   Państwowe przedsiębiorstwo wydawnictw kartografi-
       cznych.
       Atlas klimatyczny Polski.   Warszawa, 1973.
       141p.   col.   maps.   47cm.

7665   Sahab.
       Climatic atlas of Iran.   With Univ. of Teheran.
       By M. H. Ganji.   Teheran, [1972].
       117p.   col.   maps.   42cm.

7666   Springer Verlag.
       Climate-diagram maps of the individual continents and
       the ecological climate regions of the earth.   Berlin, Hei-
       delberg, New York, 1975.
       36p.   40cm.

7667   Unesco.
       Climatic atlas of Europe.   Atlas climatique de l'Europe.
       By F. Steinhauser.   Geneva, Paris, 1970-
       in parts.   col.   maps.   60cm.

7668   University of Teheran.
       Climatic atlas of Iran.   By Ahmad Mostofi.   In English
       and Persian.   Teheran, 1965.
       117p.   col.   maps.   44cm.

7669   University of Teheran.
       Climatic atlas of Iran.   By M. H. Ganji.   Teheran,
       [1972].
       117p.   col.   maps.   42cm.

7670   U. S. S. R.   Akademia nauk.
       Klimaticheskii atlas Afriki.   Moskva, 1972.
       137p.   col.   maps.   35cm.

7671   U. S. S. R.   Akademia nauk.
       Klimaticheskii atlas S. S. S. R.   Moskva, 1960-62.
       2 vol.   col.   maps.   34cm.

7672   U. S. S. R.   Glavnoe upravlenie geodezii i kartografii.
       Agroklimaticheskii atlas mira.   Moskva, 1972.
       115p.   col.   maps.   41cm.

7673   U. S. S. R.   Nauchno-issledovatel'ski institut aeroklimatologii.
       Atlas kharakteristik vetra.   By I. G. Guterman and S. I.
       Dunayeva.   Moskva, 1967-70.
       2 vol.   35cm.

7674   World Meteorological Organization.

Climatic atlas of Europe. By F. Steinhauser. With
Cartographia. Budapest, 1970-
in parts. col. maps. 60cm.

COMMERCE see ECONOMIC

COMMUNICATION

7675 British Bureau of Television Advertising, Ltd.
The BBTA Marketing Manual of the United Kingdom 1970.
1ed. London, 1970.
1 vol. col. maps. 49cm.

7676 British Bureau of Television Advertising, Ltd.
The BBTA Marketing Manual of the United Kingdom. 2ed.
London, 1971.
1 vol. col. maps. 49cm.

7677 British Bureau of Television Advertising, Ltd.
The BBTA Marketing Manual of the United Kingdom. 3ed.
London, [1973].
1 vol. col. maps. 49cm.

7678 Elving, Bruce F.
FM atlas and station directory. U.S., Canada. Duluth,
Minn., 1971.
48p. 28cm.

7679 France. Ministère des postes et télécommunications.
Mémento de nomenclature géographique. Paris, 1967.
87p. 31cm.

7680 Generalstabens litografiska anstalt.
Post-och järnvägs karta över sverige. Stockholm, 1973.
10p. col. maps. 23cm.

7681 International Telecommunication Union.
Carte des stations terrestres ouvertes à la correspondance
publique avec les aéronefs. 1ed. Geneva, 1950.
12p. col. maps. 34cm.

7682 Norway. Postdirekforatet.
Pensumoversikt i utenriks postgeografi for kontoraspiranter;
postassistenkursene. Oslo, [1970].
16p. 32cm.

7683 Poståpnernes Landsforbund.
Post-, vej-og fylkeskarte. Oslo, [1960].
44p. col. maps. 23cm.

7684 Radio Amateur Callbook, Inc.
Radio amateurs' world atlas. Lake Bluff, Ill., 1970.
16p. col. maps. 31cm.

7685   Radio Amateur Callbook, Inc.
       Radio amateurs world atlas.   6ed.   Lake Bluff, Ill.,
       [1972].
       19p.   col.   maps.   31cm.

7686   Rand McNally & Co.
       Rand McNally road atlas and radio guide of the United
       States.   Chicago, 1950.
       88p.   col.   maps.   27cm.

7687   Rand McNally & Co.
       Rand McNally road atlas and radio guide of the United
       States.   Chicago, 1951.
       88p.   col.   maps.   27cm.

7688   Rand McNally & Co.
       Rand McNally road atlas and radio guide of the United
       States.   Chicago, 1952.
       96p.   col.   maps.   27cm.

7689   Rand McNally & Co.
       Rand McNally road atlas and radio guide of the United
       States.   Chicago, 1957.
       96p.   col.   maps.   27cm.

7690   Rand McNally & Co.
       Rand McNally road atlas and radio guide of the United
       States.   Chicago, 1958.
       96p.   col.   maps.   27cm.

7691   Rand McNally & Co.
       Zip code atlas.   Chicago, 1970.
       130p.   col.   maps.   27cm.

DEMOGRAPHY see POPULATION

DISCOVERY see HISTORY

ECOLOGY

7692   Argentina.   Ministerio de Agricultura y Gandaría.
       Mapa ecológico de la Republica Argentina.   [Atlas.]   By
       Juan Papadakis.   Buenos Aires, 1951.
       2 vol.   col.   maps.   33cm.

7693   Hammond, Inc.
       Nature atlas of America.   By Roland C. Clement.
       Maplewood, N.J., 1973.
       255p.   col.   maps.   32cm.

7694   Springer Verlag.
       Climate-diagram maps of the individual continents and the
       ecological climate regions of the earth.   Berlin, Heidelberg,

New York, 1975.
36p.   40cm.

ECONOMIC

7695   American Map Co., Inc.
       Cleartype business control atlas of the United States and
       Canada. New York, [1962].
       120p.   28cm.

7696   American Map Co., Inc.
       Cleartype business control atlas of the United States and
       Canada. New York, 1970.
       120p.   29cm.

7697   American Map Co., Inc.
       Cleartype business control atlas of the United States and
       Canada. New York, 1971.
       120p.   28cm.

7698   American Map Co., Inc.
       Cleartype business control atlas of the United States and
       Canada. New York, 1972.
       128p.   28cm.

7699   American Map Co., Inc.
       Cleartype business control atlas of the United States and
       Canada. New York, 1973.
       128p.   28cm.

7700   American Map Co., Inc.
       Cleartype business control atlas of the United States and
       Canada. New York, 1974.
       128p.   28cm.

7701   Anikasari.
       Atlas Indonesia. [In Indonesian.] Djakarta, [1971-].
       in parts.   35cm.

7702   Argentina. Instituto Geográfico Militar.
       Atlas de la República Argentina, físico, político y estadís-
       tico. 1ed. Buenos Aires, 1953.
       90p.   col. maps.   49cm.

7703   Argentina. Instituto Geográfico Militar.
       Atlas del potencial Argentino. 1ed. By J. Quargnolo.
       Buenos Aires, 1972.
       159p.   col. maps.   33cm.

7704   BLV Verlagsgesellschaft.
       Wirtschaftsgeographischer Weltatlas. 3ed. München,
       Bern, Wien, 1975.
       169p.   col. maps.   33cm.

7705   Brazil Instituto brasileiro de geografia et estatística.
       Atlas geográfico escolar.   6ed.   Rio de Janeiro, [1970].
       57p.   col.   maps.   31cm.

7706   Carleton University.
       A Computer atlas of Kenya.   By D. R. F. Taylor.   Ot-
       tawa, 1971.
       121p.   28cm.

7707   Cartographia.
       Illustrated political and economical world atlas.   3ed.
       Budapest, [1971].
       185p.   col.   maps.   34cm.

7708   Colin.
       Atlas des circonscriptions électorales en France depuis
       1875.   By Marie-Thérèse Lancelot and Alain Lancelot.
       Paris, 1970.
       95p.   35cm.

7709   Collins, William, Sons & Co., Ltd.
       An atlas of Papua and New Guinea.   By R. G. Ward and
       D. A. M. Lea.   Glasgow, 1970.
       101p.   26cm.

7710   Colombia.   Departmento Administrativo Nacional de Estadistica.
       División político-administrativa de Colombia.   By Ernesto
       Rojas Morales.   Bogotá, [1970].
       180p.   col.   maps.   27cm.

7711   Cram, George F., Co.
       Cram's easy reference business-man's atlas of the United
       States.   4ed.   Indianapolis, Ind., [1952].
       264p.   col.   maps.   38cm.

7712   Cram, George F., Co.
       Cram's easy reference business-man's atlas of the United
       States.   5ed.   Indianapolis, Ind., [1962].
       248p.   col.   maps.   38cm.

7713   Cuba.   Oficina Nacional de los Censos Demográfico y Elec-
       toral.
       Atlas censo 1953.   La Habana, [1958].
       160p.   49cm.

7714   Dreyers forlag.
       Økonomisk atlas.   By Tor Wisting.   Oslo, [1969].
       79p.   col.   maps.   29cm.

7715   Ecuador.   Junta Nacional de Planificación y Coordinación
       Económica.
       Principales aspectos socio económicos del país; informa-
       ción gráfica.   Quito, 1967.

27p.   col. maps.   58cm.

7716   E. D. A. F.
       El universo en color.   Gran atlas y geografía Edaf físico-
       político-económico.   Madrid, [1971].
       395p.   col. maps.   40cm.

7717   Edições Melhoramentos.
       Atlas das potencialidades brasileiras.   1ed.   Rio de
       Janeiro, [1974].
       158p.   38cm.

7718   Editions André Lesot.
       Atlas départemental de la France à l'usage des statis-
       ticiens, commerçants, industriels, agents de publicité,
       administrations publiques ou privées, etc.   Paris, [1970].
       1 vol.   23cm.

7719   Editions Stauffacher.
       Neuer Weltatlas.   By E. T. Rimli.   With Haack.   Zürich,
       1972.
       444p.   col. maps.   44cm.

7720   Editoria Estrada.
       Atlas del potencial Argentino.   1ed.   By J. Quargnolo.
       Buenos Aires, 1972.
       159p.   col. maps.   33cm.

7721   Editorial Teide.
       Atlas universal geo-económico.   With Istituto Geografico
       De Agostini.   Barcelona, [1973].
       160p.   col. maps.   31cm.

7722   France.   Électricité de France.
       Atlas: réseau general d'énergie électrique de France.
       Paris, 1969.
       1 vol.   col. maps.   34cm.

7723   France.   Électricité de France.
       Atlas, réseau général d'énergie électrique de France.
       Paris, 1971.
       116p.   col. maps.   34cm.

7724   France.   La Documentation Française.
       Atlas de la formation professionelle.   France.   Paris,
       [1969].
       2 vol.   col. maps.   65cm.

7725   France.   La Documentation Française.
       Atlas économique et social pour l'aménagement du
       territoire.   By T. Hautreux.   Paris, 1966-69.
       3 vol.   col. maps.   56cm.

7726   France.   Ministère de l'Éducation nationale.
       Atlas de l'Éducation nationale.   La Celle-Saint Cloud, 1970.
       3 vol.   col.   maps.   72cm.

7727   Generalstabens litografiska anstalt.
       Vä värld Latinamerika.   Politisk-ekonomisk atlas.   By
       Leif Söderström and Gunnar Schalin.   Stockholm, 1968.
       1 vol.   col.   maps.   22cm.

7728   Generalstabens litografiska anstalt.
       Vär värld Nordamerika.   Politisk-ekonomisk atlas.   By
       Leif Söderström and Gunnar Schalin.   Stockholm, 1971.
       70p.   col.   maps.   22cm.

7729   Generalstabens litografiska anstalt.
       Vär värld Fydasien; politisk-ekonomisk atlas.   By Eivor
       Samuelss n.   Stockholm, [1973].
       72p.   col.   maps.   22cm.

7730   Geographia, Ltd.
       Geographia road atlas of Great Britain.   Commercial
       atlas of Great Britain.   London, [1969].
       94p.   col.   maps.   28cm.

7731   Ghana.   Survey Dept.
       National atlas of Ghana.   By E. A. Boateng.   Accra,
       1960-1970.
       15p.   col.   maps.   64cm.

7732   Gisbert y Cía, S. A.
       Atlas económico de Bolivia.   By Alfredo Ayala Z.   La
       Paz, 1954.
       10p.   col.   maps.   30cm.

7733   Gt. Britain.   Ministry of Housing and Local Government.
       Atlas of planning maps of England and Wales.   London,
       1965-70.
       in parts.   col.   maps.   44cm.

7734   Gower Economic Publications.
       Business atlas of Great Britain.   Epping, Essex, [1974].
       186p.   28cm.

7735   Gower Economic Publications.
       Business atlas of Western Europe.   Epping, 1974.
       144p.   col.   maps.   29cm.

7736   Gyldendal.
       Atlas of economic geography.   7ed.   By J. Humlum and
       H. S. Thomsen.   København, 1975.
       139p.   col.   maps.   27cm.

7737   Gyldendal.

Kulturgeografisk atlas. 7ed. By Johannes Humlum.
Kφbenhavn, 1971.
2 vol. col. maps. 27cm.

7738 Gyldendal.
Kulturgeografisk atlas. By Johannes Humlum. Kφbenhavn,
1975.
2 vol. col. maps. 27cm.

7739 Gyldendal.
Lille erhvervsgeografisk atlas. By Johannes Humlum.
Kφbenhavn, 1972.
39p. col. maps. 31cm.

7740 Haack, Hermann.
Weltatlas. Die Staaten der Erde und ihre Wirtschaft. 9ed.
By Edgar Lehmann. Gotha, Leipzig, 1969.
176p. col. maps. 35cm.

7741 Hammond, C. S. & Co., Inc.
Hammond's indexed atlas of the United States. New York,
1952.
160p. col. maps. 32cm.

7742 Indonesia. Badan Atlas Nasional.
Badan atlas nasional. Djakarta, [1968].
in parts. 30cm.

7743 Indonesia. Direktorat Land Use.
Atlas Indonesia, buku kedna ekonomi. [Indonesian
economic atlas.] (In Indonesian.) By I. Made Sandy.
Djakarta, 1971.
26p. col. maps. 35cm.

7744 Institut cartographique européan.
Carte politique de la Belgique. Atlas des élections
législatives du 31 mars 1968. By Wilfred Dewachter.
Bruxelles, 1970.
79p. col. maps. 30cm.

7745 International Bank for Reconstruction and Development.
World bank atlas; population, per capita product and
growth rate. 5ed. Washington, D.C., 1970.
16p. col. maps. 28cm.

7746 International Bank for Reconstruction and Development.
World bank atlas: population, per capita product, and
growth rate. 6ed. Washington, D.C., 1971.
13p. col. maps. 28cm.

7747 International Society for Educational Information.
Atlas of Japan. Physical, economic and Social. 1ed.
(in English.) By R. Isida. Tokyo, 1970.
128p. col. maps. 37cm.

7748   International Society for Educational Information.
       Atlas of Japan. Physical, economic and social.   2ed.
       (in English.) By R. Isida. Tokyo, 1974.
       128p. col. maps. 37cm.

7749   Israel. Central Bureau of Statistics.
       Israel. Atlas of industry and crafts. Jerusalem, 1965.
       1 vol. col. maps. 29cm.

7750   Istituto Geografico De Agostini.
       Atlante della produzione e dei commerci. By Umberto
       Bonapace and Giuseppe Motta. Novara, [1967].
       120p. col. maps. 31cm.

7751   Istituto Geografico De Agostini.
       Atlante della produzione e dei commerci. By Umberto
       Bonapace and Giuseppe Motta. Novara, 1970.
       120p. col. maps. 31cm.

7752   Istituto Geografico De Agostini.
       Atlante della produzione e dei commerci. By Umberto
       Bonapace and Giuseppe Motta. Novara, 1971.
       120p. col. maps. 31cm.

7753   Istituto Geografico De Agostini.
       Atlante della produzione e dei commerci. By Umberto
       Bonapace and Giuseppe Motta. Novara, [1973].
       120p. col. maps. 31cm.

7754   Istituto Geografico De Agostini.
       Atlante geografico economico. By Umberto Bonapace and
       Giuseppe Motta. Novara, 1974.
       262p. col. maps. 36cm.

7755   Istituto Geografico De Agostini.
       Atlas universal geo-económico. Barcelona, [1973].
       160p. col. maps. 31cm.

7756   Istituto Geografico De Agostini.
       La terra. Grande atlante geografico economico storico.
       Novara, 1965.
       3 vol. col. maps. 40cm.

7757   Jacaranda.
       Papua New Guinea resource atlas. By Edgard Ford.
       Milton, Q., 1974.
       56p. col. maps. 60cm.

7758   Jacaranda.
       The Jacaranda social studies resources atlas for New Zea-
       land. 1ed. By E. R. Bloomfield and C. A. Watson.
       Milton, 1972.
       92p. col. maps. 28cm.

7759   Japan. Geographical Survey Institute.
       National atlas of Japan. Tokyo, 1972.
       1 vol. col. maps. 80cm.

7760   Johnston, W. & A. K. & G. W. Bacon, Ltd.
       Dimension 3. Political, physical and economic world
       atlas. Edinburgh, 1969.
       64p. col. maps. 28cm.

7761   Journaux, A.
       Atlas mondial. Caen, 1970.
       16p. col. maps. 31cm.

7762   Kapelusz y Cía.
       Atlas Humboldt: América del Norte, del Sur, Central y
       Antillana, físico, político, económico. 10ed. Buenos
       Aires, [1959].
       66p. col. maps. 26cm.

7763   Kapelusz y Cía.
       Atlas Humboldt: América del Norte, del Sur, Central y
       Antillana, físico, político, económico. 10ed. Buenos
       Aires, [1964].
       66p. col. maps. 26cm.

7764   Kapelusz y Cía.
       Coloratlas Kapelusz, América central y Antillas: físico,
       político, económico, estadístico. Buenos Aires, [1970].
       28p. col. maps. 32cm.

7765   Kapelusz y Cía.
       Coloratlas Kapelusz Mundi: físico, político, económico,
       estadístico. Buenos Aires, 1971.
       78p. col. maps. 32cm.

7766   Kapelusz y Cía.
       Coloratlas regional Argentina: físico, político, económico.
       1ed. Buenos Aires, [1973].
       68p. col. maps. 32cm.

7767   Kartográfiai Vállalat.
       Képes politikai és gazdasági Világatlasz. By Sándor Radó.
       Budapest, 1971.
       414p. col. maps. 34cm.

7768   Kokusai Kyōiku Jōhō Sentā.
       Atlas of Japan: physical, economic, and social. By R.
       Isida. Tokyo, 1970.
       128p. col. maps. 37cm.

7769   Kümmerly & Frey.
       Computer atlas der Schweiz. By A. Kilchenmann, D.
       Steiner, O. Matt and E. Gächter. Bern, 1972.
       72p. 30cm.

7770   Kümmerly & Frey.
       Computer atlas of Switzerland. Population; Housing; Oc-
       cupation; Agriculture. Bern, 1972.
       72p. 30cm.

7771   Kümmerly & Frey.
       KF Atlas. Naturbild und Wirtschaft der Erde. By
       Georges Grosjean. Bern, 1970.
       206p. col. maps. 32cm.

7772   Kümmerly & Frey.
       Wirtschaftsgeographischer Weltatlas. 2ed. By Hans
       Boesch. Bern, 1969.
       89p. col. maps. 34cm.

7773   Malawi. Dept. of Surveys.
       Maps illustrating development projects, 1970-1973.
       Blantyre, [1970].
       17p. col. maps. 49cm.

7774   Malawi. Dept. of Surveys.
       Maps illustrating development projects, 1972-1973/4.
       Blantyre, [1972].
       25p. col. maps. 49cm.

7775   Mariam, Mesfin Wolde.
       An atlas of Ethiopia. Addis Ababa, [1970].
       84p. col. maps. 28cm.

7776   Mariam, Mesfin Wolde.
       An atlas of Ethiopia. Rev. ed. Addis Ababa, 1970.
       84p. col. maps. 28cm.

7777   Mariam, Mesfin Wolde.
       Ethiopia: maps and figures. Addis Ababa, [1961].
       14p. 28cm.

7778   McGraw-Hill Book Co.
       Atlas of China. By Chiao-min Hsieh and Christopher L.
       Salter. New York, [1973].
       282p. 31cm.

7779   Mexico. Comisión Federal de Electricidad.
       Red nacional eléctrica y centrales generadoras en la
       República Mexicana. México, 1971.
       10p. 39cm.

7780   Military Vehicles & Engineering Establishment.
       A land system atlas of Swaziland. By G. Murdoch.
       Christchurch, 1971.
       49p. col. maps. 47.5cm.

7781   Miller Freeman.

Atlas of Western European pulp and paper industry.
Brussels, 1974.
9p.   29cm.

7782   Oxford Polytechnic.
France.   A socio-economic atlas.   Oxford, 1972.
48p.   col. maps.   28cm.

7783   Oxford University Press.
Oxford economic atlas of the world.   4ed.   By D. B.
Jones.   London, 1972.
415p.   col. maps.   38cm.

7784   Oxford University Press.
Oxford regional economic atlas.   Africa.   Paperback ed.
London, 1970.
1 vol.   col. maps.   25cm.

7785   Oxford University Press.
Oxford regional economic atlas of the Middle East and
North Africa.   London, 1960.
135p.   col. maps.   27cm.

7786   Oxford University Press.
Oxford regional economic atlas of the U. S. and Canada.
2ed.   London, 1975.
180p.   col. maps.   27cm.

7787   Oxford University Press.
Oxford regional economic atlas of the U. S. S. R. and Eastern Europe.   London, [1960].
134p.   col. maps.   26cm.

7788   Oxford University Press.
Oxford regional economic atlas of Western Europe.   By
K. M. Clayton and I. B. F. Kormoss.   London, 1971.
160p.   col. maps.   26cm.

7789   Oxford University Press.
Oxford regional economic atlas of Western Europe.   By
K. M. Clayton and I. B. F. Kormoss.   London, 1972.
160p.   col. maps.   26cm.

7790   Oxford University Press.
Oxford regional economic atlas.   The Middle East and
North Africa.   London, 1970.
135p.   col. maps.   27cm.

7791   Oxford University Press.
Oxford regional economic atlas.   The Middle East and
North Africa.   Paperback ed.   London, 1970.
1 vol.   col. maps.   25cm.

7792   Oxford University Press.
       Oxford regional economic atlas.   The U.S.S.R. and
       Eastern Europe.   London, [1969].
       134p.   col. maps.   26cm.

7793   Oxford University Press.
       Oxford regional economic atlas.   The U.S.S.R. and
       Eastern Europe.   Paperback ed.   London, 1969.
       134p.   col. maps.   20cm.

7794   Oxford University Press.
       The shorter Oxford economic atlas of the world.   London,
       New York, 1966.
       128p.   col. maps.   26cm.

7795   Oxford University Press.
       Shorter Oxford economic atlas of the world.   4ed.   Lon-
       don, 1971.
       128p.   col. maps.   26cm.

7796   Oxford University Press.
       The U.S.S.R. and Eastern Europe.   [Atlas.]   With
       Economist Intelligence Unit, Ltd.   London, [1969].
       134p.   col. maps.   27cm.

7797   Philip, George & Son, Ltd.
       Modern school economic atlas.   By Harold Fullard.   Lon-
       don, 1975.
       176p.   col. maps.   23cm.

7798   Philip, George & Son, Ltd.
       Philips commercial course atlas.   By Harold Fullard.
       London, 1966.
       117p.   col. maps.   29cm.

7799   Philip, George & Son, Ltd.
       Philips' commercial course atlas.   By Harold Fullard.
       London, [1970].
       30p.   col. maps.   29cm.

7800   Poland.   Glowny urząd statystyczny.
       Atlas statystyczny.   1ed.   By Janusz Stepiński.   War-
       szawa, 1970.
       197p.   col. maps.   28cm.

7801   Poland.   Państwowe zaklady wydawnictw szkolnych.
       Polska XXV; ludność, przemyśl, rolnictwo, transport,
       kultura, o świata, zdrowie, na mapach.   1ed.   By J.
       Ostrowski.   Warszawa, [1969].
       16p.   col. maps.   29cm.

7802   Portugal.   Ministerio do trabalho.
       Atlas sócio-econômico.   Lisboa, 1974-
       in parts.   44cm.

7803 Rand McNally & Co.
      Rand McNally commercial atlas and marketing guide.
      102ed.   Chicago, 1971.
      657p.   col. maps.   53cm.

7804 Rand McNally & Co.
      Rand McNally commercial atlas and marketing guide.
      103ed.   Chicago, 1972.
      667p.   col. maps.   53cm.

7805 Rand McNally & Co.
      Rand McNally commercial atlas and marketing guide.
      104ed.   Chicago, 1973.
      667p.   col. maps.   53cm.

7806 Rand McNally & Co.
      Rand McNally commercial atlas and marketing guide.
      105ed.   Chicago, 1974.
      669p.   col. maps.   53cm.

7807 Rand McNally & Co.
      Rand McNally commercial atlas and marketing guide.
      106ed.   Chicago, 1975.
      669p.   col. maps.   53cm.

7808 Rand McNally & Co.
      Rand McNally sales control atlas of the United States.
      New York, Chicago, 1959.
      96p.   col. maps.   31cm.

7809 Rand McNally & Co.
      Rand McNally zip code atlas; state maps and marketing
      data for the newest system of marketing units--the 561
      zip code sectional areas.   By Richard L. Forstall.
      Chicago, [1970].
      136p.   col. maps.   28cm.

7810 Sahab.
      Atlas -i nuwin -i gāhān dar asr-i fadā.   Teheran, [1972].
      130p.   col. maps.   29cm.

7811 Salvador.   Estadistica y censos.
      El Salvador--atlas de resursos fisicos.   San Salvador,
      1969.
      1 vol.   col. maps.   72cm.

7812 Scotland.   Scottish Development Dept.
      Planning maps series: Scotland.   Edinburgh, 1970-
      1 vol.   col. maps.   43cm.

7813 Scriptoria.
      Politieke kaart van Belgie.   By Wilfried Dewachter.
      Antwerpen, 1969.
      79p.   col. maps.   29cm.

7814   State University of New York.
        Computer atlas of Bangla Desh.   By Paul R. Baumann
        and Charles W. Woolever.   Oneonta, N.Y., 1972.
        84p.   29cm.

7815   Survey of Kenya.
        National atlas of Kenya.   3ed.   Nairobi, 1970.
        103p.   col. maps.   41cm.

7816   Survey of Kenya.
        National atlas of Kenya.   Nairobi, 1971.
        103p.   col. maps.   41cm.

7817   Tanzania.   Bureau of Resource Assessment and Land-Use
        Planning.
        Regional economic atlas, mainland Tanzania.   Dar es
        Salaam, 1968.
        70p.   25cm.

7818   U. A. R.-Egypt.   al-Jihas al-Markazi lil-Ta'bi'ah al'Ammah
        wa-al-Ihsa.
        United Arab Republic statistical atlas, 1952-1966.   Cairo,
        1968.
        123p.   col. maps.   35cm.

7819   United Nations.
        Energy atlas of Asia and the Far East.   New York, 1970.
        28p.   col. maps.   38cm.

7820   University of Michigan Press.
        Economic atlas of the Soviet Union.   2ed.   By George
        Kish.   Ann Arbor, Mich., [1971].
        90p.   col. maps.   27cm.

7821   University of Papua and New Guinea.
        An atlas of Papua and New Guinea.   By R. Gerard Ward
        and David A. M. Lea.   With Collins.   Port Moresby,
        [1970].
        101p.   26cm.

7822   University of Papua and New Guinea.
        Atlas of Papua and New Guinea.   Port Moresby, 1970-
        in parts.   32cm.

7823   University of Wales Press.
        Tropical Africa.   An atlas for rural development.   By
        H. R. J. Davies.   Cardiff, 1973.
        81p.   col. maps.   42cm.

7824   Uruguay.   Comisión de Integración Eléctrica Regional.
        Atlas del desarrollo energético de América del Sur.   3ed.
        Montevideo, 1971.
        43p.   col. maps.   76cm.

7825 U. S. Central Intelligence Agency.
      <u>Indochina atlas.</u> Washington, D. C. , 1970.
      14p. col. maps. 46cm.

7826 U. S. Engineer Resources Inventory Center.
      <u>Costa Rica: análisis regional de recursos físicos,</u>
      <u>Centroamérica y Panamá.</u> 1ed. Washington, D. C. , 1965.
      1 vol. col. maps. 34cm.

7827 U. S. Engineer Resources Inventory Center.
      <u>Nicaragua; análisis regional de recursos físicos, Centro-</u>
      <u>américa y Panamá.</u> 1ed. Washington, D. C. , 1966.
      1 vol. col. maps. 34cm.

7828 U. S. Engineer Resources Inventory Center.
      <u>Resource atlas project--Thailand.</u> Washington, D. C. ,
      1969-71.
      2 vol. col. maps. 34cm.

7829 U. S. S. R. Glavnoe upravlenie geodezii i kartografii.
      <u>Atlas obrazovania i razvitiya S. S. S. R.</u> Moskva, 1972.
      112p. col. maps. 34cm.

7839 U. S. S. R. Glavnoe upravlenie geodezii i kartografii.
      <u>Atlas S. S. S. R. v deviatoi piatiletke.</u> Moskva, 1972.
      40p. col. maps. 29cm.

7831 Yavneh.
      <u>Atlas fisi, medini, velkalkali.</u> By Moshe Brawer. Tel
      Aviv, 1969.
      128p. col. maps. 35cm.

7832 Zanichelli, Nicola.
      <u>Atlante geografico.</u> By G. Nangeroni and L. Ricci.
      Bologna, 1966.
      244p. col. maps. 34cm.

ETHNOGRAPHY

7833 France. Centre national de la recherche scientifique.
      <u>Atlas linguistique et ethnographique.</u> Paris, 1972-
      in parts. col. maps. 50cm.

7834 Poland. Akademia nauk.
      <u>Polski atlas etnograficzny.</u> Zeszyt próbny. Wrocław,
      1958.
      in parts. col. maps. 49cm.

7835 Poland. Państwowe przedsiębiorstwo wydawnictw kartografi-
      cznych.
      <u>Narodowy atlas Polski.</u> Warszawa, 1973-75.
      in parts. col. maps. 40cm.

EXPLORATION   see   HISTORY

FORESTRY

7836   France.   Service de l'économie forestière.
       Atlas forestièr.   Paris, 1968.
       79p.   col.   maps.   32cm.

7837   Parey Verlag.
       Weltforstatlas.   By Claus Wiebecke.   Hamburg, 1971.
       in parts.   col.   maps.   42cm.

7838   U. S.   Department of Agriculture.
       Atlas of United States trees.   By Elbert L. Little, Jr.
       Washington, D. C., 1971.
       in parts.   36cm.

7839   U. S.   Forest Service.
       Atlas of United States trees.   By Elbert L. Little, Jr.
       Washington, D. C., 1971-
       in parts.   36cm.

GEOLOGY

7840   Hamlyn.
       Gemhunting atlas of Australia.   Sydney, New York, 1973.
       260p.   col.   maps.   27cm.

7841   Malawi.   Geological Survey.
       Geological atlas of Malawi.   By R. T. Cannon.   Zomba,
       1970-
       in parts.   col.   maps.   64cm.

7842   Norway.   Vassdrags-og Elektrisitetsvesen.
       Glacier atlas of Southern and Northern Norway.   Oslo,
       1968-73.
       2 vol.   col.   maps.   42cm..

7843   Poland.   Instytut geologiczny.
       Atlas mineralogiczny Polski.   Warszawa, 1971.
       1 portf.   col.   maps.   30cm.

7844   Poland.   Wydawn.   Geologiczne.
       Atlas litologiczno-surowcowy Polski.   Warszawa, 1973-
       in parts.   31cm.

7845   Poland.   Wydawn.   Geologiczne.
       Atlas map górniczych.   Katowice, 1971.
       17p.   col.   maps.   31cm.

7846   Poland.   Wydawn.   Geologiczne.
       Atlas mineralogeniczny Polski.   By Roman Osika.
       Warszawa, 1970.

16p.   col. maps.   30cm.

7847   Poland.   Wydawn.   Geologiczne.
       Mineralogenic atlas of Poland.   By Roman Osika.   War-
       szawa, 1970.
       20p.   col. maps.   30cm.

7848   Stanford, Edward.
       Stanford's geological atlas of Great Britain.   By T.
       Eastwood.   London, 1966.
       296p.   25cm.

7849   U. S.   Central Intelligence Agency.
       U. S. S. R. atlas of transmission pipelines for natural gas.
       Washington, D. C., 1963.
       66p.   col. maps.   57cm.

7850   U. S.   Geological Survey.
       Atlas of Asia and Eastern Europe to support detection of
       underground nuclear testing.   Washington, D. C., 1966-69.
       5 vol.   col. maps.   62cm.

7851   Vietnam.   National Geographic Center.
       Geological atlas of Vietnam, Cambodia and Laos.   Saigon,
       1962-63.
       in parts.   col. maps.   33cm.

7852   Wiley, John & Sons.
       Atlas of paleogeographic maps of North America.   By
       Charles Schuchert.   New York, [1955].
       177p.   30cm.

7853   Wiley, John & Sons.
       Atlas of world physical features.   By Rodman Eldredge
       Snead.   New York, [1972].
       176p.   col. maps.   29cm.

HISTORY

7854   Aldus-Jupiter.
       Atlas of discovery.   By Gail Roberts.   With Geographical
       Projects.   London, 1973.
       192p.   col. maps.   31cm.

7855   Anubar.
       Atlas historico; cómo se formó España.   2ed.   By
       Antonio Ubieto Arteta.   Valencia, 1970.
       148p.   col. maps.   31cm.

7856   Arnold, E.
       A historical atlas 1789-1971 for first examinations.   2ed.
       London, 1971.
       64p.   col. maps.   26cm.

7857 Arnold, E.
      A student's atlas of modern history. 2ed. By R. R.
      Sellman. London, 1972.
      106p. 28cm.

7858 Arnold, E.
      An atlas of African history. By J. D. Fage. London,
      [1970].
      64p. 29cm.

7859 Arnold, E.
      An atlas of African history. By J. D. Fage. London,
      1973.
      64p. 29cm.

7860 Arnold, E.
      An outline atlas of world history. By R. R. Sellman.
      London, 1970.
      127p. 28cm.

7861 Austria. Bundesdenkmalamt.
      Atlas der historischen Schutzzonen in Österreich. Graz,
      1970.
      1 vol. 35cm.

7862 Barnes & Noble, Inc.
      An atlas of North American affairs. By D. K. Adams
      and H. B. Rodgers. New York, [1969].
      135p. 22cm.

7863 Barnes & Noble, Inc.
      Historical atlas of the world. With Cappelens Forlag.
      New York, 1970.
      108p. col. maps. 21cm.

7864 Barnes & Noble, Inc.
      Shepherd's historical atlas. 9ed. N.Y., 1973.
      226p. col. maps. 27cm.

7865 Bayerischer Schulbuch Verlag.
      Grosser historischer Weltatlas. München 1954-[70].
      3 vol. col. maps. 34cm.

7866 Bayerischer Schulbuch Verlag.
      Grosser historischer Weltatlas. 5ed. München, [1972-].
      1 vol. col. maps. 34cm.

7867 Bayerischer Schulbuch Verlag.
      Grosser historischer Weltatlas. II Teil. Mittelalter.
      By Josef Engel. München, 1970.
      213p. col. maps. 34cm.

7868 Bayerischer Schulbuch Verlag.

Grosser historischer Weltatlas. III Teil: Neuzeit. By
Josef Engel. München, 1962.
1 vol. col. maps. 34cm.

7869 Beazley, Mitchell, Ltd.
The Mitchell Beazley world atlas of exploration. London,
1975.
1 vol. col. maps. 28cm.

7870 Bibliograf, S. A.
Atlas historico basico SPES. Barcelona, [1975].
48p. col. maps. 24cm.

7871 Blackie & Son, Ltd.
Atlas of European political history. 1ed. By P. G.
Dickson Jones. Glasgow, 1973.
30p. col. maps. 25cm.

7872 Brazil. Ministério da educação e cultura.
Atlas histórico e geográfico brasileiro. 2ed. Rio de
Janeiro, 1970.
66p. col. maps. 32cm.

7873 Cambridge University Press.
The new Cambridge modern history; volume XIV, atlas.
By H. C. Darby and Harold Fullard. Cambridge, 1970.
319p. col. maps. 24cm.

7874 Cappelens, J. W. Forlag, A. S.
Historisk skoleatlas. By Oddvar Bjørklund. Oslo, 1968.
48p. col. maps. 21cm.

7875 Centre de Psychologie et de Pédagogie.
Atlas historique du Canada. By D. G. G. Kerr. Transl.
by Pierre Tousignant. Montreal, 1967.
120p. col. maps. 31cm.

7876 Chambers, W. & R., Ltd.
Historical atlas of the world. By Oddvar Bjørklund.
With Cappelen Forlag. Edinburgh, 1970.
134p. col. maps. 21cm.

7877 Compañia Internacional Editora.
Atlas geográfico histórico CIESA. Barcelona, [1972].
2 vol. col. maps. 31cm.

7878 Cram, George F., Co.
Cram modern world atlas. With Hammond. Indianapolis,
Ind., [1971].
358p. col. maps. 32cm.

7879 Crowell-Collier Press.
The atlas of world history. From the beginning to

Alexander the Great. By Colin and Sarah McEvedy.
New York, [1970-].
in parts. col. maps. 29cm.

7880 Crown.
Atlas of discovery. With Geographical Projects. New
York, 1973.
192p. col. maps. 31cm.

7881 Czechoslovakia. Akademia věd.
Atlas chekhoslovatskoy istorii. (In Russian.) Praha,
1972.
40p. col. maps. 32cm.

7882 Czechoslovakia. Kartografické nakladatelství.
Školský atlas světových dějin. 6ed. Praha, 1972.
95p. col. maps. 31cm.

7883 Czechoslovakia. Ustřední správa geodézie a kartografie.
Školní atlas Československých dějin. 5ed. Praha, 1969.
75p. col. maps. 31cm.

7884 Czechoslovakia. Ustřední správa geodézie a kartografie.
Školní atlas Československých dějin. Praha, 1971.
75p. col. maps. 31cm.

7885 de Bussy, J. H.
Politieke wereldatlas. 2ed. By S. A. Leeflang.
Amsterdam, 1960.
65p. 21cm.

7886 Denoyer-Geppert Co.
American history atlas. 9ed. Chicago, [1953].
48p. col. maps. 28cm.

7887 Denoyer-Geppert Co.
Denoyer-Geppert atlas of American history. 1ed. By
Edgar B. Wesley. Chicago, [1957].
32p. col. maps. 28cm.

7888 Denoyer-Geppert Co.
Mapas historicos de Europa y del mundo. By James H.
Breasted, Carl F. Huth and Samuel B. Harding. Chicago,
1970.
55p. col. maps. 28cm.

7889 Denoyer-Geppert Co.
Muir's historical atlas of the world. With Philip. Chicago, 1958.
1 vol. col. maps. 29cm.

7890 Denoyer-Geppert Co.
Our United States; its history in maps. By Edgar B.

Wesley. Chicago, [1957].
96p. col. maps. 28cm.

7891   Denoyer-Geppert Co.
       Our United States; its history in maps.   2ed.   By Edgar
       B. Wesley. Chicago, [1961].
       96p. col. maps. 28cm.

7892   Denoyer-Geppert Co.
       Our United States; its history in maps.   3ed.   By Edgar
       Bruce Wesley. Chicago, [1965].
       96p. col. maps. 28cm.

7893   Denoyer-Geppert Co.
       Our United States; its history in maps.   By Edgar Bruce
       Wesley. Chicago, 1968.
       96p. col. maps. 28cm.

7894   Denoyer-Geppert Co.
       Our United States; its history in maps.   4ed.   By Edgar
       Bruce Wesley. Chicago, 1971.
       96p. col. maps. 28cm.

7895   Denoyer-Geppert Co.
       The history of Africa in maps.   By Harry A. Gailey.
       Chicago, [1971].
       96p. 28cm.

7896   Deutscher Taschenbuch Verlag.
       DTV Atlas zur Weltgeschichte.   By Hermann Kinder and
       Werner Hilgemann. München, [1970].
       2 vol. col. maps. 18cm.

7897   Deutscher Taschenbuch Verlag.
       DTV Atlas zur Weltgeschichte.   By Hermann Kinder und
       Werner Hilgemann. München, 1973.
       287p. col. maps. 18cm.

7898   Deutscher Taschenbuch Verlag.
       DTV-Perthes-Weltatlas.   München, Darmstadt, 1973-
       in parts. col. maps. 20cm.

7899   Editions Bordas.
       Atlas général Bordas, historique et géographique.   By
       Pierre Serryn and R. Blasselle. With Hölzel. Paris,
       Wien, 1972.
       215p. col. maps. 32cm.

7900   Editions Bordas.
       Atlas historique et géographique.   By Pierre Serryn and
       René Blasselle. Paris, [1970].
       240p. col. maps. 32cm.

7901   Editions Bordas.
       Nouvel atlas historique.   By Pierre Serryn and René
       Blasselle.   Paris, [1970].
       72p.   col. maps.   32cm.

7902   Editions Bordas.
       Nouvel atlas Bordas historique et géographique.   By
       Pierre Serryn and René Blasselle.   Paris, 1973.
       172p.   col. maps.   32cm.

7903   Editorial Teide.
       Atlas de historia de España.   Barcelona, 1973.
       102p.   col. maps.   28cm.

7904   Faber & Faber.
       An historical atlas of Wales.   By William Rees.   London,
       1972.
       71p.   26cm.

7905   Faber & Faber.
       An historical atlas of Wales from early to modern times.
       By William Rees.   London, 1972.
       141p.   25cm.

7906   Fabritius.
       Historisk verdensatlas.   By Willy Karlsen and Lars
       Stølen.   Oslo, [1970].
       51p.   col. maps.   32cm.

7907   France.   Centre national de la recherche scientifique.
       Atlas préhistorique du Maroc.   Paris, 1973-
       in parts.   col. maps.   46cm.

7908   Generalstabens litografiska anstalt.
       En delad varld.   Stockholm, 1971.
       1 vol.   col. maps.   22cm.

7909   Geographic and Drafting Institute.
       Atlas of Iran.   White Revolution Proceeds and Progresses.
       Teheran, 1971.
       190p.   col. maps.   35cm.

7910   Gyldendal.
       Gyldendals historiske atlas.   København, 1968.
       56p.   col. maps.   27.5cm.

7911   Haack, Hermann.
       Atlas zur Geschichte.   1ed.   Gotha, 1973-75.
       2 vol.   col. maps.   29cm.

7912   Hammond, C. S. & Co., Inc.
       The march of civilization in maps and pictures.   Maple-
       wood, N.J.   1959.

146p.   col.   maps.   32cm.

7913   Hammond, Inc.
       American history atlas.   Maplewood, N.J., 1969.
       40p.   col.   maps.   31cm.

7914   Hammond, Inc.
       Historical atlas.   Maplewood, N.J., 1972.
       48p.   col.   maps.   31cm.

7915   Hammond, Inc.
       History atlas of America.   Maplewood, N.J., [1971].
       31p.   col.   maps.   26cm.

7916   Hammond, Inc.
       Man and history.   [Atlas.]   Maplewood, N.J., [1971].
       192p.   col.   maps.   29cm.

7917   Hammond, Inc.
       United States history atlas.   Maplewood, N.J., [1971].
       64p.   col.   maps.   31cm.

7918   Hammond, Inc.
       United States history atlas.   Maplewood, N.J., 1973.
       64p.   col.   maps.   31cm.

7919   Harrap.
       A sketch map geography of North-West Europe.   By
       Dorothy E. Cocks.   London, 1971.
       48p.   25cm.

7920   Harrap.
       A sketch-map history of the two world wars and after
       1914-1973.   7ed.   London, 1973.
       1 vol.   25cm.

7921   Hart-Davis.
       The atlas of world history.   By Colin and Sarah McEvedy.
       London, 1970-
       in parts.   col.   maps.   29cm.

7922   Hart-Davis.
       The atlas of world history: Vol. I: From the Beginning
       to Alexander the Great.   By Colin and Sarah McEvedy.
       London, 1970.
       62p.   col.   maps.   29cm.

7923   Hart-Davis.
       The atlas of world history: Vol. III: The Dark Ages.
       By Colin and Sarah McEvedy.   London, 1972.
       62p.   col.   maps.   29cm.

7924   Heinemann.

A map history of the British people, 1700 to 1970. By
Brian Catchpole. London, 1971.
170p. 26cm.

7925 Heinemann.
      A military atlas of the first world war. London, 1975.
      1 vol. 26cm.

7926 Hippocrene Books.
      A world atlas of military history. By Arthur Banks.
      London, 1973-
      4 vol. 26cm.

7927 Hölder, Pichler, Tempsky.
      Historischer Weltatlas zur allgemeinen und Österreichischen
      Geschichte. 46ed. By Egon Lendl, Wilhelm Wagner,
      Rudolf Klein. Wien, 1969.
      146p. col. maps. 27cm.

7928 Iran. Danighgah.
      Atlas-i-tarikhi Iran. Historical atlas of Iran. Teheran,
      1971.
      76p. col. maps. 28cm.

7929 Iran. Ministry of Interior.
      Atlas of Iran. White Revolution. 2ed. Teheran, 1973.
      197p. col. maps. 35cm.

7930 Istituto Geografico De Agostini.
      Atlante storico. 4ed. By Ugo Dèttore. Novara, 1968.
      56p. col. maps. 30cm.

7931 Istituto Geografico De Agostini.
      Atlante storico. Novara, [1972].
      80p. col. maps. 34cm.

7932 Istituto Geografico De Agostini.
      Atlante storico. Novara, 1973.
      80p. col. maps. 34cm.

7933 Istituto Geografico De Agostini.
      Atlante storico grande unico. Novara, 1968.
      80p. col. maps. 33cm.

7934 Istituto Geografico De Agostini.
      Atlante storico illustrato. Novara, [1974].
      103p. col. maps. 37cm.

7935 Istituto Geografico De Agostini.
      Atlante storico per la scuola media. By Ugo Dèttore.
      Novara, 1965.
      in parts. col. maps. 30cm.

7936   Istituto Geografico De Agostini.
        La terra. Grande atlante geografico economico storico.
        Novara, 1965.
        3 vol.   col.   maps.   40cm.

7937   Istituto Geografico De Agostini.
        Piccolo atlante storico.   Novara, 1968.
        164p.   col.   maps.   26cm.

7938   Istituto Geografico De Agostini.
        Piccolo atlante storico.   Novara, [1973].
        1 vol.   col.   maps.   26cm.

7939   Karolidēs, Paulos.
        Historikos atlas.   By D. Dēmētrakos.   Athens, [1960].
        2 vol.   col.   maps.   34cm.

7940   Kartográfiai Vállalat.
        Képes történelmi atlasz.   By Sándor Radó.   Budapest,
        1970.
        24p.   col.   maps.   28cm.

7941   Kartográfiai Vállalat.
        Képes történelmi atlasz.   4ed.   By Sándor Radó.   Buda-
        pest, 1973.
        24p.   col.   maps.   28cm.

7942   Kartográfiai Vállalat.
        Történelmi atlasz.   Budapest, [1971].
        33p.   col.   maps.   29cm.

7943   Kartográfiai Vállalat.
        Történelmi atlasz.   14ed.   Budapest, 1973.
        32p.   col.   maps.   29cm.

7944   Kartografie.
        Školní atlas světových dějin.   6ed.   Praha, 1971.
        97p.   col.   maps.   30cm.

7945   Kartografie.
        Školní atlas světových dějin.   7ed.   Praha, 1971.
        92p.   col.   maps.   30cm.

7946   Kartografie.
        Školní atlas světových dějin.   8ed.   By Petr Cafourek.
        Praha, 1973.
        74p.   col.   maps.   30cm.

7947   Kartografie.
        Školský atlas Československých dějín.   9ed.   Praha,
        1973.
        44p.   col.   maps.   30cm.

7948   List, P.
       Harms Geschichtsatlas mit Bildern.   By Werner Schmitt-
       diel.   München, [1973].
       49p.   col. maps.   31cm.

7949   Litografía Arco.
       Atlas de mapas antiguos de Colombia.   By Eduardo
       Acevedo Latorre.   Bogotá, 1971.
       169p.   col. maps.   46cm.

7950   Livraria Sá da Costa.
       Novo atlas escolar português, histórico-geográfico.   11ed.
       By João Soares.   Lisboa, 1971.
       85p.   col. maps.   34cm.

7951   Macmillan.
       Atlas of the Arab-Israeli conflict.   1ed.   By Martin Gil-
       bert.   New York, 1974.
       103p.   24cm.

7952   Macmillan.
       Atlas of the Arab-Israeli conflict.   New York, 1975.
       101p.   24cm.

7953   Macmillan.
       Ancient history atlas.   1ed.   By Michael Grant.   New
       York, [1972].
       87p.   24cm.

7954   Macmillan.
       An outline atlas of world history.   By R. R. Sellman.
       Toronto, 1970.
       127p.   24cm.

7955   Macmillan.
       British history atlas.   By Martin Gilbert.   New York,
       1968.
       118p.   24cm.

7956   Macmillan.
       British history atlas.   By Martin Gilbert.   New York,
       [1971].
       118p.   24cm.

7957   Macmillan.
       First world war atlas.   1ed.   By Martin Gilbert.   New
       York, [1970].
       197p.   24cm.

7958   Macmillan.
       Jewish history atlas.   By Martin Gilbert.   New York,
       1973.
       126p.   24cm.

7959   Macmillan.
     Russian history atlas.   1ed.   By Martin Gilbert.   New
     York, [1972].
     188p.   25cm.

7960   Macmillan.
     The classical world.   By Colin and Sarah McEvedy.   New
     York, 1973.
     64p.   col.   maps.   25cm.

7961   Macmillan.
     The dark ages.   By Colin and Sarah McEvedy.   New
     York, 1973.
     64p.   col.   maps.   25cm.

7962   McGraw Hill Book Co.
     Africa on maps dating from the twelfth to the eighteenth
     century.   New York, 1970.
     77p.   col.   maps.   53cm.

7963   Methuen.
     An atlas of Irish history.   By Ruth Dudley Edwards.
     London, 1973.
     261p.   25cm.

7964   Methuen.
     An atlas of North American affairs.   By David Keith
     Adams and H. B. Rodgers.   London, 1969.
     135p.   22cm.

7965   Methuen.
     An atlas of North American affairs.   By D. K. Adams
     and H. B. Rodgers.   Toronto, 1970.
     136p.   22cm.

7966   Murray, J.
     Sketch-maps in modern history, 1789-1970.   4ed.   By
     D. G. Perry and R. B. Kohler.   London, 1971.
     64p.   25cm.

7967   National Trust.
     The what to see atlas, showing places of historic,
     architectural & scenic interest in England, Wales, and
     Northern Ireland.   5ed.   With Bartholomew.   London,
     [1970].
     60p.   col.   maps.   25cm.

7968   National Trust.
     The what to see atlas, showing places of historic,
     architectural and scenic interest in England, Wales and
     Northern Ireland.   With Bartholomew.   London, 1971.
     60p.   col.   maps.   25cm.

7969   National Trust.
       The what to see atlas, showing places of historic,
       architectural and scenic interest in England, Wales and
       Northern Ireland.   5ed.   With Bartholomew.   London,
       [1974].
       60p.   col.   maps.   25cm.

7970   Nelson, Thomas & Sons, Ltd.
       Nelson's new history atlas.   By Peter Belbin and Don
       Pottinger.   London, 1969.
       32p.   col.   maps.   28cm.

7971   Nelson, Thomas & Sons, Ltd.
       Shorter atlas of the classical world.   By H. H. Scullard.
       London, 1967.
       239p.   col.   maps.   21cm.

7972   N. I. Sh. Mjete Mësimore e Sportive "Hamid Shijaku."
       Historia e mejestes per klasen e vi te shkolles tetevjecare
       harta.   Tiranë, 1970.
       16p.   col.   maps.   29cm.

7973   Oxford University Press.
       A map history of Australia.   2ed.   By Ian Wynd and
       Joyce Wood.   Melbourne, London, [1967].
       60p.   col.   maps.   25cm.

7974   Oxford University Press.
       Atlas of European history.   By Edward Whiting Fox.
       London, 1956.
       64p.   col.   maps.   26cm.

7975   Pan American Institute of Geography & History.
       Atlas de América.   Buenos Aires, 1955.
       66p.   col.   maps.   36cm.

7976   Penguin Books.
       The Penguin atlas of ancient history.   By Colin McEvedy.
       Harmondsworth, Middlesex, [1961].
       96p.   col.   maps.   23cm.

7977   Penguin Books.
       The Penguin atlas of modern history.   By Colin McEvedy.
       Harmondsworth, Middlesex, [1972].
       96p.   col.   maps.   23cm.

7978   Penguin Books.
       The Penguin atlas of world history.   Harmondsworth,
       Middlesex, 1974.
       96p.   col.   maps.   23cm.

7979   Pergamon Press, Ltd.
       Pergamon general historical atlas.   1ed.   By A. C. Cave

and B. Trinder.   Oxford, 1970.
85p.   col. maps.   28cm.

7980   Pergamon Press, Ltd.
Pergamon general historical atlas.   By A. C. Cave and
B. Trinder.   Oxford, 1971.
88p.   col. maps.   28cm.

7981   Peru.   Instituto Nacional de Planificación.
Atlas histórico geográfico y de paisajes peruanos.   By
Carlos Peñaherrera del Aguila.   Lima, [1970].
737p.   col. maps.   58cm.

7982   Philip, George & Son, Ltd.
Atlas of modern history.   London, 1970.
72p.   col. maps.   28cm.

7983   Philip, George & Son, Ltd.
Muir's atlas of ancient and classical history.   By R. F.
Treharne and Harold Fullard.   London, 1965.
36p.   col. maps.   28cm.

7984   Philip, George & Son, Ltd.
Muir's historical atlas: ancient, medieval and modern.
By R. F. Treharne and Harold Fullard.   London, 1966.
172p.   col. maps.   28cm.

7985   Philip, George & Son, Ltd.
Muir's historical atlas: ancient, medieval and modern.
By R. F. Treharne and Harold Fullard.   London, 1971.
172p.   col. maps.   28cm.

7986   Philip, George & Son, Ltd.
Muir's historical atlas, mediaeval & modern.   By George
Goodall and R. F. Treharne.   London, 1962.
68p.   col. maps.   29cm.

7987   Philip, George & Son, Ltd.
Shepherd's historical atlas.   9ed.   London, 1970.
227p.   col. maps.   26.5cm.

7988   Philip, George & Son, Ltd.
The 'Observer' atlas of world affairs: a guide to major
tensions and conflicts.   By Andrew Wilson.   London, 1971.
111p.   col. maps.   28cm.

7989   Piper, R. & Co.
Piper's world history in maps, data and pictures.   Historical atlas.   München, 1970.
700p.   col. maps.   28cm.

7990   Poland.   Akademia nauk.
Atlas historyczny Polski.   1ed.   Warszawa, [1961].

2 vol.   col.   maps.   31cm.

7991   Poland.   Centralny urzad geodezii i kartografii.
        Maly atlas historiczny.   Warszawa, 1952.
        12p.   col.   maps.   30cm.

7992   Poland.   Centralny urzad geodezii i kartografii.
        Maly atlas historiczny.   Warszawa, 1953.
        12p.   col.   maps.   30cm.

7993   Poland.   Centralny urzad geodezii i kartografii.
        Maly atlas historiczny.   Warszawa, 1954.
        12p.   col.   maps.   30cm.

7994   Poland.   Państwowe przedsiębiorstwo wydawnictw kartografi-
        cznych.
        Atlas do historii Polski.   Warszawa, 1966-
        in parts.   col.   maps.   30cm.

7995   Poland.   Państwowe przedsiębiorstwo wydawnictw kartografi-
        cznych.
        Atlas do historii starozytnej.   By L. Piotrowicz.   War-
        szawa, 1957.
        1 vol.   col.   maps.   30cm.

7996   Poland.   Państwowe przedsiębiorstwo wydawnictw kartografi-
        cznych.
        Atlas do historii starozytnej.   By L. Piotrowicz.   War-
        szawa, 1959.
        1 vol.   col.   maps.   30cm.

7997   Poland.   Państwowe przedsiębiorstwo wydawnictw kartografi-
        cznych.
        Atlas do historii starozytnej.   By L. Piotrowicz.   War-
        szawa, 1960.
        1 vol.   col.   maps.   30cm.

7998   Poland.   Państwowe przedsiębiorstwo wydawnictw kartografi-
        cznych.
        Atlas do historii starozytnej.   By L. Piotrowicz.   War-
        szawa, 1961.
        1 vol.   col.   maps.   30cm.

7999   Poland.   Państwowe przedsiębiorstwo wydawnictw kartografi-
        cznych.
        Atlas do historii starozytnej.   By L. Piotrowicz.   War-
        szawa, 1962.
        1 vol.   col.   maps.   30cm.

8000   Poland.   Państwowe przedsiębiorstwo wydawnictw kartografi-
        cznych.
        Atlas do historii starozytnej.   By L. Piotrowicz.   War-
        szawa, 1965.

1 vol. col. maps. 30cm.

8001 Poland. Państwowe przedsiębiorstwo wydawnictw kartograficznych.
Atlas do historii starozytnej. By L. Piotrowicz. Warszawa, 1966.
1 vol. col. maps. 30cm.

8002 Poland. Państwowe przedsiębiorstwo wydawnictw kartograficznych.
Atlas do historii starozytnej. By L. Piotrowicz. Warszawa, 1968.
12p. col. maps. 30cm.

8003 Poland. Państwowe przedsiębiorstwo wydawnictw kartograficznych.
Atlas do historii starozytnej. By L. Piotrowicz. Warszawa, 1971.
12p. col. maps. 30cm.

8004 Poland. Państwowe przedsiębiorstwo wydawnictw kartograficznych.
Atlas historyczny Polski. 2ed. By Wladyslaw Czapliniski and Tadeusz Ladogorski. Warszawa, [1970].
54p. col. maps. 32cm.

8005 Poland. Państwowe przedsiębiorstwo wydawnictw kartograficznych.
Atlas historyczny Polski. 3ed. Warszawa, 1973.
55p. col. maps. 32cm.

8006 Poland. Państwowe przedsiębiorstwo wydawnictw kartograficznych.
Atlas historyczny swiata. By Józef Wolski. Warszawa, 1974.
224p. col. maps. 30cm.

8007 Poland. Państwowe przedsiębiorstwo wydawnictw kartograficznych.
Atlas przemian politydznych swiata w XX Wieku. By Zofia Dworak. Warszawa, 1970.
59p. col. maps. 32cm.

8008 Poland. Państwowe przedsiębiorstwo wydawnictw kartograficznych.
Maly atlas historyczny. Warszawa, 1956.
12p. col. maps. 30cm.

8009 Poland. Państwowe przedsiębiorstwo wydawnictw kartograficznych.
Maly atlas historyczny. Warszawa, 1957.
1 vol. col. maps. 30cm.

8010   Poland.   Państwowe przedsiębiorstwo wydawnictw kartografi-
       cznych.
       Maly atlas historyczny.   Warszawa, 1958.
       1 vol.   col.   maps.   30cm.

8011   Poland.   Państwowe przedsiębiorstwo wydawnictw kartografi-
       cznych.
       Maly atlas historyczny.   Warszawa, 1959.
       1 vol.   col.   maps.   30cm.

8012   Poland.   Państwowe przedsiębiorstwo wydawnictw kartografi-
       cznych.
       Maly atlas historyczny.   Warszawa, 1960.
       1 vol.   col.   maps.   30cm.

8013   Poland.   Państwowe przedsiębiorstwo wydawnictw kartografi-
       cznych.
       Maly atlas historyczny.   Warszawa, 1961.
       1 vol.   col.   maps.   30cm.

8014   Poland.   Państwowe przedsiębiorstwo wydawnictw kartografi-
       cznych.
       Maly atlas historyczny.   Warszawa, 1962.
       1 vol.   col.   maps.   30cm.

8015   Poland.   Państwowe przedsiębiorstwo wydawnictw kartografi-
       cznych.
       Maly atlas historyczny.   Warszawa, 1966.
       1 vol.   col.   maps.   30cm.

8016   Poland.   Państwowe przedsiębiorstwo wydawnictw kartografi-
       cznych.
       Maly atlas historyczny.   Warszawa, 1967.
       1 vol.   col.   maps.   30cm.

8017   Poland.   Państwowe przedsiębiorstwo wydawnictw kartografi-
       cznych.
       Maly atlas historyczny.   Warszawa, 1968.
       1 vol.   col.   maps.   30cm.

8018   Poland.   Państwowe przedsiębiorstwo wydawnictw kartografi-
       cznych.
       Maly atlas historyczny.   Warszawa, 1969.
       12p.   col.   maps.   30cm.

8019   Poland.   Państwowe przedsiębiorstwo wydawnictw kartografi-
       cznych.
       Maly atlas historyczny.   Warszawa, 1970.
       12p.   col.   maps.   30cm.

8020   Poland.   Państwowe przedsiębiorstwo wydawnictw kartografi-
       cznych.
       Maly atlas historyczny.   Warszawa, 1971.

     12p.   col. maps.   30cm.

8021   Poland.   Państwowe przedsiębiorstwo wydawnictw kartograficznych.
     Maly atlas historyczny.   Warszawa, 1972.
     12p.   col. maps.   30cm.

8022   Praeger, Frederick A.
     An atlas of Latin American affairs.   By Ronald M.
Schneider.   New York, 1966.
     136p.   22cm.

8023   Praeger, Frederick A.
     An atlas of Latin American affairs.   By Ronald M.
Schneider.   New York, 1970.
     136p.   22cm.

8024   Putnam's, G. P. , Sons.
     Atlas of the second world war.   1ed.   By Peter Young.
New York, [1974].
     288p.   col. maps.   29cm.

8025   Rand McNally & Co.
     Atlas of the American Revolution.   By Kenneth Nebenzahl.
Chicago, [1974].
     218p.   col. maps.   35cm.

8026   Rand McNally & Co.
     Rand McNally world atlas of exploration.   By Eric Newby.
Chicago, 1975.
     288p.   col. maps.   28cm.

8027   Rand McNally & Co.
     These states united: atlas of American history.   Chicago,
[1974].
     64p.   col. maps.   29cm.

8028   Romania.   Editura di Stat Didactică şi Pedagogică.
     Atlas istoric.   Bucureşti, 1971.
     200p.   col. maps.   34cm.

8029   Sahab.
     Atlas of ancient and historical maps of Iran.   Teheran,
[1973].
     200p.   col. maps.   35cm.

8030   Sahab.
     Atlas of Iran.   White Revolution Proceeds and Progresses.
Teheran, 1971.
     191p.   col. maps.   35cm.

8031   Sahab.
     Atlas of Iran.   White Revolution Proceeds and Progresses.

2ed.   Teheran, 1974.
197p.   col. maps.   35cm.

8032 Sauerländer, H. R.
       Historischer atlas zur Welt-und Schweizer Geschichte.
       7ed. By F. W. Putzger.   Aarau, 1969.
       146p.   col. maps.   27cm.

8033 Seeley Service & Co.
       A world atlas of military history.   By Arthur Banks.
       London, 1974-
       in parts.   26cm.

8034 Slovenska Kartografia.
       Školský atlas Československých dejin.   9ed.   Bratislava,
       1973.
       75p.   col. maps.   33cm.

8035 Slovenska Kartografia.
       Školský atlas svetových dejin.   7ed.   Bratislava, 1972.
       95p.   col. maps.   33cm.

8036 Söderström, W.
       Historian Kartasto.   4ed.   By Jarl Gustafson.   Porvoo,
       [1970].
       48p.   col. maps.   29cm.

8037 Söderström, W.
       Historian Kartasto.   By Jarl Gustafson.   Porvoo, 1971.
       48p.   col. maps.   29cm.

8038 Stock.
       Grand atlas historique.   By Pierre Montrouge.   Paris,
       1969.
       590p.   col. maps.   26cm.

8039 Südwest Verlag.
       Der Grosse Atlas zum 2. Weltkrieg.   München, 1974.
       288p.   col. maps.   31cm.

8040 Svenska bokförlaget.
       Atlas til historien.   3ed.   By Bengt Y. Gustafson.
       Stockholm, [1970].
       60p.   col. maps.   30cm.

8041 Taplinger Publishing Co.
       A map history of world war I.   By Arthur Banks.   New
       York, 1975.
       1 vol.   26cm.

8042 Učila.
       Povijesni atlas.   By Zvonimir Dugački.   Zagreb, 1969.
       66p.   col. maps.   30cm.

8043   University of London Press.
       A student's atlas of African history.   By Derek A. Wilson.
       London, 1971.
       64p.   28cm.

8044   University of Teheran.
       Historical atlas of Iran.   Teheran, 1971.
       1 vol.   col.   maps.   28cm.

8045   University of Wales Press.
       Historical atlas of Wales.   2ed.   By J. Idwal Jones (in
       Welsh).   Cardiff, 1972.
       137p.   25cm.

8046   University Tutorial Press.
       A student's atlas of African history.   By Derek A. Wilson.
       London, 1971.
       1 vol.   28cm.

8047   U. S. S. R.   Glavnoe upravlenie geodezii i kartografii.
       Atlas istorii dvernego mira dlya V klassa strednei shkoly.
       Moskva, 1971.
       12p.   col.   maps.   26cm.

8048   U. S. S. R.   Glavnoe upravlenie geodezii i kartografii.
       Atlas istorii S. S. S. R.   dlya IV klassa.   Moskva, 1971.
       12p.   col.   maps.   26cm.

8049   U. S. S. R.   Glavnoe upravlenie geodezii i kartografii.
       Atlas istorii S. S. S. R.   Part I dlya VII klassa.   Moskva,
       1971.
       16p.   col.   maps.   25cm.

8050   U. S. S. R.   Glavnoe upravlenie geodezii i kartografii.
       Atlas istorii S. S. S. R.   Part II dlya VIII klassa.   Moskva,
       1971.
       11p.   col.   maps.   26cm.

8051   U. S. S. R.   Glavnoe upravlenie geodezii i kartografii.
       Atlas istorii S. S. S. R.   Part III, dlya IX-X klassov.
       Moskva, 1971.
       20p.   col.   maps.   26cm.

8052   U. S. S. R.   Glavnoe upravlenie geodezii i kartografii.
       Atlas istorii strednich vekov dlya VI klassa stredneii
       shkoly.   Moskva, 1971.
       16p.   col.   maps.   26cm.

8053   U. S. S. R.   Glavnoe upravlenie geodezii i kartografii.
       Atlas novoi istorii.   Part I. dlya VIII klassa.   Moskva,
       1971.
       16p.   col.   maps.   26cm.

8054   U. S. S. R. Glavnoe upravlenie geodezii i kartografii.
       Atlas novoi istorii. Part II, dlya IX klassa. Moskva,
       1971.
       16p. col. maps. 26cm.

8055   U. S. S. R. Glavnoe upravlenie geodezii i kartografii.
       Atlas noveishich istorii, dlya X klassa. Moskva, 1971.
       20p. col. maps. 26cm.

8056   U. S. S. R. Glavnoe upravlenie geodezii i kartografii.
       Atlas vsemirnoi istorii. Vol. I. Moskva, 1972.
       158p. col. maps. 50cm.

8057   Velhagen & Klasing.
       Putzger Historischer Weltatlas. Bielefeld, 1969.
       194p. col. maps. 27cm.

8058   Weidenfeld & Nicolson.
       Ancient history atlas. By Michael Grant. London, 1971.
       127p. 26cm.

8059   Weidenfeld & Nicolson.
       Atlas of the second world war. By Peter Young.
       London, 1973.
       281p. 26cm.

8060   Weidenfeld & Nicolson.
       Atlas of the second world war. By Peter Young. Lon-
       don, 1975.
       288p. 26cm.

8061   Weidenfeld & Nicolson.
       First World War atlas. By Martin Gilbert. London,
       1970.
       159p. 26cm.

8062   Weidenfeld & Nicolson.
       Recent history atlas 1860-1960. By Martin Gilbert. Lon-
       don, 1970.
       1 vol. 25cm.

8063   Weidenfeld & Nicolson.
       Russian history atlas. By Martin Gilbert. London, 1972.
       175p. 26cm.

8064   Weidenfeld & Nicolson.
       World atlas of military history. By Arthur Banks. Lon-
       don, 1973-
       5 vol. 26cm.

8065   Wesmael-Charlier.
       Atlas der algemene geschiedenis. By Franz Hayt. Na-
       mur, [1971].

152p.   col.   maps.   26cm.

8066 Wesmael-Charlier.
      Atlas der algemene geschiedenis.   By Franz Hayt.
      Namur, 1974.
      151p.   col.   maps.   26cm.

8067 Wesmael-Charlier.
      Atlas d'histoire universelle (et d'histoire de Belgique).
      By Franz Hayt.   Namur, [1969].
      152p.   col.   maps.   26cm.

8068 Wesmael-Charlier.
      Atlas d'histoire universelle et d'histoire de Belgique.   By
      Franz Hayt.   Namur, 1970.
      144p.   col.   maps.   26cm.

8069 Wesmael-Charlier.
      Cultuurhistorische atlas.   Het document in kaart.   By
      L. Th. Maes E. Bradt and R. Cazier.   Namur, [1970].
      1 vol.   32cm.

8070 Wesmael-Charlier.
      Culturhistorische atlas.   Het document in kaart.   By
      L. Th. Maes, E. Bradt and R. Cazier.   Namur, 1972.
      63p.   32cm.

8071 Westermann, Georg.
      Völker, Staaten und Kulturen.   Ein Kartenwerk zur
      Geschichte.   Braunschweig, 1957.
      98p.   col.   maps.   30cm.

8072 Westermann, Georg.
      Völker, Staaten und Kulturen.   Ein Kartenwerk zur
      Geschichte.   Braunschweig, 1969.
      146p.   col.   maps.   30cm.

8073 Westermann, Georg.
      Völker, Staaten und Kulturen.   Ein Kartenwerk zur
      Geschichte.   13ed.   By Hans-Erich Stier.   Braunschweig,
      1970.
      136p.   col.   maps.   30cm.

8074 Westermann, Georg.
      Westermann Geschichtsatlas: Politik, Wirtschaft, Kultur.
      1ed.   By Wolfgang Birkenfeld.   Braunschweig, [1971].
      51p.   col.   maps.   29cm.

8075 Westermann, Georg.
      Westermann Geschichtsatlas: Politik, Wirtschaft, Kultur.
      2ed.   By Wolfgang Birkenfeld.   Braunschweig, 1972.
      51p.   col.   maps.   29cm.

8076 Westermann, Georg.
      Westermann Geschichtsatlas: Politik, Wirtschaft, Kultur.
      3ed. By Wolfgang Birkenfeld. Braunschweig, 1973.
      51p. col. maps. 29cm.

8077 Wheaton & Co., Ltd.
      Wheaton's atlas of British and world history. 2ed. Exe-
      ter, 1972.
      52p. col. maps. 25cm.

8078 W. S. O. Y.
      Historisk atlas. By Jarl Gustafson. Porvoo, Helsinki,
      1971.
      38p. col. maps. 26cm.

8079 Yale University Press.
      Atlas of Russian history: eleven centuries of changing
      borders. Rev. ed. By Allen F. Chew. New Haven,
      1970.
      127p. 28cm.

HYDROGRAPHY

8080 Canada. Inland Waters Branch.
      Hydrological atlas of Canada; preliminary maps. Ottawa,
      1969.
      1 portf. 31cm.

8081 Congo. Comissariat Général au Plan.
      Atlas du Congo. Brazzaville, 1969.
      15p. col. maps. 62cm.

8082 France. Direction des ports maritimes et des voies naviga-
      bles.
      Liaisons fluviales Mer-du-Nord-Mediterranée. Paris,
      [1969].
      1 vol. col. maps. 42cm.

8083 U. S. Department of Agriculture.
      Atlas of the river basins of the United States. 2ed.
      Washington, D. C., 1970.
      82p. col. maps. 56cm.

8084 Water Information Center, Inc.
      Water atlas of the United States. 3ed. Port Washington,
      N. Y., 1973.
      200p. col. maps. 34cm.

INDUSTRIAL see ECONOMIC

IRRIGATION

8085 India. Ministry of Irrigation and Power.

Irrigation atlas of India.   Delhi, 1969.
1 vol.   30cm.

8086   India.   Ministry of Irrigation and Power.
Irrigation atlas of India.   Calcutta, 1972.
1 vol.   30cm.

LANGUAGE

8087   Bulgaria.   Akademiya na naukite.
Bulgarski dialekten atlas.   (In Bulgarian.)   Sofia, 1964-
in parts.   col.   maps.   50cm.

8088   France.   Centre national de la recherche scientifique.
Atlas linguistique de la France par régions.   Vol. 1:
de l'ouest.   Paris, 1971-
in parts.   col.   maps.   45. 5cm.

8089   France.   Centre national de la recherche scientifique.
Atlas linguistique et ethnographique.   Paris, 1972-
in parts.   col.   maps.   50cm.

8090   Romania.   Academia Republicii Socialiste.
Atlasul lingvistic român.   Serie nova.   Vol. VII.   Bucuresti, 1972.
398p.   col.   maps.   37cm.

MARINE

8091   Lloyd's Corp. of.
Lloyd's maritime atlas.   7ed.   London, 1969.
166p.   col.   maps.   25cm.

8092   Lloyd's Corp. of.
Lloyd's maritime atlas.   8ed.   London, 1971.
166p.   col.   maps.   25cm.

8093   Lloyd's Corp. of.
Lloyd's maritime atlas.   9ed.   Lor .on, 1974.
166p.   col.   maps.   25cm.

8094   Philip, George & Son, Ltd.
World atlas of shipping.   By W. D. Ewart and H. Fullard.
London, 1972.
277p.   col.   maps.   29cm.

8095   Philip, George & Son, Ltd.
World atlas of shipping.   By W. D. Ewart and H. Fullard.
London, 1973.
277p.   col.   maps.   29cm.

8096   St. Martin's Press.
World atlas of shipping: sea and shipping.   By W. D.

Ewart and Harold Fullard. With Philip. New York, London, [1973].
296p. col. maps. 29cm.

MEDICAL

8097 Panama. Asecoría en Geografía y Ecología.
      <u>Atlas de geografía médica.</u> Salud, 1970.
      60p. col. maps. 74cm.

MILITARY <u>see</u> HISTORY

MINERAL <u>see</u> GEOLOGY

MINING <u>see</u> GEOLOGY

MOUNTAINEERING

8098 Nelson, Thomas & Sons, Ltd.
      <u>World atlas of mountaineering.</u> By Wilfred Noyce and
      Ian McMorrin. London, 1969.
      224p. col. maps. 27cm.

OCEANOGRAPHY

8099 Chile. Instituto hidrografico de la armada.
      <u>Atlas oceanografico de Chile.</u> Valparaiso, 1972.
      21p. col. maps. 45cm.

8100 Pergamon Press, Ltd.
      <u>The world ocean atlas.</u> By Sergei G. Gorshkov. Oxford,
      New York, 1975.
      in parts. col. maps. 46cm.

8101 U.S. Naval Oceanographic Office.
      <u>Oceanographic atlas of the polar seas.</u> Part I: Antarctic.
      Washington, D.C., 1970.
      69p. col. maps. 40cm.

8102 U.S. Naval Oceanographic Office.
      <u>Oceanographic atlas of the polar seas.</u> Part II: Arctic.
      Washington, D.C., 1968.
      1 vol. col. maps. 40cm.

OIL <u>see</u> GEOLOGY

OREOGRAPHY

8103 Meyer, Kartographisches Institut.
      <u>Meyers grosser physischer Weltatlas.</u> Band 4: Atlas
      <u>zur physischen Geographie; Oreographie.</u> By Karlheinz
      Wagner. Mannheim, [1971].
      67p. col. maps. 30cm.

PALEOGRAPHY

8104   Poland.   Wydawn.   Geologiczne.
       Atlas litologiczno-paleograficzny obszaród platformowych
       Polski.   Warszawa, 1974-
       in parts.   31cm.

8105   Wiley, John & Sons.
       Atlas of paleogeographic maps of North America.   By
       Charles Schuchert.   New York, [1955].
       177p.   30cm.

PETROLEUM   see   GEOLOGY

POPULATION

8106   Canada.   Dept. of Indian Affairs and Northern Development.
       Atlas of Indian reserves & settlements of Canada.   Ottawa,
       1971.
       1 vol.   col. maps.   39cm.

8107   France.   Centre national de la recherche scientifique.
       Atlas de la population rurale.   France.   Paris, 1968.
       176p.   col. maps.   34cm.

8108   India.   Census Commission.
       Census of India, 1961.   Census Atlas.   By A. Mitra.
       New Delhi, 1970.
       423p.   col. maps.   52cm.

8109   India.   Census Commission.
       Census of India 1961.   Census Atlas.   By Sen Gupta.
       Delhi, 1971.
       423p.   col. maps.   52cm.

8110   Uruguay.   Dirección General de Estadística y Censos.   De-
       partmento de Cartografía.
       Mapas departmentales.   Montevideo, [1969].
       22p.   29cm.

8111   Zambia.   National Council for Scientific Research.
       Atlas of the population of Zambia.   By Mary E. Jackman
       and D. Hywel Davies.   Lusaka, 1971.
       10p.   col. maps.   54cm.

RADIO   see   COMMUNICATION

RAILROAD   see   TRANSPORTATION

ROAD

8112   Al-Ma-Prisma, Ltd.
       Mobil road maps of Greece: Hellas.   Athens, [1971].

16p. col. maps. 24cm.

8113 American Heritage.
        AA Illustrated road book of Scotland; with gazetteer,
        itineraries, maps and town plans. New York, 1971.
        288p. col. maps. 25cm.

8114 American Hotel Register Co.
        Leahy's hotel-motel guide and travel atlas of the United
        States, Canada and Mexico. 96ed. Chicago, 1971.
        278p. col. maps. 38cm.

8115 American Hotel Register Co.
        Leahy's hotel-motel guide and travel atlas of the United
        States, Canada and Mexico. 97ed. Chicago, 1972.
        278p. col. maps. 38cm.

8116 American Hotel Register Co.
        Leahy's hotel-motel guide and travel atlas of the United
        States, Canada and Mexico. 98ed. Chicago, 1973.
        278p. col. maps. 38cm.

8117 American Hotel Register Co.
        Leahy's hotel-motel guide and travel atlas of the United
        States, Canada and Mexico. 99ed. Chicago, 1974.
        296p. col. maps. 38cm.

8118 American Hotel Register Co.
        Leahy's hotel-motel guide and travel atlas of the United
        States, Canada and Mexico. 100ed. Chicago, 1975.
        296p. col. maps. 38cm.

8119 American Map Co., Inc.
        Cleartype transcontinental highway atlas; United States,
        Canada, Mexico. New York, [1950].
        16p. col. maps. 40cm.

8120 American Oil Co.
        American road atlas. With Diversified Map Corp. Ra-
        cine, Wisc., [1971].
        114p. col. maps. 28cm.

8121 Artists & Writers Press.
        Holiday Inn travel guide and road atlas. With General
        Drafting. New York, [1961].
        80p. col. maps. 28cm.

8122 Asociación Nacional Automovilística.
        Atlas: rutas de México; routes of Mexico. 5ed. México,
        1971.
        2 vol. col. maps. 24cm.

8123 Asociación Nacional Automovilística.

Atlas: rutas de Mexico; routes of Mexico. 6ed. México,
[1973].
2 vol. col. maps. 24cm.

8124 Automobile Association.
AA Illustrated road book of Scotland; with gazetteer,
itineraries, maps and town plans. London, 1971.
288p. col. maps. 25cm.

8125 Automobile Association.
Road book of France. 1ed. London, 1969.
535p. col. maps. 25cm.

8126 Automobile Association.
Road book of France. 2ed. London, 1970.
535p. col. maps. 25cm.

8127 Automobile Association of Malaya.
Malaysia road atlas; road atlas showing all motor roads
in Malaysia. 3ed. Penang, 1971.
28p. col. maps. 25cm.

8128 Automobile Association of South Africa.
Road atlas and touring guide of southern Africa. 3ed.
Johannesburg, [1968].
200p. col. maps. 25cm.

8129 Automobile Club d'Italia.
Autostrade italiane. Roma, [1973].
44p. col. maps. 26cm.

8130 Automóvil Club de Chile.
Atlas caminero de Chile. 1ed. By José Francisco Silva
C. Santiago, 1971.
1 vol. col. maps. 33cm.

8131 Balkanturist.
Automobile map of Bulgaria. Sofia, 1958.
32p. col. maps. 17cm.

8132 Bartholomew, John & Son, Ltd.
Bartholomew road atlas. Britain. Edinburgh, 1971-72.
112p. col. maps. 30cm.

8133 Bartholomew, John & Son, Ltd.
Bartholomew road atlas. Britain. Edinburgh, 1973.
112p. col. maps. 30cm.

8134 Bartholomew, John & Son, Ltd.
Companion road atlas of British Isles. Edinburgh, [1971].
112p. col. maps. 30cm.

8135 Bartholomew, John & Son, Ltd.

        Motorway atlas of Great Britain.   Edinburgh, 1972.
        48p. col. maps. 31cm.

8136   Bartholomew, John & Son, Ltd.
        Motorways atlas of Great Britain.   Edinburgh, 1973.
        48p. col. maps. 31cm.

8137   Bartholomew, John & Son. Ltd.
        Road atlas Britain.   Edinburgh, [1971].
        112p. col. maps. 28cm.

8138   Bartholomew, John & Son, Ltd.
        Road atlas Britain.   Edinburgh, 1974.
        112p. col. maps. 28cm.

8139   Bartholomew, John & Son, Ltd.
        Road atlas Britain.   Edinburgh, 1975.
        112p. col. maps. 28cm.

8140   Bartholomew, John & Son, Ltd.
        Road atlas Europe.   Edinburgh, [1970].
        136p. col. maps. 30cm.

8141   Bartholomew, John & Son, Ltd.
        Road atlas Europe.   Edinburgh, 1971.
        136p. col. maps. 30cm.

8142   Bartholomew, John & Son, Ltd.
        Road atlas Europe.   Edinburgh, 1972.
        136p. col. maps. 30cm.

8143   Bartholomew, John & Son, Ltd.
        Road atlas Europe.   Edinburgh, 1973.
        136p. col. maps. 30cm.

8144   Bartholomew, John & Son, Ltd.
        Road atlas Europe.   Edinburgh, 1974.
        136p. col. maps. 30cm.

8145   Bartholomew, John & Son, Ltd.
        Road atlas Europe.   Edinburgh, 1975.
        136p. col. maps. 30cm.

8146   Bartholomew, John & Son, Ltd.
        Road atlas of Great Britain.   Edinburgh, 1969.
        112p. col. maps. 25cm.

8147   Bartholomew, John & Son, Ltd.
        Roadmaster travel maps of Britain.   Edinburgh, 1970.
        1 vol. col. maps. 25cm.

8148   Bernces Förlag.
        Bernces reseatlas.   Malmö, [1972].

190p.   col.   maps.   31cm.

8149   Bertelsmann, C.
    Autoatlas Bertelsmann.   Deutschland-Europa.   Gütersloh,
    1970.
    386p.   col.   maps.   27cm.

8150   Bertelsmann, C.
    Autoatlas Bertelsmann.   Deutschland-Europa.   Gütersloh,
    1971.
    386p.   col.   maps.   27cm.

8151   Bertelsmann, C.
    Autoatlas Bertelsmann.   Deutschland-Europa.   Gütersloh,
    [1973].
    380p.   col.   maps.   27cm.

8152   Blondel La Rougery.
    Atlas des routes de France.   Paris, 1968.
    32p.   col.   maps.   24cm.

8153   Blondel La Rougery.
    Atlas des routes de France.   Paris, 1969.
    32p.   col.   maps.   24cm.

8154   BP Southern Africa Pty., Ltd.
    BP padkaarte.   Road maps.   Cape Town, [195-].
    14p.   col.   maps.   29cm.

8155   BP Southern Africa Pty., Ltd.
    BP road maps.   Padkaarte.   Cape Town, [1970].
    22p.   col.   maps.   29cm.

8156   BP Southern Africa Pty., Ltd.
    Road maps.   Padkaarte.   Cape Town, [1967].
    22p.   col.   maps.   29cm.

8157   Brazil.   Departamento nacional de estradas de rodagem.
    Atlas rodoviário provisório.   Rio de Janeiro, [1970].
    2 vol.   49cm.

8158   Brown & Bigelow.
    Automobile Travel-map road atlas for easier traveling.
    St. Paul, Minn., [1950].
    48p.   col.   maps.   26cm.

8159   Brown & Bigelow.
    Travel-map road atlas.   St. Paul, Minn., [1951].
    48p.   col.   maps.   26cm.

8160   Bulgaria.   Glavno upravlenie po geodezià i kartografià.
    Avtomobilei atlas Bulgaria.   Sofia, 1970.
    51p.   col.   maps.   21cm.

8161   Bulgaria.   Glavno upravlenie po gedeziâ i kartografiâ.
       Avtomobilei atlas Bulgaria.   2ed.   Sofia, 1971.
       52p.   col.   maps.   21cm.

8162   Buyōdō Co., Ltd.
       Road atlas.   Japan.   (In Japanese.)   Tokyo, 1970.
       4 vol.   col.   maps.   26cm.

8163   Carta.
       Carta's Israel motor atlas.   Jerusalem, [1970].
       57p.   col.   maps.   21cm.

8164   Carta.
       Carta's Israel road guide.   2ed.   Jerusalem, 1965.
       68p.   col.   maps.   24cm.

8165   Carta.
       Carta's Israel road guide.   Jerusalem, [1972].
       75p.   col.   maps.   28cm.

8166   Cartografía Pirelli.
       Guía Pirelli di carreteras: España.   Barcelona, [1971].
       40p.   col.   maps.   31cm.

8167   Cartographia.
       Autoatlas von Ungarn.   Road atlas of Hungary.   Budapest,
       1973.
       118p.   col.   maps.   26cm.

8168   Cartographia.
       Road atlas of Hungary.   Budapest, 1972.
       118p.   col.   maps.   26.5cm.

8169   Cartographia.
       Road atlas of Hungary.   By Hegyi Gyula.   Budapest,
       1973.
       118p.   col.   maps.   26.5cm.

8170   Chile.   Departamento de Caminos.
       Cartas camineras provinciales.   Santiago de Chile, 1951.
       1 vol.   col.   maps.   33cm.

8171   Collins, William, Sons & Co., Ltd.
       Collins road atlas, Britain & Ireland.   Glasgow, 1974.
       97p.   col.   maps.   28cm.

8172   Collins, William, Sons & Co., Ltd.
       Collins road atlas, Britain & Ireland.   Glasgow, 1975.
       97p.   col.   maps.   28cm.

8173   Compañia Shell de Venezuela.
       Carreteras de Venezuela.   3ed.   Caracas, [1960].
       23p.   19cm.

8174   Continental Gummiwerke Kartographischer Verlag.
       <u>Continental Atlas. Deutschland, Europa.</u> 36ed. Han-
       nover, 1969.
       555p. col. maps. 26cm.

8175   Continental Gummiwerke Kartographischer Verlag.
       <u>Continental Atlas. Deutschland, Europa.</u> 37ed. Han-
       nover, 1970.
       611p. col. maps. 26cm.

8176   Continental Gummiwerke Kartographischer Verlag.
       <u>Conti-Strassenatlas Deutschland.</u> Hannover, 1973.
       239p. col. maps. 26cm.

8177   Continental Gummiwerke Kartographischer Verlag.
       <u>Der grosse Continental-Atlas.</u> Hannover, Stuttgart, 1971.
       639p. col. maps. 26cm.

8178   Continental Gummiwerke Kartographischer Verlag.
       <u>Der grosse Continental-Atlas.</u> 39ed. Hannover, Stuttgart,
       1972.
       601p. col. maps. 26cm.

8179   Cram, George F., Co.
       <u>Cram's road atlas of the United States, Canada, Mexico.</u>
       Indianapolis, Ind., 1958.
       64p. col. maps. 31cm.

8180   Cram, George F., Co.
       <u>Cram's road atlas of the United States, Canada, Mexico.</u>
       Indianapolis, Ind., [1960].
       64p. col. maps. 31cm.

8181   Cuba. Instituto Cubano de Cartografía y Catastro.
       <u>Red de carreteras de la República de Cuba en planos
       provinciales y accesos de la ciudad de la Habana.</u> Ha-
       vana, 1957.
       8p. 35cm.

8182   Czechoslovakia. Kartografické nakladatelství.
       <u>Autoatlas ČSSR.</u> Praha, 1971.
       171p. col. maps. 31cm.

8183   Das Beste, G.M.B.H.
       <u>Reader's Digest ADAC Autoreisebuch. Atlas von den
       Alpen bis zur Nordsee.</u> Stuttgart, Zürich, Wien, 1968.
       440p. col. maps. 31cm.

8184   Das Beste, G.M.B.H.
       <u>Reader's Digest ADAC Autoreisebuch. Atlas von den
       Alpen bis zur Nordsee.</u> 4ed. Stuttgart, Zürich, Wien,
       1970.
       440p. col. maps. 31cm.

8185   Delta éditions.
       Tchécoslovaquie. Cartes et plans. By Philippe Froment.
       Paris, 1968.
       144p. col. maps. 18cm.

8186   Det Bedste fra Reader's Digest AS.
       Det Bedste fra Reader's Digest. København, 1969.
       516p. col. maps. 29cm.

8187   Det Beste A. S.
       Det Bestes bilbok. Oslo, 1969.
       392p. col. maps. 29cm.

8188   Diversified Map Corporation.
       American road atlas. [U. S.] With American Oil Co.
       St. Louis, Mo., 1971.
       114p. col. maps. 28cm.

8189   Diversified Map Corporation.
       American road atlas. With Western Pub. Co., St.
       Louis, Mo., [1971].
       114p. col. maps. 28cm.

8190   Diversified Map Corporation.
       Diversified Map Corporation road atlas. St. Louis, Mo.,
       1968.
       84p. col. maps. 23cm.

8191   Diversified Map Corporation.
       Interstate atlas. United States, Canada, Mexico. St.
       Louis, Mo., 1969.
       64p. col. maps. 23cm.

8192   Diversified Map Corporation.
       Pocket road atlas of the United States, Canada and Mexico.
       St. Louis, Mo., 1969.
       64p. col. maps. 21. 5cm.

8193   Diversified Map Corporation.
       Road atlas of the United States, Canada, and Mexico. St.
       Louis, Mo., 1968.
       144p. col. maps. 34cm.

8194   Diversified Map Corporation.
       The new Grosset road atlas of the United States, Canada
       and Mexico. St. Louis, [1973].
       128p. col. maps. 34cm.

8195   Donnelley, R. R. & Sons, Co.
       Best Western 1969 travel guide and atlas. Chicago, 1969.
       48p. col. maps. 31cm.

8196   Donnelley, R. R. & Sons, Co.
       Best Western 1970 travel guide and atlas.   Chicago, 1970.
       48p.   col.   maps.   31cm.

8197   Donnelley, R. R. & Sons, Co.
       Best Western 1971 travel guide and atlas.   Chicago, [1971].
       48p.   col.   maps.   31cm.

8198   Donnelley, R. R. & Sons, Co.
       Best Western motels, 1972 travel guide and atlas.   [North
       America.]   Chicago, 1972.
       48p.   col.   maps.   31cm.

8199   Donnelley, R. R. & Sons, Co.
       1973 travel guide and atlas.   Chicago, [1973].
       48p.   col.   maps.   31cm.

8200   Donnelley, R. R. & Sons, Co.
       Shell USA travel guide.   Chicago, [1970].
       31p.   col.   maps.   26cm.

8201   Donnelley, R. R. & Sons, Co.
       Shell USA travel guide.   Chicago, 1971.
       31p.   col.   maps.   26cm.

8202   Dutton, E. P. & Co.
       EURoad; the complete guide to motoring in Europe.   By
       Bert W. Lief.   New York, 1971.
       72p.   col.   maps.   28cm.

8203   Editions Bordas.
       Atlas routier et touristique.   Paris, 1970.
       1 vol.   col.   maps.   28cm.

8204   Editorial Everest.
       Mapa Everest de carreteras España y Portugal.   Leon,
       [1971].
       86p.   col.   maps.   25cm.

8205   Editura Stadion.
       România.   Ghid-atlas turistic.   By Mihai Iancu and D.
       Popescu.   Bucureşti, 1971.
       160p.   col.   maps.   24cm.

8206   Editura Stadion.
       România.   Tourist guide and atlas.   Bucureşti, 1971.
       80p.   col.   maps.   32cm.

8207   Esso, A. G.
       Europe Atlas.   Hamburg, 1968.
       96p.   col.   maps.   30cm.

8208   Esso, A. G.

Europa-Atlas. Hamburg, [1969].
96p. col. maps. 30cm.

8209 Esso, A. G.
Europa-Atlas. Ausgabe 1970/71. Hamburg, [1970].
96p. col. maps. 30cm.

8210 Esso, A. G.
Europa-Atlas. Hamburg, [1971].
96p. col. maps. 30cm.

8211 Esso, A. G.
Taschen-Atlas Deutschland. Hamburg, [1972].
64p. col. maps. 25cm.

8212 Esso Petroleum Co., Ltd.
Esso road atlas of Great Britain and Ireland. 1972/73
ed. With Stanford. London, 1971.
254p. col. maps. 28cm.

8213 European Road Guide, Inc.
1971-1972 Motoring atlas, Europe and Israel. Larch-
mont, N.Y., 1971.
78p. 28cm.

8214 Falk Verlag.
Autostrassen Atlas der Bundesrepublik Deutschland.
Hamburg, [1968].
68p. col. maps. 25cm.

8215 Falk Verlag.
Autostrassen Atlas der Bundesrepublik Deutschland. Hamburg, 1969.
68p. col. maps. 25cm.

8216 Falk Verlag.
Autostrassen Atlas der Bundesrepublik Deutschland. 72ed.
Hamburg, 1972.
72p. col. maps. 25cm.

8217 Falk Verlag.
Europa. Auto-Atlas. Hamburg, 1975.
41p. col. maps. 25cm.

8218 Falk Verlag.
Phoenix Autoatlas Bundesrepublik Deutschland. Hamburg,
1973.
72p. col. maps. 25cm.

8219 Falk Verlag.
Phoenix Autoatlas. Bundesrepublik Deutschland. Hamburg,
1974.
72p. col. maps. 25cm.

8220 Falk Verlag.
Phoenix Autoatlas. Bundesrepublik Deutschland. Hamburg, 1975.
72p. col. maps. 25cm.

8221 Farmers Insurance Group.
National road atlas. With H. M. Gousha. Los Angeles, Calif., 1961.
64p. col. maps. 26cm.

8222 Fietz, W. G.
Strassenatlas: Deutschland und Europa. Frankfurt, [1972].
71p. col. maps. 27cm.

8223 Firestone de la Argentina, S. A.
Mapa Firestone; red caminera de la República Argentina. Buenos Aires, [1950].
15p. col. maps. 28cm.

8224 Firestone-Hispania, S. A.
Firestone-Hispania atlas de España y Portugal. San Sebastian, [1971].
80p. col. maps. 27cm.

8225 Firestone-Hispania, S. A.
Firestone-Hispania atlas de España y Portugal. San Sebastián, [1972].
79p. col. maps. 27cm.

8226 Firestone-Hispania, S. A.
Firestone-Hispania atlas de España y Portugal. San Sebastián, 1974.
79p. col. maps. 27cm.

8227 Freytag, Berndt & Artaria.
Auto-Atlas Österreich 1:200,000. Wien, [1970].
111p. col. maps. 26cm.

8228 Freytag, Berndt & Artaria.
Auto-Atlas Österreich 1:200,000. Wien, [1972].
111p. col. maps. 26cm.

8229 Freytag, Berndt & Artaria.
Auto-Atlas Österreich 1:200,000. Wien, 1975.
103p. col. maps. 26cm.

8230 Freytag, Berndt & Artaria.
Europa Auto Atlas: Europe et Méditerranée. Road atlas. Wien, [1972].
216p. col. maps. 26cm.

8231 General Drafting Co.

HTC travel atlas. With Humble Travel Club. Houston,
Texas, 1970.
96p. col. maps. 29cm.

8232 General Drafting Co.
HTC travel atlas. With Humble Travel Club. Houston,
Texas, [1971].
84p. col. maps. 29cm.

8233 General Drafting Co.
Travel atlas. With Exxon Travel Club. Houston, Tex.,
[1973].
84p. col. maps. 29cm.

8234 General Drafting Co.
Travel atlas [North America]. With Humble Travel
Club. New York, [1970].
84p. col. maps. 29cm.

8235 General Drafting Co.
Travel atlas [North America]. With Humble Travel Club.
New York, [1971].
84p. col. maps. 29cm.

8236 Generalstabens litografiska anstalt.
KAK Bilatlas. Stockholm, 1969.
296p. col. maps. 31cm.

8237 Generalstabens litografiska anstalt.
KAK Bilatlas. Stockholm, [1972].
1 vol. col. maps. 31cm.

8238 Generalstabens litografiska anstalt.
KAK Bilatlas. Stockholm, 1973.
1 vol. col. maps. 31cm.

8239 Generalstabens litografiska anstalt.
KAK bilkartor. Road atlas of Sweden. Autoatlas von
Schweden. Atlas routier de Suède. Stockholm, [1966].
1 vol. col. maps. 31cm.

8240 Geographia, Ltd.
AA Great Britain road atlas. London, [1973].
247p. col. maps. 30cm.

8241 Geographia, Ltd.
European motoring atlas and guide. London, [1970].
89p. col. maps. 29cm.

8242 Geographia, Ltd.
Geographia commercial gazetteer and atlas of Great
Britain. London, 1970.
2 vol. col. maps. 25cm.

8243   Geographia, Ltd.
        Geographia commercial gazetteer and atlas of Great
        Britain. London, [1972].
        2 vol. col. maps. 25cm.

8244   Geographia, Ltd.
        Geographia road atlas of Great Britain. Commercial
        atlas of Great Britain. London, [1969].
        94p. col. maps. 28cm.

8245   Geographia, Ltd.
        Geographia road atlas of Great Britain. G. B. motoring
        atlas. London, [1969].
        94p. col. maps. 28cm.

8246   Geographia, Ltd.
        Geographia road atlas of Great Britain. London, [1972].
        94p. col. maps. 28cm.

8247   Geographia, Ltd.
        Great Britain touring atlas and guide. 8ed. London,
        [1972].
        68p. col. maps. 28cm.

8248   Germany. Militärgeographisches Amt.
        BW-Kraftfahrer Atlas. Bonn, 1969.
        2 vol. col. maps. 30cm.

8249   Goushá, H. M. , Co.
        American highway atlas. Chicago, [1955].
        98p. col. maps. 46cm.

8250   Goushá, H. M. , Co.
        American highway atlas. Chicago, [1956].
        98p. col. maps. 46cm.

8251   Goushá, H. M. , Co.
        American highway atlas. 3ed. New York, [1957].
        102p. col. maps. 46cm.

8252   Goushá, H. M. , Co.
        American highway atlas. 4ed. New York, [1959].
        103p. col. maps. 46cm.

8253   Goushá, H. M. , Co.
        American highway atlas. 5ed. New York, [1960].
        103p. col. maps. 46cm.

8254   Goushá, H. M. , Co.
        American highway atlas. Chicago, [1961].
        103p. col. maps. 46cm.

8255   Goushá, H. M. , Co.

National road atlas, United States, Canada, Mexico.
Chicago, San Jose, Calif., [1957].
48p.   col.   maps.   26cm.

8256   Goushá, H. M., Co.
New redi-r.ap road atlas.   With Brown & Bigelow.
Chicago, S: \ Jose, Calif., [1951].
32p.   col.   iaps.   26cm.

8257   Goushá, H. M. Co.
New redi-map; maps of the 48 states.   With Brown &
Bigelow.   Chicago, [1952].
32p.   col.   maps.   26cm.

8258   Goushá, H. M., Co.
New redi-map road atlas with maps of 48 states.   With
Brown & Bigelow.   Chicago, San Jose, Calif., [1954].
48p.   col.   maps.   26cm.

8259   Goushá, H. M., Co.
Redi-map road atlas with maps of 48 states.   With Brown
& Bigelow.   Chicago, San Jose, Calif., [1955].
48p.   col.   maps.   26cm.

8260   Goushá, H. M., Co.
Redi-map road atlas with maps of 48 states.   With Brown
& Bigelow.   Chicago, San Jose, Calif., [1956].
48p.   col.   maps.   26cm.

8261   Goushá, H. M., Co.
United States road atlas.   San Jose, Calif., [1962].
64p.   col.   maps.   26cm.

8262   Goushá, H. M., Co.
Vacation guide and road atlas.   United States, Canada,
Mexico.   With Brown & Bigelow.   Chicago, San Jose,
Calif., [1957].
48p.   col.   maps.   26cm.

8263   Goushá, H. M., Co.
Vacation guide and road atlas.   United States, Canada
and Mexico.   With Brown & Bigelow.   Chicago, San
Jose, Calif., [1958].
48p.   col.   maps.   26cm.

8264   Gregory's Guides & Maps Pty., Ltd.
The Ampol touring atlas of Australia.   Sydney, 1969.
122p.   col.   maps.   32cm.

8265   Gregory's Guides & Maps Pty., Ltd.
The Ampol touring atlas of Australia.   2ed.   Sydney,
[1970].
122p.   col.   maps.   32cm.

8266   Gregory's Guides & Maps Pty., Ltd.
       The Ampol touring atlas of Australia.   3ed.   Sydney, 1971.
       122p.   col.   maps.   32cm.

8267   Gregory's Guides & Maps Pty., Ltd.
       Touring atlas of Australia.   By Charles Sriber.   Sydney,
       [1970].
       122p.   col.   maps.   32cm.

8268   Haack, Hermann.
       Verkehrsatlas.   Deutsche Demokratische Republik.   1ed.
       By H. Langer.   Gotha, 1971.
       216p.   col.   maps.   18cm.

8269   Haack, Hermann.
       Verkehrsatlas.   Deutsche Demokratische Republik.   By H.
       Langer.   Gotha, 1972.
       220p.   col.   maps.   18cm.

8270   Hachette.
       Atlas routier et touristique: France, Belgique, Luxem-
       bourg, Suisse.   With Bordas.   Paris, [1970].
       76p.   col.   maps.   30cm.

8271   Hallwag, A. G.
       Autropa atlas.   Bern, 1970.
       89p.   col.   maps.   25cm.

8272   Hallwag, A. G.
       Autropa atlas.   Bern, [1971].
       89p.   col.   maps.   25cm.

8273   Hallwag, A. G.
       Autropa atlas.   Bern, 1972.
       84p.   col.   maps.   25cm.

8274   Hallwag, A. G.
       Europa-Auto-Atlas.   Bern, [1970].
       210p.   col.   maps.   26cm.

8275   Hallwag, A. G.
       Europa-Auto-Atlas.   Bern, Stuttgart, [1971].
       210p.   col.   maps.   26cm.

8276   Hallwag, A. G.
       Europa-Auto-Atlas.   Bern, [1972].
       216p.   col.   maps.   26cm.

8277   Hallwag, A. G.
       Europa-Auto-Atlas.   Bern, [1973].
       224p.   col.   maps.   26cm.

8278   Hallwag, A. G.

      Europa-Auto-Atlas.   Bern, 1974.
      220p. col. maps. 26cm.

8279 Hallwag, A. G.
      Europa-Auto-Atlas.   Bern, 1975.
      220p. col. maps. 26cm.

8280 Hallwag, A. G.
      Europa Touring. Automobilführer von Europa.   Bern,
      Stuttgart, [1970].
      822p. col. maps. 26cm.

8281 Hallwag, A. G.
      Europa Touring. Automobilführer von Europa.   Bern,
      Stuttgart, [1971].
      822p. col. maps. 26cm.

8282 Hallwag, A. G.
      Europa Touring. Automobilführer von Europa.   Bern,
      Stuttgart, 1972.
      822p. col. maps. 26cm.

8283 Hallwag, A. G.
      Europa Touring. Automobilführer von Europa.   Bern,
      Stuttgart, [1973].
      822p. col. maps. 26cm.

8284 Hallwag, A. G.
      Europa Touring. Automobilführer von Europa.   Bern,
      Stuttgart, 1974.
      822p. col. maps. 26cm.

8285 Hallwag, A. G.
      Europa Touring. Automobilführer von Europa.   Bern,
      Stuttgart, 1975.
      865p. col. maps. 26cm.

8286 Hamlyn.
      AA road atlas of New Zealand.   Auckland, 1974.
      124p. col. maps. 29cm.

8287 Hamlyn.
      Road atlas of Australia.   Sydney, 1972.
      128p. col. maps. 26cm.

8288 Hamlyn.
      The motorists touring maps and gazetteer.   London, 1972.
      163p. col. maps. 28cm.

8289 Hammond, C. S. & Co., Inc.
      Hammond's road atlas and city street guide of the United
      States, Canada, Mexico. Maplewood, N. J., 1962.
      96p. col. maps. 31cm.

8290   Hammond, C. S. & Co., Inc.
        Hammond road atlas of the United States, Canada, Mexico.
        Maplewood, N. J., 1966.
        48p. col. maps. 32cm.

8291   Hammond, Inc.
        Hammond compact road atlas and vacation guide. Maple-
        wood, N. J., [1973].
        48p. col. maps. 22cm.

8292   Hammond, Inc.
        Pictorial travel atlas of scenic America. By E. L. Jor-
        dan. Maplewood, N. J., 1973.
        288p. col. maps. 28cm.

8293   Hammond, Inc.
        Road atlas and travel guide, U. S. Maplewood, N. J., 1971.
        48p. col. maps. 28cm.

8294   Hartford Fire Insurance Co.
        United States road atlas, including Canada and Mexico.
        With H. M. Gousha. Hartford, Conn., [1959].
        56p. col. maps. 26cm.

8295   Hartford Fire Insurance Co.
        United States road atlas, including Canada and Mexico.
        With H. M. Gousha. Hartford, Conn., [1960].
        56p. col. maps. 26cm.

8296   Humble Travel Club.
        HTC travel atlas. With General Drafting Co. Houston,
        Texas, [1971].
        84p. col. maps. 29cm.

8297   Industrias Kaiser Argentina, S. A.
        Atlas vial IKA. Buenos Aires, 1960.
        111p. col. maps. 23cm.

8298   Innocenti.
        Carta automobilistica d'Italia. With De Agostini. Milano,
        [1972].
        28p. col. maps. 22cm.

8299   International Road Federation.
        Main European arteries (E roads): traffic census maps,
        1965. Grands itinéraires européens; Europäische Haupt-
        verkehrsadern. Geneva, 1968.
        19p. col. maps. 29cm.

8300   Istituto Geografico De Agostini.
        Atlante stradale d'Italia. Novara, 1969.
        182p. col. maps. 27cm.

8301   Istituto Geografico De Agostini.
        Atlante stradale d'Italia. Novara, 1971.
        1 vol. col. maps. 27cm.

8302   Istituto Geografico De Agostini.
        Atlante stradale d'Italia. Novara, [1972].
        188p. col. maps. 27cm.

8303   Istituto Geografico De Agostini.
        Carta automobilistica d'Italia. Novara, [1971].
        20p. col. maps. 24cm.

8304   Istituto Geografico De Agostini.
        Guida del servizio Fiat Italia. Novara, [1970].
        114p. col. maps. 25cm.

8305   Istituto Geografico De Agostini.
        Guida del servizio Fiat Italia. Novara, [1971].
        86p. col. maps. 25cm.

8306   Johnston, W. & A. K. & G. W. Bacon, Ltd.
        Autoway atlas. Great Britain and Ireland. London, 1969.
        1 vol. col. maps. 26cm.

8307   Johnston, W. & A. K. & G. W. Bacon, Ltd.
        Pocket road atlas of Ireland. London, 1968.
        1 vol. col. maps. 18cm.

8308   Johnston & Bacon
        A & B roads and motorways atlas of Great Britain. 4ed.
        Edinburgh, 1973.
        48p. col. maps. 33cm.

8309   Johnston & Bacon.
        3 miles to 1 inch road atlas of Great Britain. Edinburgh,
        London, [1971].
        112p. col. maps. 30cm.

8310   Johnston & Bacon.
        3 miles to 1 inch road atlas of Great Britain. 7ed.
        Edinburgh, London, 1973.
        373p. col. maps. 30cm.

8311   JRO Verlag.
        Der Grosse JRO Auto Atlas. JRO Autoführer der
        Bundesrepublik Deutschland. 24ed. München, 1964.
        658p. col. maps. 24.5cm.

8312   JRO Verlag.
        JRO Autoatlas. Deutschland, Europäische Reiseländer.
        München, [1971].
        1 vol. col. maps. 25cm.

8313 Jugoslavenski leksikografski zavod.
Jugoslavija; auto atlas. By Petar Mardešić. Zagreb,
[1969].
1 vol. col. maps. 24cm.

8314 Jugoslavenski leksikografski zavod.
Jugoslavija; auto atlas. 5ed. Zagreb, 1970.
56p. col. maps. 24cm.

8315 Jugoslavenski leksikografski zavod.
Jugoslavija; auto atlas. 7ed. Zagreb, [1971].
56p. col. maps. 24cm.

8316 Jugoslavenski leksikografski zavod.
Jugoslavija; auto atlas. 8ed. Zagreb, [1971].
52p. col. maps. 24cm.

8317 Jugoslavenski leksikografski zavod.
Jugoslavija; auto atlas. 10ed. Zagreb, [1971].
56p. col. maps. 24cm.

8318 Jugoslavenski lekisografski zavod.
Jugoslavija; auto atlas. 1ed. Zagreb, 1973.
110p. col. maps. 24cm.

8319 Kartlitografen, AB.
Mobil bilkarta. Danderyd, [1970].
29p. col. maps. 33cm.

8320 Kartlitografen, AB.
Mobil bilkarta. Danderyd, [1971].
29p. col. maps. 33cm.

8321 Kartográfiai Vállalat.
Magyarország autóatlasza. 1ed. Budapest, 1972.
220p. col. maps. 21cm.

8322 Kartográfiai Vállalat.
Magyarország autóatlasza. Budapest, 1973.
220p. col. maps. 21cm.

8323 Kartografie.
Autoatlas ČSSR. 7ed. Praha, 1973.
183p. col. maps. 25cm.

8324 Kongelik Novsk automobilklub.
KNA Kart-og reisehändbok. Oslo, 1971.
327p. col. maps. 26cm.

8325 König, Hans, Verlag.
Deutscher Ferien Atlas. Frankfurt am Main, 1969.
105p. col. maps. 24cm.

8326 König, Hans, Verlag.
      Fina Europa Atlas. Bergen-Enkheim, 1969.
      114p. col. maps. 25cm.

8327 König, Hans, Verlag.
      Strassenatlas Deutschland-Europa. Frankfurt am Main,
      1971.
      1 vol. col. maps. 29cm.

8328 Kümmerly & Frey.
      Auto Europa, road atlas. Bern, [1971].
      241p. col. maps. 25cm.

8329 Kümmerly & Frey.
      Auto-Europa. Strassenatlas. Bern, 1969.
      218p. col. maps. 25cm.

8330 Kümmerly & Frey.
      Europa. Europe. Strassenatlas. Bern, 1969.
      84p. col. maps. 23cm.

8331 Kümmerly & Frey.
      Europa. Europe. Strassenatlas. Bern, 1970.
      260p. col. maps. 26cm.

8332 Kümmerly & Frey.
      Europa. Europe. Strassenatlas. Bern, 1971.
      260p. col. maps. 26cm.

8333 Kümmerly & Frey.
      Europa. Europe. Strassenatlas. Bern, [1972].
      260p. col. maps. 26cm.

8334 Kümmerly & Frey.
      Europa. Europe. Strassenatlas. Bern, [1973].
      266p. col. maps. 26cm.

8335 Kümmerly & Frey.
      Europa. Grosser Strassen-und Reiseatlas. Bern, 1973.
      165p. col. maps. 30cm.

8336 Kümmerly & Frey.
      Europe, atlas routier. Bern, [1968].
      140p. col. maps. 23cm.

8337 Kümmerly & Frey.
      Europe road atlas. Bern, [1971].
      140p. col. maps. 23cm.

8338 Kümmerly & Frey.
      Schweiz und angrenzende Länder, Strassenatlas. Bern,
      [1963].
      60p. col. maps. 23cm.

8339   Lademann forlagsaktieselskab.
       Lademanns rejseatlas.   By Svend-Aage Hansen.   With
       Kümmerly & Frey.   København, 1972.
       192p.   col.   maps.   31cm.

8340   Landkartenverlag, VEB.
       Atlas für Motortouristik der Deutschen Demokratischen
       Republik.   Berlin, [1973].
       224p.   col.   maps.   26cm.

8341   Landkartenverlag, VEB.
       Reiseatlas der Deutschen Demokratischen Republik.   4ed.
       Berlin, 1970.
       176p.   col.   maps.   26cm.

8342   Landkartenverlag, VEB.
       Reiseatlas der Deutschen Demokratischen Republik.   4ed.
       Berlin, [1971].
       176p.   col.   maps.   26cm.

8343   Landkartenverlag, VEB.
       Reiseatlas der Deutschen Demokratischen Republik.   4ed.
       Berlin, 1972.
       176p.   col.   maps.   26cm.

8344   Landkartenverlag, VEB.
       Reiseatlas der Deutschen Demokratischen Republik.   5ed.
       Berlin, 1973.
       176p.   col.   maps.   26cm.

8345   Landkartenverlag, VEB.
       Reiseatlas der Deutschen Demokratischen Republik.   6ed.
       Berlin, 1973.
       176p.   col.   maps.   26cm.

8346   Lief, B. W.
       EURoad: the complete guide to motoring in Europe.   New
       York, [1971].
       72p.   col.   maps.   28cm.

8347   Lief, B. W.
       Volvo road atlas; the complete guide to motoring in
       Europe.   New York, [1971].
       72p.   col.   maps.   28cm.

8348   Maanmittaushallitus.
       Suomi.   Finland.   Yleiskartta 1:400,000.   Helsinki,
       1966-72.
       31p.   col.   maps.   35cm.

8349   Maanmittaushallitus.
       Suomi.   Finland.   Yleiskartta 1:400,000 general karta.
       6ed.   Helsinki, 1968.

121p.   col. maps.   25cm.

8350   Maanmittaushallitus.
       Suomi. Finland. Yleiskarttalehtiö 1:400,000 generalkart-
       blocket. Helsinki, [1968-72].
       31p. col. maps. 35cm.

8351   Maanmittaushallitus.
       Suomi. Finland. Yleiskarttalehtiö 1:400,000.   Finland;
       generalkartblocket. Helsinki, [1969].
       34p. col. maps. 35cm.

8352   Maanmittaushallitus.
       Yleiskarttalehtiö-Generalkartblocket.   Helsinki, 1968.
       31p. col. maps. 35cm.

8353   Mairs Geographischer Verlag.
       Der grosse Continental-Atlas. Deutschland, Europa.
       Stuttgart, 1971.
       576p. col. maps. 26cm.

8354   Mairs Geographischer Verlag.
       Der grosse Continental-Atlas. Deutschland, Europa.
       Stuttgart, 1972.
       576p. col. maps. 26cm.

8355   Mairs Geographischer Verlag.
       Der grosse Continental-Atlas. Deutschland, Europa.
       Stuttgart, 1973.
       576p. col. maps. 26cm.

8356   Mairs Geographischer Verlag.
       Der grosse Continental-Atlas. Deutschland, Europa.
       Stuttgart, 1974.
       576p. col. maps. 26cm.

8357   Mairs Geographischer Verlag.
       Der grosse Continental-Atlas. Deutschland, Europa.
       Stuttgart, 1975.
       576p. col. maps. 26cm.

8358   Mairs Geographischer Verlag.
       Der Grosse Shell Atlas. Deutschland, Europa. 1970/71.
       Stuttgart, 1970.
       317p. col. maps. 27cm.

8359   Mairs Geographischer Verlag.
       Der Grosse Shell-Atlas. Deutschland, Europa. 1971/72.
       Stuttgart, 1971.
       317p. col. maps. 27cm.

8360   Mairs Geographischer Verlag.
       Der Grosse Shell Atlas. Deutschland und Europa. Stutt-

gart, 1972.
526p. col. maps. 27cm.

8361 Mairs Geographischer Verlag.
Der grosse Shell Atlas. Deutschland und Europa. Stuttgart, 1973.
513p. col. maps. 27cm.

8362 Mairs Geographischer Verlag.
Der grosse Shell Atlas. Deutschland und Europa. Stuttgart, 1974.
513p. col. maps. 27cm.

8363 Mairs Geographischer Verlag.
Der grosse Shell Atlas. Deutschland und Europa. Stuttgart, 1975.
513p. col. maps. 27cm.

8364 Mairs Geographischer Verlag.
Shell atlas of Europe. Stuttgart, [1971].
229p. col. maps. 27cm.

8365 Mairs Geographischer Verlag.
Shell Reiseatlas Deutschland. Stuttgart, 1975.
206p. col. maps. 30cm.

8366 Mairs Geographischer Verlag.
VARTA Atlas Deutschland/Europa. Stuttgart, [1974].
1 vol. col. maps. 30cm.

8367 Map Productions, Ltd.
BMC Route Planner. London, [1970].
64p. col. maps. 28cm.

8368 Map Productions, Ltd.
Fina route planning atlas. Great Britain. London, 1969.
64p. col. maps. 28cm.

8369 Map Productions, Ltd.
Fina route planning atlas. Great Britain. London, [1970].
64p. col. maps. 28cm.

8370 Map Productions, Ltd.
Great Britain Motorways. London, [1972].
1 vol. col. maps. 27cm.

8371 Map Productions, Ltd.
Great Britain. Route Planning [atlas]. London, [1971].
64p. col. maps. 28cm.

8372 Map Productions, Ltd.
Great Britain. Route Planning maps. London, [1972].
139p. col. maps. 28cm.

8373   Map Productions, Ltd.
       Motorways: A new atlas to illustrate the motorway system
       of Great Britain. London, [1970].
       1 vol. col. maps. 27cm.

8374   Map Studio Productions, pty. , Ltd.
       Road atlas of Southern Africa. With Shell South Africa.
       Johannesburg, 1970.
       64p. col. maps. 27.5cm.

8375   Marketing International.
       International airline & road atlas. 1ed. Frankfurt am
       Main, [1971].
       1 vol. col. maps. 30cm.

8376   Mexico. Ministerio de Comunicaciones y Obras Públicas.
       Atlas de la república Mexicana con los caminos a cargo
       de la dirección nacional de caminos. México, 1952.
       31p. 42cm.

8377   Mexico. Secretaría de Comunicaciones y Transportes.
       Cartas e información sobre vías generales de comunicación
       de las entidades federativas. México, 1964.
       2 vol. 44cm.

8378   Michelin et Cie.
       Atlas des routes de France. Paris, [1971].
       1 vol. col. maps. 26cm.

8379   Michelin et Cie.
       Michelin atlas des autoroutes de France. Paris, 1970.
       46p. col. maps. 26cm.

8380   Michelin et Cie.
       Michelin atlas des autoroutes de France. Paris, [1971].
       54p. col. maps. 26cm.

8381   Michelin et Cie.
       Michelin atlas des autoroutes de France. Paris, [1973].
       66p. col. maps. 26cm.

8382   Mobil Oil, AB.
       Mobil bilkarta. Danderyd, [1971].
       29p. col. maps. 33cm.

8383   Mobil Oil Hellas.
       Mobil road maps of Greece. Athens, 1971.
       20p. col. maps. 24cm.

8384   Mondadori.
       Rand McNally road atlas of Europe. Chicago, 1973.
       104p. col. maps. 28cm.

8385 Motormännens riksförbund.
      M:S vägvisare: Sverige.   9ed.   By Harry Ljunberg.
      Stockholm, 1971.
      304p. col. maps. 25cm.

8386 National Bus Traffic Association.
      Atlas of motor bus routes and express blocks no. A-602.
      Chicago, 1956.
      72p. 40cm.

8387 National Bus Traffic Association.
      Atlas of motor bus routes; showing operations of intercity
      bus carriers in the United States, Canada, Mexico. Chi-
      cago, [1953].
      81p. 46cm.

8388 National Safety Council.
      National Safety Council road atlas, travel safety guide.
      With H. M. Goushá. Chicago, [1964].
      64p. col. maps. 28cm.

8389 National Safety Council.
      Travel safety guide and road atlas. With Goushá. Chi-
      cago, [1967].
      64p. col. maps. 28cm.

8390 Philip, George & Son, Ltd.
      BP road atlas of Great Britain.   London, 1971.
      160p. col. maps. 28cm.

8391 Philip, George & Son, Ltd.
      BP road atlas of Great Britain.   London, 1972.
      160p. col. maps. 28cm.

8392 Philip, George & Son, Ltd.
      Esso road atlas of Great Britain and Ireland.   London,
      1972.
      253p. col. maps. 29cm.

8393 Philip, George & Son, Ltd.
      Esso road atlas of Great Britain and Ireland.   London,
      1974.
      260p. col. maps. 29cm.

8394 Philip, George & Son, Ltd.
      Motorist's touring maps and gazetteer.   London, [1971].
      146p. col. maps. 29cm.

8395 Philip, George & Son, Ltd.
      National atlas. Road maps and town plans--Great Britain.
      London, 1971.
      192p. col. maps. 29cm.

8396   Philip, George & Son, Ltd.
       National road atlas of Great Britain.   London, [1971].
       103p. col. maps. 28cm.

8397   Philip, George & Son, Ltd.
       Philips' road atlas Europe.   1ed.   London, 1972.
       239p. col. maps. 29cm.

8398   Philip, George & Son, Ltd.
       Shell road atlas, Great Britain: with special London sec-
       tion. London, 1971.
       160p. col. maps. 29cm.

8399   Philip, George & Son, Ltd.
       Shell road atlas, Great Britain: with special London sec-
       tion. London, 1972.
       160p. col. maps. 29cm.

8400   Philip, George & Son, Ltd.
       Shell road atlas of Great Britain.   London, [1971].
       144p. col. maps. 28cm.

8401   Poland. Państwowe przedsiębiorstwo wydawnictw kartografi-
       cznych.
       Atlas samochodowy Polski. 2ed. Warszawa, 1959.
       155p. col. maps. 23cm.

8402   Poland. Państwowe przedsiębiorstwo wydawnictw kartografi-
       cznych.
       Atlas samochodowy Polski. Warszawa, 1970.
       156p. col. maps. 23cm.

8403   Poland. Państwowe przedsiębiorstwo wydawnictw kartografi-
       cznych.
       Atlas samochodowy Polski. Warszawa, 1971.
       156p. col. maps. 23cm.

8404   Poland. Państwowe przedsiębiorstwo wydawnictw kartografi-
       cznych.
       Atlas samochodowy Polski. Warszawa, 1972.
       201p. col. maps. 23cm.

8405   Postånpernes Landsforbund.
       Post-, vej-og fylkeskarte. Oslo, [1960].
       44p. col. maps. 23cm.

8406   Rand McNally & Co.
       Canada road atlas. By Paul Tiddens. Chicago, 1974.
       64p. col. maps. 38cm.

8407   Rand McNally & Co.
       Chevrolet's family travel guide. Chicago, 1968.
       128p. col. maps. 28cm.

8408   Rand McNally & Co.
       Rand McNally illustrated road guide.   Chicago, 1956.
       48p.   col. maps.   23cm.

8409   Rand McNally & Co.
       Rand McNally interstate highway atlas.   Pocket ed.   Chi-
       cago, 1971.
       32p.   col. maps.   20cm.

8410   Rand McNally & Co.
       Rand McNally interstate highway atlas.   Pocket ed.   Chi-
       cago, 1972.
       32p.   col. maps.   20cm.

8411   Rand McNally & Co.
       Rand McNally interstate road atlas.   Chicago, 1974.
       96p.   col. maps.   28cm.

8412   Rand McNally & Co.
       Rand McNally road atlas and radio guide of the United
       States.   Chicago, 1950.
       88p.   col. maps.   27cm.

8413   Rand McNally & Co.
       Rand McNally road atlas and radio guide of the United
       States.   Chicago, 1951.
       88p.   col. maps.   27cm.

8414   Rand McNally & Co.
       Rand McNally road atlas and radio guide of the United
       States.   Chicago, 1952.
       96p.   col. maps.   27cm.

8415   Rand McNally & Co.
       Rand McNally road atlas and radio guide of the United
       States.   Chicago, 1957.
       96p.   col. maps.   27cm.

8416   Rand McNally & Co.
       Rand McNally road atlas and radio guide of the United
       States.   Chicago, 1958.
       96p.   col. maps.   27cm.

8417   Rand McNally & Co.
       Rand McNally road atlas.   Golden anniversary ed.   Chi-
       cago, 1974.
       160p.   col. maps.   40cm.

8418   Rand McNally & Co.
       Rand McNally road atlas of Europe.   Chicago, 1971.
       96p.   col. maps.   28cm.

8419   Rand McNally & Co.

      Rand McNally road atlas of Europe.   Chicago, 1972.
      104p. col. maps. 28cm.

8420 Rand McNally & Co.
      Rand McNally road atlas of Europe.   Chicago, 1973.
      104p. col. maps. 28cm.

8421 Rand McNally & Co.
      Rand McNally road atlas of Europe.   Chicago, 1974.
      104p. col. maps. 28cm.

8422 Rand McNally, GMBH.
      Rand McNally road atlas of Europe.   Chicago, 1971.
      96p. col. maps. 28cm.

8423 Rand McNally, GMBH.
      Rand McNally road atlas of Europe.   Chicago, 1972.
      104p. col. maps. 28cm.

8424 Rand McNally & Co.
      Rand McNally road atlas, United States, Canada, Mexico.
      Chicago, 1971.
      118p. col. maps. 40cm.

8425 Rand McNally & Co.
      Rand McNally road atlas, United States, Canada, Mexico.
      Chicago, 1972.
      128p. col. maps. 40cm.

8426 Rand McNally & Co.
      Rand McNally road atlas, United States, Canada, Mexico.
      Chicago, 1973.
      128p. col. maps. 40cm.

8427 Rand McNally & Co.
      Rand McNally road atlas, United States, Canada, Mexico.
      Chicago, 1974.
      160p. col. maps. 40cm.

8428 Rand McNally & Co.
      Rand McNally road atlas, United States, Canada, Mexico.
      Chicago, 1975.
      160p. col. maps. 40cm.

8429 Rand McNally & Co.
      Rand McNally road atlas, U.S., Canada, Mexico. 50 an-
      niversary ed. Chicago, 1974.
      136p. col. maps. 40cm.

8430 Rand McNally & Co.
      Rand McNally travel atlas. Chicago, 1974.
      224p. col. maps. 27cm.

8431 Rand McNally & Co.
      Road atlas & travel guide, United States, Canada, Mexico.
      Chicago, 1971.
      96p. col. maps. 27cm.

8432 Rand McNally & Co.
      Road atlas & travel guide, United States, Canada, Mexico.
      Chicago, 1972.
      96p. col. maps. 27cm.

8433 Rand McNally & Co.
      Texaco international road atlas. New York, 1959.
      48p. col. maps. 25cm.

8434 Rand McNally & Co.
      Texaco international road atlas. New York, 1961.
      48p. col. maps. 25cm.

8435 Rand McNally & Co.
      Texaco touring maps. New York, [1952].
      52p. col. maps. 82cm.

8436 Rand McNally & Co.
      Texaco travel atlas: United States, Canada, Mexico.
      Chicago, [1971].
      224p. col. maps. 38cm.

8437 Rand McNally & Co.
      Texaco travel atlas: United States, Canada, Mexico.
      Chicago, 1972.
      224p. col. maps. 38cm.

8438 Rand McNally & Co.
      Texaco travel atlas: United States, Canada, Mexico.
      Chicago, [1973].
      224p. col. maps. 38cm.

8439 Ravenstein Geographische Verlagsanstalt.
      Reiseatlas Deutschland und Europa. Frankfurt, 1971.
      67p. col. maps. 29cm.

8440 Ravenstein Geographische Verlagsanstalt.
      Reiseatlas Deutschland und Europa. Frankfurt, 1975.
      66p. col. maps. 29cm.

8441 Ravenstein Geographische Verlagsanstalt.
      Strassen; der aktuelle Auto-Atlas Deutschland und Europa.
      Frankfurt am Main, [1968].
      66p. col. maps. 29cm.

8442 Ravenstein Geographische Verlagsanstalt.
      Strassen der aktuelle Auto-Atlas Deutschland und Europa.
      Frankfurt am Main, 1969.
      66p. col. maps. 29cm.

8443   Ravenstein Geographische Verlagsanstalt.
       Strassen; der aktuelle Auto-Atlas. Deutschland und Europa.
       Frankfurt, 1970.
       66p. col. maps. 29cm.

8444   Ravenstein Geographische Verlagsanstalt.
       Strassen; der aktuelle Auto-Atlas Deutschland und Europa.
       Frankfurt, 1971.
       66p. col. maps. 29cm.

8445   Ravenstein Geographische Verlagsanstalt.
       Strassen; der aktuelle Auto-Atlas Deutschland und Europa.
       Frankfurt, 1972.
       66p. col. maps. 29cm.

8446   Ravenstein Geographische Verlagsanstalt.
       Strassen; der aktuelle Auto-Atlas Deutschland und Europa.
       Frankfurt, 1973.
       68p. col. maps. 29cm.

8447   Ravenstein Geographische Verlagsanstalt.
       Strassen; der aktuelle Auto-Atlas Deutschland und Europa.
       Frankfurt, 1974.
       66p. col. maps. 29cm.

8448   Ravenstein Geographische Verlagsanstalt.
       Strassen; der aktuelle Auto-Atlas Deutschland und Europa.
       Frankfurt, 1975.
       66p. col. maps. 29cm.

8449   Reader's Digest A. B.
       Det Bästas bilbok. Stockholm, [1969].
       392p. col. maps. 29cm.

8450   Reader's Digest Association, Ltd.
       The Reader's Digest A. A. book of the road. 3ed. London,
       [1972].
       412p. col. maps. 28cm.

8451   Reader's Digest, N. V.
       Het Beste boek voor de weg. Amsterdam, [1969].
       1 vol. col. maps. 29cm.

8452   Reader's Digest, N. V.
       Het Beste boek voor de weg. 2ed. Amsterdam, [1970].
       1 vol. col. maps. 29cm.

8453   Reise und Verkehrsverlag.
       Grosser Auto-Atlas: international. Stuttgart, 1975.
       503p. col. maps. 27cm.

8454   Reise und Verkehrsverlag.
       Strassenatlas: Deutschland, Europa. Berlin, [1973].

169p.   col. maps.   26cm.

8455   Reise und Verkehrsverlag.
       Strassenatlas: Deutschland, Europa.   Berlin, 1974.
       208p.   col. maps.   26cm.

8456   Rolph-McNally, Ltd.
       Canadian road atlas.   Bramalea, Ont., 1972-
       48p.   col. maps.   37cm.

8457   Royal Automobile Club.
       Road atlas of Europe.   London, 1972.
       124p.   col. maps.   28cm.

8458   Royal Automobile Club.
       Road map of Ireland.   With Bartholomew.   London, [1969].
       16p.   col. maps.   22cm.

8459   Sahab.
       Travel atlas of Iran.   Teheran, 1970.
       99p.   col. maps.   24cm.

8460   Selecções do Reader's Digest.
       O livro da estrada; seleções do Reader's Digest.   Lisboa,
       [1969].
       338p.   col. maps.   29cm.

8461   Sélection du Reader's Digest, S. A. R. L.
       Guide de la route Europe.   Paris, [1969].
       1 vol.   col. maps.   29cm.

8462   Sélection du Reader's Digest, S. A. R. L.
       Guide de la route: France, Belgique, Suisse.   Paris,
       [1969].
       455p.   col. maps.   29cm.

8463   Shell Caribbean Petroleum Company.
       Carreteras de Venezuela.   Caracas, [1951].
       19p.   18cm.

8464   Shell Co. of New Zealand.
       Shell road maps of New Zealand.   Wellington, 1972.
       44p.   col. maps.   28cm.

8465   Shell Co. of Turkey, Ltd.
       Motorist guide to Turkey.   Istanbul, [1971].
       228p.   col. maps.   21cm.

8466   Shell Moçambique, Ltd.
       Estradas de Moçambique.   Lourenço Marques, [1969].
       12p.   col. maps.   23cm.

8467   Skelly Oil Co.

Skelly highway atlas.   With H. M. Goushá.   Tulsa, Okla.,
[1959].
56p.   col. maps.   26cm.

8468   Slovenska Kartografia.
       Autoatlas ČSSR.   1ed.   Bratislava, 1971.
       18p.   col. maps.   25cm.

8469   Slovenska Kartografia.
       Autoatlas ČSSR.   2ed.   Bratislava, 1972.
       18p.   col. maps.   25cm.

8470   Slovenska Kartografia.
       Autoatlas ČSSR.   3ed.   Bratislava, 1973.
       169p.   col. maps.   25cm.

8471   Spain.   Ministerio de Obras Públicas.
       España: Mapa oficial de carreteras.   8ed.   Madrid,
       [1969].
       114p.   col. maps.   32cm.

8472   Spain.   Ministerio de Obras Públicas.
       España: Mapa oficial de carreteras.   9ed.   Madrid,
       [1971].
       90p.   col. maps.   32cm.

8473   Spain.   Ministerio de Obras Públicas.
       España: Mapa oficial de carreteras.   9ed.   Madrid, 1972.
       90p.   col. maps.   32cm.

8474   Spain.   Ministerio de Obras Públicas.
       España: Mapa oficial de carreteras.   10ed.   Madrid, 1973.
       86p.   col. maps.   32cm.

8475   Spain.   Ministerio de Obras Públicas.
       España: Mapa oficial de carreteras.   11ed.   Madrid,
       1974.
       86p.   col. maps.   32cm.

8476   Spectrum.
       Spectrum wegenatlas.   Utrecht, 1974.
       104p.   col. maps.   39cm.

8477   Stanford, Edward.
       Esso road atlas of Great Britain and Ireland.   1970-71 ed.
       London, 1970.
       253p.   col. maps.   28cm.

8478   Stanford, Edward.
       Esso road atlas of Great Britain and Ireland.   1972-73 ed.
       London, 1971.
       254p.   col. maps.   28cm.

8479 Stanford, Edward.
      Esso road atlas of Great Britain and Ireland. London, 1973.
      254p. col. maps. 28cm.

8480 Tammi.
      Euroopan autoilukartasto. Helsinki, 1969.
      225p. col. maps. 31cm.

8481 Touring Club Italiano.
      Atlante automobilistico. Milano, 1971.
      in parts. col. maps. 32cm.

8482 Touring Club Italiano.
      Atlante automobilistico. Milano, 1974.
      3 vol. col. maps. 32cm.

8483 Turistička Štampa.
      Road map, Yugoslavia. 2ed. Beograd, 1958.
      132p. col. maps. 29cm.

8484 U. A. R. Egypt. Survey of Egypt.
      U. A. R. tourist atlas. Cairo, [1971].
      69p. col. maps. 30cm.

8485 Učila.
      Autoatlas Jugoslavije. Zagreb, 1965.
      27p. col. maps. 23cm.

8486 U. S. S. R. Glavnoe upravlenie geodezii i kartografii.
      Atlas avtomobilnykh dorog S. S. S. R. 1ed. Moskva, 1959.
      165p. col. maps. 27cm.

8487 U. S. S. R. Glavnoe upravlenie geodezii i kartografii.
      Atlas avtomobilnykh dorog S. S. S. R. 2ed. Moskva, 1960.
      165p. col. maps. 27cm.

8488 U. S. S. R. Glavnoe upravlenie geodezii i kartografii.
      Atlas avtomobilnykh dorog S. S. S. R. 3ed. Moskva, 1960.
      165p. col. maps. 27cm.

8489 U. S. S. R. Glavnoe upravlenie geodezii i kartografii.
      Atlas avtomobilnykh dorog S. S. S. R. 2ed. Moskva, 1969.
      167p. col. maps. 27cm.

8490 U. S. S. R. Glavnoe upravlenie geodezii i kartografii.
      Atlas avtomobilnykh dorog S. S. S. R. 2ed. By N. T.
      Markova. Moskva, 1970.
      171p. col. maps. 27cm.

8491 U. S. S. R. Glavnoe upravlenie geodezii i kartografii.
      Atlas avtomobilnykh dorog S. S. S. R. 3ed. By N. T.
      Markova. Moskva, 1971.
      167p. col. maps. 27cm.

8492 U. S. S. R. Glavnoe upravlenie geodezii i kartografii.
      <u>Atlas avtomobilnykh dorog S. S. S. R.</u> 4ed. By N. T.
      Markova. Moskva, 1972.
      171p. col. maps. 27cm.

8493 U. S. S. R. Glavnoe upravlenie geodezii i kartografii.
      <u>Atlas avtomobilnykh dorog S. S. S. R.</u> 4ed. Moskva, 1973.
      167p. col. maps. 27cm.

8494 U. S. S. R. Glavnoe upravlenie geodezii i kartografii.
      <u>Automobilinie marshrute europeiskaya chaste.</u> Moskva,
      1973.
      39p. col. maps. 27cm.

8495 Warajiya Kabushiki Kaisha.
      <u>Zenkoku Doro Chizucho.</u> (Japan road atlas). Osaka, 1970.
      250p. col. maps. 26cm.

8496 Western Pub. Co.
      <u>American road atlas.</u> With Diversified Map Corp. Wayne,
      N. J. , [1971].
      114p. col. maps. 28cm.

SHIPPING see MARINE

SOIL

8497 Warne, F.
      <u>Warne's natural history atlas of Great Britain.</u> By Charles
      King. London, 1970.
      50p. col. maps. 25cm.

STATISTICAL see ECONOMIC

TRADE see ECONOMIC

TRAFFIC see TRANSPORTATION

TRANSPORTATION

8498 Air Canada.
      <u>Air Canada routes.</u> Ottawa, [1966].
      18p. col. maps. 23cm.

8499 Allan.
      <u>British rail atlas.</u> London, 1965.
      83p. col. maps. 24cm.

8500 Allan.
      <u>British railways pre-grouping atlas and gazetteer.</u> Shep-
      perton, 1972.
      84p. col. maps. 24cm.

8501   Allan.
       British railways pre-grouping atlas and gazetteer.   5ed.
       London, [1973].
       84p. col. maps. 24cm.

8502   American Youth Hostels.
       North American bicycle atlas. By Virginia Ward and
       Mary Williams. With Hammond. Maplewood, N. J.,
       [1969].
       127p. 24cm.

8503   American Youth Hostels.
       North American bicycle atlas. 2ed. By Virginia Ward
       and Mary Williams. New York, [1971].
       191p. 24cm.

8504   American Youth Hostels.
       North American bicycle atlas. 3ed. By Virginia Ward
       and Mary Williams. New York, [1973].
       191p. 24cm.

8505   David & Charles.
       A railway atlas of Ireland. 1ed. Newton Abbot, 1972.
       40p. 25cm.

8506   David & Charles.
       A railway atlas of Ireland. Newton Abbot, 1974.
       40p. 25cm.

8507   Generalstabens litografiska anstalt.
       Post-och järnvägs karta över Sverige. Stockholm, 1973.
       10p. col. maps. 23cm.

8508   Germany. Deutsche Reichsbahn.
       Deutsche Reichsbahn. Wegkarten. Berlin, [1968].
       42p. col. maps. 32cm.

8509   Hammond, Inc.
       American Youth Hostel's North American bicycle atlas.
       Maplewood, N. J., [1969].
       127p. 24cm.

8510   International Road Federation.
       Main European arteries (E roads): traffic census maps,
       1965. Grands itinéraires européens; Europäische Haupt-
       verkehrsadern. Geneva, 1968.
       19p. col. maps. 29cm.

8511   Istituto Geografico De Agostini.
       Atlantino di rotta. Alitalia. Roma, Novara, 1968.
       16p. col. maps. 22.5cm.

8512   Istituto Geografico De Agostini.

Atlantino di rotta.   Alitalia.   Roma, Novara, 1971.
16p.   col.   maps.   22.5cm.

8513   Istituto Geografico De Agostini.
       Route maps, Alitalia.   Novara, [1971].
       16p.   col.   maps.   22cm.

8514   Istituto Geografico De Agostini.
       Route maps, Alitalia.   Novara, [1973].
       16p.   col.   maps.   22cm.

8515   Koninklijke Luchtvaart Maatschappij, N. V.
       KLM flight companion.   Amsterdam, [1971].
       16p.   col.   maps.   26cm.

8516   Marketing International.
       International airline and road atlas.   1ed.   Frankfurt am
       Main, [1971].
       1 vol.   col.   maps.   30cm.

8517   Rand McNally & Co.
       Rand McNally handy railroad atlas of the United States.
       Chicago, 1971.
       64p.   31cm.

8518   Rand McNally & Co.
       Rand McNally handy railroad atlas of the United States.
       Chicago, 1973.
       64p.   31cm.

8519   Técnica Aérea e Fotogramétrica.
       Rotas/routes, TAP.   Lisboa, [1970].
       19p.   col.   maps.   26cm.

8520   United Nations.   Economic Commission for Europe.
       Census of motor traffic on main international traffic
       arteries, 1965.   [Atlas.]   Geneva, [1967].
       10p.   col.   maps.   28cm.

8521   U. S. S. R.   Glavnoe upravlenie geodezii i kartografii.
       Atlas skhem zheleznykh dorog S. S. S. R.   Moskva, 1972.
       101p.   col.   maps.   16cm.

8522   U. S. S. R.   Glavnoe upravlenie geodezii i kartografii.
       Zheleznye dorogi S. S. S. R.   4ed.   Moskva, 1969.
       148p.   col.   maps.   16cm.

8523   U. S. S. R.   Glavnoe upravlenie geodezii i kartografii.
       Zheleznye dorogi S. S. S. R.   5ed.   Moskva, 1970.
       148p.   col.   maps.   16cm.

8524   U. S. S. R.   Glavnoe upravlenie geodezii i kartografii.
       Zheleznye dorogi S. S. S. R.   6ed.   Moskva, 1971.

150p.   col.   maps.   16cm.

8525 Wyt.
      Atlas van de tramwegen in Nederland.   Rotterdam, 1973.
      32p.   28cm.

UNIVERSE

8526 Bartholomew, John & Son, Ltd.
      Exploration universe; an atlas of our environment.   By
      William Kinnear and James R. Carson.   Edinburgh, 1972.
      47p.   col.   maps.   31cm.

8527 Bartholomew, John & Son, Ltd.
      Problems of our planet.   An atlas of earth and man.
      Edinburgh, 1975.
      1 vol.   col.   maps.   38cm.

8528 Beazley, Mitchell, Ltd.
      The atlas of the universe.   By Patrick Moore.   London,
      1970.
      272p.   col.   maps.   36cm.

8529 Beazley, Mitchell, Ltd.
      The atlas of the universe.   By Patrick Moore.   London,
      1971.
      272p.   col.   maps.   36cm.

8530 Cram, George F., Co.
      Student atlas: Earth science and outer space.   Indianapolis,
      Ind., [1971].
      34p.   col.   maps.   32cm.

8531 Crown.
      The Space-Age Photographic atlas.   By Ken Fitzgerald.
      New York, 1970.
      246p.   32cm.

8532 Philip, George & Son, Ltd.
      Around the world.   A view from space [atlas].   London,
      [1971].
      125p.   col.   maps.   29cm.

8533 Philip, George & Son, Ltd.
      Moon flight atlas.   2ed.   By Patrick Moore.   London,
      1970.
      64p.   34cm.

8534 Philip, George & Son, Ltd.
      The atlas of the universe.   1ed.   By Patrick Moore.
      London, 1970.
      272p.   col.   maps.   36cm.

8535   Philip, George & Son, Ltd.
       The atlas of the universe.   2ed.   By Patrick Moore.
       London, 1971.
       272p.   col.   maps.   36cm.

8536   Rand McNally & Co.
       Atlas of the universe.   1st Canadian ed.   By Stuart
       Kaminsky and Charles Yoder.   Chicago, 1971.
       1 vol.   col.   maps.   36cm.

8537   Rand McNally & Co.
       The atlas of the universe.   By Patrick Moore.   Chicago,
       1970.
       272p.   col.   maps.   36cm.

8538   Rand McNally & Co.
       The atlas of the universe.   2ed.   By Patrick Moore.
       Chicago, 1971.
       272p.   col.   maps.   36cm.

8539   Taplinger Publishing Co.
       A new photographic atlas of the moon.   By Zdeněk Kopal.
       New York, [1971].
       311p.   32cm.

8540   U.S. Geological Survey.
       Geologic atlas of the moon.   Washington, D.C., 1972-
       in parts.   col.   maps.   40cm.

VEGETATION   see   AGRICULTURE

WATERWAYS

8541   Cranfield & Bonfiel Books.
       Waterways atlas of the British Isles.   2ed.   London,
       1968.
       53p.   col.   maps.   24cm.

8542   France.   Direction des ports maritimes et des voies naviga-
       bles.
       Liaisons fluviales Mer-du-Nord-Mediterranée.   Paris,
       [1969].
       1 vol.   col.   maps.   42cm.

ZOOGEOGRAPHY

8543   Beazley, Mitchell, Ltd.
       The Mitchell Beazley atlas of world wildlife.   London,
       1973.
       208p.   col.   maps.   37cm.

8544   Bee Research Organisation.
       Preliminary bumble bee atlas.   London, 1973.
       31p.   20.5cm.

8545   Day, John, Co.
     .   Atlas of animal migration.   By Catherine Jarman.   With
        Geographical Projects.   New York, [1972].
        124p.   col. maps.   31cm.

8546   Day, John, Co.
        Atlas of wild life.   By Jacqueline Nayman.   With
        Geographical Projects.   New York, [1972].
        124p.   col. maps.   31cm.

8547   Geographical Projects.
        Atlas of animal migration.   By Catherine Jarman.   Lon-
        don, [1972].
        124p.   col. maps.   31cm.

8548   Geographical Projects.
        Atlas of wild life.   By Jacqueline Nayman.   London,
        [1972].
        124p.   col. maps.   31cm.

8549   Rand McNally & Co.
        The Rand McNally atlas of world wildlife.   Chicago,
        [1973].
        208p.   col. maps.   37cm.

COMPREHENSIVE LIST OF PUBLISHERS

AFRICA

Angola
 Edições Spal   Luanda

Botswana
 Botswana.   Govt. Printer   Gaborone

Cameroun
 Institut de recherches scientifiques
   du Cameroun   Yaoundé

Chad
 Chad.   Institut national tschadien pour les
   sciences humaines   N'djamena

Ethiopia
 Mariam, Mesfin Wolde   Addis Ababa

Ghana
 Ghana.   Census Office   Accra
 Ghana.   Meteorological Services   Legon
 Ghana.   Survey Dept.   Accra

Ivory Coast
 Ministère du plan de Côte d'Ivoire   Abidjan
 Société pour le développement de la
   Côte d'Ivoire   Abidjan

Kenya
 Marco Surveys, Ltd.   Nairobi
 Royal East African Automobile Assoc.   Nairobi
 Survey of Kenya   Nairobi

Malagasy
 Malagasy.   Bureau pour le développement
   de la production agricole   Tananarive
 Malagasy.   L'Association des géographes
   de Madagascar   Tananarive

Malawi
 Malawi.   Dept. of Surveys   Blantyre

Malawi. Geological Survey   Zomba

Morocco
    Morocco. Comité national de géographie   Rabat

Mozambique
    Empresa Moderna   Lourenço Marques
    Shell Moçambique, Ltd.   Lourenço Marques

Nigeria
    Commission for Technical Cooperation in
        Africa South of the Sahara   Lagos
    Nigeria. Federal Surveys   Lagos
    Nigeria. Survey Dept.   Lagos

Rhodesia
    Collins, M. O. (Pvt), Ltd.   Salisbury
    Rhodesia. Department of Trigonometrical
        and Topographical Surveys   Salisbury

Senegal
    Institut fondamental d'Afrique noire   Dakar
    Institut français d'Afrique noire   Dakar
    Organisation of African Unity   Dakar
    Senegal. Ministère du plan et du
        développement   Dakar

Sierra Leone
    Sierra Leone. Survey and Lands Dept.   Freetown
    Sierra Leone. Survey and Lands Division Freetown

South Africa
    Afrika Instituut   Pretoria
    Atlantik Refining Company of Africa   Cape Town
    Automobile Association of South Africa   Johannesburg
    B. P. Southern Africa Pty, Ltd.   Cape Town
    Juta & Co., Ltd.   Cape Town
    Map Studio Productions, Pty, Ltd.   Cape Town
    Nationale Boekhandel   Cape Town
    Shell Company of South Africa, Ltd.   Cape Town
    South Africa. Department of Planning   Pretoria
    South Africa. Government Printer Office Pretoria
    South Africa. National Council for Social
        Research   Pretoria
    Timmins, H. B.   Cape Town
    Tourist Publications   Cape Town
    Van Schaik's Bookstore   Pretoria
    Varia Books   Alberton

Tanzania
    Tanganyika. Department of Lands and
        Surveys   Dar Es Salaam
    Tanzania. Bureau of Resource Assessment

and Land-Use Planning	Dar Es Salaam
Tanzania. Ministry of Lands, Housing & Urban Development. Survey & Mapping Division	Dar Es Salaam
Tanzania. Ministry of Lands, Settlement and Water Development	Dar Es Salaam
Tanzania Publishing House, Ltd.	Dar Es Salaam

Uganda
East African Institute of Social Research	Kampala
Uganda. Department of Lands and Surveys	Kampala

United Arab Republic-Egypt
Dar Al-Ma'Arif	Cairo
Hilâl	Cairo
Institut français d'archéologie orientale	Cairo
U. A. R. -Egypt. al-Jihaz al-Markazi lil-Ta'bi'ah al'Ammah wa-al-Ihsa	Cairo
U. A. R. Egypt. Survey of Egypt	Cairo

Zaïre
Congo. Commissariat général au plan	Brazzaville
Congo. Institut national pour l'étude agronomique	Brazzaville

Zambia
Northern Rhodesia. Survey Dept.	Lusaka
Zambia. Ministry of Lands and Mines	Lusaka
Zambia. National Council for Scientific Research	Lusaka

ASIA

Afghanistan
Afghanistan. Cartographic Inst.	Kabul

China
China. Academy of Sciences	Peking
China. Geographical Institute	Shanghai
Chinese Map Publ.	Peking
Hsin Ya Shu Tien	Shanghai
Kuang Hua Yü Ti Hsüeh Shê	Peking
Shih Chieh Yü Ti Hsüeh Shê	Shanghai
Ta Chung Ti Hsüeh Shê	Shanghai
Ta Lu Yü Ti Shê	Shanghai
Ti-Tu Chu-Pan Shê	Shanghai
Ya Kuang Yü Ti Hsüeh Shê	Shanghai

Hong Kong
Hai Kuang Ch'u Pan Shê	Hong Kong
Hong Kong, Govt. Printer	Hong Kong
Hong Kong University Press	Hong Kong

Hsin Kuang Yü Ti Hsüeh Shê	Hong Kong
Liang, Ch'i-Shan	Hong Kong
Macmillan Publishers (HK) Ltd.	Hong Kong
Shih Chieh Ch'u Pan Shê	Hong Kong
Ta Chung Shu Chü	Hong Kong

India
India. Book House	Bombay
India. Census Commission	New Delhi
India. Directorate General of Health Services	Delhi
India. Directorate of Economics and Statistics	Delhi
India. Information and Broadcasting Ministry	Calcutta
India. Meteorological Dept.	New Delhi
India. Ministry of Agriculture	Delhi
India. Ministry of Education and Scientific Research	Calcutta
India. Ministry of Irrigation and Power	Delhi
India. National Atlas Organization	Calcutta
India. Survey of India.	Dehra Dun
Indian Book Depot & Map House	Delhi
Indian Central Cotton Committee	Bombay
Indian Central Jute Committee	Calcutta
Indian Central Oilseeds Committee	Hyderabad
Ramnarain Sons Limited	Bombay

Indonesia
Anikasari	Djakarta
Bachtar, A.	Djakarta
Ganaco, N. V.	Bandung
Ichtiar	Djakarta
Indonesia. Army Topographical Directorate	Djakarta
Indonesia. Badan Atlas Nasional	Djakarta
Indonesia. Direktorat Land Use	Djakarta
Majdu, Firma	Medan
Noordhoff-Kolff, N. V.	Djakarta
Pembina	Djakarta
Pemusatan	Bandung
Pradnja-Paramita	Djakarta
Tjempaka, P. T.	Djakarta

Iran
Geographic & Drafting Institute	Teheran
Guruhi Jughrafiya	Teheran
Iran. Danishgah	Teheran
Iran. Ministry of Interior	Teheran
Sahab	Teheran
University of Teheran	Teheran

Iraq
Sadiq Salih	Baghdad

Surveys Press	Baghdad

Israel

ADI, Ltd.	Tel Aviv
Ahiever	Jerusalem
Anokh, Hanok	Tel Aviv
Ben-Eliyahu, Ephraim	Jerusalem
Carta	Jerusalem
Israel. Central Bureau of Statistics	Jerusalem
Israel. Department of Surveys	Jerusalem
Israel. Mahleket Ha-Medidot	Jerusalem
Israel. Ministry of Labour	Jerusalem
Israel. Ministry of Surveys	Tel Aviv
Israel. Tseva Haganah Le-Yisrael	Jerusalem
Israel. University Press	Jerusalem
Szapiro, J.	Tel Aviv
Universitas	Jerusalem
Yavneh	Tel Aviv

Japan

Buyōdō Co., Ltd.	Tokyo
Heibonsha	Tokyo
International Society for Educational Information	Tokyo
Japan. Geographical Survey Institute	Tokyo
Japan. Meteorological Agency	Tokyo
Japan. Un'Yashō Kankōkyoku	Tokyo
Jimbunsha	Tokyo
Kishō Kyōkai	Tokyo
Kokusai Chicaku Kyōkai	Tokyo
Kokusai Kyōiku Jōhō Sentā	Tokyo
Nihon Kyōzu Kabushiki Kaisha	Tokyo
Nitchi Shuppan Kabushiki Kaisha	Tokyo
Reader's Digest of Japan, Ltd.	Tokyo
Teikoku-Shoin Co., Ltd.	Tokyo
Tōbunsha	Tokyo
Tokyo Chizu K. K.	Tokyo
Tōsei Shuppan Kabushiki Kaisha	Tokyo
Warajiya Kabushiki Kaisha	Osaka
Zenkoko Jichitai Kenkyukai	Tokyo
Zenkoku Kyoiku Tosho	Tokyo
Zenkoku Ryokaku Jidōsha Yōran Henshūshitsu	Tokyo
Zenkyozu	Tokyo

Jordan

Jordan. Meteorological Dept.	Amman

Korea

Kim, Sang-Jin	Seoul
Sosŏ Publishing Co.	Seoul
Taehan Sŏrim	Seoul

Laos
    Laos. National Geographic Center   Vientiane

Lebanon
    Lebanon. Direction des Affaires
      Géographiques   Beyrouth
    Lebanon. Ministère du Plan   Beyrouth
    Lebanon. Service Météorologique   Beyrouth
    Lebanon. Wizārat al-Taşmin al-'Āmm   Beyrouth

Malaysia
    Automobile Association of Malaya   Penang
    Borneo Literature Bureau   Kuching
    Malaysia. Directorate of National Mapping Singapore

Nepal
    Nepal. Ministry of Information and
      Broadcasting   Kathmandu

Pakistan
    Pakistan. Dept. of Advertising, Films and
      Publications   Karachi

Philippines
    Caltex (Philippines)   Manila
    Phil-Asian Publishers, Inc.   Manila
    Philippines. Agriculture and Natural
      Resources Dept.   Manila
    Philippines. Bureau of Public Works   Manila
    Philippines. Office of the President   Manila

Singapore
    Tien Wah Press, Ltd.   Singapore

Sri Lanka
    Atlas and Map Industries   Colombo

Taiwan
    China. National War College   Taipei
    Fu Min Geographical Institute of Economic
      Development   Taipei
    Sha, Hsüeh Chün   Taipei
    T'ai-Wan Ta Hsiüeh   Taipei
    Taiwan. National University   Taipei

Thailand
    Thailand. Department of Commercial
      Intelligence   Bangkok
    Thailand. Royal Thai Survey Department   Bangkok

Vietnam
    Vietnam. Dept. of Survey and Mapping   Hanoi
    Vietnam. Information Section   Saigon

Vietnam.   National Geographic Center   Saigon
Vietnam.   Nha G'a'm-Dôc Khï-Tu'o'ng   Saigon

AUSTRALASIA

Australia
    Ampol Petroleum, Ltd.   Sydney
    Angus & Robertson   Sydney
    Australia.   Bureau of Mineral Resources,
      Geology and Geophysics   Adelaide
    Australia.   Department of National
      Development   Canberra
    Australia.   Division of Soils, Commonwealth
      Scientific and Industrial Research Organiza-
      tion   Canberra
    Australian Educational Foundation, Pty, Ltd.   Sydney
    B. P. Australia, Ltd.   Melbourne
    Colorgravure   Melbourne
    Gregory's Guides & Maps Pty, Ltd.   Sydney
    Jacaranda   Brisbane
    Martindale Press   Sydney
    Motor Manual   Melbourne
    Reader's Digest Association, Pty, Ltd.   Sydney
    Robinson, H. E. C. Pty, Ltd.   Sydney
    The Age   Melbourne

New Zealand
    Military Vehicles & Engineering Establish-
      ment   Christchurch
    New Zealand.   Atlas Committee   Wellington
    New Zealand.   Government Printing Office   Auckland
    New Zealand.   Local Government Commission   Wellington
    New Zealand.   National Airways Corporation   Wellington
    New Zealand.   Town and Country Planning
      Branch   Wellington
    Reed, A. W. & A. H.   Wellington
    Shell Co. of New Zealand   Wellington
    Shell Oil New Zealand, Ltd.   Wellington

Papua and New Guinea
    University of Papua and New Guinea   Port Moresby

EUROPE

Albania
    Albania.   Ministria e Aresimit dhe Kultures   Tiranë
    N. I. Sh. Mjete Mesimore e Sportive
      "Hamid Shijaku"   Tiranë

Austria
    Austria.   Akademie der Wissenschaften   Wien

Austria. Bundesdenkmalamt   Graz
Auto-Motor-und Radfahrerbund
    Österreichs   Wien
Buchgemeinschaft Donauland   Wien
Dom Verlag   Wien
Freytag-Berndt & Artaria   Wien
Geographisches Institut Wien   Wien
Hölder, Pichler Tempsky   Wien
Hölzel, Ed. Verlag   Wien
Internationaler Holzmarkt   Wien
Kaiser   Klagenfurt
Society of the Divine Word   Mödling
St. Gabriel Verlag   Mödling

Belgium
    Asedi   Bruxelles
Belgium. Académie royale des sciences
    d'outre-mer   Bruxelles
Belgium. Centre d'information et de
    documentation du Congo belge et du
    Ruanda-Urundi   Bruxelles
Belgium. Centre national de recherches
    scientifiques souterraines   Liège
Belgium. Comité national de géographie   Bruxelles
Belgium. Ministère des travaux publics
    et de la reconstruction   Bruxelles
Contact   Anvers
De Sikkel   Anvers
Editions Meddens   Bruxelles
Editions R. de Rouck   Bruxelles
European Communities.   Press and Informa-
    tion Service   Bruxelles
Institut cartographique européan   Bruxelles
L'Institut national pour l'étude agronomique
    du Congo   Bruxelles
Mantniers, P.   Bruxelles
Miller Freeman   Bruxelles
Plantyn   Anvers
Scriptoria   Anvers
Standaard Uitjeverij   Anvers
Transportikronier   Anvers
Visscher   Bruxelles
Wesmael-Charlier   Namur

Bulgaria
    Balkanturist   Sofia
Bulgaria. Akademya na Naukite   Sofia
Bulgaria. Glavno Upravlenie po Geodeziă
    i Kartografiă   Sofia
Bulgaria. Muzei na Revolutsidnnoto
    Dvizhenie v Bŭlgariiă   Sofia

Czechoslovakia

Czechoslovakia.	Akademie Věd	Praha
Czechoslovakia.	Kartografické Nakladatelství	Praha
Czechoslovakia.	Komenium	Praha
Czechoslovakia.	Ministerstvo Národní Obrany	Praha
Czechoslovakia.	Státní Nakl. Učebnic	Praha
Czechoslovakia.	Státní Pedagogické Nakl	Praha
Czechoslovakia.	Státní Zeměměřický a Kartografický Ústav	Praha
Czechoslovakia.	Ustřední Správa Geodesie a Kartografie	Praha
Czechoslovakia.	Ustřední Ústav Geologický	Praha
Kartografie		Praha
Melantrich		Praha
Orbis		Praha
Slovenska Kartografia		Bratislava

Denmark

Denmark. Geodaetisk Institut	København
Det Beste fra Reader's Digest AS	København
Gjellerups Forlag	København
Grafisk Forlag	København
Gyldendal	København
Haase	København
Hirschsprungs Forlag	København
Imperial Press	København
Importbøger	København
Lademann forlagsaktieselskab	København
Martins Forlag	København
Munksgaard	København
Normanns Forlag	Odense
Politikens Forlag	København
Reader's Digest, AB	København
Reitzels, C. A. Forlag	København
Schultz	København
Skandinavisk Bogforlag	København
Skrifola	København

Finland

Maanmittaushallitus	Helsinki
Otava	Helsinki
Söderström, Werner	Helsinki
Suomen Maantietellinen Seura	Helsinki
Tammi	Helsinki
Valistus	Helsinki
Weilin & Co.	Helsinki
W. S. O. Y.	Helsinki
Yhtyneet Kuvalehdet	Helsinki

France

Blondel la Rougery	Paris

Bordas, H.	Paris
Colin	Paris
Delagrave	Paris
Delta éditions	Paris
Didot-Bottin	Paris
Editions Alain	Paris
Editions André Lesot	Paris
Editions Bordas	Paris
Editions du Centurion	Paris
Editions de l'Ecole	Paris
Editions de Lyon	Lyon
Editions jeune Afrique	Paris
Editions Sequoia	Paris
Encyclopaedia universalis	Paris
Foldex (France), Ltd.	Paris
France. Centre de recherches historique	Paris
France. Centre national de la recherche scientifique	Paris
France. Comité national de géographie	Paris
France. Commissariat général à la productivité	Paris
France. Conseil national du patronat français	Paris
France. Direction de la météorologie nationale	Paris
France. Direction des ports maritimes et de voies navigables	Paris
France. Electricité de France	Paris
France. Ministère de l'éducation nationale	La Celle-Saint Cloud
France. Institut géographique national	Paris
France. La Documentation française	Paris
France. Ministère de l'équipement	Paris
France. Ministère des postes et télécommunications	Paris
France. Service de l'économie forestière	Paris
France. Sociéte nationale des chemins de fer français	Paris
Gallimard	Paris
Grange Batelière	Paris
Hachette	Paris
Hatier	Paris
IAC	Lyon
Imprimeries Oberthur	Rennes
Informations et conjoncture	Paris
Journaux, André	Caen
Laffont	Paris
Larousse	Paris
Le Carrousel publicité	Tours
Librairie générale française	Paris
Librairie Mellottée	Paris
Livre de poche	Paris
L'Oeuvre de la propagation de la foi	Paris

Michelin et Cie	Paris
Mouton & Co.	Paris
Nathan, Fernand	Paris
Nouvelles de l'enseignement	Paris
Office Général du Livre	Paris
Peugeot	Paris
Quillet, A.	Paris
Sélection du Reader's Digest S. A. R. L.	Paris
Société des pétroles Shell Berre	Paris
Société européenne d'études et d'informations	Paris
Société française des pétroles BP	Courbevoie, Seine
Stock	Paris
Tallandier	Paris
Vilo	Paris

Germany

Accumulatoren-Fabrik, A. G.	Hannover
Akademie Verlag	Berlin
Allgemeiner deutscher Automobil-Club	Kiel
Atlantik Verlag	Frankfurt
Autokarten und Reiseführer Verlag	Kiel
Bayerischer Schulbuch Verlag	München
Benziger & Co.	Einsiedeln
Bertelsmann, C.	Gütersloh
Beste, G. M. B. H.	Stuttgart
BLV Verlagsgesellschaft	München
BP Benzin & Petroleum Gesellschaft	Hamburg
Brockhaus, F. A.	Wiesbaden
Codex Verlag	Gundholzen
Columbus Verlag Oestergaard	Berlin
Continental Gummiwerke kartographischer Verlag	Hannover
Deutsche Lufthansa	Köln
Deutsche Viscobil Öl Gesellschaft	Hamburg
Deutscher Bücherbund	Stuttgart
Deutscher Taschenbuch Verlag	München
Deutscher Zentralverlag VEB	Berlin
Droemer	München
Elwert Verlag	Marburg
Esso, A. G.	Hamburg
Europäischer Buchklub	Stuttgart
Fachbuchverlag, G. M. B. H.	Leipzig
Falk Verlag	Hamburg
Fietz, W. G.	Frankfurt
Fischer, G.	Jena
Flemings Verlag	Hamburg
Frankfurt. Institut für angewandte Geodäsie	Frankfurt
Frankfurt. Soziographisches Institut der Universität	Frankfurt
Freytag, G.	München
Germany. Akademie für Raumforschung und Landesplannung	Hannover

Germany. Deutsche Reichsbahn	Berlin
Germany. Deutscher Wetterdienst	Hamburg
Germany. Militärgeographisches Amt	Bonn
Germany. Statistisches Bundesamt, Institut für Landeskunde und Institut für Raumforschung	Mainz
Goldmann Verlag	München
Haack, Hermann	Gotha
Haller Verlag	Berlin
Herder Verlag	Freiburg
Hirt Verlag	Kiel
Humboldt Verlag	Stuttgart
Institut für thematische Kartographie der deutschen Kreiskartenverlagsanstalt	München
JRO Verlag	München
Keysersche Verlagsbuchhandlung, G. M. B. H.	Heidelberg
Klett Verlag	Stuttgart
Knaur, Th. Nachf.	München
Kohlhammer Verlag	Mainz
König, Hans, Verlag	Frankfurt
Landkartenverlag VEB	Berlin
Lehrmittel Verlag	Offenburg
Lingen	Köln
List, P.	München
Lux Verlag	München
Mairs Geographischer Verlag	Stuttgart
Marketing International	Frankfurt
Meyer, Kartographisches Institut	Mannheim
Mohn	Gütersloh
Nomos Verlagsgesellschaft	Baden-Baden
Olbers Gesellschaft	Bremen
Oldenburger Verlagshaus	Oldenburg
Parey Verlag	Hamburg
Perthes, Justus	Gotha
Pfahl Verlag	Laupheim
Piper, R. & Co.	München
Ravenstein geographische Verlagsanstalt	Frankfurt
Reise und Verkehrsverlag	Stuttgart
Ruhr-Stickstoff, A. G.	Bochum
Siemens & Halske, A. G.	München
Springer Verlag	Berlin
Steiner Verlag	Wiesbaden
Südwest Verlag	München
Ullstein	Berlin
VEB bibliographisches Institut	Leipzig
Velhagen & Klasing	Bielefeld
Verlag Die Gabe	Gütersloh
Verlag Enzyklopädie	Leipzig
Verlag lebendiges Wissen	München
Verlag Sport & Technik	Berlin
Verlag Zeit im Bild	Dresden
Volk und Wissen Verlag	Berlin
Wenschow	München

Westermann, Georg   Braunschweig
Weststadt Verlag   München

Greece
Al-Ma-Prisma, Ltd.   Athens
Greece.   Ministry of National Economy   Athens
Greece.   National Statistical Service   Athens
Greece.   Statistikon Graphelon   Athens
Hellēnike Leschē Autokinētou kai
   Periēgēsēon   Athens
Karolidaēs, Paulos   Athens
Mobil Oil Hellas   Athens

Great Britain
African Magazine   London
Aldus-Jupiter   London
Allan   London
Arnold, E.   London
Austin Motor Co., Ltd.   Birmingham
Automobile Association   London
Bancroft & Co.   London
Beazley Mitchell, Ltd.   London
Bee Research Organisation   London
Berlitz   London
Blackie & Son, Ltd.   London
Blond Educational, Ltd.   London
British Bureau of Television Advertising, Ltd.   London
British Motor Corp., Ltd.   London
British Sulphur Corp., Ltd.   London
Burns & Oates, Ltd.   London
Cambridge University Press   Cambridge
Cassell   London
Caxton Pub. Co.   London
Clarendon Press   Oxford
Collet   London
Cranfield & Bonfiel Books   London
Daily Express   London
David & Charles   Newton Abbot
Dent, J. M.   London
Ebury Press   London
Economist Intelligence Unit, Ltd.   London
English University Press, Ltd.   London
ESSO Petroleum Co., Ltd.   London
Evans Brothers   London
Faber & Faber   London
Gatrell, A. W. & Co., Ltd.   London
Geographers' Map Co.   Sevenoakes, Kent
Geographia, Ltd.   London
Geographical Projects, Ltd.   London
Geo Publishing Co.   Oxford
Gollancz, Victor   London
Gower Economic Publications   Epping
Gt. Britain.   Meteorological Office   London

Gt. Britain. Ministry of Agriculture, Fisheries & Food	London
Gt. Britain. Ministry of Housing and Local Government	London
Hamlyn	London
Harrap	London
Hart-Davis	London
Heinemann	London
Heyden & Son, Ltd.	London
Hippocrene Books	London
Hulton Educational Publications, Ltd.	London
Humphrey, H. A., Ltd.	London
Kings College School	London
Lloyd's Corp. of	London
Longmans Green	London
Lutterworth Press	London
MacDonald & Co., Ltd.	London
Macdonald & Evans	London
Macdonald Education	London
Macmillan & Co., Ltd.	London
Macmillan South Africa, Ltd.	Basingstoke
Map Productions Ltd.	London
Meiklejohn	London
Methuen	London
Michelin Tyre Co.	Stoke-on-Trent
Murray, John	London
National Trust	London
Nelson-Doubleday	London
Nelson, Thomas & Sons, Ltd.	London
Newnes, George, Ltd.	London
Nuffield Organization	Oxford
Odhams Press Ltd.	London
Oxford Polytechnic	Oxford
Oxford University Press	London
Pan Books	London
Penguin Books	Harmondsworth
Pergamon Press, Ltd.	Oxford
Philip, George & Son, Ltd.	London
Railway Publications, Ltd.	London
Reader's Digest Association, Ltd.	London
Religious Education Press	Oxford
Royal Automobile Club	London
Seeley Service & Co.	London
Shell-Mex & BP Ltd.	London
Stanford, Edward	London
Technical Press, Ltd.	London
Thames and Hudson, Ltd.	London
The Times Publishing Co.	London
Thomas, A.	Preston
Times of London	London
University of London Press	London
University Tutorial Press	London

Ward, Lock	London
Warne, F.	London
Weidenfeld & Nicolson	London
Wheaton & Co. , Ltd.	Exeter

Hungary

Cartographia	Budapest
Geodéziai és Kartográfiai Intézet	Budapest
Kartográfiai Vállalat	Budapest
Országos Meteorológiai Intézet	Budapest
Ronai, Andras	Budapest
Tervgazdhsági Könyvkiadó	Budapest
World Meteorological Organization	Budapest

Iceland

Rikisútgáfa Námsbóka	Reykjavik

Ireland

Dublin Institute for Advanced Studies	Dublin
Educational Company of Ireland, Ltd.	Dublin

Italy

AGIP	Milano
Automobile Club d'Italia	Roma
Consociazione Turistica Italiana	Milano
Curcio, A.	Roma
Edizioni Cremonese	Roma
Fabri	Milano
Fédération Internationale de l'Automobile	Roma
Innocenti	Milano
Istituto Geografico de Agostini	Novara
Istituto Geografico Editoriale Italiano	Roma
Istituto Italiano per L'Africa	Roma
Italatlas	Roma
Italgeo	Milano
Italy. Direzione Generale della Statistica	Roma
Italy. Istituto Geografico Militare	Firenze
Minerva Italica	Bergamo
Mondadori	Milano
Paravia, G. B.	Torino
Poligrafiche Bolis	Bergamo
Pont. institutum orientalium studi orum	Roma
Principato Giuseppe	Milano
Societa Cartografica G. De Agostini	Milano
Societa Editrice Internazionale	Torino
Studi Geo-Cartografici	Milano
Studio F. M. B.	Bologna
Touring Club Italiano	Milano
United Nations. Food and Agricultural Organization	Roma
Vallardi, A.	Milano
Zanchelli, Nicola	Bologna

Luxembourg
  Luxembourg.   Ministère de l'éducation
    nationale   Luxembourg

Netherlands
  Bootsma   's Gravenhage
  Bosch & Keuning   Baarn
  Brug Uitgeversbedrijf, N. V.   Amsterdam
  De Bussy, J. H.   Amsterdam
  Dijkstra   Zeist
  Djambatan   Amsterdam
  Duwaer, J. F. & Zonen   Amsterdam
  Elsevier   Amsterdam
  Katholier Sociaal-Kerkelijk Instituut   's Gravenhage
  Kluwer   Wageningen
  Koninklijke Luchtvaart Maatschappij, N. V.   Amsterdam
  Muelenhoff, J. M.   Amsterdam
  Netherlands.   Bureau voor Wegen en
    Verkeersstatistiek   's Gravenhage
  Netherlands.   Department van Landbouw
    en Visscherij   Zwolle
  Netherlands.   Dienst Verkeersonderzoek   's Gravenhage
  Netherlands.   Meteorologisch Institut   de Bilt
  Netherlands.   Ministerie van Marine   's Gravenhage
  Netherlands.   Staatsdrukkerij-en
    Uitgeverijbedrijf   's Gravenhage
  Netherlands.   Volkskundecommissie der
    Koninklijke Nederlandse Akademie van
    Wetenschappen   's Gravenhage
  Nijgh & Van Ditmar   Rotterdam
  Noordhoff, P.   Groningen
  Omnium   Waalwijk
  Oosthoek   Wageningen
  Reader's Digest, NV   Amsterdam
  Smulders' Drukkerijen, N. V.   's Gravenhage
  Spectrum   Utrecht
  Stenvert   Apeldoorn
  Ten Brink, H.   Meppel
  Thieme, W. J.   Zutphen
  Uitgeverij de Bezige Bij   Amsterdam
  Versluys   Amsterdam
  Wolters, J. B.   Groningen
  Wyt   Rotterdam

Norway
  Ashehoug & Co.   Oslo
  Beste, A. S.   Oslo
  Cappelens, J. W. Forlag, A. S.   Oslo
  Damm, N. W. & Son   Oslo
  Dreyers Forlag   Oslo
  Fabritius   Oslo
  Fonna   Oslo
  Kongelig Norsk Automobilklub   Oslo

Nomi Forlag	Oslo
Norway. Postdirektoratet	Oslo
Norway. Poststyret	Olso
Norway. Statistik Sentralbyrå	Oslo
Norway. Vassdrags- og Elektrisitetsvesen	Oslo
Norway. Vegdirektoratet	Oslo
Postapnernes Landsforbund	Oslo

Poland
Książnica-Atlas	Wrocław
Poland. Akademia Nauk	Warszawa
Poland. Centralny Urząd Geodezii i Kartografii	Warszawa
Poland. Glowny urząd statystyczny	Warszawa
Poland. Instytut Geologiczny	Warszawa
Poland. Państwowe Przedsiębiorstwo Wydawnictw Kartograficznych	Warszawa
Poland. Państwowe Wydawnictw Naukowe	Warszawa
Poland. Państwowe zaklady wydawnictw szkolnych	Warszawa
Poland. Służba Topograficzna Wojska Polskiego	Warszawa
Poland. Wydawnictw Geologiczne	Warszawa
Poland. Wydawnictw Ministerstva Obrony Narodowej	Warszawa
Romer, Eugeniusz	Wrocław
Trzaska, Evert i Michalski, S. A.	Warszawa
Warszawa Universytet	Warszawa
Wjedza Powszechna	Krakow

Portugal
Editorial Everest	Leon
Instituto de Estudos Geograficos	Coimbra
Livraria Popular de F. Franco	Lisboa
Livraria Sá da Costa	Lisboa
Livraria Simões Lopes	Porto
Porto Editora	Porto
Portugal. Junta de Investigações do Ultramar	Lisboa
Silva, J. R.	Lisboa
Portugal. Ministerio do trabalho	Lisboa
Selecções do Reader's Digest	Lisboa
Técnica Aérea e Fotogramétrica	Lisboa
Verbo	Lisboa

Romania
Editura Stadion	Bucuresti
Romania. Academia Republicii Socialiste	Bucuresti
Romania. Asociatia Automobiliştilor Din R. P. R.	Bucuresti
Romania. Editura Academiei Republici Populare Romine	Bucuresti
Romania. Editura de Stat Pentru	

Literatură Ştiinţifică   Bucuresti
Romania. Editura di Stat Didactică şi
Pedagogică   Bucuresti
Romania. Editura Stiintifica   Bucuresti
Romania. Institutul Meteorologie   Bucuresti

Scotland
Bartholomew, John & Son, Ltd.   Edinburgh
Chambers, W. & R., Ltd.   Edinburgh
Collins, Clear-Type Press   Glasgow
Collins, William, Sons & Co., Ltd.   Glasgow
Edinburgh University Press   Edinburgh
Johnston, W. & A. K. & G. W. Bacon, Ltd.   Edinburgh
McDougall's Educational Co., Ltd.   Edinburgh
Oliver & Boyd   Edinburgh
Scotland. Scottish Development Dept.   Edinburgh

Spain
Aguilar, S. A., de Ediciones   Madrid
Anubar   Valencia
Atheneum   Barcelona
Bibliograf, S. A.   Barcelona
Bosch   Barcelona
Cartografía Pirelli   Barcelona
Compañía Internacional Editora   Barcelona
Compañia Mercantil Anónima Lineas
Aéreas Españolas   Madrid
E. D. A. F.   Madrid
Editorial Bello   Valencia
Editorial Francisco Seix, S. A.   Barcelona
Editorial Luis Vives, S. A.   Zaragoza
Editorial Miguel A. Salvatella   Barcelona
Editorial Rivadeneyra   Madrid
Editorial Seix Barral, S. A.   Barcelona
Editorial Teide   Barcelona
Editorial Vergara   Barcelona
Editorial Vincens-Vives   Barcelona
Firestone-Hispania, S. A.   Bilbao
Hernando   Madrid
Jover   Barcelona
Litografía de Fernández   Madrid
Martin, A.   Barcelona
Neguri Editorial   Bilbao
Salinas Bellver, Salvador   Madrid
Spain. Cámeras Oficiales de Comercio,
Industria y Navegación   Madrid
Spain. Comité Español de Riegos y
Drenajes   Madrid
Spain. Consejo Superior de Investigaciones
Científicas   Madrid
Spain. Direción General de Marruecos y
Colonias e Instituto de Estudios Africanos   Madrid
Spain. Direción General de Montes,

Caza y Pesca Fluvial	Madrid
Spain. Ejercito Servicio Geografico	Madrid
Spain. Instituto Geográfico y Catastral	Madrid
Spain. Ministerio de Obras Públicas	Madrid
Villarroya San Mateo, Antonio	Madrid

Sweden

Akademiförlaget	Göteborg
Aldus	Stockholm
Allhem	Malmö
Bergvalls Förlag	Stockholm
Bernces Förlag	Malmö
Bonnier	Stockholm
Carlson, A. V.	Stockholm
Esselte Map Service	Stockholm
Generalstabens Litografiska Anstalt	Stockholm
Gumperts Förlag	Göteborg
Kartlitografen, AB	Danderyd
Kungliga Automobil Klubben	Stockholm
Lantbruksförbundets Tidskriftsaktiebolag	Stockholm
Läromedelsförlagen	Stockholm
Mobil Oil, AB	Danderyd
Motormännens Riksförbund	Stockholm
Natur och Kultur Bokförlaget	Stockholm
Raben & Sjögren	Stockholm
Royal Automobile Club Sweden	Stockholm
Sohlmans Förlag, A. B.	Stockholm
Svenska Bokförlaget Norstedts	Stockholm
Sveriges Köpmannaförbund	Stockholm
Tidens Förlag	Stockholm

Switzerland

Buchclub Ex Libris	Zürich
Buchverlag Verlandsdruckerei	Bern
Editions Rencontre	Lausanne
Editions Stauffacher	Zürich
Europa im Automobile A. G.	Zürich
Hallwag, A. G.	Bern
International Road Federation	Geneva
International Telecommunication Union	Geneva
Kantonaler Lehrmittel Verlag	Zürich
Kümmerly & Frey	Bern
Librairie Payot	Lausanne
Literärisches Institut	Basel
Nagel Publishers	Geneva
Orell Füssli, A. G.	Zürich
Sauerländer, H. R.	Aarau
Schweizer Reisekasse	Bern
Schweizer Volks-Buchgemeinde	Luzern
Schweizerische Gesellschaft für Volkskunde	Basel
Switzerland. Konferenz der Kantonalen Erziehungsdirektoren	Zürich
Switzerland. Landestopographie	Wabern-Bern

Unesco   Geneva
United Nations Economic Commission
   for Europa   Geneva

Turkey
   Bir Yayinevi   Istanbul
   Kanaat Kitabevi   Istanbul
   Kanaat Yayinlari   Istanbul
   Maarif Basimevi   Istanbul
   Milli Egitim Bakanliği   Istanbul
   Milli Egitim Basimevi   Istanbul
   Shell Co. of Turkey, Ltd.   Istanbul
   University of Itanbul   Istanbul

U.S.S.R.
   Novoe Vremya   Moskva
   U.S.S.R. Akademiia Nauk   Kiev
   U.S.S.R. Gidronet   Leningrad
   U.S.S.R. Glavnoe Upravlenie Geodezii i
      Kartografii   Moskva
   U.S.S.R. Nauchno-issledovatel'ski
      Institut Aeroklimatologii   Moskva
   U.S.S.R. Voyenno-Morskoe Ministerstvo   Moskva
   U.S.S.R. Voyenno-Topograficheskoe
      Upravlenie   Moskva

Wales
   Gwasg Prifysgol Cymru   Caerdydd
   Hughes & Son   Wrezham
   University of Wales Press   Cardiff

Yugoslavia
   Državana Založba Slovenije   Ljubljana
   Geokarta   Beograd
   Jugoslavenski Leksikografski Zavod   Zagreb
   Leksikografski Zavod Fnrj   Zagreb
   Mladinska Knjiga   Ljubljana
   Rad   Beograd
   Savremena Shkola   Beograd
   Seljačka Sloga   Zagreb
   Školska Knjiga   Zagreb
   Turistička Stampa   Beograd
   Učila   Zagreb
   Vuk Karadžić   Beograd
   Yugoslavia. Vojno-Istoriski Institut   Beograd
   Znanje   Zagreb

NORTH AMERICA

Canada
   Air Canada   Ottawa
   Canada. Dept. of Citizenship and

Immigration	Ottawa
Canada. Department of Energy, Mines & Resources	Ottawa
Canada. Dept. of Indian Affairs and Northern Development	Ottawa
Canada. Inland Waters Branch	Ottawa
Canada. Department of Mines and Technical Surveys	Ottawa
Canada. Department of Transport	Ottawa
Canada. Surveys and Mapping Branch	Ottawa
Carleton University	Ottawa
Centre de Psychologie et de Pédagogie	Montreal
Dent, J. M.	Toronto
Editions du Renouveau Pédagogique	Montreal
Editions françaises	Québec
Encyclopedia Canadiana	Ottawa
Longmans, Green	Toronto
Rolph-McNally, Ltd.	Bramlea
Ryerson Press	Toronto
Vilas Industries	Toronto

Costa Rica

Costa Rica. Ministerio de Economia y Hacienda	San José

Cuba

Cuba. Academia de Ciencias	Havana
Cuba. Instituto Cubano de Cartografía y Catastro	Havana
Cuba. Oficina Nacional de los Cencos Demográfico y Electoral	Havana
Instituto Cubano del Libro	Havana

El Salvador

Salvador. Direción General de Cartografía	San Salvador
Salvador. Estadistica y Cencos	San Salvador
Salvador. Universidade Federal da Bahia, Centro de Estudos Afro-Orientais	San Salvador

Guatemala

Editorial Escolar "Piedra Santa"	Guatemala
Guatemala. Dirección General de Cartografia	Guatemala
Guatemala. Instituto Geográfico Nacional	Guatemala
Guatemala. Ministerio de Educación Pública	Guatemala
Guatemala. Observatorio Meteorológico y Estación Sismográfia	Guatemala
Obiols, Alfredo	Guatemala

Jamaica

Jamaica Pub. House	Kingston
Jamaica. Scientific Research Council	Kingston

Jamaica.   Town Planning Dept.   Kingston

Mexico
   Asociación Nacional Automovilística   México, D. F.
   Clute, J. W.   México, D. F.
   Compañía Hulera Euzkadi, S. A.   México, D. F.
   Ediciones Ateneo   México, D. F.
   Edi-Mapas de Mexico   México, D. F.
   Editorial Grijalbo   México, D. F.
   Editorial Patria, S. A.   México, D. F.
   Editorial Porrúa, S. A.   Mexico, D. F.
   Editorial Progreso   México, D. F.
   Fondo de Cultura Económica   México, D. F.
   Jackson, W. M., Inc.   México, D. F.
   Mexico.   Centro de Estudios y
     Documentación Sociales   México, D. F.
   Mexico.   Comisión Federal de
     Electricidad   México, D. F.
   Mexico.   Comisión Nacional de Caminos
     Vecinales   México, D. F.
   Mexico.   Fondo de Cultura Economica   México, D. F.
   Mexico.   Instituto Mexicano de Investiga-
     ciones Economicas   México, D. F.
   Mexico.   Ministerio de Comunicaciones y
     Obras Públicas   México, D. F.
   Mexico.   Secretaría de Comunicaciones y
     Transportes   México, D. F.
   Mexico.   Universidad Nacional Autónoma   México, D. F.
   Reader's Digest Mexico, S. A.   México, D. F.

Nicaragua
   Castillo, Guillermo J.   Managua

Panama
   Ediciones Oasis   Panama
   Editora Istmeña   Panama
   Panama.   Asesoría en Geografía y Ecología   Salud
   Panama.   Comisión del Atlas de Panamá   Panama
   Sanchez y Herrera   Panama

Puerto Rico
   Puerto Rico.   Dept. of Education   San Juan

U. S. A.
   Abercrombie & Fitch   New York
   Africana Pub. Corp.   New York
   Aldine Pub. Co.   Chicago
   Alpine Geographical Press   Champaign, Ill.
   American Geographical Society   New York
   American Heritage   New York
   American Hotel Register Co.   Chicago
   American Map Co., Inc.   New York
   American Oil Co.   Racine, Wis.

American Youth Hostels	New York
Artists & Writers Press	New York
Association Press	New York
Augsburg Publishing House	Minneapolis
Baker	Grand Rapids, Mich.
Bantam Books	New York
Barnes & Noble, Inc.	New York
Better Camping Magazine	Milwaukee, Wis.
Bobley Pub. Corp.	Glen Cove, N. Y.
Bookcraft	Salt Lake City, Utah
Book Production Industries	Chicago
Book Publishers Distributing Co.	Cincinnati
Boy Scouts of America	New Brunswick, N. J.
Brown & Bigelow	St. Paul, Minn.
Brown, W. C., Co.	Dubuque, Iowa
Camping Maps, U. S. A.	Montclair, N. J.
Cárdenas Associates	Fort Lauderdale, Fla.
Catholic War Veterans	Washington, D. C.
Clapsy, E. M.	Dowagiac, Mich.
Climatic Data Press	Lemont, Pa.
Collier, P. F. & Son, Corp.	New York
Consolidated Book Publishers	Chicago
Container Corporation of America	Chicago
Continental Oil Co.	Chicago
Cooper Square Publishers	New York
Cram, George F., Co.	Indianapolis
Crowell & Co.	New York
Crown	New York
Day, John Co.	New York
Dell Pub. Co.	New York
Denoyer-Geppert Co.	Chicago
Deseret Book Co.	Salt Lake City, Utah
Diversified Map Corporation	St. Louis
Donnelley, R. R. & Sons Co.	Chicago
Dorsey Press	Homewood, Ill.
Doubleday	Garden City, N. Y.
Dover Publications	New York
Dutton, E. P. & Co.	New York
Editors Press Service	New York
Educational Book Club	Des Moines, Iowa
Elving, Bruce F.	Duluth, Minn.
Encyclopaedia Britannica	Chicago
European Road Guide, Inc.	Larchmont, N. Y.
Everton Publishers	Logan, Utah
Exxon Travel Club	Houston, Tex.
Ezy Index	New York
Farmers Insurance Group	Los Angeles
Fawcett Publications	Greenwich, Conn.
Field Enterprises Educational Corp.	Chicago
Follett Educational Corp.	Chicago
Free Press	New York
Gale Research Co.	Detroit
Garden City Books	Garden City, N. Y.

General Drafting Co.	Convent Station, N. J.
Geographical Pub. Co.	Cleveland
Ginn & Co.	Boston
Golden Press	New York
Goushá, H. M., Co.	San Jose, Calif.
Greystone Press	New York
Grolier Society	New York
Grosset & Dunlap	New York
Halcyon House	Garden City, N. Y.
Hammond, Inc.	Maplewood, N. J.
Hanover House	Garden City, N. Y.
Harper & Row	New York
Hartford Fire Insurance Co.	Hartford, Conn.
Harvard University Press	Cambridge, Mass.
Hawthorne Books	New York
Hearst Magazines, Inc.	New York
Hitt Label Co.	Los Angeles
Holt	New York
Houghton Mifflin Co.	Boston
Household Goods Carriers' Bureau	Washington, D. C.
Humble Travel Club	Houston, Tex.
Indiana University. Dept. of Geography	Bloomington, Ind.
Industrial Atlas Corporation	New York
International Bank for Reconstruction and Development	Washington, D. C.
International Publications Service	New York
Kalmbach Publishing Co.	Milwaukee, Wis.
Koplinger-Washington Editors, Inc.	Washington, D. C.
Lexicon Publications, Inc.	Chicago
Lief, B. W.	New York
Macmillan Co.	New York
McGraw-Hill Book Co.	New York
Merriam, G. & C. Co.	Springfield, Mass.
Merrill, C. E. Co.	Columbus, Ohio
Moore, William L.	Mt. Vernon, Ill.
Munger Oil Information Service	Los Angeles
National Bus Traffic Association	Chicago
National Geographic Society	Washington, D. C.
National Safety Council	Chicago
Nelson-Doubleday	New York
News Map of the Week, Inc.	Skokie, Ill.
New York Herald Tribune	New York
Nystrom	Chicago
Oceana Publications	Dobbs Ferry, N. Y.
Odyssey Books	New York
Orbis Terrarum	New York
Ottenheimer Publishers, Inc.	Baltimore
Pan American Airways	New York
Pan American Union	Washington, D. C.
Permabooks	New York
Petroleum Publishing Co.	Tulsa, Okla.
Philadelphia Inquirer	Philadelphia
Pocket Books	New York

Praeger, Frederick A.	New York
Prentice-Hall	New York
Princeton University Press	Princeton, N. J.
Putnam's, G. P. Sons	New York
Quadrangle Books	New York
Radio Amateur Callbook, Inc.	Chicago
Rand McNally & Co.	Chicago
Rand McNally, G. M. B. H.	Chicago
Reader's Digest Association	Pleasantville, N. Y.
Replogle Globes, Inc.	Chicago
Sadlier, W. H.	New York
Scholastic Book Service	New York
School and Library Publ. Co.	Sycamore, Ill.
Scott, Foresman & Co.	Glenview, Ill.
Scribner, C.	New York
Sears Roebuck	Chicago
Simmons-Boardman Books	New York
Simon & Schuster	New York
Skelley Oil Co.	Tulsa, Okla.
Spencer Press, Inc.	Chicago
Standard International Library	New York
Standard Reference Works Pub. Co.	Brooklyn, N. Y.
State University of New York	Oneonta, N. Y.
Stein, Jack	Dayton, Ohio
St. Martin's Press	New York
Taplinger Publishing Co.	New York
Texana	Los Angeles
The New York Times	New York
Time, Inc.	New York
Time-Life Books	New York
United Nations	New York
Universal Guild	New York
University of Chicago Press	Chicago
University of Michigan Press	Ann Arbor, Mich.
University of Texas	Austin, Tex.
U. S. Aeronautical Chart and Information Center	St. Louis
U. S. Aid Mission to Laos	Washington, D. C.
U. S. Army Natick Laboratories	Natick, Mass.
U. S. Central Intelligence Agency	Washington, D. C.
U. S. Defense Mapping Agency	Washington, D. C.
U. S. Department of Agriculture	Washington, D. C.
U. S. Department of Commerce	Washington, D. C.
U. S. Economic Development Administration	Washington, D. C.
U. S. Engineer Agency of Resources Inventories	Washington, D. C.
U. S. Engineer Resources Inventory Center	Washington, D. C.
U. S. Forest Service	Washington, D. C.
U. S. Geological Survey	Washington, D. C.
U. S. Military Academy	West Point, N. Y.
U. S. National Ocean Survey	Washington, D. C.
U. S. Naval Oceanographic Office	Washington, D. C.
U. S. Topographic Command	Washington, D. C.

U. S. Weather Bureau	Washington, D. C.
Van Nostrand Co.	Princeton, N. J.
Walker, Gerald E.	Berkeley, Calif.
Water Information Center, Inc.	Port Washington, N. Y.
Watts	New York
Welch Scientific Co.	Chicago
Western Pub. Co.	Wayne, N. J.
Westminster Press	Philadelphia
Whittemore Associates	Needham Heights, Mass.
Wiley, John & Sons	New York
Wise, W. H.	New York
World Pub. Co.	Cleveland
Yale University Press	New Haven, Conn.
Young Readers Press	New York
Zondervan Pub. House	Grand Rapids, Mich.

SOUTH AMERICA

Argentina

Antonio, Roberto O.	Buenos Aires
Argentina. Departamento de Agrometeorología	Buenos Aires
Argentina. Instituto Geográfico Militar	Buenos Aires
Argentina. Ministerio de Agricultura y Gandaría	Buenos Aires
Argentina. Servicio Meteorológico Nacional	Buenos Aires
Automóvil Club Argentino	Buenos Aires
Ediciones G. L. G.	Buenos Aires
Ediciones Libreria del Colegio	Buenos Aires
Editorial Campano	Buenos Aires
Editorial Codex	Buenos Aires
Editorial Estrada	Buenos Aires
Editorial Mapa	Buenos Aires
Firestone de la Argentina SA	Buenos Aires
Ford Motor Argentina	Buenos Aires
Granda, J. C.	Buenos Aires
Industrias Kaiser Argentina, S. A.	Buenos Aires
Kapelusz y Cía	Buenos Aires
Pan American Institute of Geography & History	Buenos Aires
Peuser, Ediciones Geográficas	Buenos Aires

Bolivia

Camacho Lara, René R.	La Paz
Ediciones Condarco	La Paz
Gisbert y Cía, S. A.	La Paz

Brazil

Alves, Francisco	Rio de Janeiro
Brazil. Companha Nacional de Material de Ensino	Rio de Janeiro
Brazil. Conselho Nacional de Geografia	Rio de Janeiro

Brazil. Departamento Nacional de Estradas de Rodagem	Rio de Janeiro
Brazil. Instituto Brasileiro de Geografia e Estatistica	Rio de Janeiro
Brazil. Ministerio da Agricultura	Rio de Janeiro
Brazil. Ministerio da Educação e Cultura	Rio de Janeiro
Brazil. Servico de Meteorologia	Rio de Janeiro
Brazil. Servico Nacional de Recenseamento	Rio de Janeiro
Companha Editôra Nacional	São Paulo
Edições Melhoramentos	São Paulo
Editôra Civilização Brasiliera, S. A.	Rio de Janeiro
Editôra do Brazil	São Paulo
Editôra FTD	São Paulo
Editôra Globo	Rio de Janeiro
Editôra Liceu	Rio de Janeiro
Editôra Minerva	Rio de Janeiro
Editôra Ypiranga	Rio de Janeiro
Livros Cadernos	Rio de Janeiro
Puma	Rio de Janeiro
Schaeffer, Juan E.	Rio de Janeiro

Chile

Automóvil Club de Chile	Santiago
Chile. Departmento de Caminos	Santiago
Chile. Instituto Geografico Militar	
Chile. Instituto Hidrografico de la Armada	Válparaiso
Empresa Editora Zig Zag	Santiago
Kaplán Cojano, Oscar	Santiago
Liga Chileno-Alemana	Santiago

Colombia

Codazzi, Instituto Geográfico	Bogotá
Colombia. Banco de la Republica. Departmento de Investigaciones Economicas	Bogotá
Colombia. Departmento Administrativo Nacional de Estadística	Bogotá
Colombia. Ministerio de Obras Publicas	Bogotá
Compañía Suramericana de Seguros	Medellín
Editorial Colina	Medellín
Litografía Arco	Bogotá

Ecuador

Ecuador. Junta Nacional de Planificación y Coordinación Económica	Quito
Ecuador. Ministerio de Relaciones Exteriores	Quito
Publicationes Educativas Ariel	Guayaquil
SAM	Quito

Paraguay

Ferreira Gubetich, Hugo	Asunción

Machuca Martinez, Marcelino   Asunción
Ponte, Alberto da   Asunción

Peru
Compañía de Seguros "Atlas"   Lima
Editorial F. T. D.   Lima
Librería e Imprenta "Guía Lascano"   Lima
Peru. Dirección de Caminos   Lima
Peru. Instituto Nacional de Planificación   Lima
Peru. Ministerio de Trabajo y Asuntos
   Indigenas   Lima

Surinam
Duif en Schalken   Paramaribo
Kessel, M. S. van   Paramaribo

Uruguay
Barreiro & Ramos   Montevideo
Martín, Pedro   Montevideo
Monteverde, A.   Montevideo
Uruguay. Comisión de Integración
   Eléctrica Regional   Montevideo
Uruguay. Dirección General de Estadística
   y Censos. Departmento de Cartografía   Montevideo

Venezuela
Compañía Shell de Venezuela   Caracas
Discolar   Caracas
Ediciones Nueva Cadiz   Caracas
Litografía Miangolarra Hnos   Caracas
Minerva Books   Caracas
Pensamiento, Vivo   Caracas
Shell Caribbean Petroleum Company   Caracas
Venezuela. Consejo Nacional de Validad   Caracas
Venezuela. Dirección de Cartografía
   Nacional   Caracas
Venezuela. Direccion de Plantificacion
   Agropecuaria   Caracas
Venezuela. Ministerio de Agricultura   Caracas
Venezuela. Ministerio de la Defensa   Caracas
Venezuela. Ministerio de Obras Públicas   Caracas

COMPREHENSIVE INDEX OF PUBLISHERS

3716, 3717, 3718, 3719, 4110, 4111, 4112, 4113, 4114, 4115,
4116, 4117, 5006, 5007, 5008, 5009, 5010, 5011, 5012, 5013,
7274, 7402, 7640
Alves, Francisco (Rio de Janeiro, Brazil)   310, 1606, 5692, 7554
American Geographical Society (New York, N.Y., U.S.A.)   1893,
4945, 4959, 6398
American Heritage (New York, N.Y., U.S.A.)   3720, 4494, 7154,
8113
American Hotel Register Co. (Chicago, Ill., U.S.A.)   3454, 3455,
3456, 3457, 3458, 3459, 3460, 3461, 3462, 3463, 3464, 3465,
3466, 3467, 3468, 3469, 3470, 3471, 3472, 3473, 3474, 3595,
3596, 3597, 3598, 3599, 3600, 3601, 3602, 3603, 3604, 3605,
3606, 3607, 3608, 3609, 3610, 3611, 3612, 3613, 3614, 3615,
3721, 3722, 3723, 3724, 3725, 3726, 3727, 3728, 3729, 3730,
3731, 3732, 3733, 3734, 3735, 3736, 3737, 3738, 3739, 3740,
3741, 5014, 5015, 5016, 5017, 5018, 5019, 5020, 5021, 5022,
5023, 5024, 5025, 5026, 5027, 5028, 5029, 5030, 5031, 5032,
5033, 5034, 7275, 7276, 7277, 7278, 7279, 7280, 7281, 7282,
7283, 7284, 7285, 7286, 7355, 7356, 7357, 7358, 7359, 7403,
7404, 7405, 7406, 7407, 8114, 8115, 8116, 8117, 8118
American Map Co., Inc. (New York, N.Y., U.S.A.)   704, 785,
1016, 1141, 1142, 1143, 1217, 1272, 1400, 1419, 1501, 1607,
1713, 1948, 3475, 3476, 3477, 3742, 3743, 3744, 3976, 3980,
4214, 4215, 4216, 7280, 7360, 7408, 7409, 7410, 7411, 7412,
7413, 7414, 7695, 7696, 7697, 7698, 7699, 7700, 8119
American Oil Co. (Racine, Wisc., U.S.A.)   6548, 7415, 7435,
8120, 8188
American Youth Hostels (New York, N.Y., U.S.A.)   6549, 6550,
6551, 8502, 8503, 8504
Ampol Petroleum, Ltd. (Sydney, Australia)   2527, 5035
Angus & Robertson (Sydney, Australia)   1949, 2528
Anikasari (Djakarta, Indonesia)   6687, 7701
Anokh, Hanok (Tel Aviv, Israel)   516
Antonio, Roberto O. (Buenos Aires, Argentina)   3905
Anubar (Valencia, Spain)   7165, 7855
Argentina.   Departamento de Agrometeorología (Buenos Aires,
Argentina)   7533, 7648
Argentina.   Instituto Geográfico Militar (Buenos Aires, Argentina)
2155, 3906, 3907, 3908, 3909, 3910, 3911, 4217, 5036, 5505,
7534, 7535, 7536, 7537, 7538, 7702, 7703
Argentina.   Ministerio de Agricultura y Gandaría (Buenos Aires,
Argentina)   7539, 7692
Argentina.   Servicio Meteorológico Nacional (Buenos Aires, Ar-
gentina)   7540, 7649
Ariel, Publicationes Educativas see Publicaciones Educativas Ariel
Arnold, E. (London, England)   1788, 1897, 4495, 4496, 4497, 4498,
4499, 6362, 6363, 7856, 7857, 7858, 7859, 7860
Artists & Writers Press (New York, N.Y., U.S.A.)   6552, 7416,
8121
Aschehoug & Co. (Oslo, Norway)   1144, 1273, 1774, 4500, 5624,
5649, 5693, 7098, 7099
Asedi (Bruxelles, Belgium)   1608, 2659
Asociación Nacional Automovilística (México, D.F., México)   3616,

3617, 3618, 5037, 5038, 5039, 7361, 7362, 8122, 8123
Association Press (New York, N. Y., U. S. A.) 4047
Ateneo Ediciones see Ediciones Ateneo
Atheneum (Barcelona, Spain) 1502
Atlantik Refining Company of Africa (Cape Town, South Africa)
2234, 2257, 5040
Atlantik Verlag (Frankfurt, Germany) 1, 2, 84, 86, 160, 228, 229,
230, 231, 270, 311, 380, 453, 454, 455, 456, 705, 737, 2785,
2786, 2787, 2788, 2789, 4218, 4501, 4502, 4503
Atlas and Map Industries (Colombo, Sri Lanka) 6047, 6748, 6749,
6750
Augsburg Publishing House (Minneapolis, Minn., U. S. A.) 4048,
4504
Austin Motor Co., Ltd. (Birmingham, England) 2944, 2945, 2946,
2947, 2948, 2949, 2950, 5041, 5042, 5043, 5044, 5045, 5046,
5047
Australia. Bureau of Mineral Resources, Geology and Geophysics
(Adelaide, Australia) 1936, 4470
Australia. Department of National Development (Canberra, Aus-
tralia) 2529, 2530, 4219, 4220
Australia. Division of Soils, Commonwealth Scientific and Industrial
Research Organization (Canberra, Australia) 2531, 5499
Australian Educational Foundation, Pty., Ltd. (Sydney, Australia)
931, 2532
Austria. Akademie der Wissenschaften (Wien, Austria) 2604,
2605, 4451
Austria. Bundesdenkmalamt (Graz, Austria) 6789, 7861
Autokarten und Reiseführer Verlag (Kiel, Germany) 2790, 5048
Automobile Association (London, England) 3051, 5049, 6864, 6865,
7155, 8124, 8125, 8126
Automobile Association of Malaya (Penang, Malaysia) 2489, 5050,
6733, 8127
Automobile Association of South Africa (Johannesburg, South Africa)
1789, 1790, 2258, 5051, 5052, 6364, 6634, 8128
Automobile Club d'Italia (Roma, Italy) 1950, 1951, 3063, 3064,
5053, 5054, 5055, 5056, 7074, 8129
Auto-Motor-und Radfahrerbund Österreichs (Wien, Austria) 1952,
1953, 5057, 5058
Automóvil Club Argentino (Buenos Aires, Argentina) 3912, 5059
Automóvil Club de Chile (Santiago de Chile, Chile) 7567, 8130

Bachtiar, A. (Djakarta, Indonesia) 232, 2392
Bacon, G. W., Ltd. see Johnston, W. & A. K. (Edinburgh,
Scotland)
Baker (Grand Rapids, Mich., U. S. A.) 7625
Balkanturist (Sofia, Bulgaria) 6818, 8131
Bancroft & Co. (London, England) 1274, 5636, 5650, 7380
Bantam Books (New York, N. Y., U. S. A.) 1145
Barnes & Noble, Inc. (New York, N. Y., U. S. A.) 772, 2135,
4221, 4505, 4506, 4507, 4508, 4509, 4510, 4511, 4512, 4513,
4514, 4515, 4516, 4517, 7862, 7863, 7864
Barreiro & Ramos (Montevideo, Uruguay) 7588
Bartholomew, John & Son, Ltd. (Edinburgh, Scotland) 3, 52, 53,

54, 55, 75, 87, 93, 161, 233, 234, 278, 279, 280, 312, 348,
381, 403, 437, 457, 493, 494, 517, 518, 558, 601, 613, 706,
744, 773, 774, 808, 809, 822, 859, 914, 927, 932, 978, 1017,
1018, 1019, 1030, 1085, 1143, 1146, 1221, 1356, 1357, 1400,
1401, 1503, 1543, 1584, 1609, 1692, 1918, 1919, 1942, 1943,
1954, 1955, 2951, 2952, 2953, 2954, 2955, 2956, 2957, 2958,
2959, 2960, 2961, 2962, 2963, 2998, 3006, 3204, 3206, 3413,
3424, 3487, 3488, 4342, 4518, 4571, 4572, 4730, 4755, 4756,
5060, 5061, 5062, 5063, 5064, 5065, 5066, 5067, 5068, 5069,
5070, 5071, 5072, 5073, 5074, 5363, 5365, 5550, 5585, 5609,
5613, 5639, 5746, 5747, 5821, 5822, 5869, 5870, 5943, 5978,
6022, 6048, 6049, 6139, 6155, 6156, 6157, 6175, 6176, 6177,
6225, 6229, 6230, 6265, 6266, 6322, 6323, 6413, 6414, 6415,
6416, 6417, 6418, 6419, 6420, 6538, 6546, 6672, 6965, 6966,
6967, 6968, 6969, 6970, 6971, 6972, 6973, 6974, 7019, 7020,
7021, 7070. 7254, 7255, 7256, 7967, 7968, 7969, 8132, 8133,
8134, 8135, 8136, 8137, 8138, 8139, 8140, 8141, 8142, 8143,
8144, 8145, 8146, 8147, 8458, 8526, 8527
Bayerischer Schulbuch Verlag (München, Germany) 4519, 4520,
    4521, 4522, 4523, 4524, 7865, 7866, 7867, 7868
Beazley, Mitchell, Ltd. (London, England) 5748, 5871, 5872, 6050,
    6131, 6178, 6179, 6324, 7601, 7618, 7619, 7869, 8528, 8529,
    8543
Bee Research Organisation (London, England) 6975, 8544
Belgium. Académie Royale des Sciences d'Outre-Mer (Bruxelles,
    Belgium) 2181, 2192, 2193, 2239
Belgium. Centre d'Information et de Documentation du Congo Belge
    et du Ruanda-Urundi (Bruxelles, Belgium) 2182, 2183, 2194,
    2195, 2240, 2241
Belgium. Centre National de Recherches Scientifiques Souterraines
    (Liège, Belgium) 2660, 4134
Belgium. Comité National de Géographie (Bruxelles, Belgium)
    2661
Belgium. Ministère des Travaux Publics et de la Reconstruction
    (Bruxelles, Belgium) 2662, 4222
Bello, Editorial see Editorial Bello
Ben-Eliyahu, Ephraïm (Jerusalem, Israel) 2422, 4049
Benziger & Co. (Einsiedeln, Germany) 4050, 4525
Bergvalls Förlag (Stockholm, Sweden) 162, 458, 775, 933, 1147,
    5873
Berlitz (London, England) 6180
Bernces Förlag (Malmö, Sweden) 934, 6421, 8148
Bertelsmann, C. (Gütersloh, Germany) 313, 602, 776, 839, 840,
    868, 915, 946, 1020, 1021, 1022, 1084, 1148, 1275, 1276, 1277,
    1278, 1402, 1403, 1404, 1504, 1505, 1506, 1507, 1774, 1956,
    1957, 1958, 1959, 2072, 2791, 2792, 2793, 5075, 5076, 5077,
    5694, 5749. 5750, 5874, 6051, 6052, 6181, 6182, 6183, 6247,
    6267, 6325, 6422, 6423, 6424, 6896, 6897, 6898, 8149, 8150,
    8151
Beste, A. S. (Oslo, Norway) 1023, 1149, 1378, 6842, 7103, 7181,
    8187
Beste, G. M. B. H. (Stuttgart, Germany) 1610, 6431, 6432, 8183,
    8184

Brazil)   3935, 4225
Brink, H. Ten see Ten Brink, H.
British Bureau of Television Advertising, Ltd. (London, England)
    6976, 6977, 6978, 7675, 7676, 7677
British Motor Corp. , Ltd. (London, England) 2967, 2973, 5087,
    5181
British Sulphur Corp. , Ltd. (London, England) 1283, 1715, 3991,
    3992, 5880, 6184, 7602, 7603
Brockhaus, F. A. (Wiesbaden, Germany) 778, 1150
Brown & Bigelow (St. Paul, Minn. , U. S. A.) 7374, 7375, 7417,
    7418, 7457, 7458, 7459, 7460, 7461, 7463, 7464, 8158, 8159,
    8256, 8257, 8258, 8259, 8260, 8262, 8263
Brown, W. C. Co. (Dubuque, Iowa, U. S. A.) 779, 1611, 1792,
    3747, 4024, 4025, 4138, 7650
Brug Uitgeversbedrijf, N. V. (Amsterdam, Netherlands) 707, 708,
    936, 1508, 3091, 3092, 3093
Buchclub Ex Libris (Zürich, Switzerland) 1509
Buchgemeinschaft Donauland (Wien, Austria) 520, 1151, 1284, 1964,
    2606, 2607, 5088
Buchverlag Verlandsdruckerei (Bern, Switzerland) 3282, 3993
Bulgaria. Akademiya na Naukite (Sofia, Bulgaria) 2679, 4533,
    6819, 6820, 8087
Bulgaria. Glavno Upravlenie po Geodezia i Kartografia (Sofia,
    Bulgaria) 709, 1024, 1612, 2680, 2681, 2682, 5089, 5695,
    6821, 6822, 6823, 8160, 8161
Bulgaria. Muzei na Revoliutsionnoto Dvizhenie Bŭlgariia (Sofia,
    Bulgaria) 2683, 4534
Burnes & Oates, Ltd. (London, England) 4051, 4052
Buyōdō Co. , Ltd. (Tokyo, Japan) 6717, 8162

Cadernos see Livros Cadernos
Caltex (Philippines) (Manila, Philippines) 2508, 5090
Camacho Lara, René R. (La Paz, Bolivia) 3922
Cambridge University Press (Cambridge, England) 7873
Campano, Editorial see Editorial Campano
Camping Maps, U. S. A. (Montclair, N. J. , U. S. A.) 3619, 3748,
    3749, 4120, 4121, 7287, 7419, 7420, 7421, 7641, 7642, 7643,
    7644
Canada. Dept. of Citizenship and Immigration (Ottawa, Canada)
    7288
Canada. Department of Energy, Mines & Resources (Ottawa,
    Canada) 3479, 3480, 7289
Canada. Dept. of Indian Affairs and Northern Development (Ottawa,
    Canada) 7290, 8106
Canada. Department of Mines and Technical Surveys (Ottawa,
    Canada) 3481, 7291
Canada. Department of Transport (Ottawa, Canada) 3482, 4139,
    7292, 7651
Canada. Inland Waters Branch (Ottawa, Canada) 7293, 8080
Canada. Surveys and Mapping Branch (Ottawa, Canada) 3483,
    7294, 7295, 7296
Cappelens, J. W. Forlag, A. S. (Oslo, Norway) 89, 237, 382,
    1152, 1153, 1405, 1406, 1613, 1775, 3128, 3129, 3130, 3131,

3132, 3133, 3134, 4535, 5091, 5655, 5656, 5696, 5753, 6055,
6268, 7100, 7101, 7102, 7626, 7863, 7874, 7876
Cárdenas Associates (Fort Lauderdale, Fla. , U. S. A.)   6056
Carleton University (Ottawa, Canada)   6599, 7706
Carlson, A. V. (Stockholm, Sweden)   4, 3261, 3262, 3263
Carta (Jerusalem, Israel)   2423, 2424, 2425, 4053, 4054, 4076,
5092, 5093, 6709, 6710, 6711, 8163, 8164, 8165
Cartografía Pirelli (Barcelona, Spain)   7166, 8166
Cartographia (Budapest, Hungary)   604, 686, 3036, 5881, 5882,
6426, 6547, 7043, 7044, 7045, 7652, 7674, 7707, 8167, 8168,
8169
Cassell (London, England)   843, 4226
Castillo, Guillermo J. (Managua, Nicaragua)   3704
Catholic War Veterans (Washington, D. C. , U. S. A.)   4055, 4536
Caxton Pub. Co. (London, England)   780, 937
Centre de Psychólogie et de Pédagogie (Montréal, Canada)   7297,
7875
Chad. Institut National Tchadien pour les Sciences Humaines
(N'djamena, Chad)   6588
Chambers, W. & R. , Ltd. (Edinburgh, Scotland)   5753, 7876
Chile. Departmento de Caminos (Santiago de Chile, Chile)   7568,
8170
Chile. Instituto Geografico Militar (Santiago de Chile, Chile)   3946,
3947, 3948, 5094, 7569, 7570
Chile. Instituto Hidrografico de la Armada (Valparaiso, Chile)
7571, 8099
China. Academy of Sciences (Peking, China)   2320, 4973
China. Geographical Institute (Shanghai, China)   2321
China. National War College (Taipei, Taiwan)   1285, 2322, 2518
Chinese Map Publ. (Peking, China)   2323
Clapsy, E. M. (Dowagiac, Mich. , U. S. A.)   2534
Clarendon Press see Oxford University Press
Climatic Data Press (Lemont, Pa. , U. S. A.)   7363, 7645
Clute, J. W. (México, D. F. , México)   5754
Codazzi, Instituto Geográfico (Bogotá, Colombia)   3953, 3954,
7574, 7575
Codex Verlag (Gundholzen, Germany)   1898, 2218, 2306, 2307, 2426,
2935, 3321, 4027, 4028, 4029, 4030, 4031, 4032
Colin (Paris, France)   90, 164, 383, 781, 2733, 2734, 2735,
4537, 4538, 4539, 4540, 4541, 4542, 4543, 4544, 6868, 7708
Collet (London, England)   1510
Collier, P. F. & Son, Corp. (New York, N. Y. , U. S. A.)   238,
384, 521, 605, 4227, 4228
Collins Clear-Type Press (Glasgow, Scotland)   844, 845, 1154
Collins-Longmans see Collins, William, Sons & Co. , Ltd.
Collins, M. O. (Pvt), Ltd. (Salisbury, Rhodesia)   2235, 4229
Collins, William, Sons & Co. , Ltd. (Glasgow, Scotland)   5, 165,
166, 167, 239, 240, 241, 385, 386, 460, 522, 846, 847, 848,
849, 850, 1025, 1286, 1287, 1407, 1511, 1512, 1614, 1615,
1616, 1716, 1717, 1718, 1776, 1793, 1794, 1795, 1796, 1797,
1798, 1799, 1800, 1801, 1802, 1803, 1804, 1805, 1806, 1807,
1965, 2212, 2220, 2228, 2229, 2236, 2248, 2249, 2260, 2261,
2262, 2263, 2370, 2493, 2494, 2495, 2496, 2497, 2498, 2515,

2516, 2521, 2535, 2536, 2573, 4056, 4545, 5095, 5628, 5683,
5755, 5756, 5757, 5758, 5759, 5883, 5884, 5885, 5886, 5887,
6057, 6058, 6059, 6060, 6185, 6186, 6187, 6188, 6189, 6269,
6587, 6592, 6600, 6608, 6611, 6612, 6632, 6633, 6647, 6655,
6656, 6675, 6688, 6735, 6736, 6737, 6743, 6744, 6781, 6783,
6979, 6980, 7056, 7057, 7270, 7272, 7349, 7709, 7821, 8171,
8172
Colombia. Banco de la República. Departamento de Investigaciones
   Económicas (Bogotá, Colombia) 3955, 3994, 4230
Colombia. Departmento Administrativo Nacional de Estadística
   (Bogotá, Colombia) 7576, 7710
Colombia. Ministerio de Obras Publicas (Bogotá, Colombia) 3956,
   5096
Colorgravure (Melbourne, Australia) 6, 2537, 2538
Columbus Verlag Oestergaard (Berlin, Germany) 7, 8, 168, 269,
   304, 461, 606, 689, 851, 1026, 1288, 1408, 2796, 5097
Commission for Technical Cooperation in Africa South of the Sahara
   (Lagos, Nigeria) 1808, 4140
Companha Editora Nacional (São Paulo, Brazil) 5760
Compañia de Seguros "Atlas" (Lima, Peru) 7583
Compañia Hulera Euzkadi, S.A. (México, D.F., México) 3620,
   3621, 3622, 5098, 5099, 5100
Compañia Internacional Editora (Barcelona, Spain) 7877
Compañia Mercantil Anónima Líneas Aéreas Españolas (Madrid,
   Spain) 3237, 5506
Compañia Shell de Venezuela (Caracas, Venezuela) 7591, 8173
Compañia Suramericana de Seguros (Medellín, Colombia) 3957
Condarco Ediciones see Ediciones Condarco
Congo. Commissariat Général au Plan (Brazzaville, Congo) 6651,
   7604, 7653, 8081
Congo. Institut National pour L'étude Agronomique (Bruxelles,
   France) 6652, 7654
Consociazione Turistica Italiana (Milano, Italy) 3065, 4231
Consolidated Book Publishers (Chicago, Ill., U.S.A.) 1155
Contact (Antwerpen, Belgium) 91
Container Corporation of America (Chicago, Ill., U.S.A.) 242
Continental Gummiwerke Kartographischer Verlag (Hannover, Ger-
   many) 1966, 1967, 1968, 1969, 1970, 1971, 2608, 2663, 2664,
   2797, 2798, 2799, 2800, 2801, 2802, 2803, 2804, 2805, 2806,
   2807, 2808, 3066, 3082, 3083, 3283, 5101, 5102, 5103, 5104,
   5105, 5106, 5107, 5108, 5109, 5110, 5111, 5112, 5113, 5114,
   5115, 5116, 6427, 6428, 6429, 6430, 6899, 6900, 6901, 6902,
   6903, 8174, 8175, 8176, 8177, 8178
Continental Oil Co. (Chicago, Ill., U.S.A.) 3767, 3768, 5189,
   5190
Compano, Editorial see Editorial Compano
Cooper Square Publishers (New York, N.Y., U.S.A.) 2156, 4232,
   4546
Costa Rica. Ministerio de Economia y Hacienda (San José, Costa
   Rica) 3579, 4233
Cram, George F., Co. (Indianapolia, Ind., U.S.A.) 9, 10, 169,
   314, 387, 462, 852, 853, 938, 1156, 4057, 5888, 5889, 6061,
   7298, 7299, 7364, 7365, 7422, 7423, 7424, 7425, 7711, 7712,

1292, 1411, 1810, 1811, 1899, 1900, 1972, 1973, 1974, 1975,
2324, 3325, 3326, 3327, 3750, 3751, 4557, 4558, 4559, 4560,
4561, 4562, 4563, 4564, 4565, 4566, 4567, 5570, 5597, 5630,
5762, 5892, 6368, 6400, 6401, 6402, 6433, 7214, 7428, 7429,
7430, 7431, 7432, 7433, 7434, 7886, 7887, 7888, 7889, 7890,
7891, 7892, 7893, 7894, 7895
Dent, J. M. (London, England & Toronto, Canada) 93, 612, 613,
   614, 858, 859, 1030, 1293, 3484, 3485, 3486, 3487, 3488, 4568,
   4569, 4570, 4571, 4572, 5631, 5893, 6190, 7300, 7301, 7302
Deseret Book Co. (Salt Lake City, Utah, U. S. A.) 2970, 3052,
   3414, 4466, 4467
De Sikkel (Anvers, Belgium) 1412, 5658, 6804
Det Bedste fra Reader's Digest AS (København, Denmark) 6434,
   8186
Det Beste A. S. see Beste A. S.
Deutsche Lufthansa (Köln, Germany) 1618, 5507
Deutsche Viscobil Öl Gesellschaft (Hamburg, Germany) 2809, 5127
Deutscher Bücherbund (Stuttgart, Germany) 1513, 1619, 4573, 6271
Deutscher Taschenbuch Verlag (München, Germany) 4574, 4575,
   4576, 4577, 6191, 6328, 7896, 7897, 7898
Deutscher Zentralverlag VEB (Berlin, Germany) 2810, 5128
Didot-Bottin (Paris, France) 2736, 2737
Die Gabe Verlag see Verlag Die Gabe
Dijkstra (Zeist, Netherlands) 1976, 1977, 3094, 4235, 5577
Discolar (Caracas, Venezuela) 785, 3977
Diversified Map Corporation (St. Louis, Mo. , U. S. A.) 2136, 2137,
   3489, 3490, 3502, 3503, 3504, 3623, 3624, 3639, 3640, 3641,
   3752, 3753, 3754, 3779, 3780, 3781, 5129, 5130, 5131, 5201,
   5202, 5203, 6548, 7303, 7304, 7305, 7306, 7366, 7367, 7368,
   7369, 7415, 7435, 7436, 7437, 7438, 7439, 7440, 7441, 7532,
   8120, 8188, 8189, 8190, 8191, 8192, 8193, 8194, 8496
Djambatan (Amsterdam, Netherlands) 94, 173, 246, 247, 388, 527,
   708, 956, 957, 1812, 1813, 1901, 1902, 1903, 1912, 1928, 1929,
   2319, 2325, 2393, 2394, 2395, 2396, 2397, 4058, 4236, 4400,
   4401, 4493, 4578, 4579, 4580, 4581, 4582, 4661, 5894, 6689,
   6690
Dom Verlag (Wien, Austria) 2609, 4059, 4583
Donnelley, R. R. & Sons Co. (Chicago, Ill. , U. S. A.) 6553, 6554,
   6555, 6556, 7442, 7443, 7444, 8195, 8196, 8197, 8198, 8199,
   8200, 8201
Dorsey Press (Homewood, Ill. , U. S. A.) 3755, 4584
Doubleday (Garden City, N. Y. , U. S. A.) 315, 466, 467, 528, 615,
   941, 942, 1180, 1719, 4060, 4585, 5763, 5895, 5896, 6064,
   6065, 6272
Dover Publications (New York, N. Y. , U. S. A.) 5548
Dreyers Forlag (Oslo, Norway) 174, 1294, 3135, 4061, 7104, 7714
Droemer (München, Germany) 13, 95, 529, 1157, 4237, 4238,
   4979, 5897
Državana Založba Slovenije (Ljubljana, Yugoslavia) 175, 4239
Dublin Institute for Advanced Studies (Dublin, Ireland) 3053, 4938
Duif en Schalken (Paramaribo, Surinam) 3974
Dutton, E. P. & Co. (New York, N. Y. , U. S. A.) 1295, 4586,
   4587, 6435, 8202

Duwaer, J. F. & Zonen (Amsterdam, Netherlands) 3095

East African Institute of Social Research (Kampala, Uganda) 1814,
  2292, 4026, 4980
Ebury Press (London, England) 3203, 5132
Economist Intelligence Unit, Ltd. (London, England) 7219, 7796
Ecuador. Junta Nacional de Planificación y Coordinación Económica
  (Quito, Ecuador) 7579, 7715
Ecuador. Ministerio de Relaciones Exteriores (Quito, Ecuador)
  3959, 4588
E. D. A. F. (Madrid, Spain) 1620, 1720, 4240, 5898, 7716
Ediciones Ateneo (México, D. F., México) 3625
Ediciones Condarco (La Paz, Bolivia) 2157, 4589
Ediciones de Aguilar, S. A. see Aguilar, S. A. De Ediciones
Ediciones Geográficas Peuser see Peuser, Ediciones Geográficas
Ediciones G. L. G. (Buenos Aires, Argentina) 7541
Ediciones Libreria del Colegio (Buenos Aires, Argentina) 530
Ediciones Nueva Cadiz (Caracas, Venezuela) 3978, 7592, 7593,
  7594
Ediciones Oasis (Panama, Panama) 3705, 7398
Edições Melhoramentos (São Paulo, Brazil) 14, 316, 531, 943,
  1158, 1413, 1514, 1621, 3936, 3937, 3938, 3939, 3940, 3941,
  3942, 5586, 5697, 5764, 5899, 6066, 7559, 7560, 7561, 7562,
  7563, 7564, 7717
Edições Spal (Luanda, Angola) 2180
Edi-Mapas de México (México, D. F., México) 3626, 3627, 3628,
  5133, 5508
Edinburgh University Press (Edinburgh, Scotland) 2326, 4590
Editions Alain (Paris, France) 2203
Editions André Lesot (Paris, France) 6869, 7718
Editions Bordas (Paris, France) 248, 317, 532, 616, 617, 860,
  1159, 1160, 1296, 1414, 1415, 1622, 1721, 2738, 2739, 2740,
  2741, 2742, 2743, 2744, 2745, 4241, 4591, 4592, 4593, 5765,
  5766, 5767, 5900, 6067, 6436, 6805, 6870, 6883, 7089, 7194,
  7859, 7900, 7901, 7902, 8203, 8270
Editions de l'Ecole (Paris, France) 1978
Editions de Lyon (Lyon, France) 1979, 2042, 4242
Editions du Centurion (Paris, France) 4062
Editions du Renouveau Pédagogique (Montreal, Canada) 1515, 3491,
  5659, 5768
Editions française (Québec, Canada) 5901, 7307
Editions Jeune Afrique (Paris, France) 6369, 6650
Editions Meddens (Bruxelles, Belgium) 1980, 4594
Editions R. De Rouck (Bruxelles, Belgium) 2184, 2196, 2242,
  4595
Editions Rencontre (Lausanne, Switzerland) 468, 4243
Editions Sequoia (Paris, France) 786, 944, 1416, 1981, 4596, 4597
Editions Stauffacher (Zürich, Switzerland) 618, 945, 1297, 5769,
  6068, 7719
Editôra Civilização Brasileira, S. A. (Rio de Janeiro, Brazil) 176
Editôra do Brazil (São Paulo, Brazil) 3943
Editôra F. T. D. (São Paulo, Brazil) 4598
Editôra Globo (Rio de Janeiro, Brazil) 3944, 3945, 7565

Editôra Istmeña (Panama, Panama) 7399
Editôra Liceu (Rio de Janeiro, Brazil) 1623
Editôra Minerva (Rio de Janeiro, Brazil) 787
Editora Porto see Porto Editora
Editôra Ypiranga (Rio de Janeiro, Brazil) 1516
Editorial Bello (Valencia, Spain) 788
Editorial Campano (Buenos Aires, Argentina) 2158
Editorial Codex (Buenos Aires, Argentina) 5632, 5698
Editorial Colina (Medellín, Colombia) 7577
Editorial Escolar "Piedra Santa" (Guatemala, Guatemala) 3587
Editorial Estrada (Buenos Aires, Argentina) 7542, 7720
Editorial Everest (Leon, Portugal) 7136, 7167, 8204
Editorial Francisco Seix, S.A. (Barcelona, Spain) 533
Editorial F.T.D. (Lima, Peru) 1517, 3964, 5699, 7584
Editorial Grijalbo (México, D.F., México) 619
Editorial Luis Vives, S.A. (Zaragoza, Spain) 15, 318, 319, 715,
    3238, 3239, 3240, 4599, 7168
Editorial Mapa (Buenos Aires, Argentina) 3913, 3914, 3915, 5134,
    5135, 5136
Editorial Miguel A. Salvatella (Barcelona, Spain) 861
Editorial Patria, S.A. (México, D.F., México) 3629
Editorial Porrúa, S.A. (México, D.F., México) 3630, 7370, 7371
Editorial Progreso (México, D.F., México) 3631, 4600, 7372
Editorial Rivadeneyra (Madrid, Spain) 5770
Editorial Seix Barral, S.A. (Barcelona, Spain) 249, 320, 469,
    3241, 3242, 3243, 3581, 3958, 3965, 4244, 4245, 4246, 7345
Editorial Teide (Barcelona, Spain) 16, 17, 620, 1161, 3244, 4247,
    4601, 4602, 6069, 6192, 7169, 7721, 7903
Editorial Vergara (Barcelona, Spain) 946
Editorial Vincens-Vives (Barcelona, Spain) 5598, 5771
Editors Press Service (New York, N.Y., U.S.A.) 716, 789
Editura Stadion (Bucuresti, Romania) 7148, 7149, 8205, 8206
Edizioni Cremonese (Roma, Italy) 717
Educational Book Club (Des Moines, Iowa, U.S.A.) 862, 947, 948,
    1031, 1162
Educational Company of Ireland, Ltd. (Dublin, Ireland) 3054, 7060,
    7061, 7062, 7063
Elsevier (Amsterdam, Netherlands) 18, 19, 20, 534, 922, 1001,
    1032, 1033, 1034, 1163, 1164, 1298, 1417, 1624, 1625, 1815,
    1982, 1983, 1984, 1986, 1987, 2159, 2185, 2186, 2197, 2198,
    2243, 2244, 2308, 2427, 2665, 2666, 2667, 2746, 3084, 3096,
    3097, 3328, 3995, 3996, 3997, 4033, 4034, 4035, 4063, 4064,
    4103, 4142, 4248, 4603, 4604, 4605, 4606, 4607, 4608, 4609,
    4610, 4611, 4612, 4613, 4614, 4615, 4877, 5700, 5701, 6070,
    6273, 6712
Elving, Bruce F. (Duluth, Minn., U.S.A.) 7308, 7445, 7678
Elwert Verlag (Marburg, Germany) 2811, 2812, 3085, 4452, 4939,
    4940
Empresa Editora Zig-Zap (Santiago de Chile, Chile) 177, 535, 3949
Empresa Moderna (Lourenço Marques, Mozambique) 2225
Encyclopaedia Britannica (Chicago, Ill., U.S.A.) 96, 178, 321,
    389, 718, 863, 1035, 1165, 1166, 1299, 1418, 1518, 1626, 1722,
    1723, 1777, 5702, 6071, 6274

Fondo de Cultura Económica (México, D. F., México) 2138, 2160
Fonna (Oslo, Norway) 952, 3136
Ford Motor Argentina (Buenos Aires, Argentina) 3916, 5163
France. Centre de Recherches historique (Paris, France) 5908,
    7606
France. Centre national de la recherche scientifique (Paris,
    France) 6621, 6871, 6872, 6873, 7833, 7907, 8088, 8089, 8107
France. Comité National de Géographie (Paris, France) 2748
France. Commissariat Général à la Productivité (Paris, France)
    2749, 4252
France. Conseil National du Patronat Français (Paris, France)
    2750, 4253
France. Direction de la météorologie nationale (Paris, France)
    6874, 6875, 7655, 7656
France. Direction des ports maritimes et de voies navigables
    (Paris, France) 6444, 8082, 8542
France. Electricité de France (Paris, France) 6876, 6877, 7722,
    7723
France. Institut Géographique National (Paris, France) 3086,
    6369
France. La Documentation Française (Paris, France) 2751, 2752,
    2753, 2754, 4254, 4255, 4928, 4929, 4976, 6878, 6879, 7724,
    7725
France. Ministère de l'Education nationale (La Celle-Saint Cloud,
    France) 6880, 7726
France. Ministère de l'Équipement (Paris, France) 2755, 4146
France. Ministère des Postes et Télécommunications (Paris,
    France) 2756, 4176, 6881, 7679
France. Service de l'Économie Forestière (Paris, France) 2757,
    4458, 6882, 7836
France. Société Nationale des Chemins de Fer Français (Paris,
    France) 2758, 5510
Franco, Livraria Popular De F. see Livraria Popular De F.
    Franco
Frankfurt. Institut für Angewandte Geodäsie (Frankfurt, Germany)
    2001
Frankfurt. Soziographisches Institut der Universität (Frankfurt,
    Germany) 2074, 4325
Free Press (New York, N.Y., U.S.A.) 6370, 6371
Freytag-Berndt & Artaria (Wien, Austria) 21, 97, 181, 391, 470,
    621, 1520, 1629, 1726, 2612, 2613, 2614, 2615, 2616, 2617,
    2618, 2619, 2620, 2621, 5164, 5165, 5166, 5167, 5168, 5169,
    5170, 5171, 5705, 5909, 6195, 6445, 6790, 6791, 6792, 6793,
    6794, 8227, 8228, 8229, 8230
Freytag, G. (München, Germany) 324, 392, 471
F. T. D. Editôra see Editôra F. T. D.
F. T. D. Editorial see Editorial F. T. D.
Fu-Min Geographical Institute of Economic Development (Taipei,
    Taiwan) 2519

Gale Research Co. (Detroit, Mich., U.S.A.) 6985
Gallimard (Paris, France) 2759
Ganaco, N. V. (Bandung, Indonesia) 472, 622, 791, 2398, 2399,

Globo Editôra see Editôra Globo
Golden Press (New York, N.Y., U.S.A.) 1524, 5578, 5579, 5616
Goldmann Verlag (München, Germany) 393, 538, 867, 1042, 1304, 1635, 6197
Gollancz, Victor (London, England) 1817
Goushá, H. M. Co. (San José, Calif., U.S.A.) 2139, 2140, 2141, 3493, 3494, 3495, 3496, 3497, 3498, 3499, 3500, 3632, 3633, 3634, 3635, 3636, 3637, 3638, 3757, 3758, 3759, 3766, 3767, 3768, 3769, 3770, 3771, 3772, 3773, 3774, 3775, 3776, 3777, 3778, 5155, 5156, 5157, 5188, 5189, 5190, 5191, 5192, 5193, 5194, 5195, 5196, 5197, 5198, 5199, 5200, 6561, 6562, 6563, 6564, 6565, 6566, 6577, 7309, 7310, 7311, 7314, 7315, 7373, 7374, 7375, 7378, 7379, 7446, 7450, 7451, 7452, 7453, 7454, 7455, 7456, 7457, 7458, 7459, 7460, 7461, 7462, 7463, 7464, 7476, 7477, 7483, 7484, 7524, 8221, 8249, 8250, 8251, 8252, 8253, 8254, 8255, 8256, 8257, 8258, 8259, 8260, 8261, 8262, 8263, 8294, 8295, 8388, 8389, 8467
Gower Economic Publications (Epping, England) 6451, 6994, 7734, 7735
Grafisk Forlag (København, Denmakr) 868
Granda, J. C. (Buenos Aires, Argentina) 1636
Grange Batelière (Paris, France) 6198
Greece. Ministry of National Economy (Athens, Greece) 2936
Greece. National Statistical Service (Athens, Greece) 2937, 2938, 4260
Greece. Statistikon Graphelon (Athens, Greece) 2939, 4261
Gregory's Guides & Maps Pty. Ltd. (Sydney, Australia) 6760, 6761, 6762, 6763, 8264, 8265, 8266, 8267
Greystone Press (New York, N.Y., U.S.A.) 1424
Grijalbo, Editorial see Editorial Grijalbo
Grolier Society (New York, N.Y., U.S.A.) 183, 252, 1190, 3501, 5778, 5839
Grosset & Dunlap (New York, N.Y., U.S.A.) 869, 1525, 3502, 3503, 3504, 3639, 3640, 3641, 3779, 3780, 3781, 5201, 5202, 5203, 6275
Gt. Britain. Meteorological Office (London, England) 2980, 4148
Gt. Britain. Ministry of Agriculture, Fisheries & Food (London, England) 2981, 3420, 4937
Gt. Britain. Ministry of Housing and Local Government (London, England) 2982, 3421, 6993, 7253, 7733
Guatemala. Dirección General de Cartografia (Guatemala, Guatemala) 3588
Guatemala. Instituto Geográfico Nacional (Guatemala, Guatemala) 3589, 7347
Guatemala. Ministerio de Educación Pública (Guatemala, Guatemala) 3590
Guatemala. Observatorio Meteorológico y Estacion Sismográfia (Guatemala, Guatemala) 3591, 4149
Guia Lascano see Librería e Imprenta "Guía Lascano"
Gumperts Förlag (Göteborg, Sweden) 24, 25, 184, 870, 4262
Guruhi Jughrafiya (Teheran, Iran) 2419, 4150
Gwasg Prifysgol Cymru (Caerdydd, Wales) 3422, 4630
Gyldendal (København, Denmark) 26, 27, 101, 720, 871, 956, 957, 1043, 1044, 1045, 1172, 1173, 1305, 1306, 1526, 1637, 1638,

3509, 3510, 3511, 3512, 3513, 3514, 3515, 3642, 3643, 3644,
3645, 3646, 3647, 3709, 3710, 3746, 3782, 3783, 3784, 3785,
3786, 3787, 3788, 3789, 3790, 3791, 3792, 3793, 3794, 3795,
3796, 3797, 4065, 4066, 4067, 4120, 4274, 4275, 4634, 4635,
4636, 4637, 4638, 4639, 4640, 4641, 4642, 4643, 4644, 4645,
4646, 4647, 4648, 4649, 4650, 4651, 4652, 4653, 4654, 4655,
4656, 4657, 4658, 4659, 4823, 5083, 5218, 5219, 5220, 5221,
5222, 5223, 5519, 5534, 5576, 5580, 5587, 5634, 5711, 5754,
5763, 5784, 5786, 5787, 5788, 5813, 5888, 5894, 5896, 5921,
5922, 5923, 5924, 5925, 5926, 5927, 5928, 5929, 5930, 5931,
5932, 5933, 5934, 5935, 5936, 5937, 5938, 5939, 5940, 5941,
5975, 5977, 6064, 6065, 6081, 6082, 6083, 6084, 6085, 6086,
6087, 6088, 6089, 6090, 6091, 6092, 6093, 6094, 6201, 6202,
6203, 6204, 6205, 6206, 6207, 6208, 6209, 6210, 6227, 6272
6275, 6279, 6280, 6281, 6282, 6283, 6284, 6294, 6314, 6333,
6334, 6335, 6336, 6549, 6567, 6568, 6569, 6766, 7312, 7313,
7376, 7377, 7465, 7466, 7467, 7468, 7469, 7470, 7471, 7472,
7473, 7474, 7475, 7480, 7693, 7741, 7878, 7912, 7913, 7914,
7915, 7916, 7917, 7918, 8289, 8290, 8291, 8292, 8293, 8502, 8509
Hanover House (Garden City, N.Y., U.S.A.)   485, 486, 549, 550,
   633, 727, 728
Harper & Row (New York, N.Y., U.S.A.)   2143, 4068, 4660
Harrap (London, England)   6467, 7919, 7920
Hart-Davis (London, England)   5789, 7921, 7922, 7923
Hartford Fire Insurance Co. (Hartford, Conn., U.S.A.)   7314,
   7315, 7378, 7379, 7476, 7477, 8294, 8295
Harvard University Press (Cambridge, Mass., U.S.A.)   3798,
   3799, 4069, 4151, 4152, 4661
Hatier (Paris, France)   1648, 5712
Hawthorne Books (New York, N.Y., U.S.A.)   4070
Hearst Magazines, Inc. (New York, N.Y., U.S.A.)   3800, 4276
Heibonsha (Tokyo, Japan)   6718, 6719
Heinemann (London, England)   2012, 2013, 3329, 3330, 4662, 4663,
   6767, 6996, 7924, 7925
Hellēnike Leschē Autokinētou Kai Periēgēseon (Athens, Greece)
   2940, 2941, 2942, 5224, 5225, 5226
Herder Verlag (Freiburg, Germany)   634, 1065, 1192, 1438, 1553,
   1649, 1742, 5790, 5791, 6095, 6211, 6285, 7628
Hernando (Madrid, Spain)   114, 3248
Heyden & Son, Ltd. (London, England)   6096
Hilâl (Cairo, U.A.R.-Egypt)   963, 4153, 4277
Hippocrene Books (London, England)   7926
Hirschsprungs Forlag (København, Denmark)   729
Hirt Verlag (Kiel, Germany)   6097
Hitt Label Co. (Los Angeles, Calif., U.S.A.)   38
Hölder, Pichler, Tempsky (Wien, Austria)   2622, 2623, 2624,
   2625, 2626, 2627, 4664, 4665, 4666, 4667, 4668, 4669, 6795,
   7927
Holt (New York, N.Y., U.S.A.)   3801, 4670, 5751, 5792, 5793,
   5794
Hölzel, Ed. Verlag (Wien, Austria)   39, 115, 195, 267, 268, 337,
   402, 487, 551, 635, 636, 638, 730, 741, 799, 880, 881, 964,
   974, 1066, 1086, 1170, 1193, 1194, 1995, 1196, 1197, 1198,

Jugoslavenski Leksikografski Zavod (Zagreb Yugoslavia) 1076, 1445,
   1446, 3429, 3430, 5254, 5255, 5716, 5806, 5953, 6293, 7259,
   7260, 7261, 7262, 7263, 7264, 8313, 8314, 8315, 8316, 8317,
   8318
Juta & Co., Ltd. (Cape Town, South Africa) 2264, 4690

Kaiser (Klagenfurt, Austria) 1341
Kalmbach Publishing Co. (Milwaukee, Wisc., U.S.A.) 3516, 3804,
   4123, 5256
Kanaat Kitabevi (Istanbul, Turkey) 43
Kanaat Yayinlari (Istanbul, Turkey) 638, 886, 1342, 1343, 1344,
   2024, 2025, 4691, 4692, 5571, 7209
Kantonaler Lehrmittel Verlag (Zurich, Switzerland) 343, 553, 639,
   640, 970, 3285, 3286, 3287, 3288, 3289, 5954
Kapelusz y Cía (Buenos Aires, Argentina) 1208, 4042, 4297, 5955,
   6570, 6571, 6572, 6580, 6581, 7545, 7546, 7547, 7762, 7763,
   7764, 7765, 7766
Kaplán Cojano, Oscar (Santiago de Chile, Chile) 802, 5956
Karolidēs, Paulos (Athens, Greece) 7939
Kartlitografen, AB (Danderyd, Sweden) 7187, 7188, 8319, 8320
Kartográfiai Vállalat (Budapest, Hungary) 407, 408, 554, 619, 641,
   642, 643, 687, 733, 887, 971, 972, 973, 1077, 1078, 1345,
   1346, 1347, 1447, 1448, 1449, 1550, 1653, 1654, 1655, 2026,
   3037, 3038, 3039, 3040, 3041, 3042, 3043, 3044, 3045, 3046,
   4298, 4299, 4300, 4301, 4693, 4694, 5257, 5258, 5259, 5260,
   5261, 5262, 5263, 5264, 5265, 5672, 5673, 5807, 5808, 5957,
   5958, 5959, 5960, 6110, 6223, 6224, 7046, 7047, 7048, 7049,
   7050, 7051, 7052, 7053, 7054, 7767, 7940, 7941, 7942, 7943,
   8321, 8322
Kartografické nakladatelství see Czechoslovakia. Kartografické
   nakladatelství
Kartografie (Praha, Czechoslovakia) 6097, 6111, 6112, 6113, 6829,
   6830, 6831, 6832, 6833, 7944, 7945, 7946, 7947, 8323
Kartographisches Institut Meyer see Meyer Kartographisches
   Institut
Katholiek Sociaal-Kerkelijk Instituut ('s Gravenhage, Netherlands)
   2027, 4302, 4989
Kessel, M. S. van (Paramaribo, Surinam) 7587
Keyser see Keysersche Verlagsbuchhandlung, G. M. B. H.
Keysersche Verlagsbuchhandlung, G. M. B. H. (Heidelberg, Germany)
   344, 409, 555, 556, 644, 974, 1079, 1209, 1210, 1551, 1656,
   4695, 5809
Kim, Sang-Jin (Seoul, Korea) 2481
Kings College School (London, England) 3593, 4004
Kiplinger-Washington Editors, Inc. (Washington, D.C., U.S.A.)
   1080, 1211
Kishō Kyōkai (Tokyo, Japan) 2451, 4155
Klett Verlag (Stuttgart, Germany) 275, 492
Kluwer (Wageningen Netherlands) 6225
Knaur, Th. Nachf. (München, Germany) 410, 5961, 6114
Kohlhammer Verlag (Mainz, Germany) 2860
Kokusai Chicaku Kyōkai (Tokyo, Japan) 2452
Kokusai Kyōiku Jōhō Sentā (Tokyo, Japan) 6725, 7768

3309, 3310
Libreria del Colegio Ediciones see Ediciones Libreria del Colegio
Librería e Imprenta "Guía Lascano" (Lima, Peru) 3966, 3967,
    3968, 3969, 3970, 3971
Librería y Casa Editorial Hernando see Hernando
Liceu Editora see Editora Liceu
Lief, B. W. (New York, N. Y., U. S. A.) 6484, 6485, 8346, 8347
Liga Chileno-Alemana (Santiago de Chile, Chile) 3950, 3951, 4699,
    4700
Lingen (Köln, Germany) 1658, 6337
L'Institut National pour l'Étude Agronomique du Congo (Bruxelles,
    Belgium) 2187, 2199, 2245, 4006, 5500
List, P. see also Atlantik Verlag (München, Germany) 977,
    1081, 1082, 1214, 1349, 1454, 1552, 1659, 1660, 2871, 2872,
    2873, 2874, 2875, 2876, 2877, 4314, 4315, 4701, 4702, 4703,
    4704, 4705, 5718, 6338, 6931, 7948
Literarisches Institut (Basel, Switzerland) 1553
Litografía Arco (Bogota, Colombia) 7578, 7949
Litografía de Fernández (Madrid, Spain) 123
Litografía Miangolarra Hnos (Caracas, Venezuela) 7595, 7596,
    7597
Livraria Francisco Alves see Alves, Francisco
Livraria Popular de F. Franco (Lisboa, Portugal) 45, 738, 4316
Livraria Sá da Costa (Lisboa, Portugal) 347, 739, 1554, 3189,
    3190, 3191, 4706, 4707, 5967, 7140, 7950
Livraria Simões Lopes (Porto, Portugal) 46, 648
Livre de Poche (Paris, France) 1661, 5674, 5675
Livros Cadernos (Rio de Janeiro, Brazil) 805, 7566
Lloyd's, Corp. of (London, England) 124, 277, 649, 889, 1215,
    1455, 4946, 4947, 4948, 4949, 4950, 4951, 5719, 5968, 6295,
    8091, 8092, 8093
L'Oeuvre de la Propagation de la Foi (Paris, France) 4074
Longmans, Green (London, England & Toronto, Canada) 47, 1824,
    2265, 6486, 6487, 6488
Lopes, Livraria Simões see Livraria Simões Lopes
Lutterworth Press (London, England) 4075
Lux Verlag (München, Germany) 4708, 4709
Luxembourg. Ministère de l'Éducation Nationale (Luxembourg)
    7090

Maanmittaushallitus (Helsinki, Finland) 2727, 5305, 6847, 6848,
    6849, 6850, 6851, 8348, 8349, 8350, 8351, 8352
Maarif Basimevi (Istanbul, Turkey) 5567, 7210
MacDonald & Co., Ltd. (London, England) 650
Macdonald & Evans (London, England) 6489
Macdonald Education (London, England) 6490, 7001
Machuca Martinez, Marcelino (Asunción, Paraguay) 3963, 4710
Macmillan & Co., Ltd. (London, England) 48, 806, 1825, 1826,
    1827, 1828, 1829, 1830, 1831, 1832, 1833, 1834, 1835, 1906,
    1907, 1908, 1909, 1910, 1911, 1912, 1913, 1914, 1939, 1940,
    1941, 2043, 2044, 2045, 2046, 2047, 2048, 2144, 2145, 2146,
    2147, 2161, 2162, 2163, 2164, 2165, 2166, 2167, 2168, 2169,
    2170, 2171, 2217, 2299, 2542, 2543, 2575, 2576, 2577, 2993,

McGraw-Hill Book Co. (New York, N. Y. , U. S. A.) 52, 53, 278,
    348, 493, 978, 1084, 1085, 1662, 2439, 4077, 4719, 5720, 5815,
    6339, 6376, 6670, 7616, 7778, 7962
Meddens Editions see Editions Meddens
Meiklejohn (London, England) 54, 55, 279, 280, 494, 558
Melantrich (Praha, Czechoslovakia) 3331
Melhoramentos, Edições see Edições Melhoramentos
Mellottée see Libraire Mellottée
Merriam, G. & C. Co. (Springfield, Mass. , U. S. A.) 6227, 7480
Merrill, C. E. Co. (Columbus, Ohio, U. S. A.) 56, 1216
Methuen (London, England) 1838, 2172, 3332, 4322, 4720, 4721,
    4722, 4723, 4724, 4725, 4726, 6574, 7067, 7963, 7964, 7965
Meulenhoff, J. M. (Amsterdam, Netherlands) 741, 1086, 1555,
    1663, 1664, 3098, 3099, 3100, 3101, 3102, 6116, 6809
México.   Centro de Estudios y Documentación Sociales (México,
    D. F. , México) 5602
México.   Comisión Federal de Electricidad (México, D. F. , México)
    7381, 7779
México.   Comisión Nacional de Caminos Vecinales (México, D. F. ,
    México) 3648, 3649, 5336, 5337
México.   Fondo de Cultura Economica (México, D. F. , México)
    3650, 4727
México.   Instituto Mexicano de Investigacíones Economicas (México,
    D. F. , México) 3651, 4104, 4323, 4990
México.   Ministerio de Communicaciones y Obras Públicas (México,
    D. F. , México) 3652, 3653, 4179, 4180, 5526, 5527, 7382, 8376
México.   Secretaría de Comunicaciones y Transportes (México,
    D. F. , México) 3654, 4181, 5528, 7383, 8377
México.   Universidad Nacional Autónoma (México, D. F. , México)
    3655, 3656, 4158
Meyer, Kartographisches Institut (Mannheim, Germany) 979, 1087,
    1351, 1456, 1556, 1665, 1750, 1751, 1781, 4043, 4102, 4159,
    4476, 4491, 4966, 4969, 5501, 5638, 5816, 5817, 5818, 5970,
    5971, 6296, 6297, 8103
Michelin et Cie (Paris, France) 2769, 2770, 2771, 2772, 2773,
    2774, 4126, 5338, 5339, 5340, 5341, 5342, 5343, 6889, 6890,
    6891, 6892, 8378, 8379, 8380, 8381
Michelin Tyre Co. (Stoke-on-Trent, England) 2997, 5344
Military Vehicles & Engineering Establishment (Christchurch, New
    Zealand) 6642, 7780
Miller Freeman (Bruxelles, Belgium) 6506, 7781
Milli Eğitim Bakanliği (Istanbul, Turkey) 5588, 5677, 7211, 7212
Milli Egitim Basimevi (Istanbul, Turkey) 57, 3322
Minerva Books (Caracas, Venezuela) 1217, 3980
Minerva, Editôra see Editôra Minerva
Minerva Italica (Bergamo, Italy) 4728
Mladinska Knjiga (Ljubljana, Yugoslavia) 6117
Mobil Oil, AB (Danderyd, Sweden) 7190, 8382
Mobil Oil Hellas (Athens, Greece) 6961, 8383
Moderna, Empresa see Empresa Moderna
Mohn (Gütersloh, Germany) 4729
Mondadori (Milano, Italy) 5972, 6507, 8384
Monteverde, A. (Montevideo, Uruguay) 891, 1352

Moore, William L. (Mt. Vernon, Ill., U.S.A.) 1353
Morocco. Comité National de Géographie (Rabat, Morocco) 2224
Motormännens Riksförbund (Stockholm, Sweden) 3276, 3277, 3278,
    3279, 3280, 5345, 5346, 5347, 5348, 5349, 7191, 8385
Motor Manual (Melbourne, Australia) 2544, 2545, 2546, 2547,
    2548, 2549, 2550, 5350, 5351, 5352, 5353, 5354, 5355, 5356
Mouton & Co. (Paris, France) 5973, 7610
Munger Oil Information Service (Los Angeles, Calif., U.S.A.)
    1839, 1915, 4477
Munksgaard (København, Denmark) 1666
Murray, John (London, England) 1088, 2072, 6740, 6747, 7966

Nagel Publishers (Geneva, Switzerland) 1667
Nathan, Fernand (Paris, France) 58, 412, 559, 742, 743, 1089,
    1218, 1668, 2191, 2201, 2298, 3250, 6228, 6508, 6618
National Bus Traffic Association (Chicago, Ill., U.S.A.) 3518,
    3657, 3809, 5357, 5529, 7317, 7384, 7481, 7482, 8386, 8387
National Geographic Society (Washington, D.C., U.S.A.) 651, 1090,
    1457, 3810, 3811, 5819, 6340
National Safety Council (Chicago, Ill., U.S.A.) 3500, 3638, 3778,
    5200, 7483, 7484, 8388, 8389
National Trust (London, England) 2988, 2999, 3424, 4730, 4731,
    7019, 7020, 7021, 7254, 7255, 7256, 7967, 7968, 7969
Nationale Boekhandel (Kaapstad, South Africa) 2268, 4732
Natur Och Kultur Bokförlaget (Stockholm, Sweden) 495
Neguri Editorial (Bilbao, Spain) 6298
Nelson-Doubleday (New York, N.Y., U.S.A. and London, England)
    1189, 1219, 2541, 2551
Nelson, Thomas & Sons, Ltd. (London, England) 652, 807, 892,
    980, 1091, 1354, 1355, 1458, 1459, 1557, 1669, 1670, 1840,
    1841, 1916, 2207, 2208, 2209, 2210, 2213, 2222, 2230, 2250,
    2251, 2293, 2300, 2301, 2311, 2552, 3000, 3001, 3002, 3003,
    3004, 3005, 3519, 3520, 3521, 3522, 3523, 3524, 3658, 3659,
    3972, 4037, 4078, 4079, 4080, 4081, 4106, 4733, 4734, 4735,
    4736, 4737, 4738, 4739, 4962, 4963, 4964, 4991, 5358, 5678,
    5721, 6118, 6119, 6377, 6597, 7022, 7318, 7637, 7970, 7971,
    8098
Nepal. Ministry of Information and Broadcasting (Kathmandu,
    Nepal) 2502
Netherlands. Bureau voor Wegen en Verkeersstatistiek ('s Graven-
    hage, Netherlands) 3103, 5359
Netherlands. Department van Landbouw en Visscherij (Zwolle,
    Netherlands) 3104, 4409
Netherlands. Dienst Verkeersonderzoek ('s Gravenhage, Nether-
    lands) 3105, 5360
Netherlands. Meteorologisch Institut (de Bilt, Netherlands) 7093,
    7663
Netherlands. Ministerie van Marine ('s Gravenhage, Netherlands)
    2599, 4160
Netherlands. Staatsdrukkerij-en Uitgeverijbedrijf ('s Gravenhage,
    Netherlands) 2669, 3087, 3106, 3107, 3108, 3109, 3110, 4161,
    4931, 4952, 5361, 5362
Netherlands. Volkskundecommissie der Koninklijke Nederlandse

Akademie van Wetenschappen ('s Gravenhage, Netherlands) 3111, 4453
Newnes George, Ltd. (London, England) 560, 1220, 1558, 2073, 3006, 3007, 3204, 3205, 3206, 5363, 5364, 5365, 5366
News Map of the Week, Inc. (Skokie, Ill., U.S.A.) 1460
New York Herald Tribune (New York, N.Y., U.S.A.) 1092
New Zealand. Atlas Committee (Wellington, New Zealand) 2578, 2579
New Zealand. Government Printing Office (Auckland, New Zealand) 6777
New Zealand. Local Government Commission (Wellington, New Zealand) 6778
New Zealand. National Airways Corporation (Wellington, New Zealand) 2580, 2581, 5530, 5531
New Zealand. Town and Country Planning Branch (Wellington, New Zealand) 2582, 4324
Nigeria. Federal Surveys (Lagos, Nigeria) 2231, 2232, 6627, 6628
Nigeria. Survey Dept. (Lagos, Nigeria) 2233
Nihon Kyōzu Kabushiki Kaisha (Tokyo, Japan) 2453
Nijgh & Van Ditmar (Rotterdam, Netherlands) 127, 7094
N. I. Sh. Mjete Mesimore e Sportive "Hamid Shijaku" (Tiranë, Albania) 2603, 4740, 5603, 5820, 5974, 6509, 6785, 6786, 6787, 6788, 7972
Nitchi Shuppan Kabushiki Kaisha (Tokyo, Japan) 2454, 2455, 2456, 2457, 2458, 2459, 2460, 2461, 2462, 2463
Nomi Forlag (Oslo, Norway) 7631
Nomos Verlagsgesellschaft (Baden-Baden, Germany) 2074, 4325
Noordhoff, P. (Groningen, Netherlands) 59, 349, 350, 413, 1461, 2407, 2408, 3112, 4741
Noordhoff-Kolff, N. V. (Djakarta, Indonesia) 281, 561, 653, 2404, 2405, 2406
Normanns Forlag (Odense, Denmark) 4742
Northern Rhodesia. Survey Dept. (Lusaka, Zambia) 2312
Norway. Postdirektoratet (Oslo, Norway) 7108, 7682
Norway. Poststyret (Oslo, Norway) 3139, 4182
Norway. Statistik Sentralbyrå (Oslo, Norway) 3140, 4992
Norway. Vassdrags-og Elektrisitetsvesen (Oslo, Norway) 7109, 7842
Norway. Vegdirektoratet (Oslo, Norway) 3141, 5532
Nouvelles de l'Enseignement (Paris, France) 2775, 4326
Novoe Vremya (Moskva, U.S.S.R.) 2148, 2173
Nueva Cadiz Ediciones see Ediciones Nueva Cadiz
Nuffield Organization (Oxford, England) 2075, 3008, 3009, 5367, 5368, 5369
Nystrom (Chicago, Ill., U.S.A.) 5722, 5975, 5976, 5977

Oasis Ediciones see Ediciones Oasis
Oberthur, Imprimeries see Imprimeries Oberthur
Obiols, Alfredo (Guatemala, Guatemala) 3582
Oceana Publications (Dobbs Ferry, N.Y., U.S.A.) 1093, 4743
Odhams Press, Ltd. (London, England) 60, 562, 2076, 3010, 3060, 5370
Odyssey Books (New York, N.Y., U.S.A.) 1462
Oestergaard, Columbus Verlag see Columbus Verlag Oestergaard

Penguin Books (Harmondsworth, England)   499, 4757, 6300, 7976, 7977, 7978
Pensamiento Vivo (Caracas, Venezuela)   3981, 4348
Pergamon Press, Ltd. (Oxford, England)   1466, 1675, 5618, 5679, 5984, 6342, 7979, 7980, 8100
Permabooks (New York, N. Y. , U. S. A.)   61
Perthes, Justus (Gotha, Germany)   203, 204, 5563
Peru. Dirección de Caminos (Lima, Peru)   3973, 5372
Peru. Instituto Nacional de Planificación (Lima, Peru)   7585, 7981
Peru. Ministerio de Trabajo y Asuntos Indigenas (Lima, Peru)   7586
Petroleum Publishing Co. (Tulsa, Okla. , U. S. A.)   3531, 3532, 3815, 3816, 4478, 4479
Peugeot (Paris, France)   2776, 5373
Peuser, Ediciones Geográficas (Buenos Aires, Argentina)   131, 417, 1561, 1754, 3917, 3918, 3919, 3920, 3921, 5828, 6125, 7548, 7549, 7550
Pfahl Verlag (Laupheim, Germany)   132, 205, 352, 418, 419, 566, 567, 658, 659, 660, 813, 1225, 4349, 4350, 4351, 4758, 4759
Philadelphia Inquirer (Philadelphia, Penna. , U. S. A.)   133
Phil-Asian Publishers, Inc. (Manila, Philippines)   2509, 4760
Philip, George & Son, Ltd. (London, England)   24, 25, 62, 63, 64, 65, 134, 135, 136, 184, 206, 207, 208, 209, 210, 222, 283, 284, 285, 286, 287, 288, 353, 354, 355, 356, 420, 421, 422, 423, 500, 501, 502, 568, 569, 570, 571, 587, 661, 662, 663, 675, 714, 747, 748, 749, 750, 751, 765, 772, 814, 815, 816, 817, 823, 895, 896, 897, 898, 899, 983, 984, 1100, 1101, 1107, 1121, 1167, 1226, 1227, 1228, 1294, 1361, 1362, 1363, 1364, 1368, 1467, 1468, 1469, 1562, 1563, 1564, 1565, 1566, 1567, 1568, 1676, 1677, 1712, 1755, 1756, 1757, 1758, 1810, 1849, 1850, 1851, 1852, 1853, 1854, 1855, 1856, 1857, 1858, 1859, 1860, 1861, 1862, 1863, 1864, 1865, 1866, 1867, 1868, 1869, 2269, 2270, 2271, 2272, 2273, 2274, 2275, 2276, 2277, 2278, 2279, 2280, 2281, 2282, 2283, 2284, 2285, 2289, 2291, 2334, 2557, 2558, 2559, 2560, 2561, 2562, 2563, 2564, 2565, 2566, 2567, 2568, 3014, 3015, 3016, 3017, 3018, 3019, 3020, 3021, 3135, 3336, 3337, 3533, 3534, 3574, 3817, 3818, 4083, 4084, 4085, 4086, 4087, 4352, 4761, 4762, 4763, 4764, 4765, 4766, 4767, 4768, 4769, 4770, 4771, 4772, 4773, 4774, 4775, 4776, 4777, 4778, 4889, 4953, 4954, 4955, 5374, 5375, 5376, 5377, 5378, 5379, 5380, 5381, 5570, 5582, 5604, 5605, 5610, 5619, 5641, 5642, 5643, 5644, 5648, 5680, 5691, 5727, 5781, 5829, 5830, 5831, 5832, 5833, 5867, 5868, 5985, 5986, 5987, 5988, 5989, 5990, 5991, 5992, 5993, 5994, 5995, 5996, 5997, 5998, 6050, 6126, 6127, 6128, 6129, 6130, 6131, 6132, 6133, 6134, 6178, 6226, 6234, 6235, 6236, 6237, 6238, 6239, 6240, 6241, 6242, 6252, 6262, 6301, 6302, 6343, 6344, 6345, 6346, 6384, 6385, 6386, 6387, 6388, 6389, 6513, 6601, 6640, 6641, 7023, 7024, 7025, 7026, 7027, 7028, 7029, 7030, 7031, 7032, 7033, 7068, 7069, 7214, 7220, 7620, 7621, 7627, 7797, 7798, 7799, 7889, 7982, 7983, 7984, 7985, 7986, 7987, 7988, 8094, 8095, 8390, 8391, 8392, 8393, 8394, 8395, 8396, 8397, 8398, 8399, 8400, 8532, 8533, 8534, 8535

Philippines.   Agriculture and Natural Resources Dept. (Manila,
   Philippines)   2510, 4010
Philippines.   Bureau of Public Works (Manila, Philippines)   2511,
   5382
Philippines.   Office of the President (Manila, Philippines)   2512,
   4353
Piper, R. &. Co. (München, Germany)   7989
Plantyn (Anvers, Belgium)   2083
Pocket Books (New York, N. Y., U. S. A.)   140, 900
Poland.   Akademia Nauk (Warszawa, Poland)   3146, 3147, 3148,
   3149, 3150, 3151, 3151, 4107, 4108, 4450, 4779, 4780, 4941,
   4993, 7112, 7113, 7834, 7990
Poland.   Centralny Urzad Geodezii i Kartografii (Warszawa, Poland)
   424, 425, 503, 3152, 4781, 5564, 7991, 7992, 7993
Poland.   Glowny Urząd Statystyczny (Warszawa, Poland)   5834, 7114,
   7800
Poland.   Instytut Geologiczny (Warszawa, Poland)   3153, 3154,
   3155, 3156, 3157, 4480, 4481, 4482, 4483, 4484, 7115, 7843
Poland.   Państwowe Przedsiębiorstwo Wydawnictw Kartograficznych
   (Warszawa, Poland)   289, 504, 572, 573, 664, 665, 666, 752,
   818, 901, 985, 1102, 1103, 1104, 1105, 1106, 1229, 1230, 1231,
   1365, 1366, 1367, 1470, 1471, 1569, 1570, 1678, 1759, 3158,
   3159, 3160, 3161, 3162, 3163, 3164, 3165, 3166, 3167, 3168,
   3169, 3170, 3171, 3172, 3173, 3174, 3175, 3176, 3177, 3178,
   3179, 3180, 4782, 4783, 4784, 4785, 4786, 5383, 5384, 5385,
   5386, 5387, 5388, 5572, 5573, 5574, 5583, 5589, 5590, 5591,
   5594, 5595, 5606, 5620, 5681, 5682, 5728, 5729, 5730, 5731,
   5835, 5836, 5837, 5999, 6000, 6001, 6002, 6135, 6136, 6137,
   6243, 6303, 7116, 7117, 7118, 7119, 7120, 7121, 7122, 7123,
   7124, 7125, 7126, 7127, 7128, 7129, 7664, 7835, 7994, 7995,
   7996, 7997, 7998, 7999, 8000, 8001, 8002, 8003, 8004, 8005,
   8006, 8007, 8008, 8009, 8010, 8011, 8012, 8013, 8014, 8015,
   8016, 8017, 8018, 8019, 8020, 8021, 8401, 8402, 8403, 8404
Poland.   Państwowe Wydawnictw Naukowe (Warszawa, Poland)   986,
   3181, 4109
Poland.   Państwowe Zaklady Wydawnictw Szkolnych (Warszawa, Poland)   7130, 7801
Poland.   Służba Topograficzna Wojska Polskiego (Warszawa, Poland)
   1232, 1675
Poland.   Wydawn. Geologiczne (Warszawa, Poland)   7131, 7132,
   7133, 7134, 7135, 7844, 7845, 7846, 7847, 8104
Poland.   Wydawn. Ministerstva Obrony Narodowej (Warszawa,
   Poland)   357
Poligrafiche Bolis (Bergamo, Italy)   1894, 3076
Politikens Forlag (København, Denmark)   211, 358, 753, 987, 1107,
   1368, 4787, 5732, 6304
Pont. institutum orientalium studi orum (Rome, Italy)   7634
Ponte, Alberto da (Asunción, Paraguay)   7582
Porrúa, S. A. Editorial see Editorial Porrúa, S. A.
Porto Editora (Porto, Portugal)   1369, 1571, 6138
Portugal.   Junta de Investigações do Ultramar (Lisboa, Portugal)
   4088, 4089
Portugal.   Ministerio do Trabalho (Lisboa, Portugal)   7141, 7802

Poståpnernes Landsforbund (Oslo, Norway)   3142, 4183, 7110,
    7683, 8405
Pradnja-Paramita (Djakarta, Indonesia)   2411
Praeger, Frederick A. (New York, N.Y., U.S.A.)   574, 754, 819,
    988, 1108, 1233, 1870, 1871, 1873, 1922, 1923, 1944, 2084,
    2085, 2174, 2513, 2569, 2586, 3338, 3339, 3819, 3820, 4354,
    4788, 4789, 4790, 4791, 4792, 4793, 4794, 4795, 4796, 4797,
    4798, 4799, 4800, 4801, 4802, 4803, 6583, 6584, 8022, 8023
Prentice-Hall (New York, N.Y., U.S.A.)   212, 359, 667, 1109,
    4011, 4485
Princeton University Press (Princeton, N.J., U.S.A.)   4090, 4091,
    4092, 4804, 4805, 4806
Principato, Giuseppe (Milano, Italy)   1234
Progreso, Editorial see Editorial Progreso
Publicaciones Educativas Ariel (Guayaquil, Ecuador)   3960, 7580
Puerto Rico. Dept. of Education (San Juan, Puerto Rico)   3709,
    3710
Puma (Rio de Janeiro, Brazil)   1679
Putnam's, G. P., Sons (New York, N.Y., U.S.A.)   8024

Quadrangle Books (New York, N.Y., U.S.A.)   6139
Quillet, A. (Paris, France)   137, 4355

Rabén & Sjögren (Stockholm, Sweden)   2086, 5389
Rad (Beograd, Yugoslavia)   6514, 7265
Radio Amateur Callbook, Inc. (Chicago, Ill., U.S.A.)   1680, 4184,
    5838, 6140, 7684, 7685
Railway Publications, Ltd. (London, England)   3022, 3023, 3024,
    3025, 5535, 5536, 5537, 5538
Ramnarain Sons Limited (Bombay, India)   6665, 6686, 7611
Rand McNally & Co. (Chicago, Ill., U.S.A.)   66, 67, 68, 138,
    139, 140, 141, 142, 213, 214, 215, 216, 290, 291, 292, 293,
    426, 427, 428, 429, 430, 575, 576, 577, 578, 579, 580, 581,
    603, 668, 669, 670, 671, 755, 756, 757, 758, 759, 820, 821,
    862, 869, 900, 902, 903, 904, 905, 906, 907, 908, 909, 910,
    917, 948, 951, 989, 990, 991, 992, 993, 994, 995, 996, 1110,
    1111, 1112, 1113, 1114, 1155, 1162, 1168, 1235, 1236, 1237,
    1238, 1239, 1240, 1241, 1242, 1243, 1244, 1301, 1370, 1371,
    1372, 1373, 1374, 1375, 1376, 1377, 1420, 1472, 1473, 1474,
    1475, 1476, 1482, 1572, 1573, 1574, 1575, 1576, 1577, 1681,
    1682, 1683, 1684, 1685, 1686, 1678, 1691, 1723, 1760, 1761,
    1762, 1782, 1783, 2087, 3454, 3455, 3456, 3457, 3458, 3459,
    3460, 3461, 3462, 3463, 3464, 3465, 3466, 3467, 3468, 3469,
    3470, 3471, 3472, 3473, 3474, 3535, 3536, 3537, 3538, 3539,
    3540, 3541, 3542, 3543, 3544, 3545, 3546, 3547, 3548, 3549,
    3550, 3551, 3552, 3553, 3554, 3555, 3556, 3557, 3558, 3559,
    3560, 3561, 3562, 3563, 3564, 3565, 3566, 3567, 3568, 3569,
    3570, 3571, 3572, 3573, 3595, 3596, 3597, 3598, 3599, 3600,
    3601, 3602, 3603, 3604, 3605, 3606, 3607, 3608, 3609, 3610,
    3611, 3612, 3613, 3614, 3615, 3661, 3662, 3663, 3664, 3665,
    3666, 3667, 3668, 3669, 3670, 3671, 3672, 3673, 3674, 3675,
    3676, 3677, 3678, 3679, 3680, 3681, 3682, 3683, 3684, 3685,
    3686, 3687, 3688, 3689, 3690, 3691, 3692, 3693, 3694, 3695,

7665, 7810, 8029, 8030, 8031, 8459
Salinas Bellver, Salvador (Madrid, Spain)   361, 672, 761
Salvador. Direción General de Cartografía (San Salvador, El
   Salvador)   3583
Salvador. Estadistica y Cencos (San Salvador, El Salvador)   3584,
   4389, 7346, 7811
Salvador. Universidade Federal da Bahia, Centro de Estudos Afro-
   Orientais (San Salvador, El Salvador)   3585, 4812
Salvatella, Editorial Miguel A. see Editorial Miguel A. Salvatella
SAM (Quito, Ecuador)   3961, 3962, 4813, 4814
Sanchez y Herrera (Panama, Panama)   7401
Sauerländer, H. R. (Aarau, Switzerland)   3314, 3315, 3316, 4815,
   4816, 4817, 7198, 8032
Savremena Shkola (Beograd, Jugoslavia)   585
Schaeffer, Juan E. (Rio de Janeiro, Brazil)   1582
Scholastic Book Service (New York, N. Y., U. S. A.)   762, 1249,
   6314
School and Library Publ. Co. (Sycamore, Ill., U. S. A.)   6016
Schultz (København, Denmark)   72
Schweizer Reisekasse (Bern, Switzerland)   2102, 3317, 5452
Schweizer Volks-Buchgemeinde (Luzern, Switzerland)   145
Schweizerische Gesellschaft für Volkskunde (Basel, Switzerland)
   3318, 4454
Scotland. Scottish Development Dept. (Edinburgh, Scotland)   7156,
   7812
Scott, Foresman & Co. (Glenview, Ill., U. S. A.)   1765, 6017
Scribner, C. (New York, N. Y., U. S. A.)   3885, 4818, 6413, 6538
Scriptoria (Anvers, Belgium)   6810, 7813
Sears, Roebuck (Chicago, Ill., U. S. A.)   362, 363, 507, 912
Seeley Service & Co. (London, England)   8033
Seix Barral Editorial see Editorial Seix Barral, S. A.
Seix Editorial see Editorial Francisco Seix, S. A.
Selecções do Reader's Digest (Lisboa, Portugal)   7142, 7175, 8460
Sélection du Reader's Digest, S. A. R. L. (Paris, France)   1479,
   1766, 2777, 5686, 5851, 6539, 6811, 6894, 6895, 7199, 8461,
   8462
Seljačka Sloga (Zagreb, Yugoslavia)   146, 147, 434
Senegal. Ministère du Plan et du Développement (Dakar, Senegal)
   2247
Sequoia, Editions see Editions Sequoia
Sha, Hsüeh-Chün (Taipei, Taiwan)   2335
Shell Caribbean Petroleum Company (Caracas, Venezuela)   7598,
   8463
Shell Co. of New Zealand (Wellington, New Zealand)   6780, 8464
Shell Company of South Africa, Ltd. (Cape Town, South Africa)
   1875, 2286, 5453, 6375, 8374
Shell Co. of Turkey Ltd. (Istanbul, Turkey)   7213, 8465
Shell-Mex & BP Ltd. (London, England)   3017, 3018, 3019, 3020,
   3029, 3207, 3425, 5377, 5378, 5379, 5380, 7035, 7157, 7257
Shell Moçambique, Ltd. (Lourenço Marques, Mozambique)   2227,
   5454, 6622, 8466
Shell Oil New Zealand, Ltd. (Wellington, New Zealand)   2592,
   2593, 2594, 5455, 5456, 5457

Shih Chieh Ch'u Pan Shê (Hong Kong) 2336
Shih Chieh Yü Ti Hsüeh Shê (Shanghai, China) 2337, 2338, 2339
Siemens & Halske, A. G. (München, Germany) 913, 1118, 4390,
    4819, 5734
Sierra Leone. Survey and Lands Dept. (Freetown, Sierra Leone)
    2252, 2254
Sierra Leone. Surveys and Lands Division (Freetown, Sierra
    Leone) 2253
Silva, J. R. (Lisboa, Portugal) 673, 4391
Simmons-Boardman Books (New York, N. Y., U. S. A.) 822, 914
Simões Lopes see Livraria Simões Lopes
Simon & Schuster (New York, N. Y., U. S. A.) 674, 6018, 7612
Skandinavisk Bogforlag (København, Denmark) 1001
Skelly Oil Co. (Tulsa, Okla., U. S. A.) 6577, 7524, 8467
Školska Knjiga (Zagreb, Yugoslavia) 6019, 6248
Skrifola (København, Denmark) 1002, 2103
Slovenska Kartografia (Bratislava, Czechoslovakia) 5852, 6020,
    6151, 6152, 6249, 6834, 6835, 6836, 6837, 6838, 8034, 8035,
    8468, 8469, 8470
Smulders' Drukkerijen, N. V. ('s Gravenhage, Netherlands) 508,
    2104
Societa Cartografica G. de Agostini (Milano, Italy) 3078, 3079,
    3982, 5458, 5459, 7599
Societa Editrice Internazionale (Torino, Italy) 586, 763
Société des Pétroles Shell Berre (Paris, France) 2778, 5460
Société Européenne d'Études et d'Informations (Paris, France)
    2105, 2106, 2107, 4392, 4393, 4394
Société Française des Pétroles BP (Courbevoie, Seine, France)
    2779, 5461
Société pour le Développement de la Côte d'Ivoire (Abidjan, Ivory
    Coast) 2211
Society of the Divine Word (Mödling, Austria) 4094
Söderström, Werner (Helsinki, Finland) 217, 435, 915, 1003, 1119,
    1120, 1381, 4820, 4821, 5735, 6857, 8036, 8037
Sohlmans Förlag, A. B. (Stockholm, Sweden) 587, 1121
Sosö Publishing Co. (Seoul, Korea) 2482
South Africa. Department of Planning (Pretoria, South Africa)
    2287, 4395
South Africa. Government Printer Office (Pretoria, South Africa)
    1876, 1877, 4165, 4166
South Africa. National Council for Social Research (Pretoria, South
    Africa) 2288
Spain. Cámeras Oficiales de Comercio, Industria y Navegación
    (Madrid, Spain) 3251, 3252, 4396, 4397
Spain. Comité Español de Riegos y Drenajes (Madrid, Spain)
    3253, 4933
Spain. Consejo Superior de Investigaciones Científicas (Madrid,
    Spain) 3192, 4944
Spain. Direción General de Marruecos y Colonias e Instituto de
    Estudios Africanos (Madrid, Spain) 1878, 4822
Spain. Direción General de Montes, Caza y Pesca Fluvial (Madrid,
    Spain) 3254, 4462
Spain. Ejercito. Servicio Geografico (Madrid, Spain) 3255, 5462

Spain. Instituto Geográfico y Catastral (Madrid, Spain) 3256
Spain. Ministerio de Obras Públicas (Madrid, Spain) 3193, 3194,
    3257, 3258, 5463, 5464, 7143, 7144, 7145, 7146, 7147, 7176,
    7177, 7178, 7179, 7180, 8471, 8472, 8473, 8474, 8475
Spal Edições see Edições Spal
Spectrum (Utrecht, Netherlands) 6250, 6356, 6540, 8476
Spencer Press, Inc. (Chicago, Ill., U.S.A.) 4823
Sport & Technik Verlag see Verlag Sport & Technik
Springer Verlag (Berlin, Germany) 1122, 4167, 6357, 7666, 7694
Standaard Uitgeverij (Anvers, Belgium) 6251, 6315, 6812, 6813
Standard International Library (New York, N.Y., U.S.A.) 509
Standard Reference Works Pub. Co. (Brooklyn, N.Y., U.S.A.)
    1382
Stanford, Edward (London, England) 675, 823, 2254, 3030, 3031,
    3061, 4486, 5465, 6983, 7036, 7037, 7038, 7039, 7040, 7064,
    7071, 7072, 7073, 7848, 8212, 8477, 8478, 8479
State University of New York (Oneonta, N.Y., U.S.A.) 6666, 7814
Stauffacher, Éditions see Éditions Stauffacher
Stein, Jack (Dayton, Ohio, U.S.A.) 4095
Steiner Verlag (Wiesbaden, Germany) 2916, 2917 4014
Stenvert (Apeldoorn, Netherlands) 2601, 3115
St. Gabriel Verlag (Mödling, Austria) 4096
St. Martin's Press (New York, N.Y., U.S.A.) 1879, 1880, 1881,
    1882, 1924, 1925, 1926, 1927, 1928, 1929, 1930, 1946, 1947,
    2108, 2149, 2150, 2151, 2175, 2176, 2177, 2595, 2596, 3032,
    4398, 4399, 4400, 4401, 4824, 4825, 6252, 8096
Stock (Paris, France) 4826, 8038
Studi Geo-Cartografici (Milano, Italy) 3080, 4402, 6153
Studio F. M. B. (Bologna, Italy) 676
Südwest Verlag (München, Germany) 824, 1123, 1250, 1251, 1252,
    2109, 4403, 4404, 5466, 6154, 8039
Suomen Maantieteellinen Seura (Helsinki, Finland) 2728
Survey of Kenya (Nairobi, Kenya) 2214, 2215, 6602, 6603, 7815,
    7816
Surveys Press (Baghdad, Iraq) 2420, 4995
Svenska Bokförlaget Norstedts (Stockholm, Sweden) 148, 218, 296,
    297, 364, 677, 1124, 1663, 3101, 4405, 4827, 7193, 8040
Sveriges Köpmannaförbund (Stockholm, Sweden) 3281, 4406
Switzerland. Konferenz der Kantonalen Erziehungsdirektoren
    (Zürich, Switzerland) 436, 3319
Switzerland, Landestopographie (Wabern-Bern, Switzerland) 3320
Szapiro, J. (Tel Aviv, Israel) 2440, 4828

Ta Chung Shu Chü (Hong Kong) 1004, 2340, 2341, 2342, 2343, 2344,
    2345
Ta Chung Ti Hsüeh Shê (Shanghai, China) 2346, 2347
Taehan Sörim (Seoul, Korea) 2483
T'ai-Wan Ta Hsüeh (Taipei, Taiwan) 2348, 4829
Taiwan. National University (Taipei, Taiwan) 2520, 4015
Tallandier (Paris, France) 1690
Ta Lu Yü Ti Shê (Shanghai, China) 2349
Tammi (Helsinki, Finland) 2110, 2111, 5467, 5468, 6541, 8480
Tanganyika. Department of Lands and Surveys (Dar Es Salaam,

U. A. R. -Egypt.   al-Jihaz al-Markazi lil-Ta'bi'ah al'Ammah wa-al-
Ihsa (Cairo, Egypt)   6648, 7818, 8484
U. A. R. -Egypt.   Survey of Egypt (Cairo, Egypt)   6649
Učila (Zagreb, Yugoslavia)   73, 221, 680, 826, 827, 1127, 1483,
3434, 3435, 3436, 3437, 3438, 4831, 5477, 5478, 5479, 5480,
5568, 5687, 6023, 6159, 6160, 6161, 7267, 7268, 7269, 8042,
8485
Uganda.   Department of Lands and Surveys. (Kampala, Uganda)
2302, 2304
Uitgeverij de Bezige Bij (Amsterdam, Netherlands)   151
Ullstein (Berlin, Germany)   2125, 2126
Unesco (Geneva, Switzerland)   6542, 7652, 7667
U. S. S. R.   Akademiia Nauk (Kiev, U. S. S. R.)   3341, 4044, 4974,
5553, 6394, 7225, 7670, 7671
U. S. S. R.   Gidromet (Leningrad, U. S. S. R.)   1784, 4020, 4172
U. S. S. R.   Glavnoe Upravlenie Geodezii i Kartografii (Moskva,
U. S. S. R.)   74, 152, 153, 154, 303, 367, 368, 369, 370, 371,
372, 440, 441, 442, 443, 444, 512, 513, 590, 591, 681, 682,
683, 684, 766, 767, 768, 769, 919, 920, 1006, 1007, 1008,
1254, 1255, 1256, 1257, 1258, 1259, 1384, 1385, 1386, 1484,
1485, 1486, 1487, 1585, 1585, 1587, 1588, 1589, 1590, 1591,
1592, 1695, 1696, 1697, 1698, 1699, 1700, 1767, 1785, 1887,
1888, 1896, 1932, 1933, 2178, 2179, 2477, 2780, 3342, 3343,
3344, 3345, 3346, 3347, 3348, 3349, 3350, 3351, 3352, 3353,
3354, 3355, 3356, 3357, 3358, 3359, 3360, 3361, 3362, 3363,
3364, 3365, 3366, 3367, 3368, 3369, 3370, 3371, 3372, 3373,
3374, 3375, 3376, 3377, 3378, 3379, 3380, 3381, 3382, 3383,
3384, 3385, 3386, 3387, 3388, 3389, 3390, 3391, 3392, 3393,
3394, 3395, 3396, 3397, 3398, 3399, 3400, 3401, 3402, 3403,
3404, 3405, 3406, 3407, 3408, 3409, 3410, 3580, 3894, 4021,
4045, 4046, 4175, 4188, 4418, 4419, 4420, 4421, 4422, 4423,
4424, 4425, 4426, 4427, 4428, 4429, 4430, 4431, 4463, 4834,
4835, 4836, 4837, 4838, 4839, 4840, 4841, 4842, 4843, 4844,
4845, 4846, 4847, 4848, 4849, 4850, 4851, 4852, 4853, 4854,
4855, 4856, 4857, 4858, 4859, 4860, 4861, 4862, 4863, 4864,
4865, 4866, 4867, 4868, 4869, 4870, 4871, 4872, 4873, 4874,
4965, 4975, 4996, 4997, 4998, 4999, 5000, 5481, 5482, 5483,
5484, 5485, 5543, 5544, 5545, 5546, 5547, 5554, 5688, 5689,
5736, 5854, 5855, 5856, 6024, 6025, 6026, 6027, 6028, 6029,
6030, 6031, 6032, 6033, 6162, 6163, 6164, 6165, 6254, 6255,
6316, 6317, 6395, 6544, 6545, 7226, 7227, 7228, 7229, 7230,
7231, 7232, 7233, 7234, 7235, 7236, 7237, 7238, 7239, 7240,
7241, 7242, 7243, 7244, 7245, 7246, 7247, 7248, 7344, 7615,
7672, 7829, 7830, 8047, 8048, 8049, 8050, 8051, 8052, 8053,
8054, 8055, 8056, 8486, 8487, 8488, 8489, 8490, 8491, 8492,
8493, 8494, 8521, 8522, 8523, 8524
U. S. S. R.   Nauchno-issledovatel'ski institut aeroklimatologii (Moskva,
U. S. S. R.)   5647, 7673
U. S. S. R.   Voyenno-Morskoe Ministerstvo (Moskva, U. S. S. R.)   4957
U. S. R. R.   Voyenno-Topograficheskoe Upravlenie (Moskva, U. S. S. R.)
685
United Nations (New York, N. Y. , U. S. A.)   6407, 7819
United Nations Economic Commission for Europe (Geneva, Switzer-

Vilo (Paris, France) 6397
Visscher (Bruxelles, Belgium) 2188, 2246
Vives, Editorial Luis, S.A. see Editorial Luis Vives, S.A.
Volk und Wissen Verlag (Berlin, Germany) 224, 305, 373, 445,
  446, 594, 595, 690, 829, 923, 1010, 1128, 1260, 1388, 1389,
  1489, 1594, 1702, 4890
Vuk Karadžić (Beograd, Yugoslavia) 1390

Walker, Gerald E. (Berkeley, Calif., U.S.A.) 2130, 2131, 4438,
  4439, 4891, 4892
Warajiya Kabushiki Kaisha (Osaka, Japan) 6727, 8495
Ward, Lock (London, England) 75
Warne, F. (London, England) 76, 6420, 6546, 7041, 8497
Warszawa Universytet (Warszawa, Poland) 1889
Water Information Center, Inc. (Port Washington, N.Y., U.S.A.)
  3895, 3896, 4935, 4936, 7531, 8084
Watts (New York, N.Y., U.S.A.) 830, 6258
Weidenfeld & Nicolson (London, England) 2443, 3034, 3897, 4893,
  4894, 4895, 4896, 8058, 8059, 8060, 8061, 8062, 8063, 8064
Weilin & Co. (Helsinki, Finland) 1391
Welch Scientific Co. (Chicago, Ill., U.S.A.) 1490
Wenschow (München, Germany) 77, 374, 447, 691, 1129, 2314
Wesmael-Charlier (Namur, Belgium) 306, 1491, 1492, 1493, 2132,
  2200, 2673, 2674, 2675, 2676, 2677, 2678, 4897, 4898, 4899,
  4900, 4901, 4902, 5858, 5859, 6166, 6167, 6814, 6815, 6816,
  6817, 8065, 8066, 8067, 8068, 8069, 8070
Westermann, Georg (Braunschweig, Germany) 78, 79, 80, 81,
  156, 157, 225, 226, 227, 307, 375, 376, 377, 448, 449, 596,
  597, 692, 693, 694, 695, 696, 831, 832, 924, 1011, 1130, 1131,
  1132, 1133, 1134, 1151, 1261, 1262, 1263, 1264, 1265, 1266,
  1392, 1494, 1595, 1596, 1597, 1703, 1704, 1769, 1770, 1771,
  1772, 1786, 2926, 2927, 2928, 2929, 2930, 2931, 2932, 2933,
  2934, 4440, 4489, 4827, 4903, 4904, 4905, 4906, 4907, 4908,
  4910, 4911, 4912, 4913, 4914, 5860, 5861, 5862, 6036, 6037,
  6038, 6039, 6040, 6168, 6169, 6259, 6319, 6320, 6321, 6359,
  6360, 8071, 8072, 8073, 8074, 8075, 8076
Western Pub. Co. (Wayne, N.J., U.S.A.) 6041, 7436, 7532,
  8189, 8496
Westminster Press (Philadelphia, Penna., U.S.A.) 4097, 4098,
  4915, 4916
Weststadt Verlag (München, Germany) 1135, 4441, 4958
Wheaton & Co., Ltd. (Exeter, England) 514, 1890, 1891, 1892,
  3035, 4917, 6260, 7042, 8077
Whittemore Associates (Needham Heights, Mass., U.S.A.) 4099
Wiley, John & Sons (New York, N.Y., U.S.A.) 3575, 3898, 3899,
  3900, 4490, 4918, 6170, 6578, 7852, 7853, 8105
Wise, W. H. (New York, N.Y., U.S.A.) 378
Wjedza Powszechna (Krakow, Poland) 1136, 2133
Wolters, J. B. (Groningen, Netherlands) 158, 308, 450, 515,
  771, 925, 926, 1137, 1267, 1268, 1393, 1394, 1395, 1496,
  1497, 1598, 1599, 1600, 1705, 2416, 2417, 2418, 3124, 3125,
  3126, 3127, 3975, 4919, 5738, 6042, 6171, 6262
World Meteorological Organization (Budapest, Hungary) 6547, 7674

World Pub. Co. (Cleveland, Ohio, U.S.A.)   927, 2152, 2153,
    2154, 3576, 3577, 3678, 3701, 3702, 3703, 3901, 3902, 3903,
    4100, 5494, 5495, 5496, 7636
W.S.O.Y. (Helsinki, Finland)   5739, 5863, 5864, 6043, 6859,
    6860, 6861, 6862, 6863, 8078
Wyt (Rotterdam, Netherlands)   7097, 8525

Ya Kuang Yü Ti Hsüeh Shê (Shanghai, China)   2360, 2361, 2362,
    2363, 2364, 2365, 2366, 2367, 2368, 2369
Yale University Press (New Haven, Conn., U.S.A.)   3411, 3412,
    4920, 4921, 7249, 8079
Yavneh (Tel Aviv, Israel)   82, 379, 451, 697, 833, 834, 835, 1012,
    1934, 1935, 2444, 2445, 4442, 4443, 4444, 4445, 4446, 6716,
    7831
Yhtyneet Kuvalehdet (Helsinki, Finland)   2729, 5497
Young Readers Press (New York, N.Y., U.S.A.)   6262
Ypiranga Editôra   see   Editôra Ypiranga
Yugoslavia.   Vojno-Istoriski Institut (Beograd, Yugoslavia)   3439,
    3440, 4922, 4923

Zambia.   Ministry of Lands and Mines (Lusaka, Zambia)   2313
Zambia.   National Council for Scientific Research (Lusaka, Zambia)
    6659, 8111
Zanichelli, Nicola (Bologna, Italy)   83, 159, 698, 1269, 5623, 6044,
    6172, 7832
Zenkoku Jichitai Kenkyūkai (Tokyo, Japan)   2478
Zenkoku Kyoiku Tosho (Tokyo, Japan)   1706, 2479, 4447
Zenkoku Ryokaku Jidōsha Yōran Henshūshitsu (Tokyo, Japan)   2480,
    5498
Zenkyozu (Tokyo, Japan)   6045
Znanje (Zagreb, Yugoslavia)   1013, 3441, 3442, 3443, 3444, 4448,
    4449, 4924, 4925, 4926
Zondervan Pub. House (Grand Rapids, Mich., U.S.A.)   4101
Zürich Kantonaler Lehrmittel Verlag   see   Kantonaler Lehrmittel
    Verlag

Fitzgerald, Ken 8531
Ford, Edgard 6782, 7757
Forstall, Richard L. 7513,
    7809
Foster, Fred Willaim 250,
    865, 1634, 1727, 5911,
    6016, 6196
Fox, Edward Whiting 2077,
    2078, 2079, 2080, 3812,
    4748, 4750, 4751, 4752,
    4753, 6510, 7974
Franciosa, Luchino 1823, 4687
Frazer, R. M. 2588, 2589,
    2590
Freitag, Anton 4051, 4052,
    4070
Froment, Philippe 6828, 8185
Frommberger, Herbert 6037
Fullard, Harold 209, 422, 500,
    502, 560, 568, 569, 570,
    571, 661, 662, 675, 747,
    748, 749, 750, 751, 765,
    772, 814, 815, 823, 843,
    895, 896, 897, 898, 899,
    983, 1100, 1101, 1167, 1226,
    1227, 1361, 1362, 1363,
    1364, 1467, 1562, 1564,
    1566, 1676, 1677, 1758,
    1765, 1810, 1849, 1850,
    1851, 1854, 1855, 1856,
    1857, 1858, 1859, 1860,
    1862, 1863, 1864, 1865,
    1866, 2272, 2273, 2274,
    2277, 2278, 2279, 2280,
    2281, 2282, 2324, 2334,
    2564, 2565, 2566, 2567,
    3326, 3327, 3337, 3533,
    3574, 4226, 4352, 4512,
    4513, 4515, 4516, 4517,
    4763, 4764, 4769, 4770,
    4771, 4889, 4953, 4954,
    4955, 5604, 5605, 5610,
    5619, 5641, 5642, 5644,
    5645, 5648, 5680, 5691,
    5727, 5830, 5833, 5868,
    5986, 5987, 5988, 5989,
    5990, 5991, 5992, 5997, 5998,
    6017, 6126, 6127, 6128, 6129,
    6133, 6134, 6226, 6235, 6236,
    6237, 6238, 6239, 6240, 6241,
    6242, 6252, 6262, 6302, 6343,
    6344, 6345, 6346, 6384, 6386,
    6387, 6388, 6389, 6601, 6640,

    6641, 7030, 7214, 7220, 7797,
    7798, 7799, 7873, 7983, 7984,
    7985, 8094, 8095, 8096

Gábor, Bognár 408
Gächter, E. 7195, 7769
Gailey, Harry A., Jr. 1811,
    4564, 7895
Gallouédec, L. 255, 540,
    4632, 4633
Gamba, Henrique 5760
Ganji, M. H. 6703, 6706,
    7665, 7669
García O. Juan Alfredo 3590
Gardner, David E. 2970, 3052,
    3202, 3414, 4465, 4466, 4467
Gardner, R. 6586
Garland, Sven Olof 1124, 4405
Gaustad, Edwin Scott 2143,
    4068, 4660
Geelan, P. J. M. 6672
Genovese, Omar I. 891, 1352
Geraghty, James J. 3895,
    3896, 4935, 4936
Gheorghiu, N. 584, 999, 3199,
    3200, 5685
Gilbert, André 245, 611, 1029
Gilbert, Martin 2438, 2443,
    2995, 3807, 3808, 3897,
    4712, 4713, 4714, 4715,
    4716, 4717, 4893, 4895,
    4896, 7009, 7010, 7215,
    7629, 7951, 7955, 7956,
    7957, 7958, 7959, 8061,
    8062, 8063
Gill, Somers 76
Gillardot, P. 2740
Ginsburg, Norton S. 918, 1712,
    2319, 4409, 4493, 5648,
    5691, 5867
Giry, Robert 2754, 4255
Gleave, J. T. 806, 2299
Gleditsch, Kristian 174, 952,
    1294, 3135, 3136
Goldmann, Wilhelm 393, 538
Goldthrope, E. J. 1814, 2292,
    4026, 4980
Gómez, Antonio López 928,
    1014, 1015, 1138, 1139,
    1140, 1270, 1271, 1396,
    1397, 1398, 1498, 1499,
    1500, 1601, 1602, 1603,
    1604, 1707, 1708, 1709,

Mabogunje, A. L. 2228, 2229
MacFadden, Clifford 11
Maes, L. Th. 4898, 8069,
    8070
Magnússon, Einar 5850, 7055
Maillo, Adolfo 5770
Malaschofsky, Alfred 269,
    304, 689
Mannerfelt, M:son 220
Mardešić, Petar 146, 147,
    434, 1013, 1076, 3441,
    4448, 4449, 5806, 7259,
    8313
Marinelli, Olinto 592, 828
Markel, Lester 6148
Markova, N. T. 7230, 7231,
    7232, 8490, 8491, 8492
Martin, Geoffrey J. 1792
Martin, Gilbert 7629
Martin, Jean 102, 476
Martin, Leo 4743
Martin, Pedro 7588
Martova, K. B. 4834
Matley, Ian M. 2085, 3338,
    4795
Matt, O. 7195, 7769
Matz, R. 2825, 3999
May, Herbert G. 4082, 7633
Mayer, F. 1494, 4489, 5861,
    5862, 6319
McBain, F. C. A. 6379
McCagg, William O. 2012,
    2085, 3329, 3338, 4662,
    4795
McDougall, Holmes 6266
McEvedy, Colin 4757, 5789,
    7879, 7921, 7922, 7923,
    7960, 7961, 7976, 7977
McEvedy, Sarah 5789, 7879,
    7921, 7922, 7923, 7960,
    7961
McLaren, Moray 3203, 5132
McLintock, A. H. 2578, 2579
McMorrin, Ian 5721, 8098
McNeill, William H. 4566,
    4567
Medved, Jakob 6117
Meer, Frederik van der see
    Van Der Meer, Frederik
Meertens, Pieter Jacobus
    3111, 4453
Meinardus, Otto 2309, 4036,
    4072

Meine, Franklin J. 163
Melentijević, Ilija 6449
Menin, Tiberio 4728
Merrill, Edward H. 4628
Michel, Rooul J. 3250
Miermans, G. G. M. 534
Mietzner, Horst 6154
Mikhailov, A. A. 4044, 4046
Millares Hernández, Jorge
    2138, 2160
Miller, David M. 3895, 3896,
    4935, 4936
Miller, Theodore R. 3898,
    4918
Mindak, H. E. 858, 3484
Mitić, Slobodan 585
Mitra, A. 6678, 8108
Mogilko, A. D. 4045
Mohrmann, Christine 4064,
    4080, 4608, 4738
Monteiro Ailland, Julio 310,
    5692, 7554
Montrouge, Pierre 8038
Moore, Patrick 5748, 5811,
    5832, 5846, 5871, 5995,
    6009, 7618, 7619, 7620,
    7621, 7623, 7624, 8528,
    8529, 8533, 8534, 8535,
    8537, 8538
Morales y Eloy, Juan 3959,
    4588
Morgan, M. R. 1819
Mori, Giuseppe 4688
Moriya, Yoshio 2468, 6726
Morris, J. A. 3004
Morrison, Joel 6306, 6349
Moser, John 5814, 6491
Mostofi, Ahmad 6705, 7668
Motta, Giuseppe 1746, 5635,
    5667, 5668, 5797, 5798,
    5945, 5946, 5947, 5949,
    5950, 6101, 6102, 6104,
    6214, 6215, 6286, 6287,
    6288, 6289, 6290, 7750,
    7751, 7752, 7753, 7754
Mougenot, Pierre 4826
Mugahya, Yunia 2301
Muir, Ramsey 4515, 4516,
    4517
Murdoch, G. 6642, 7780
Muris, Oswald 352, 419,
    566, 567, 658, 659, 660,
    813, 4349, 4758, 4759

2112, 2113, 2114, 2115,
2116, 2117, 2118, 2119,
2120, 2121, 2122, 2123,
2124, 2412, 2413, 2414,
3118, 3119, 3120, 3121,
3122, 3123
Pugliese, Enrique C. 3916,
5163
Putzger, F. W. 2626, 2627,
3316, 4668, 4669, 4817,
7198, 8032

Quargnolo, J. 7538, 7542,
7703, 7720
Quennevat, J. C. 1981, 4596

Radó, Sándor 733, 887, 972,
1077, 1345, 1449, 1654,
3036, 3037, 3042, 3043,
3044, 4299, 4301, 4693,
5262, 5263, 5672, 5808,
5959, 5960, 6110, 7048,
7767, 7940, 7941
Radovanović, Mihailo 955,
5776, 6075
Rae, Gordon 3208
Raup, Henry A. 7274, 7402,
7640
Recato, W. F. 5664, 6844
Redfearn, J. C. B. 1824,
2265
Reed, Alfred Hamish 143
Rees, William 3416, 3417,
4616, 4617, 7251, 7252,
7904, 7905
Reguera Sierra, Ernesto
1636
Reid, Joyce M. H. 4078
Reinoso, José 114
Rennard, T. A. 2264,
4690
Rentsch, Merete 987
Reynaud-Delaurier, G. 6226
Rhodes, Dale 3619, 3749,
3805, 3806, 4121, 4124,
4125, 5306, 5307, 7287,
7479, 7641, 7642, 7643,
7647
Rhodes, Glenn 3619, 3749,
3805, 3806, 4121, 4124,
4125, 5306, 5307, 7287,
7479, 7641, 7642, 7643,
7647

Ribeiro, Guaracy 3943
Riccardi, Mario 272
Riccardi, Riccardo 272, 341,
717, 939, 4686
Ricci, Leonardo 698, 5623,
7832
Ridwan, M. J. 5983, 6696
Riemeck, Renate 4744
Rimli, Eugen Theodor 468,
618, 945, 1297, 4243,
5769, 6068, 7719
Ríos Valdivia, Alejandro 177,
535, 3949
Roberts, Gail 7854
Rodgers, H. B. 2135, 2147,
4221, 4322, 6574, 7862,
7964, 7965
Roglić, Josip C. 73, 221
Rojas Morales, Ernesto 7576,
7710
Romein, J. E. 791, 2398
Romer, Eugeniusz 198, 289,
424, 425, 503, 504, 572,
573, 666, 3143, 3144, 3145,
4303, 4304, 4305, 5559,
5564, 5572, 5573, 5583,
5589, 5590, 5606
Roolvink, R. 4058, 4069,
4582, 4661
Rouable, M. 2740
Rowley, Harold Henry 1916,
4037, 4047, 4062, 4075,
4078, 4100, 4736, 7631
Rusch, H. 1977, 3094, 4235,
5577
Ryder, T. T. 6775
Rzedowski, Jan 1570, 5836,
5999

Safrai, Shmuel 4054
Sahab, Abbas 6662
Saibene, Cesare 1701, 4432,
5737, 6080
Saint-Yves, Maurice 5901,
5966, 7307, 7316
Sálamon, Bedřich 12, 170,
243, 464, 525, 608
Sale, Randall D. 3755, 4584
Salinas Bellver, Salvador 123
Salmanova, V. N. 5856, 6165
Salter, Christopher L. 6670, 7778
Samimit, Ergjin 5974, 6786
Sampedro V., Francisco 3961,